Reflections of an Oil & Gas Helicopter Pilot

A. OXENFORD

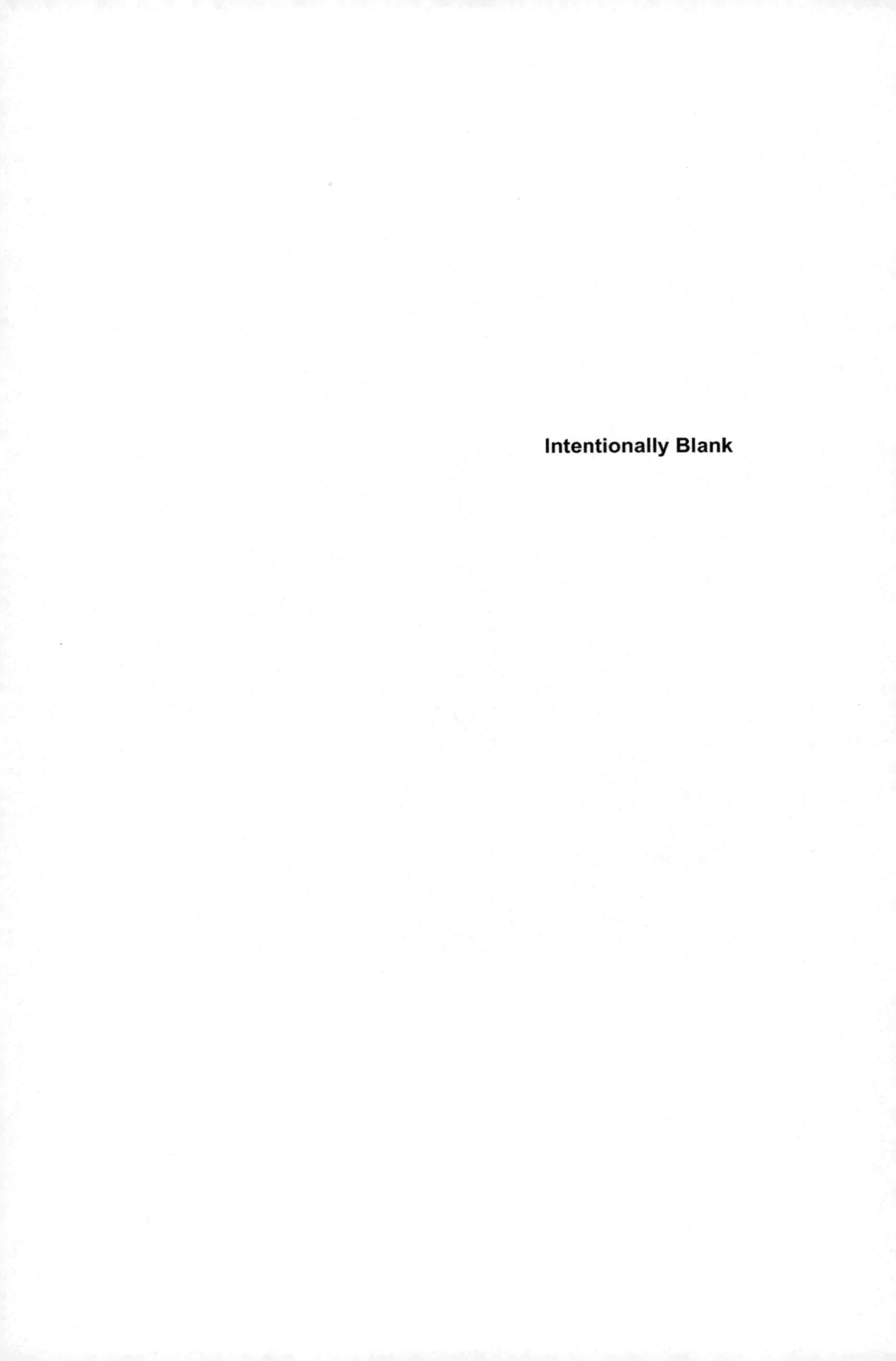

Intentionally Blank

First Edition - revised: 2023

About this Book.

This is a part historical journal, part travelogue built around the autobiography of a helicopter pilot flying medium and heavy helicopters offshore for 38 years beginning in 1975 when the UK oil boom was just taking off. To be enjoyed by the aviation community, the Oil & Gas industry and those with a spirit of adventure. How the fortunes of these interdependent organisations developed, particularly on the North Sea, from a censored, unreported world, before immersion suits and the rope around the hull to hang onto after ditching, to the introduction of safety measures, procedures and practices taken for granted today.

Reviews.

Early in this book, the author refers to the 'unreported world' of the offshore North Sea. This book helps very much to bring this world to life.
As I read it, I found myself vividly remembering what I experienced all those years ago. This book highlights what a dangerous place to work the North Sea was and still is. We were all pioneers in the job because we had to write the book as we went along, as you will see from the narrative. The colourful stories of his travels elsewhere are another highlight.
After 38 years of flying, he was asked to join the UK Search and Rescue (UK SAR) Standards Transition Team to construct and edit their operations manuals for them says a lot about the man.
The book will be enjoyed by the aviation community, all who worked in the Oil & Gas industry, and even those with an adventurist spirit. ***Major Mark Lacy. North Sea Commander with Bristow Helicopters, British International Helicopters and CHC.***

I can't praise your book enough! You've hit the right spot, describing technicalities and procedures nicely. ***Capt. Peter Jackson. RAF AI Instructor & North Sea Commander/TRE at British Airways Helicopters.***

This book is a very real insight into the world of a very different bunch of aviation professionals. I want to think I know what makes helicopter pilots tick and, in the case of the UK North Sea, motivates them to fly helicopters in what are very often the most inhospitable conditions in the world, both the weather conditions they fly in and the conditions they are expected to work for. There is absolutely no doubt in my mind that had it not been for the author and many of his colleagues, the lot of an Oil & Gas helicopter pilot would not be what it is today. Without their struggle, helicopter pilots, in general, would still be considered second class and certainly not held in the high regard that they are today.
From the first moment I started to read this book, it was apparent that the author had done extensive research and checked and re-checked his recollections.
If you are an ex-helicopter pilot, a current helicopter pilot, or an aspiring helicopter pilot in Oil & Gas/helicopters/aviation, I recommend this book. It is a very good read and well worth every penny. In turn, it is very well written by a true North Sea Commander. ***Mick Brade is a former BALPA National Officer with 17 years of special responsibility for representing members employed in the rotary section (helicopters).***

This is an amazingly accurate document and should be considered almost as a reference book on North Sea helicopter operations. I have just finished the section where you talk about lightning strikes on North Sea Helicopters. I have personal experience, having been struck three times when operating out of Unst in the S-61N and once in the AS332L out of Scatsta. In the S-61N, it just punched holes in the aircraft skin or blades, it being an all-metal aircraft, but with the AS332L, it was an entirely different matter, and the damage was substantial. We had cases where 'ball lighting' transitioned from the back of the aircraft through the cabin and out through the front, just as you describe in your book. ***Capt. Peter Cole. North Sea Commander with Bristow Helicopters.***

Wow! Your fabulous reflections totally absorbed me. What you have done is great, and if only others could appreciate all we have put up with. It was a very fulfilling experience flying helicopters, and I wouldn't have changed it for the world. Your reflections bring back so many memories. You have certainly put a lot of effort and research into writing your book, and I am pleased you have written it. I will most certainly be buying a copy to have on my bookshelf. It is a 'must have.' Well done. ***Capt. Geoff Bader. Former Royal Navy helicopter pilot and Captain with Bristow Helicopters.***

As an old, retired offshore Oil & Gas support helicopter pilot, I thoroughly enjoyed reading Andy's book. It brought back many memories of those days, some amusing, some exciting and some downright terrifying.
I never met Andy, as not only were we in different companies, but as I flew over the North Sea throughout my civil career, he spent some of his time in more exotic parts of the world. So, our paths never crossed.
For all those who have either been an O&G support helicopter pilot, are one now or are considering becoming one, this book is a "Must Read," as it covers many aspects of the business about some, me being one, knew little or nothing about. Historically, the book is of great interest, covering the industry's early beginnings, some of the characters involved and the companies created, and the political machinations rumbling on from time to time.
I can strongly recommend this book to all interested in aviation.
Capt. Roger Taite, Bristow Helicopters and Bond Helicopters. North Sea Commander, TRE (Type Rating Examiner), and Chief Pilot at Bristow Helicopters Operations, Unst, Shetland.

Foreword.

With a very special thanks to Anne for encouraging me to take up flying. And our boys, Stuart and Myles, for supporting her while I was away flying the line.

I have abridged information sourced from the AAIB (Air Accident Investigation Branch). This is to illustrate accidents and incidents more accurately in the company aircraft where I was employed. Of course, there were many involving other companies, too. Some are mentioned to provide context to the narrative where appropriate. Otherwise, as Gabriel Garcia Márquez noted: “Life is not what one lived, but what one remembers and how one remembers it in order to recount it.” The main thing is to live to tell the tale! AO.

Cover.

Transocean *Paul B. Loyd Jr.* A Harsh Environment, Semi-Sub Drilling Rig, flaring West of Shetland Isles 1997.

Photo: Author / Extract, Decca Chain Frequency Group 2A November 1983. Credit. Racal Avionics Ltd.

Table of Contents

Part 1

Chapter 1. 1975

An Experience!

The flight to a rig drilling in this area of the North Sea had claimed one rig and severely damaged another. Aberdeen, Scotland. The 4th of April 1975. At 07:20, we taxied out, adjusting the incline of the rotor head to counter a stiff crosswind, not enough to impact the top of the cab and wreck the overhead engine controls as happened at this airport a few years later. We joined the queue of other helicopters at the holding point, waiting to line up and depart from the Southerly runway. The roar from jet engines and rotor blades around us provided a background din through our ineffective Astrocom headsets. Gusts caused the aircraft to shudder. But the big American Sikorsky S-61N, G-AZDC, stayed reassuringly stable. We were airborne by 07:30 with an all-up weight of 20,500 lbs (10.5 tons). In a climbing right turn, we headed north into blue skies. Over seven hours later, we landed back here. And yes, a little wiser, too.

The first sector routed Aberdeen (Dyce) to Sumburgh in the Shetland Islands to board more passengers. These were part of a Norwegian crew change for the semi-submersible drilling rig, *Dyvi 'A'*. As most helidecks offshore, we will land in a highly obstructed environment, where space is limited with little margin for error. When fully manned, she had the usual contingent of 70, made up of crew and oil field workers. They were midway through a six-week drilling program in the block now known as the Beryl Field, some 95 miles to the southeast of Shetland. On this same field the previous year and close to midnight on New Year's Day, the semi-submersible rig *Transocean 3* capsized in storm force 10 to force-11 winds. The day before, the crew of 56 had transferred by Bristow helicopter to the rig *Transworld 61*. It, too, showed signs of collapse and had been towed away to Stavanger for shelter and repairs. The *Transocean 3*, with a leg broken off, was drifting free. They were hazards to other rigs in the area, with the wreckage passing within 100 m of the rig *West Venture*. After floating upside down for a week, and despite futile attempts by British bombers to destroy it, it sank. Meanwhile, *Beryl A*, the first of the Condeep-designed oil production platforms, was under construction in Gands Fjord near Stavanger. It will be towed out and sunk on location later in the year.

En route to Shetland, we had a good tailwind. We were riding the southerlies of a depression entering the North Sea from the west. We landed in Sumburgh with better-than-expected fuel. The captain considered it sufficient. We will wait until we arrive at the rig to refuel; just enough, none for the wife and kids. With the remaining Norwegians onboard, making up a full complement of 19 passengers, we headed back offshore. Not long after leaving Sumburgh behind, the wind began to veer into the east and freshen. And with it, our ground speed deteriorated. We checked our progress against the ten-mile increments marked on the Decca chart. And each time, we recorded a lower ground speed. After 30 miles, we were already down to a 90-knot ground speed, with a 30-knot headwind component, increasing as the wind continued to veer. It was cutting into our fuel reserves. Fuel for an onshore diversion was slipping away.
We descended out of 3,000 feet to improve our ground speed, looking for slacker winds. Passing 2,000 feet, we began to take salt on the windscreen. With the wipers on, it smeared white over the screen, leaving only small areas the washer had cleaned. Instead, the ground speed decreases to below 70 knots; the wind is freshening. We still had another 30 miles to go, at least half an hour. A subtle loss of performance to the leading edge of the main rotor blades and the compressor blades of the engines was not helping either; sea salt was packing onto them, leaving a hard glaze. Ever so slightly, we were losing aerodynamic efficiency and engine performance. We established radio contact with the rig. It was not good news. Not only were they still trying to mend their broken non-directional radio beacon (NDB), but the weather had changed. And it was not just the wind. They were in fog. Until then, I was unaware the North Sea could generate such weather, travelling up to 80 knots. And these were the ideal circumstances. A depression had snatched hot air from the continent to the southeast, conveyed it on the wind and dumped it on the North Sea. Now cooled during the winter, it was not more than +5°C, the perfect mix. As usual, we were in uniform: shirtsleeves and sweaters; the passengers were in their day clothes. Our survival would be only a matter of minutes.

Despite having insufficient fuel to return to the beach, the training captain was undeterred. He had been there before. To turn around now, he explained, we would not necessarily enjoy a good tailwind the whole way

back. The weather system was shifting to the east, taking the Easterly flow with it; we dialled up their radio beacon frequency in anticipation the rig radio operator would get it online. The needle was still resolutely parked. No ident. Then, updating the decometers for the nth time on the OE chain chart of our Mk 19 Decca navigator, the automatic direction finder, ADF, briefly flickered into life. Checking the morse code ident of their beacon 'DVA', the needle steadied, bearing 140°M against our heading of 150°M; just 10° of drift. This drift most likely reduces lower down. Now, with an even stronger beacon signal, we closed with our destination.
We completed the checks with the landing gear down, brakes on, and passengers briefed; there was no going back. We stubbed out our fags. The captain took control. We began to let down. As we levelled out at 200 feet, the occasional sighting of wind lanes, streaked white with spume, was the cue to descend farther, much farther, as it turned out, at the captain's discretion. It became darker now, a twilight zone in sight of the sea in poor forward visibility.

As a precaution, we slowed to 90 knots, as indicated on the airspeed indicator. We barely made 30 knots ground speed when the two amber master caution lights, set in the instrument combing in front of each pilot, illuminated: a warning. The low fuel lights blinked, indicating we had ten minutes of fuel remaining on either side. We continued, monitoring our approximate range on the Decca map and the beacon's bearing to the rig as the stern of a small vessel appeared on the nose. It had seen better days. A former side trawler. It had changed roles with the demise of the fishing industry and displayed a large yellow disk painted on the aft deck, the area used for winching by helicopter. Like many others, it had become a rig safety vessel. Its job was to stay downwind of the rig, anticipating collecting men overboard. And not without great difficulty. It was plunging into huge waves, the sea surging over the gunwales when it rolled. Fat chance, but it satisfied regulations. We crept by it. Oblivious to our presence, the only sign of life came from a glow in the wheelhouse. She was holding her station, an important clue. We were not too far off their rig when it briefly crossed my mind: at least we were not being tossed about riding storms, going nowhere, for weeks. The turbulence increased as we left the boat behind. The wind was now barrelling off the rig superstructure ahead. Closer and slower, we moved in. It is at times like these a radar would come in handy. The reverse currents in the gusts messed with the pitots. Our airspeed indicator needles are now quite erratic. To reduce our speed further would be aerodynamically unstable - too much wind shear.

Then, the needle in the direction finder dial began twitching violently; a steel leg emerged from the fog. Pounded by waves and shedding spindrift, it towered out of the sea above us. Time was slipping away, hovering in sight of more legs from one side of the rig to the other. And always in the event of a go-around, allowing an escape clear of obstructions into the wind. We were looking for the tell-tale protrusion of the girders bearing the helideck above, keeping one weather eye out for the larger waves rolling past just beneath us. With the wipers slapping salt spray, we caught its outline; above us, a lattice of steel beams supporting an overhang, on the southern quarter, a left-hand approach. It was my landing.
"You have control."
I took over with, "I have control."
The captain responded, "You have. And don't put it in the net."
It must have been on his mind.

Fig 1. Drillship *Glomar North Sea*.
Photo credit: ©Michael R. Reilly

(Two years earlier to the day, he had landed a Bristow S-61NR, G-AZNE, with the tail wheel in the safety net surrounding the helideck of the *Glomar North Sea,* a former ore carrier converted to a drillship. The main wheels followed, landing heavily on the deck, causing the main rotor to droop. It sheared the top of the cab off along with the engine controls. Though crew room conjecture believed it happened by inclining the disc too far when they tried to taxi forward onto the helideck. In any event, they could not shut down. The co-pilot and passengers disembarked, and after closing the doors, he took off and landed in the sea. After he had swum clear in the freezing water with only his uniform to protect him, the helicopter engines powered the rotors for another two hours. They coasted down when the fuel ran out. The aircraft rolled over and sank).

*

Climbing slowly, taking care not to lose it, we followed its motion.
"Clear to land" from the Helideck Landing Office (HLO). Acknowledging it, the skipper cautioned me to wait until the vessel had steadied between 30-foot heaves. Was I prepared for this? Whatever you do, be positive. Marking time as it crested the waves, waiting for the seventh and largest to go through, a lull followed as it slid down to wallow briefly in a long trough. It was time to move in, catch it on the descent and touch down on the deck as it briefly levelled out. Now over the bum line (a yellow segment of the landing circle viewed from our side windows), don't piss about in the hover; keep going down and land. We're on! No time to gloat. Push the collective smoothly but firmly down to compress the oleos and stabilise the aircraft, disc level and collective friction on; we'd arrived. On the deck, it was apparent the anchors were straining for supremacy. Marked by buoys in an array around us and half a mile away in the fog, this was no time to dwell. With the red anti-collision lights switched off and thumbs up to the deck crew to move in, we signalled for chocks, fists clenched with thumbs extended inwards. Overhead, lumps of fog scudded through the drilling platform, and the derrick towering out of sight.
Each incoming wave briefly appeared to engulf us, then disappeared below as the rig rose to take them; our airspeed indicators conveyed gusts, some now over 75 knots. Next, the deck crew strung a rope to prevent passengers from being blown overboard. They first fastened it to the folding handrail they had erected leading down steps off the deck. Then, bent double against the wind, they crept across the deck and fastened the bitter end to a rail of the aircraft airstair door. Tethered! The passengers disembarked.
The deck crew changed out the baggage; I checked the fuel sample for water content. Easier said than done with the salt spray soaking us, crouched in the lee of the helideck. The procedure involved filling a three-and-a-half-litre jar with fuel from the hose nozzle and swirling it around to homogenise any water suspended before syphoning a sample through a water detection capsule into a syringe. The litmus in the capsule should remain yellow. Twice, it indicated green.

A failure. Between shucking the capsule out of its tube and the test, moisture had most likely trigged the litmus. Three capsules later, a thumbs up to the captain conveyed a successful result. Back onboard in the dry, I watched the low quantity lights extinguish as the gauges registered the flow, first one tank and the other. With bacon rolls and coffee provided and the paperwork completed, we board 19, baggage and freight. Our return load. A turnaround I repeated many thousands of times over the next 38 years. Fifteen minutes after landing, we returned to Sumburgh to repeat the process: a double shuttle. I mused as you do on the final sector and sixth from Sumburgh to Aberdeen: what would the winter hold, for this was a spring day? Before last October, I had not sat in a helicopter. And this was my first commercial line flight offshore; another 7 hours and 10 minutes into my logbook.

*

We had played a small part in a vast matrix of skills, risks, and investment to access the oil and bring it ashore; the first load docked two months later in June. As the historian Christopher Harvie observed, “The country had seen no greater civilian project since navvies built 5,000 miles of railway in the late 1840s.” Apart from the oil workers we ferried over the horizon and the maritime assets supporting this effort, he continued, “The impact of oil on the British metropolitan intelligentsia and its imagination was practically zero.”

Chapter 2. 1963 - 1975

A New Trade – First Oil Ashore - Grub offshore - Automatics

Helicopters have been used in the UK sector of the Southern North Sea since 1963. Mines left over from World War II still infested it and could easily tangle in the large arrays towed by seismic survey vessels searching for gas fields. Instead, they used helicopters for these surveys.

Then, on the 17th of February 1965, Bristow Captains Bob Roffe and Alan Green flew the first crew-change helicopter flight to a rig in the UK Sector of the North Sea. They departed Sunderland Airfield in the single-engine Westland WS-55 Whirlwind 3, G-APWN, to the American Overseas Petroleum Ltd. (Amoseas) *Mr Cap* sub-leased to a Shell/Esso consortium. With a 55-foot diameter helideck, the three-legged jack-up rig was drilling on the Dogger Bank bearing 062°M and 145 nautical miles from Sunderland Airport. The twice-weekly service's success depended on having made good time to the decision point of 80 miles out to continue with a point of no return around 90 miles. Beyond the latter, there was no turning back, even if the rig went into the fog; there were no landing limitations. At the time, it was the longest over-water sector Bristow helicopter crews had ever attempted. If that was not challenging enough, the rig radio operator was notorious for enhancing his weather reports, as indeed, many were. Instead, the rig would be immersed in typical Dogger Bank weather - fog.

G-APWN, with a Bristol Siddeley Gnome 101 turboshaft engine (General Electric T-58 built under licence), was one of five constructed and is retired in the Frank Whittle Museum at Coventry Airport.

*

Before the US Army scrapped it, the drilling rig *Sea Gem* began life as a cargo pontoon. In 1964, BP acquired the pontoon and added ten legs to jack her up, a helideck, quarters for 32 persons and a drill rig. On the 17th of September 1965, she was working in the UK Sector of the Southern North Sea.

During the day, there was evidence of gas in the well. From 8,500 feet below the seabed, returning drilling fluid was frothing and bubbling. Two days later, it became apparent this could be significant. When stormy weather set in, they called a halt to drilling. On the 20th, they ran a drill-stem test to assess

flow and gas pressure. The telex to BP read, "A test in BP's North Sea well now being drilled by the *Sea Gem* 42 miles east of Humber has produced gas, but not in sufficient volume to be commercially significant. The well is being drilled deeper in the hope commercial production may be encountered." The press interpreted this as "BP Strikes Gas...... North Sea Klondike!"
By the 9th of December, they had drilled down to 10,000 feet and ignited a 40-foot flare. The first offshore gas strike in the UK sector. This well could produce ten million cubic feet of natural gas a day. Then tragedy struck.

Fig 2. Jack-up drilling rig *Sea Gem* flaring, West Sole, Southern North Sea. *Photo credit: ©Mirrorpix*

To appraise the extent of the field, they needed to move the rig two miles away to drill another step-out well. They began preparations to relocate on the 27th of December. As they lowered the barge three metres down her ten legs to sea level, the forward four jacks near the helideck moved normally; the intermediate jacks moved, but not by as much. The aft four jacks by the rig were unresponsive. They released air from the forward jack's cylinders to restore their original position. At 14:09, the two forward legs on the starboard side buckled, then collapsed under the rig's weight.

The hull split open as she listed, leaving a four-inch wide tear in her plates. The sea poured in as 15 to 20-foot waves washed the radio shack overboard. The men tried to release one life raft, but the power of the waves surging onboard was too great. When they launched another, 13 men scrambled into it. Those left behind made their way to the highest end of the barge. From there, they saw a cargo ship a mile away heading their way. It would not be long now; willing the vessel to come closer, the barge unexpectedly flipped over and tipped them into the sea to join others thrown off when she initially listed.

As the MV *Baltrover* was making her way over, she put out a distress call to alert rescue services to assist her. When she arrived, the freighter crew rescued the 13 in the life raft. Three others are rescued by boats responding to the distress call. A few miles north of the Humber estuary, an RAF Westland Whirlwind HAR.10 helicopter of 202 Search and Rescue Squadron, based at RAF Leconfield, is scrambled. Flying through winter snowstorms, Flight Sergeant Lee Smith and his crew arrived overhead to find only the hollow stump of one leg visible, surrounded by flotsam. The 24-year-old skipper recounted: “It was pandemonium”. They saw men in the water. Some are alive, others floating dead among the waves. His winchman, Flight Lieutenant John Hill, recovered two survivors close to death and lowered them onto the *Baltrover* - an exhausting manoeuvre in strong winds, with the deck rising and falling away. Sergeant John Reeson, the navigator, volunteered to go down and rescue another tangled in the wreckage – wires and metal. Despite the survivor weighing 16 stone, John brought him and the debris on board. Returning to Leconfield with their survivor, Lee faced a similar situation a few years later. Instead of the rescuer, he became the survivor when he ditched the Bristow S-61N, G-BBHN.

*

The 13 lives lost that day led to the mandatory requirement for an offshore installation manager (OIM), a rescue boat on standby, and a ‘technological revolution’ for offshore platforms to be stronger and safer to cope with the hostile North Sea environment. Not a moment too soon. On the 6th of January, BP launched their new semi-submersible rig, *Sea Quest,* down the Harland and Wolff slipway in Belfast.

Within a few weeks, she was drilling in the block as planned, yielding 50 million cubic feet of natural gas daily, equivalent to half a million tons of coal. The gas field is called West Sole. *Sea Quest* could also claim fame of her own. In May 1969, she struck oil for Amoco in the Arbroath field. Arbroath was the first oil discovery in the UK Sector of the North Sea: well No. 22/18-1, 130 miles east of Aberdeen. Later, on the 14th of September, after further tests, they officially disclosed their find to the public. The following year, 1970, *Sea Quest* discovered the BP Forties Field, 110 miles east of Aberdeen. The development of Arbroath was not viable at the time, unlike the Forties, reaching a production peak nine years later of half a million barrels/day.

*

In October 1973, the price of oil leapt from 3 to 13 US$/ per barrel, the first significant hike since World War II. Carriers collapsed, including Court Line and Cyprus Airways. Elsewhere, there were worldwide airline layoffs and redundancies. The cause: a coalition of Arab states led by Egypt crossing the ceasefire lines in the Sinai and Syria in the Golan Heights had, unannounced, attacked Israel on their holiest day: Yom-Kippur. In response to Washington and other Western allies supporting Israel, the Arab states embargoed their oil. Their timing was impeccable, as crude oil production barely met Western consumption. The Tory government imposed a three-day working week to conserve electricity. As the lights went out and stocks ran out, ferry trips to France returned with supplies of candles.

*

Early in 1974, a cargo vessel was inbound from the USA with nine new, 26-seater Sikorsky S-61N helicopters as deck cargo. BEA Helicopters (part of British European Airways before it merged that year with British Overseas Airways Corporation - BOAC to form British Airways) had ordered them. Controversially, when the vessel arrived, the Minister of Aerospace and Shipping, Trade and Industry directed the helicopters to a private enterprise - Bristow Helicopters Ltd (BHL). And Bristow needed pilots to fly them.
At 27, with a recently completed fixed-wing commercial pilot's licence with instrument rating (CPL IR) – the latter flown in a Cessna 310 twin, September 1974 was still not a good time to apply for work with the airlines. Conversely, commercial helicopter operations in the Oil & Gas industry were promising, and Bristow Helicopters had recently begun courses to convert airline pilots to fly this bonanza of helicopters. Though only a budding airline pilot, I was invited to an interview at their Redhill HQ in October. The apologetic receptionist advised me the meeting was off, though she gladly reimbursed my travel expenses from South Devon. They will be in touch.

Meanwhile, if I was interested in helicopters, I was welcome to look around them in the hangar. It could have been more encouraging. Packed inside like sardines in a tin were seven Sikorsky S-58 helicopters. They were former German Army Aviation Corps machines, part of the fleet their government had disposed of between 1972 and 1974. Speaking to an avionics engineer, Steve Hogarth, who went on to become my pilot manager, he explained they would be upgrading them. They will remove the double-banked Wright Cyclone piston radial engines and replace them with a kit developed by Sikorsky: Pratt and Whitney twin pack PT 6T3 turbine engines mated with a combining gearbox (C-Box), similar to the configuration on a Bell 212.
Fitted with an additional fuel tank on the port side, they become S-58ETs. The power assurance performance figures were disappointing when they air-tested the first one to be converted. The Sikorsky rep commented,
“Oh, we thought that might happen.” Alan Bristow, aka Big Al, was not impressed.
“Who advised me to buy these (expletive) things?”
Prophetic? Two years later, an accident destroyed one on the North Sea. G-BCRU.
Back in South Devon, news arrived at the end of the week. A fixed-wing to helicopter conversion course for those turning up was starting on Monday and an opportunity to take advantage of.

Eight former British Caledonian, Britannia, Logan Air, Cyprus Airways, and air taxi pilots attend the course learning to fly the Hiller 12c, a version similar to the type Big Al flew off whaling ships in the Antarctic, spotting prey for whaling companies. By the end of February 1975 and 100 flying hours later, we had completed the flying on the Bell 47G2 (the civil variant of the H-13 Sioux used by the Mobile Army Surgical Hospital - MASH crews in the Korean War with a litter on each skid). The conversion was sublime compared to the Middle East Airlines (MEA) CPL/IR course I joined at Air Service Training, Perth, Scotland. During lectures, the Lebanese students, Shiite Muslims, and Christian Falangists took the opportunity to warm up for their civil war the following year. The new licence to fly commercial helicopters led to the Sikorsky S-61N ground school at Aberdeen, followed by four hours of instruction in this aircraft and the proficiency day and night checks culminating with the offshore helideck landing practice. These helicopters are related to the more familiar Sea King, except the length of the cabin is stretched with a four-foot plug and includes a cargo door.
By April 1975, we were line training over routes and destinations where few existed compared with those on the more recent charts printed on the 25th

of January 2021 below. The fixed installations are illustrated; the hundreds of floating destinations with helidecks are not.

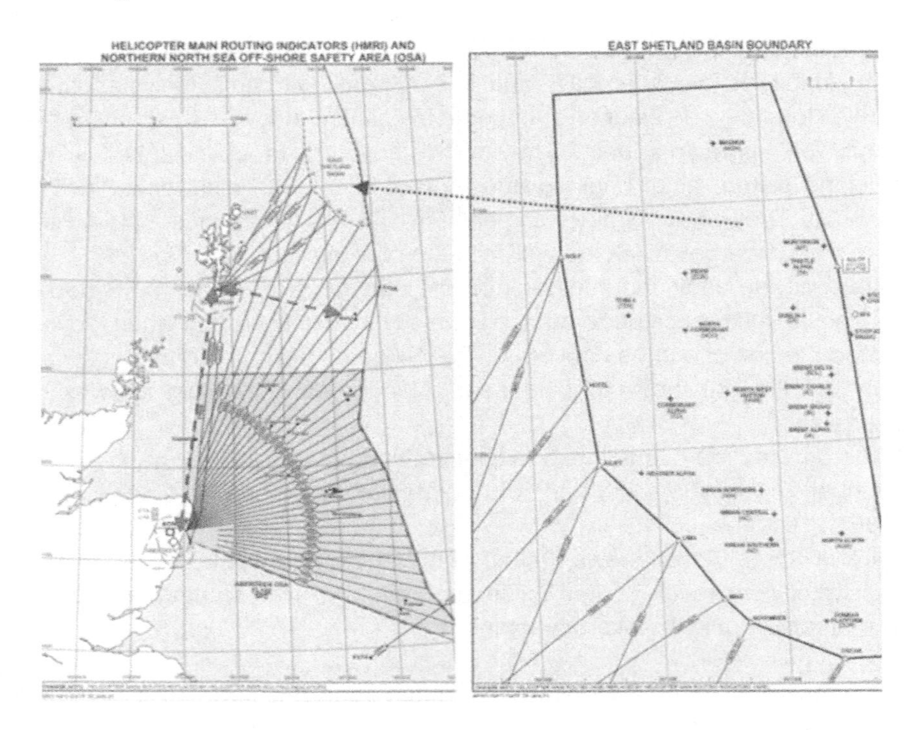

Fig 3. Aberdeen and Sumburgh Helicopter Main Route Indicators. *Credit: NATS*

HMRI to/from Sumburgh and ESB *Credit: NATS*

Red arrows show the route taken on my first line flight to *Dyvi 'A'* via Sumburgh on 4/4/75.

For one line pilot (helicopters), there was much to learn. Having enough fuel onboard other than breakdowns is the most mind-concentrating issue for all pilots, checked when they are not discussing how to improve their lot. Above all, I took away from that first line flight to stay ahead of the game, to mentally plan for the 'what if' scenario as the flight unfolds, and to bear in mind a change of circumstances like routing, loads, weather and much more. It was a practice to develop, inhabiting the subconscious and revealing it'll probably be all right. After all, the time taken to make decisions ate into any reserve fuel. Arranging a meeting around a table to discuss the next move was not an option. Making a mistake could have life-changing implications for everyone onboard.

Then, there was the natural environment of the North Sea, the like of which most had never experienced. It included airframe icing, rapidly shifting sea fog, hurricanes, mountainous seas, and severe turbulence and how to respond to these conditions when landing on helidecks of vessels working the oilfields. Next up, we learned about safety equipment and procedures. There were hardly any. Over the years, they drip-feed into the system. Finally, on multisector routings, knowing where to source the best food to enjoy on the return sector should not be discounted. Indeed, for some, including this pilot, it became a Pavlovian necessity, and knowing the right person to ask for advice helped, too. On arrival from a flight with Ron Kann, an ex-Vietnam Vet or ex-WWNam, a young co-pilot anticipating a debrief to expand his knowledge asked if the captain had any tips. "Best not to wear brown shoes with a dark suit," advised Ron.

Weather forecasting in those days before satellites was still a black art; little had changed from World War II. The synoptic chart and the shipping forecast provided the most relevant information. Then, as the headwinds freshened and different flight levels considered, checking the fuel state invariably became more frequent.
You quickly built up a picture of fuel burn by mentally calculating the ground speed over ten-mile increments marked along the track drawn on the Decca map. Thus: 5 minutes/120 knots; 6, 100 knots, and 7½ minutes, 80 knots. Now suitably informed, you knew when a refuel was due, planned accordingly to drop in on a rig for a top-up and finally backed up with an 'ops normal' call back to base. Due to the poor VHF radio coverage in the early days, high-frequency radio (HF) was the principal means of communication with the beach when cruising at 3,000 feet and when over 80 miles away, though closer in if staying low level to avoid icing up or battling into a powerful headwind. Because the radio resides next to the co-pilot's collective lever, it was his baby to use and a pain in the headset. Headsets. These sun-brittled, grey plastic Astrocom contraptions clipped onto the instrument combing when not in use, waiting for the next crew to perch on their head (it will be years from now before we receive a personal, sound-deadening Peltor headset for health considerations). No, these headsets ensured you did not miss out on the ambient racket around you and really came to life when listening out on the high-frequency radio, for they revelled in this noise. An "Ops normal" transmission, giving your flight number and position every ten minutes or 20 miles, greeted you with a continuous screeching *kshhkshhkshhkkkkkkk* carrier wave when you switched the set on. It only

stopped during voice transmission. Then back to the *kshhkshhkshhkkkkkkk* as you waited for the base to acknowledge it.
At night, when the airport Air Traffic Control (ATC) controllers had gone to bed, you had the additional *zzzzzzzzzkshhkshhzzzzzzzzzzzkshhkkkkkkk* "Copied" *kshhkkkkkkk* from the company night ops controller back at the base interrupting his sleep.

Added to the mix, some captains had idiosyncratic ways of keeping co-pilots busy. For example, a push button is just below the fuel gauges on an S-61N. When pressed, it will cycle the content needles to zero. These gauges' alternating current circuit breaker (AC CB) is among a cluster protruding from a panel just below the captain's window and hidden behind his right knee. He first requests his co-pilot to check for traffic through their (port/left-hand side) window. Then, suitably distracted, he presses the button and, in mid-cycle, pulls the circuit breaker. After some time, he casually asks him to update the arrival fuel. Thus, a running mental picture of speed and endurance came in handy to call their bluff. Pressure refuelling was an option, much as you see airliners at airports fuelling today. This method worked well until a hose broke. The aircraft was rotors running refuelling offshore. The rupture was perfectly aligned to deliver high-pressure Jet A1 kerosene directly into the port engine. When a helicopter goes tech on an offshore helideck, it often denies the means to evacuate by air. Peace in the OIM's office is unlikely to be restored until the offender's removal per G-AZNE on the 4th of April 1973. As a precaution, Bristow opted for gravity fuelling, as at the petrol station. This procedure on an S-61N requires filling the fore and aft tanks individually to balance the centre of gravity. If you wanted more, some in the centre tank, too, rather than just through one pressure refuelling connection with the ability to fill all three simultaneously.

*

And while on pressure: One foggy morning, we were lounging in the crew room waiting for the weather to clear. After all, in most companies, the captain who signs for the aircraft has the final say on whether he takes the flight. On this operation, there was no redress until you went elsewhere. Compared to the other operator, British Airways Helicopters (BAH), with its absence of coercion, the turnover of pilots spoke volumes. It comes to a head in 1977, as we shall see. At eight o'clock, the chief pilot arrived for work swinging his brown nav bag as usual. He passed us on the way to his office with something on his mind. After the morning ritual of dumping the bag on his desk, he returns to the crew room. "Get Airborne!" he bellowed. And so, we did. We made it back with a fortuitous improvement in the weather. Except for some crews who recently arrived from bases overseas, they were less fortunate. Not yet being checked out to fly according to instrument flight rules (IFR) (there was no requirement for an instrument rating then, just a company check), they turned back after entering some cloud. Result: "You're grounded (until checked out)!" No pressure, then!

*

Captain's discretion extended to the boundary of his experience and sometimes beyond. To reach the latter was quite common as the North Sea was always ready to deliver surprises; experience never stood still. The modus operandum was to assume it'll probably be all right. As it was for offshore limitations, one must also read discretion captain's discretion, for there were few limitations.

Many vessels were unsuitable for the environment. Pressed into service by a rapidly expanding industry, they included some with a low freeboard. It was best to empty the seawater from your shoes before closing the air-stair door. It made the remainder of the flight more enjoyable.

It could happen after refuelling on vessels like the diving support vessel DSV *Coupler One,* which is not of the design familiar today. A former bulk ore carrier, she was constructed on Teesside in 1955.

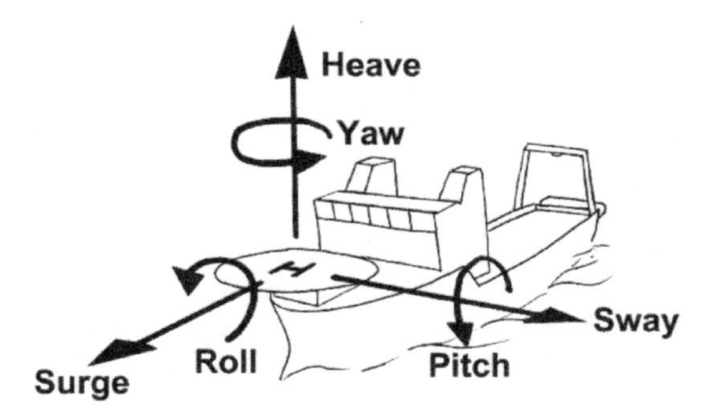

Fig 4. *Drawing Credit: UK Civil Aviation Authority*

In 1972, the owners converted this 130-metre-long ship into a diving support vessel with a helideck near the bow. With seas breaking over her, the deck crew had more sense to come out on the deck. Then, struggle to refuel a 72-foot-long helicopter, rotors running and heaving to the full extent of its oleos in response to the wild gyrations of the vessel moving in six different directions at once under your feet. Probably not. In 1982, she sailed to Vigo, Spain, and was broken up for scrap. This year, its divers were hooking up the under-sea wellheads to pipelines and risers connecting Hamilton Brothers' semi-submersible production rig *Trans World 58* (*TW58*. 108nm East-southeast from ABZ) in the Argyll Field to a Catenary Anchor Leg Mooring Facility. It looked much like a large yellow buoy. Here, shuttle tankers could load up their holds with crude oil. Landed by the MV Theogennitor on the 17th of June, it was the first North Sea oil sent ashore.

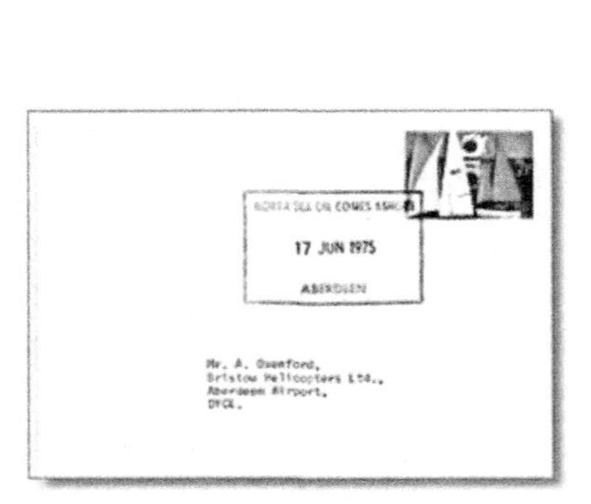

BRISTOW HELICOPTERS

17th June 1975

Dear Mr. Oxenford,

The cancellation date stamp on this envelope was specially produced for limited use to commemorate the arrival of the first North Sea Oil ashore from the U.K. sector. The first oil started flowing into the tanker 'Theogennitor' at 1235 hours on June 11th 1975 from the Transworld 58 Production Rig in the Argyll Field. The 'Theogennitor' sailed for a British Refinery on June 17th.

Hamilton Brothers Oil and Gas Company discovered and produced the Argyll Field in Block 30/24, some 180 nautical miles East/South East of Aberdeen. Hamilton Brothers is one of our Clients for whom we operate Sikorsky S61N's registration G-BCLD and G-BAKB.

On behalf of the Company I would like to thank you for your efforts which have helped to bring this about.

Yours sincerely,

J. E. Odlin
General Manager-Scotland.

Fig 5. The First North Sea Oil came ashore on the 17th of June, 1975

Dear Mr Oxenford.
The cancellation date stamp on this envelope was specially produced for limited use to commemorate the arrival of the first North Sea Oil ashore from the U.K. sector. The first oil started flowing into the tanker 'Theogennitor' at 12:35 hours on the 11th of Jun 1975 from the Transworld 58 production rig in the Argyll Field. The 'Theogennitor' sailed for a British refinery on June 17th.
Hamilton Brothers Oil & Gas Company discovered and produced the Argyll Field in Block 30/24, some 180 nautical miles East / Southeast of Aberdeen.
Hamilton Brothers are one of our clients for whom we operate Sikorsky S-61N's registration G-BCLD and G-BAKB.
On behalf of the Company, I would Like to thank you for your efforts, which have helped to bring this about.

Yours sincerely. John E. Odlin. General Manager – Scotland.

There were already four gas fields in production in the UK sector of the Southern North Sea. As you dodged the heaving undercarriage struts while refuelling, it was not a time to speculate that by October 2018, there would be a further 311 fields producing oil, gas, and condensate. Condensate is mainly comprised of propane, butane, pentane, and other fractions.

*

Taking on fuel on these occasions was, well, self-service. It is when, if you have managed to land in the first place, the captain's discretion comes to the fore: who steps into the surf? After all, this was the North Sea. The oil companies considered it an area where to venture was risky and dangerous. Most of the year, sea temperatures guarantee hypothermia. It is where they drill in water depths never attempted and then drill down another four miles under the seabed. And all this in some of the worst weather in the world. "There's nothing quite as vile as the North Sea when she's in a temper," one veteran sea captain commented. Like the rest of Scotland, there could be four seasons daily. Storms spring up and lash the sea to foam with waves between 50 and 100 feet in winds of over 90 knots. They were not uncommon, and most offshore workers took it on the chin and worked through – day and night on 12-hour shifts. After two weeks, we flew them ashore in an amphibious S-61N with its watertight hull and two sponsons, each with airtight compartments enveloping the undercarriage bay; inflatable floatation gear comes later. They were usually too tired to stay awake. And that was useful. It blocked the realisation; if their transport ditched, it rolled over. Trails demonstrated waves over six feet high do the job quite nicely. Then, their problems of escape and survival will really begin.

Navigation and letting down were approximate, hit or miss. Operators provided the rig radio rooms with a pair of pressure altimeters lodged side by side in a small wooden plywood box. As they do today, the rig radio operator relays the QNH–pressure setting to dial into your altimeter to produce the height above sea level. Except, the information passed to the crews was not always accurate. It could be up to ten millibars (300 feet) out. Like radar, it would have been useful to have a Radar Altimeter (RADALT) fitted, too. Even when eventually fitted, they were not a 'no-go' item when broken. When working, they measured a more precise distance between the helicopter and the surface below using an FM signal. After all, they were not new technology.

First invented in 1924 and successfully trialled in aircraft in 1938, they were considered an optional extra. The directors deemed an extra, if not mandated to be fitted, as an unnecessary expense. Yet they were happy for us to fly these multi-million-dollar machines all day and night into one of the more inhospitable environments in the world. Daily. One of the many Vietnam Vets working for Bristow, Jim Church, a former Seawolf, kissed the sea twice in the fog before flying on to make a more traditional approach and a drier landing on the helideck. He returned to the USA before his luck ran out. His co-pilot on one occasion was Rhys Evans. He had been on my fixed-wing to helicopter conversion course.

Along with John Learmonth, another course-mate, they returned to fly the BAC 1-11 narrow body jet for British Caledonian for, after 18 months, the fixed-wing world was recovering. Luckily, they retained their original seniority, though failure to refund the outstanding helicopter conversion bond occasioned a late-night visit with menaces to restore the balance.

*

Returning to Aberdeen in poor visibility could be challenging. As is available at some other airports, it had a low-level route. And this one was well appointed for crew and aircraft if unsuccessful. You joined the route at the mouth of the river Don. Following it upstream, a cemetery on the south bank sloped down to the river just before the Persley bridge. And if you looked up after skimming over the bridge, you might see Hutchison's scrap metal yard partly hidden by trees. The waypoint to leave the river was just past the papermills. Then, a short climb up the right bank and over the fence onto the airfield. This practice seemed to end when the airport received its approach radar towards the end of the seventies, and instrument ratings for captains became mandatory.

Aircraft radar, on the other hand, was rudimentary if fitted. Seeing the Bristow fleet of new S-61Ns lined up on the flight line was impressive, sporting their shiny black radomes. Except they were just voids. It will be some time before Bristow fits a Bendix radar set. British Airways Helicopters had cast-off Echo 290 M weather/mapping radars used by Merchantman (formerly Vickers Vanguard, a four-engine turboprop aircraft designed to replace the Viscount and now converted to freighters). Though quite good for spotting a Cumulus Nimbus cloud (Cb) at 100 miles and vessels down to 3, they were not much use on the final approach to a rig on a foggy day. Still, they were better than nothing. Navigation. The Mk19 Decca navigator harked back to World War II technology. When adopted by the Royal Navy, 'QH', its official title, was better known as Micky Mouse. An improved version, 'QM', was used to assist minesweepers in clearing the approaches to the Normandy beaches early in the morning of D-Day, the 6th of June 1944. Despite protestations from the crews enthusing on its accuracy, it was switched off on D-Day +1 to avoid detection by the Axis. Our 'rolling map' was positioned above the centre console for both pilots to see and access it. It worked well most of the time except during inclement weather and system design malfunctions. In the first instance, it simply 'loses the plot', especially when electrical storms are nearby. The needle tracing the track on the map parks in the right-hand margin and 'no longer plays ball', and the master 'cheese/spider' combination and the slave (Red, Green, and Purple) decometer needles spin into a blur. Thus, dead reckoning was the default position for a weather malfunction when beyond the range of land-based navigation beacons.

In the second instance, it could malfunction for a variety of reasons. During warm weather, the glue in the bespoke tape holding the map pages together melts. These maps wound onto a roller. It was when they fed onto a second roller the glue gave way with the sun's warmth as the flight progressed. The reel then spews up to 20 feet of maps onto the console if they have not already started disintegrating. A motor drove the maps. Sprockets with teeth engage perforations on their periphery, much as those on a 35 mm camera film. Except on a worn roll, these perforations tear and merge, allowing the teeth to spin in the void. With the teeth disengaged, the whole act grinds to a halt. Then, you reverted to a conventional Decca paper map to plot your position from the decometers.

The setup is to synchronise the pages with the appropriate key in a turret. The latter is inserted next to the chain selector, e.g., 2A, in the flight log control box on the console. Each key/page combo had a three-letter identifier. The key identifier headed a stalk. The latter inserts through a series of holes circling the periphery at the top of the turret. The turret could accommodate a set of keys, leaving these identifiers visible. Each stalk had its unique strata of metal sensors, much as a bar code, for synching with the corresponding map page. For example, the route to the Argyll Field is on the 'DWW' page of the roller map. The co-pilot was responsible for selecting the correct roll of maps, including a DWW page and the associated turret with its nest of keys with a DWW, before walking out to the aircraft. Woe would betide the pilot if a key were missing en route. Each Decca chain had its map. The example we are using to route to the Argyll would have been the Northumbrian Chain 2A.

The S-61N cockpit was large enough to unfurl the map measuring 1,340 x 930 mm, then fold it up again to the required area of the chain, then plot the rig's position and draw a line from it to the last known fix, usually, from where you had taken off. Next up was to read off the letter/number combinations from at least two of the three decometers and plot them on the map; ideally, the two intersecting with each other the best: be they combinations of red, green/ red, purple/ green, purple, and so on. And keep correcting the course every five minutes to stay in touch with the track you have drawn until you reach your destination; easier said than done in a vibrating machine pushing through turbulence on a windy day/night. Oh! Especially at night. The wander light held in one hand with the red filter selected and dimmed to protect the night vision of the flying pilot. In the other, a pencil for annotating the chart and a biro for keeping the nav log going while monitoring the instruments, listening out for other traffic, and not forgetting to make position reports on the radio from the map sliding between your knees.

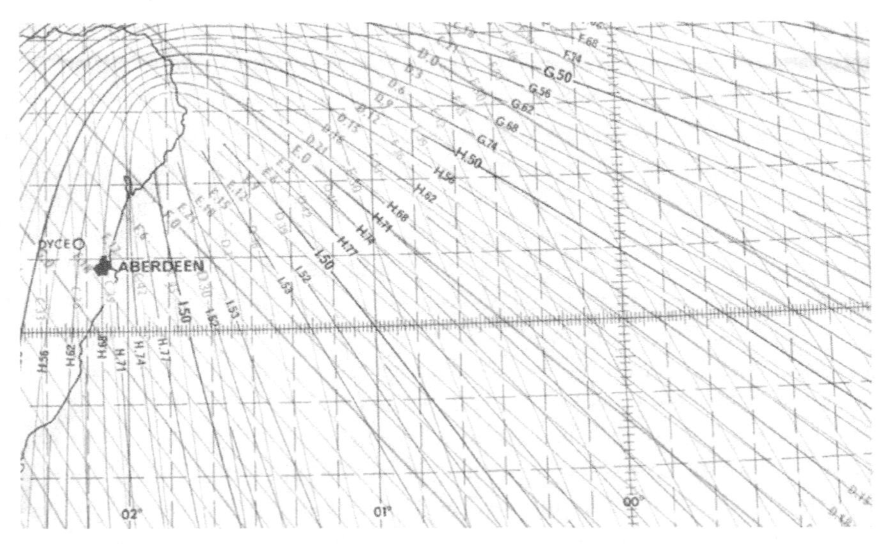

Fig 6. Decca Chain Frequency Group 6C North Scottish Chain.
They are primarily used to route to the northeast from Aberdeen. Original scale: 1:1,000,000. Printed June 1974. *Courtesy of The Decca Navigation Co. Ltd.*

Decca maps produced in the mid-1970s would not have VOR beacon radials with three-degree separation from inbound and outbound traffic marked with the distance every ten nautical miles, danger area boundaries, undersea pipelines and fixed offshore installations overlaid on later editions. Still, it gave a rough idea of where you thought you were! Rougher still, on routes to the southeast of Aberdeen, one centimetre on the roller map represents ten miles on the ground.

Sometimes, the activation key stops working, and the map grinds to a halt—the first aid to reactivate it is the same as restoring lost communication to the headsets. Remove the key from the turret or the headset jack plug from its female socket as appropriate. Then, please give it a good lick for the pantomime to continue. Eventually, the Decca navigator was replaced with area navigation (RNav) using GPS. Those pilots who had not experienced the ways of Decca freak when they received a GPS receiver autonomous integrity monitoring (RAIM) error: when insufficient satellites are in the vicinity to obtain a good signal.

For those with less experience in dead reckoning navigation and being beyond the range of picking up any onshore beacons, these occasions leave them adrift. It will cue the captain to utter, "It'll probably be all right," knowing sufficient satellites will soon become available. In the past, Aviators had the makings of sterner stuff. One was Tryggve Gran, a 26-year-old Norwegian. He prepared for the first airborne crossing of the North Sea from a fishing village 25 miles north of Aberdeen. His Bleriot XI-2 monoplane, *Ca Flotte,* arrived in Cruden Bay on the back of a steam lorry. Four days before the beginning of World War I, on the 30th of July 1914, he took off from a field outside the village. Forgetting the tram wires leading to the hotel and clearing them by a whisker, he coasted out. With only a clock, a compass and a keen sense of direction, his destination was Stavanger-Sola, Norway, 320 miles away.

Seventy minutes into the flight, sea fog precludes further progress. Gran returned and landed on the beach, only stopping when he ran into the sea. Horses recovered the aircraft for another attempt. He left again at 1:00 p.m. En route; the engine stopped after leaving a fuel pump on by mistake. Putting the little plane into a dive, he air-starts the engine. Recovering 15 feet off the sea, he touches down 4 hours and 10 minutes later in a field near Jaeren, not far from the present Stavanger-Sola airport. Leaving the engine running with a bemused farmer, he ran to telegraph the Daily Mail to announce his arrival and claim the prize for the first crossing. The farmer, who had never seen an aeroplane before, took the precaution of tethering it to a boulder. *Ca Flotte* can be seen in the Norwegian Museum of Science and Technology, Oslo.

*

Moreover, we were smart and wore airline uniforms and caps in the cockpit. We continued to do so long after the passengers had adopted immersion suits – much to the dismay of Iggy Davidson. "My last flight in the Royal Navy was in a Sea King in October 1977, wearing a full goon suit to protect me from hypothermia if I ditched. The flight involved transfers to HMS *Euryalus* and an unsuccessful search in the lower Clyde Estuary for a man overboard. Three months later, I arrived in Sumburgh over 400 miles further north to fly for British Airways Helicopters. Here, I found the crews operating over the North Sea in January with no protection whatsoever other than their uniform. Dismay doesn't really cover it! I felt distinctly uncomfortable. My first flight was with a former RAF pilot, John Baker, on the 14th; however, I wasn't going to let an ex-CRAB see it!"

An advertising company contracted by Harp Lager recognised this glamourous life when they filmed Dave Paris coming down the steps of an S-61N. Dave later went on to work for Flying Pictures. Lifestyle extended to smoking onboard. Ashtrays were in every cabin armrest, the cockpit below the jettisonable windows, and the cover over the AC circuit breaker panel adjacent to the captain's seat was handy for tapping out pipes. Then the result disappears, smouldering somewhere on the floor. By tracing the origin of the smoke, you could then stamp out the offending miscreant. Though, on one flight, we unaccountably lost a few AC services; ash and sparks had migrated inside. Offshore, every vessel and installation had a duty-free bond. Besides the weather and the return load, there will often be a request for the daily customs allowance of two packets of tobacco or cigarettes. 'Stocktaking' the bond begins with a request for some freight to be sent offshore. It would be an evening flight when the customs at small provincial airports had gone home. After unloading the freight and repacking the holds with bulging black bin liners, some passengers struggle onboard, clutching even more. Crammed with cartons of cigarettes, they strap them onto seats. Stocktaking!

Besides red-hot windscreen fires cracking the glass impregnated with gold heating filaments, fires in the cockpit were few, despite the amount of coffee spilt on the flight deck conveniently located just above the electronics bay. And then there was the food offshore. The deck crew invariably passed this through the cockpit window wrapped in tinfoil with coffee. Much as it is today. Breakfasts from two derrick barges stand out and will forever remain in the memory: two steaks and three fried eggs wedged in a freshly baked baguette. And if that did not excite the taste buds, they are backed up by the petit fours packed in a patisserie box that did. As good as Fortnum's, they were taken home for our sweethearts to enjoy. Fortuitously, American helicopter cockpits, unlike their French counterparts, are designed with plenty of room for a feast.

With the seat slid back on its rails, the cyclic stick could no longer interfere with the whole rainson d'étre for going there in the first place – to feed! And those barges? They were the Heerema derrick barge DB *Thor*, a converted oil tanker (formerly the front section of the oil tanker *Veedol* launched in 1952). At the time, DB *Thor* had the heaviest lift capacity in the world of 2,000 short tons (US ton – 100 lbs/cwt as opposed to the UK Long ton – 112 lbs/cwt). She is featured again in the next chapter when her crew saves the passengers and pilot after their helicopter crashes onto her deck. The other derrick barge was the Brown and Root DB *Hercules*, a flat-bottomed river barge of more later, were the two crane barges building the British Petroleum (BP) Forties platforms. Bristow had the BP contract, including a Bell 206 operation offshore in the field.

Fig 7. DB *Hercules* (foreground) and DB *Thor* with Forties Field Jacket.
The white domes form the bow of the raft used in transit.
Now upended with the jacket on the seabed, they are removing the raft.
Photo unattributed.

At the beginning of the summer of 1975, Peter Barnes flew G-AVIG single pilot out to the DB *Hercules* to set up the operation. They used single-engined Agusta Bell 206B (Jet Rangers) fitted with pop-out floats. As usual, offshore-based aircraft lift off to make room on the deck when a crew change aircraft comes through. On this occasion, Dave Hogg had arrived flying a Westland Wessex 60. 'IG' was already airborne shuttling and was due for a refuel. Instead, the pilot let Dave land and change out his passengers. This involves a ten-minute turnaround, 15 if taking on fuel. It was a surprise when Peter learned the Jet Ranger had ditched! She was floating perfectly on a calm sea when three overzealous vessels arrived and tried to 'save' her and rescue the pilot, Terry Burnal.

Unfortunately, a once unblemished aircraft quickly became one with significant damage. After they returned the tattered aircraft to Aberdeen, the engineers drained her tank. As can happen, there was just enough fuel to fill a Kilner jar. Many years later, I was taxiing in at Aberdeen when first one, then the other engine flamed out. With the half-hour loitering fuel reserves still indicated on the gauges, a tug towed the Aérospatiale AS332 L2 to the parking stand. Engineers traced the problem to faulty fuel calibration in the tank bladders.

Later, the operation moved to the DB *Thor,* and whenever the 206Bs were changed out, they 'escorted', as the shuttle pilots preferred to say, rather than 'were', by an S-61N to ensure they arrived.

When operational, all four Forties helidecks, *Alpha, Bravo, Charlie, and Delta,* were notorious for the difficulty experienced when landing and taking off with a strong South-Westerly wind. Buried deep down and shielded on the western side by the drilling rig on rails and the southern by the towering superstructure, a departure from the *Forties 'A'* warranted my first voyage report. Flying with Tony Barnetson, who had legs shorter than most of us, having bailed out of a fast jet and landing without his parachute deploying, he ran out of rudder control in the hover. The drilling rig was on the end of the rails closest to the helideck, and we were drifting rapidly into it. Taking control, we manoeuvred clear and continued the take-off. The report escalated to a safety report, resulting in a helideck review for these platforms. BP raised them and positioned them farther away from obstructions.

The S-61N has an Automatic Flight Control System (AFCS) to stabilise the aircraft after the pilot has trimmed in Pitch, Roll and Yaw. It made eating meals en route more enjoyable. Some years later, I accompanied an ex-Vietnam pilot to the Scandinavian Airlines System Flight Academy at Arlanda, Sweden. We flew the line in the Persian Gulf and were there for our annual Proficiency Checks (PC) in the Bell 412 simulator. It was his first time in a simulator. We went downtown Stockholm for supper the evening before the first sim session. A table outside a corner restaurant still catching the evening rays proved a good place to view life. Probably after the first bottle of white port at the end of the meal may have had a bearing on the next 24 hours. And because the man around the corner suppling blondes on bikes wheeling past our table from his box had not gone home yet - we ordered another. Back at Arlanda after breakfast, we were suitably relaxed when the simulator slot arrived: we will make our Norwegian (seaplane) instructor, Uffe Engstrom, proud.

"Never use the automatics," my co-imbiber declared, referring to the Stability Augmentation System (SAS) as we strapped in.

"Not a wise move in the sim'. Works better with it," I cautioned, "though not as good as an AFCS."
The aircraft was parked facing a nondescript building. As he lifted into the hover, the structure rapidly inverted.
"Whoa! Shit."
Now 'upside-down', unstrapped and muttering, he headed for the door. There, he waited for the machine to settle on its jacks and the door to open. A day later, he reappeared somewhat chagrined to realise earning a tick in the box, old dogs, even Vets, must learn new tricks. Well, sometimes.

*

And then there was the *ETPM 1601*, a pipe-laying and crane ship. Aft of the bow helideck, the flying bridge (I was going to write 'flying picket' when Grangemouth popped up. That will come later) included a dining room with views over the North Sea; waiters with bow ties provided silver service. It was the way then; many operators expected the helicopter to shut down on arrival, and an excellent opportunity to take advantage of their hospitality, and being a French operator, included wine. This vessel was responsible for laying part of the pipeline from the Frigg field in the Norwegian sector to the St Fergus gas terminal, a few miles north of Peterhead. From here, it routes onwards underground for distribution through other pipelines from Kirriemuir, Angus and Bathgate in East Lothian. Another pipeline came ashore south of Cruden Bay and conveyed the oil from the Forties field down to Grangemouth. Contractors temporarily requisitioned miles of farmland and moved in their heavy plant to lay the lines. After restoring the ground, the farmers had a bonanza of 4x4-inch posts used to fence off the trenches; they were left behind when the contractors moved on.

Chapter 3. 1975 - 1977

Condeep – Jump Seat Riders – Missiles - Strike! - Picketing

October 1975. Our flight routed to Stavanger-Sola, back out to the rig *Waage II*, and returned to Sola, then home.

As we coasted in amongst the islands, we happened on how the Norwegians built offshore platforms. There was much activity near Stavanger in Gands Fjord and Hinnavagen Bay. Looking closer, it was a vast construction site with at least three concrete structures under different stages of completion. They were building Condeeps. Instead of steel for the legs, they used concrete and mated the top sides to them before towing out.

Condeep (Concrete deep-water) was a marvel of product line engineering with three or four concrete legs to support the superstructure. Concrete is poured in a seamless supply into moulds, and as the legs form, they slowly sink into the fjord as construction progresses. Their steel topsides were as large as a football pitch. Each one straddled across two supertankers, much like a vast catamaran. When both components were ready for mating, the superstructure was floated over the legs, now some 170m long, then de-ballasted to lift it clear of the supporting vessels. When fully aloft and ready to go, this complete assembly will be towed out by a fleet of tugboats and sunk into its final position. Condeeps arrived in many oilfields, including the Beryl, Brent, and Cormorant Fields. At the time of writing, they are now being de-commissioned using the purpose-built *Pioneering Spirit*, the largest by-volume vessel in the world. Owned by the Allseas Group, it can remove the topside of an oilfield installation in one lift. The exceptional height of these oil production platforms was necessary as the waves could become huge, enough to wipe out the lifeboats suspended under the *Brent 'B'* topsides in one particular storm. A report published in the late 1990s determined their incidence and frequency over 100 feet high in the North Sea were only matched in one other place in the world: off the coast of South Africa. The design of these fixed installations allows them to sway in the wind and the swell to resist such weather. I first experienced this effect in a bathroom leading off the *Beryl 'A'* heli lounge. The towel on the rail before me moved like washing on a line in the wind.

Chevron constructed a one-off design at Loch Kishorn, Scotland. They carved a giant dry dock out of the hillside at Nigg Bay in preparation for *Ninian Central*. It was the world's largest manufactured movable object at 600,000 tonnes and with a 140 m diameter base. Unlike other installations, this one appeared just too large to sway. The dry dock is now where they construct offshore windmills with towers weighing over 1,000 tonnes.

*

Taking visitors and friends out on the jump seat was common practice, a jolly to see what was happening over the horizon. Though intrigued by an alternative side of aviation, British Airways crews still considered fixed-wing a more sensible option. What we did was considered by them to be downright dangerous. We did not see it that way. When I asked my father whether he had found the jump seat a bit hard after a four-hour return trip to the *Transworld 58*, he remarked, "It was no more uncomfortable than the trap we used during the Suez crisis." This event in 1956 closed the canal, a conduit for three-quarters of Europe's oil consumption. Until then, you could still buy petrol in one and two-gallon cans. The latter had 8/- (£0.40), indelibly pressed into the steel – 20p a gallon, including the tin or 5p/litre. Born in 1898, the same year as Erich Remarque, author of 'All Quiet on the Western Front', my patriarch qualified as a contender for the oldest to have flown to a North Sea oilfield, then and maybe since, though a Senior Helideck Inspector, Pete Garland, informed me he was still visiting oil rigs and super yachts to check their compliance to accept helicopters at the good old age of 77. It was not always thus.

*

Fog delayed the flights out of Aberdeen on the morning of the 21st of April 1976. It will not be until 11:52 before this Bristow Sikorsky S-58ET took off, routing to *Forties 'B'* and *'C'* and then back to Aberdeen. In common with the Bell 212 and Jet Ranger, these aircraft were flown by a single pilot. Geoff Bader was the captain of G-BCRU and had invited his neighbour, who strapped into the left-hand seat; eight other passengers, part of the crew change offshore, sat in the cabin. The turnaround on the *Forties 'B'* was normal. Here, the helideck crew changed out the passengers, baggage and freight stowed at the front of the cabin in a freight/baggage cage fixed to the aircraft forward of the main door on the starboard side. A life raft weighing approximately 130 lb was stowed on top of the cage, secured by a single strap. Geoff remained at the controls, completing the next sector's load sheet: 9 pax, 75 lb baggage, 15 lb freight and 1500 lbs of fuel. They were 550 lbs under the maximum authorised take-off weight.

Fig 8. Bristow Sikorsky S-58ET.G-BCDE (left). Note the extended range fuel tank on G-BCTX.
Photos donated by Steve Hogarth.

There was a slight delay on arrival at the *Forties 'C'*. They circled the installation to allow another helicopter to depart. It was an opportunity to choose the best approach to the helideck as the DB *Thor* was anchored alongside the *Forties 'C'* with her large crane rising 170 feet into the sky and abeam the southeastern corner of the installation. He could visualise the 210º safe approach and landing sector chevron as depicted in the diagram terminating at the helideck. The considerable obstruction created by *Thor's* crane within this sector was not unusual on the approach to North Sea installations, and it was within the pilot's discretion to accept it. Considering this limitation, the best approach path with the wind in the north and northeast, between 14 and 16 knots, meant flying over the DB *Thor* amidships to the helideck on a heading of 280ºM. The installation's towering superstructure and drilling rig blocked all other approaches outside the safety sector. Geoff set up the approach over the DB *Thor*.

As they flew past the crane down their left-hand side, it was only when close to the edge of the helideck Geoff felt a strong medium-frequency vibration through the yaw pedals and heard a rapid increase in engine speed. Witnesses saw pieces fly off the tail rotor at high speed and heard a sudden rise in engine noise. He noticed both torque meters had increased to over 100% without him increasing the collective pitch. The helicopter then started yawing uncontrollably to the right.

Geoff assumed there had been some sort of tail rotor failure and attempted to land on the *Forties 'C's* helideck. The aircraft, however, was out of control. The starboard landing gear leg impacted the helideck, ruptured the forward fuel cell, broke off and, with the aircraft, fell off the helideck in a South-

Easterly direction. The helicopter crashed between *Thor's* crane and the engine room deckhouse 140 feet below. She just missed some 40-gallon drums of lubricating oil stored next to oxygen and acetylene cylinders on the deck.

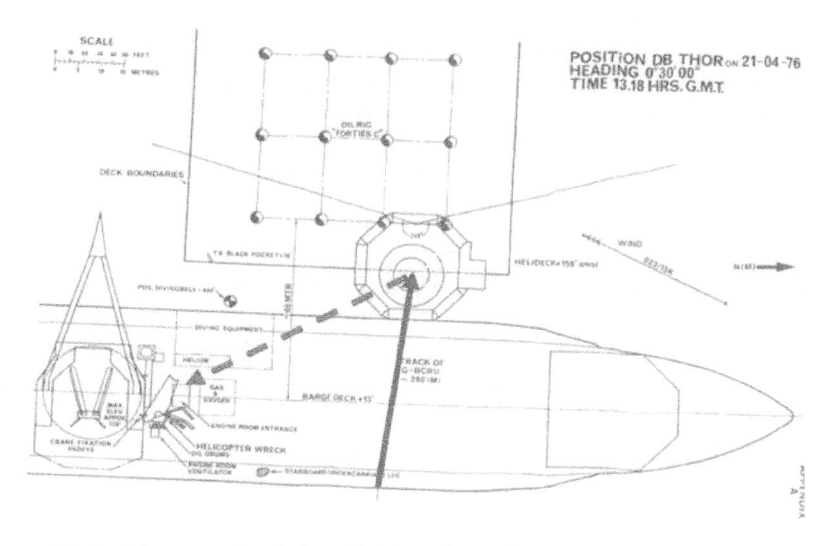

Fig 9. Diagram depicting flight path and wreck site of G-BCRU.
Diagram Credit: AAIB.

'RU' came to rest on her port side. Soon after impact, a fire broke out in the area of the ruptured tank on the starboard (top) side of the aircraft and spread onto the deck. Geoff operated the engine compartment fire extinguishers, and *Thor's* crew members rapidly responded using foam, carbon dioxide, powder appliances, and water hoses. The fire hoses from the *Forties 'C'* were also trained on the fire. Though concussed and with lacerations to his scalp, Geoff's neighbour was quickly helped out of the cockpit by two of *Thor's* crewmembers. But Geoff was stuck by his left foot. He described how "The cockpit floor had pushed up, trapping my leg between the floor and the instrument panel. My left leg bones were broken between the ankle and the knee, causing the leg to lie at some crazy angle that was very much not the norm. The ensuing fire produced thick black smoke and made it impossible to see. I remember pulling my flying overall over my face to stop me from breathing in too much smoke. The flames burnt my left foot." He also had a severe head injury (a depressed skull fracture). Their head injuries were consistent, with them striking their heads on the overhead controls and panel and the transmission tunnel between their seats.

Meanwhile, the fire was consuming the nose doors and much of the equipment and engines in the nose compartment. It was also invading the forward end of the passenger cabin, filling it with dense black smoke. The *Thor* crew opened both emergency exits and could only slide the starboard door back halfway; the detached tail pylon partially obstructed it. A passenger removed the access hatch from the cabin into the tail cone to allow escape through the ruptured rear fuselage. Seven injured passengers (three minor, four seriously) escaped through these exits. Ten minutes after impact, Geoff was still trapped and in great danger from the flames. They extinguished the fire at this point, and Geoff was cut free from the cockpit. "I will be forever grateful to them. They were brilliant!"

After the inferno was under control and the dense smoke had cleared, *Thor's* crew noticed the life raft had become dislodged on impact. It had triggered its CO_2 inflation air supply and had allowed the baggage to spill out of the cage. Behind the cargo, they eventually found the remaining passenger hidden by the semi-inflated dingy. *Thor's* crew gives all ten men first aid before being treated by a doctor flown over from a nearby ship. They then flew ashore to the Aberdeen Royal Infirmary accompanied by another doctor who had flown out from Aberdeen. The passenger discovered under the dingy did not survive his severe burns; Geoff spent five days in intensive care. Numerous bone splinters and fragments had penetrated his cranial meninges and lodged in his brain. It will be many months before the Civil Aviation Authority (CAA) allowed him back to fly the line; they feared the damage to his brain could be a precursor of epileptic fits. Finally, after Dave Warren had given him an S-61N conversion, on the 25th of April 1978, he was back on the line. Geoff's neighbour recovered fully, except for a scar on his head. Later in life, when he had gone bald, a tuft of hair grew to remind him of that 'jolly' offshore in April 1976.

The probable cause of the accident, based upon the limited physical evidence available regarding tail rotor damage, was the tail rotor instability arising from some undetermined cause, resulting in the whole tail rotor assembly becoming detached within one revolution. This instability is known as ‘Tail Rotor Buzz’ and most likely occurs under the following conditions:

1. high all-up weight;
2. high power;
3. high tail rotor pitch angle;
4. wind from the starboard quarter and between 15 – 25 knots;
5. low forward airspeed.

These conditions cause the flapping tail rotor blades seeking equality to hit the mechanical stops, resulting in a massive increase in drag and vibration. This action tended to slow the main rotor down and the engines to full power to correct this. All in a few seconds, one tail rotor blade detached, and the whole rotor and gearbox parted company with the aircraft.
As Geoff pointed out,
"Due to the difficulty of the approach, I had set up all the conditions operating within the flight envelope. It was unknown then that reducing the tail rotor pitch by applying the yaw pedal got you out of the situation.
There were three other possible incidences of tail rotor buzz later, but everyone was aware of it and the recovery action by then."

*

There is an advisory route from Aberdeen to Sumburgh, with danger areas on either side and an air traffic advisory service. Air and naval forces use these areas for live firing. On this occasion, heading north with Bill Roy (DFC and bar), a Vietnam vet and former Seawolf, the danger areas flanking it were NOTAMed (Notice to Airmen) as active. Even though we took care to remain on the route, should we have requested the advisory service? To the east, we could see a carrier force steaming west. We associated them with potential air activity. And it happened very quickly. Our first warning was missiles flashing past from east to west, just half a mile ahead. Then, a few seconds later, and at the same level and much closer, an F-4 Phantom.
“Did you see that, Bill?” Of course, he did, and then he replied matter-of-factory,
“Usually, missiles passing through the cabin detonate well clear of the aircraft. It is when they hit the gearbox you have a problem.”
“So, no problem, Bill?”
“No problem.”
As we continued north, I thought about my lack of experience flying in a dangerous environment and another 12 years before Bill would reveal the source of his nonchalant advice.
On contacting Sumburgh Approach, we asked for their weather. Fog! We looked at each other and put the same question:
“Did you check the weather before you left?”
It was not a scheduled flight, and we had been on standby. When we arrived at flight planning, we assumed the other had. Without diversion fuel, we had the choice: check if the top of Fitful Head nearby at 1,000 feet above sea level was above the fog. It was a popular place in the day to land and shut

down until the weather at the airport improved; Land Rovers would recover the passengers and crew. Or let down to the airfield using the new Instrument Landing System (ILS). We elected to approach the Westerly Runway 27. Before they installed the ILS, pilots followed a line of buoys in the fog to guide them to the airfield. These markers were painted in dayglow colours and anchored in the water leading to runway 27. Sodium flares on either side of the threshold marked the beginning of the runway. As Pete Benson recounted: "It was not unusual to drop down to 20 feet, reduce speed to 35 knots or translational lift speed to recover quickly, then, with the flares in sight, climb onto the runway – elevation 30 feet above sea level. It worked well until I was surprised to find a Douglas DC-3 parked on the runaway a few yards from the threshold in the fog!" The ILS on runway 27 also had a trick up its sleeve. The vertical beam is offset slightly to the right of the runway. There was no other option.

The pavement ended in the Atlantic and the North Sea on the other. From the east, the beam takes you into Virkie Pool, bordering the north shore of the runway. At a tangent to the pool running southwest is a disused Runway 04/22. You know you are close to the Runway 22 threshold when you pass the small jetty jutting into the pool from the north shore. The runway leads to the apron between the BAH and Bristow hangars.

Fig 10. Bristow and BAH/BIH Hangars with disused runway leading to them from Virkie Pool in the background

Photo© kindly provided by Kieran Murray Snr, SAR Crewman, Sumburgh, LSI.

To cut a short story shorter, we climbed onto the disused as you do and taxied down it to refuel outside the hangars. Later in the day, the weather picked up a bit. It was now on limits. So, after the crew change offshore, we returned to refuel before they closed, then headed on south to Aberdeen.

Just before we QSY'd (changed radio frequency) en route, the controller thanked us for coming. We had been their only movements all day.

1976. One of the first safety items introduced this year is the UVic Thermafloat jacket. The construction was nylon-coated neoprene designed by the University of Victoria, BC, hence UVic. They came in orange for Bristow and dark blue for BAH. Their design included a crotch flap, much like a paratrooper's jacket. This flap was to stop the jacket from riding up around the armpits when you jumped into the air/sea as appropriate. Normally stowed at the back of the jacket, it hung down when released. Then pulled forward between the legs and secured by poppers at the front. Being bulky, we rarely wore them onboard except during the winter when the temperamental paraffin heater on the S-61N had failed. They did, however, come to the fore for keeping the weather out on the picket line and, of course, for sailing in wet dinghies like lasers. Some years later, after the passengers had adopted immersion suits, the aircrew replaced their UVic jackets. The initial immersion suit trials were not promising. As one pilot pointed out on return from a rig, "You came back into ops having been trialling a new Multifab immersion suit with a vent on the shoulder and pronounced it unsuitable on the grounds that you had nearly gassed yourself after eight pints of heavy and a vindaloo the previous evening!" It was a relief for the boil-in-a-bag aircrew, as Pete Jackson succinctly described our predicament when it was decreed their use would be seasonal. So long as it was not night-time and the sea temperature was warmer than +10°C, one could substitute them for overalls. The idea was sound, except it did not consider the rising sea temperature lagging well behind the sun's heat, broiling the crew under the Plexiglas. On the North Sea, it is not long before you are back into 'rubber' again.

Across the North Sea, Helikopter Service, operating out of Bergen-Flesland and Stavanger-Sola, was grateful for any assistance to fly the line. Crews commuted from all over the world. This shortage led to a few Aberdeen captains popping across the North Sea on time off; the Norwegians offered a significant bounty to moonlight. It was prudent to keep this practice below the radar for obvious reasons, not least for Flight Time Limitations (FTLs) – the legal requirements not to be exceeded without good reason. And Big Al. From time to time, he visited the base, leaving his HS-125 business jet parked outside on the ramp.

On one occasion, I was planning a flight when he appeared out of the corner of my eye from the direction of flight ops. Passing through the planning room, he stopped just past me.

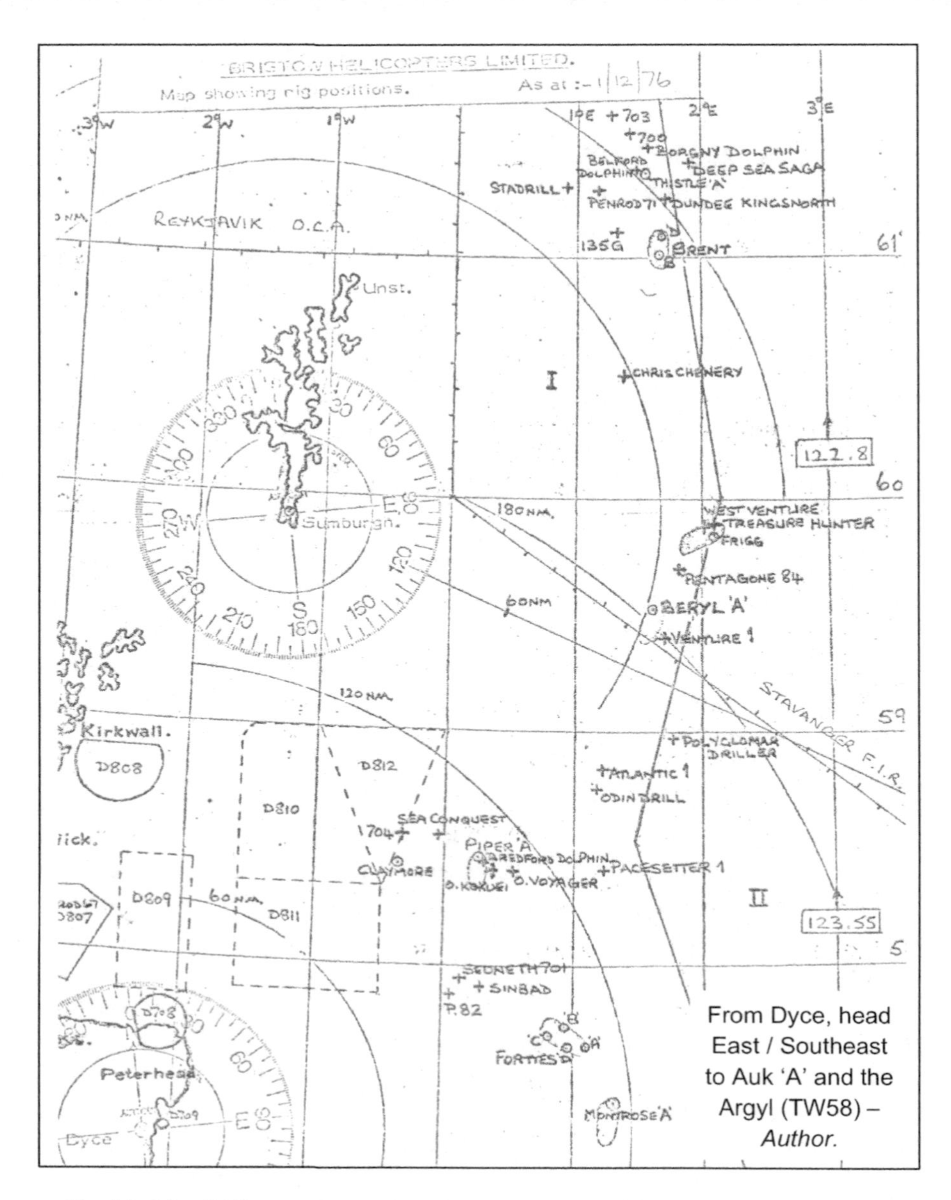

From Dyce, head East / Southeast to Auk 'A' and the Argyl (TW58) – *Author.*

Fig 11. The BHL pre-flight planning map on 1/12/1976 shows 26 drilling rig positions and 12 North Sea production platforms. *Author's collection.* (Today, I am crewed with Barry Bird in G-BBVB to the drilling rig *Sea Conquest,* and in the afternoon, to *Forties 'A'* in G-BBHL).

Dick Rae, a Vietnam vet, sported an impressive black afro hairstyle; you could lose drumsticks in it; he was coming from the opposite direction when Big Al blocked Dick's path. In no uncertain terms, he informed Dick his hair had to go. At this point, Rick Peterson, another Vietnam vet and Marine Corps Boeing Vertol CH-47A Chinook pilot, appeared behind Big Al. Tapping him on the shoulder with a,
"Hey, man. Leave my buddy alone,"
Big Al swung around. His eyes glared at the size 14 shoes, then moved up to focus briefly on an outstretched hand. It offered a handshake backed up with,
"Hi! I'm Rick. Who are you?" from above.
The glare moved farther up a notch until it arrived at Rick's face, for Rick was at least a foot taller. And here to meet him was that disarming smile Rick permanently wore. Even Big Al, who took on the world and usually won, knew when to back off. Much to the amazement of the few who witnessed this unique event. As Big Al sorted out the rest of his organisation, Rick left later in the year to return home to Hawaii. He had accepted the post as marketing manager of Aloha (unkindly referred to as 'ragtop') Airlines. Twelve years later, he will have a challenge on his hands. 'Rag top' in a sense, on the 28th of April 1988, significant dis-bonding and fatigue damage on one of their Boeing B-737-200 aircraft caused an explosive decompression. Part of the upper fuselage of the cabin ripped off. As convertibles do, it exposed some passengers on Flight 243 to the sky above. Sadly, a flight attendant was sucked out of the void and never found. The captain landed the aircraft safely with the remaining crew and 65 passengers still onboard. If anyone could restore the confidence of passengers to fly again with Aloha, then Rick was the man. His smile conquered all.

*

Two years after joining Bristow, the Aberdeen pilots sought union recognition – BALPA, the British Airline Pilots' Association. A mere pilots' association was insufficient to negotiate anything of worth. The principal reason for recognition was to achieve parity with the competition, BAH, for they had good conditions of employment. These include rates of pay on parity with narrow-body jet pilots based at Heathrow, a staff vacancy notice system, health, loss of licence and life insurance policies. The latter amounted to 15 times the salary; staff travel on a par with British Airways fixed-wing crews, and an excellent final salary pension scheme besides allowances and overtime boosting income by up to 50%. The latter had paradoxically come about through government austerity measures since the sixties and continued well into the seventies. It affected the public in ways unimaginable today. One example applied to those wishing to leave the county for a holiday. We were limited to taking £50.00 per annum abroad and recorded in the back of your passport. It does not seem a lot, though it could buy over a month's skiing in the Vorarlberg mountains of Austria. Ten bob (50p) a night in a farmhouse with punch cards for the lifts operated by the farmer on the breakfast table still left £35.00 for wieners, bratwurst and glühwein.

*

The UK economy continued to deteriorate when finally, the Labour Government accepted help from the International Monetary Fund in 1976. This loan was conditional on government organisations taking a pay freeze, including BAH. It was the largest ever loan to a country to date, and a year later, the freeze had morphed into a pay cap. The cap was limited to 5% to control inflation. The tipping point came during the 'winter of discontent' (1978/79) when the public sector took to the picket lines demanding an end to the cap. The prime minister of the Labour Party, Jim Callahan, downplayed the situation upon returning from a holiday in Guadeloupe. The Sun newspaper interpreted this to comment: "Crisis. What crisis?" Jim kept an ace in his pocket: North Sea oil and a fleet of helicopters and workboats serving it to buoy the economy and enable the country to float through the 'Crisis'.

BAH introduced new allowances or enhanced existing ones to compensate for the pay cap. It was known for a crew in danger of missing out on a meal allowance to fly from the East Shetland Basin (ESB) oilfields around the *West* Coast of Shetland back to Sumburgh. Then the Union tackled overtime and days off lost. The introduction of trigger points enables claims in many ways (any flying hours over 600 was one trigger of the 900 permitted per annum). In some cases, giving up a day off without due notice would, through devious administration, accrue an additional three in compensation – all paid for at a generous rate. Allowances became so comprehensive you could live off them. Though Bristow tracked the BAH pay scales, the pilots had poor or non-existent terms and conditions, allowances, or ways to trigger overtime. Any financial assistance that is due, such as danger money provided by the oil companies for the crews to fly in West Africa and other hot spots, was never distributed. Finally, BAH only hired foreign pilots if they had UK national spouses.

Bristow had a different business model. Despite a high pilot turnover, the company had two distinct advantages over BAH. Many foreign pilots made up the Bristow crew room, most of whom had fought in the recently concluded war in Vietnam. These pilots had broken their journey home to visit Europe on their time off—the Grand Tour. For Bristow, why bother about crew allowances and conditions with an endless supply of pilots demobbed from the war? With the newly acquired helicopters transferred from BEA Helicopters in 1974 and the foreign aircrew to fly them, they retained this advantage until 1977, when the tables turned in favour of BAH.

And this is how it happened. By April 1977, things had come to a head. A poll was taken in Aberdeen by a senior Captain, Dick Metcalfe. This base was where the main effort for recognition was centred. In the event of industrial action, over 85% of pilots signed a pledge to take it. Given the generally low morale, there was no specific reason to meet when it went ahead, just the proverbial straw on the camel's back. And then it happened: strike.

I was working a detachment from Aberdeen in Sumburgh and had just come off a flight. It was the evening on the 13th of April when at least half the Aberdeen fleet of S-61Ns diverted and stayed the night on the island. Their crews joined us at the bar in the BA Sumburgh Club in an eclectic atmosphere. (The club is a Scandinavian wooden building. It never gave up its smell of pine woods. British Airways owned, it included a restaurant and accommodation overlooking the West Voe, a narrow sea inlet). After all, it was a radical move by responsible people, mostly ex-armed forces commissioned officers. There are no invites for other bases ensuring cohesive action, an Aberdeen pilots-only affair. This warmup was the prelude to the announcement on the following day of a strike. Terry Wolfe-Milner QGM, a Canadian and Chief Pilot at Sumburgh, knew he could do nothing about the Aberdeen pilots and persuaded me to desist.

Terry was awarded the Queen's Gallantry Medal for recovering four men off the *Beryl 'A's SPM* (Single Point Mooring) buoy. Technicians were still commissioning the SPM after it had arrived in September 1975. On the 5th of December, it broke free in winds up to 65 knots. Terry and his co-pilot, Charlie Beilby, were outbound to fly the evening shuttle between the semi-sub drilling rig *Sedco 704*, *Beryl' A'* and rig *Dyvi 'A'*. Now, two-way with the *704*, the radio operator interrupted the numbers for the shuttle and informed them the SPM was adrift. They return to Sumburgh to mount the winch to G-BDII and board Winchman Phil Johns, Winch Operator Gerald Flaws, and his assistant Peter Moir. At 18:49, they depart Sumburgh and arrive back in the field, overhead the SPM at 19:23. To avoid striking the loading arm with the tail rotor and remain in sight of the deck in the dark, it was necessary to hover 60 degrees off the wind. At the same time, Terry is following the deck illuminated by the rotatable landing lights with guidance from Gerald. It is rolling and significantly, moving a considerable horizontal distance to and fro. They made 12 attempts to recover the men. By 19:45, they were all on board and landed on the *Beryl 'A'* five minutes later. Only then did they resume the shuttle, landing back in Sumburgh at 22:00. Phil is awarded the Queen's Commendation for Bravery. Gerald's expert conning? It goes unrewarded.

Terry taught me to shuttle. The instruction began during the construction of the *Thistle 'A'*. As with many others, the jacket arrives on location welded to a specially fabricated pontoon. In an ideal world, it then upends, sinking vertically into a precise position over the capped wellheads poking out of the seabed. In the case of some others, notably one in the Frigg field, it was so far out of whack it completely missed the wellheads and was never used. The topsides are now ready to be constructed. And *Thistle 'A'* was unique in the North Sea as to what happened next. It built itself. First, they mount a pedestal crane on one of the legs. This crane shortly snapped off, drowning the driver, a common occurrence offshore in the early days. After they mounted another to lift the various components off barges, they removed it on completion. Of course, during the build, there was no accommodation onboard for the construction workers; they had to be moved to and fro the *Belford Dolphin,* originally a semi-sub flotel, anchored alongside.

To move over 100 men each way could be time-consuming. Instead, Terry demonstrated a quick solution: Lift into the hover, climb upwards and backwards until the next deck came into view, let down, and land.

Elsewhere in the oilfields on windy days, making a circuit to land when shuttling was usual. Terry taught me to be economical with the air space and save time by eliminating the downwind segment beyond the destination, always remaining aerodynamically safe. Even in the 90-knot winds, I will have to deal with later when shuttling at night. Sometimes, a shuttle could take over four hours, a lone aircraft working the East Shetland Basin until another helicopter pilot comes on the ADF radio with, "Help me make it through the night .... let the devil take tomorrow, but tonight I need a friend," before flying back to base. (Written by Kris Kristofferson on an oil rig off Lafayette, LA, in 1970 when flying for Petroleum Helicopters International, Inc. - PHI, and recorded in Nashville, TN while working 7/7).

After taking off, the initial part of the procedure was to fly into the wind until you reached the normal operating speed (VNO) for an S-61N of 121 knots IAS (indicated airspeed), now making only 30 knots ground speed. On

reaching VNO, setting up a rate-one turn (30° bank) was now aerodynamically safe. The importance of this precaution is revealed later. Then continue at this rate until, at night, you can see your destination's lights. Keep turning. By now, you should ideally be passing through the downwind segment of the turn with the ground speed briefly at 210 knots. At this juncture, select a more specific point, ideally, the helideck if it has become visible. Then, use it to pivot the nose, adjust the bank rate accordingly, and set up a descent. Still turning, the ground speed is reducing as you cross over the wind. The turn should be complete by the time you are on short finals. Now, with that 90-knot headwind back again on the nose, you only have a 30-knot ground speed to wash off. The aircraft should be level and short of the committal point adjacent to the helideck by this time. Perfectly set up to land. The wind did all the work. It was just a case of using it intelligently - no need for the wind to blow you into the next parish farther down the downwind leg. Then, face a long slog into the wind through the turbulence on finals. As I had been working on his operation, he felt he had a case for keeping a homegrown shuttle pilot.
In the morning, we were refused travel by the oil company carriers; instead, BALPA funded seats south for us with British Airways. Aberdeen Air Traffic Control reciprocates and refuses to allow a private jet with Big Al onboard to enter their airspace. They relented when he came on the radio with what Lord McDonald later described in the subsequent enquiry as "A man whose language was more suited to the barrack room than the boardroom" and gave the flight permission to land. On arrival in Aberdeen, around 55 pilots formed a picket line out of the over 100 expected, probably because the vehicle chosen to precipitate action was somewhat unexpected, and the individual concerned was possibly not the most 'popular pixie in the wood'. Before joining Bristow, he had flown the line for BAH and was next in seniority to bid for a command. No opportunities appeared. Crewing was becoming a problem due to a lack of captains. Then he left. A staff vacancy notice for several captains to bring the crewing ratio back in balance was published the next day. The same day, he joined Bristow.
There were many reasons to act. The background crystallising this action interfered with this pilot's two-year rolling contract, providing him with an element of base security. As bad luck would have it, the personnel department in Redhill directed him to relocate abroad 18 months into his Aberdeen contract. A keen sailor, he had other plans: to sail his yacht in the Norwegian Fjords during the summer. This reluctance to move culminated in flight ops giving him a telex with his pre-flight planning instructions. He'd is fired. Redress in Redhill was swift. The head of personnel, Jack Brannon,

had a magnetic whiteboard in his office. A spreadsheet recording every pilot in the company on a magnetic strip. Not only his name, rank, pay scale and other details but also on which of Bristow's worldwide operations he was working. A sympathetic pilot took the initiative and made a clean sweep. When Jack arrived in the morning, the board was quite clean. The empire was in a heap on the floor.

Despite a relatively poor turnout, the resolution was firm. Ninety-five per cent of the participants were former officers, warrant officers and non-commissioned officers of Her Majesty and the US and Australian Armed forces, the latter vets of the Vietnam War, a future Lord and one of Big Al's former chief pilots from the early days of the Persian Gulf. A gentlemen's strike – as reported to the Press and Journal by the Grampian Police as they formed us into a huddle to have the most visual impact on television news channels. Industrial action was initially led (and here, their serving ranks are included as an indication it was not a belligerent exercise conducted by die-hard militant subversives) by Major Fred Pidcock. Towards the end of the first week, he handed over to US Navy Commander Bob Britts, a Vietnam vet and former Seawolf. (Think of a stand-in for Marlin Brando in 'On the Waterfront'). It will be the last time he flew 9M-ARV, a Malaysian registered S-61N he brought over from Terengganu, Malaysia. During this period, Bill Roy had invited me to stay, along with a fellow co-pilot, Howard Mersey, who would later become a CAA Flight Operations Inspector. He had rented a wing of Skene House, owned by Lady Hamilton, near Dunecht, west of Aberdeen. Bill owned just three items: a white MGC convertible sports car, a rocking chair, and a Bang & Olufsen TV with a remote control (hi-tech for 1977); at the same time, something was missing. He corrected this on the first day by collecting a case of Glenmorangie on the way home. Over the coming days, this new addition held a temporary position between the rocking chair and the TV. From here, we watched the newsreels of our progress inside when not forming the line outside the airport. A bedroom at the Airport Skean Dhu Hotel became the nerve centre for the strike; BALPA recorded it will be 40 years before the next one by Thomas Cook Airlines in 2017. The BALPA General Secretary Mark Young, with his hard-working secretary/assistant Molly, directed the effort. The police also assisted us throughout the country to teach first-timers how to picket the airport, road, and railway track access to refineries, as Ron Young explained. The instruction on picketing roundabouts leading to refineries was a parody of an instruction from the William Goldman film when Percy Garris stopped on his mule going down the mountain from the silver mine to the bank to collect the payroll. Turning around to the Hole in the Wall Gang in disgust, he spat: "Morons," stretching his neck out and spitting again for emphasis, "I've got morons on my team. Nobody is going to rob us going down the mountain. We have got no money. On the way back, then you can sweat," spit. And so, it was with roundabouts. Here, the police pointed out this simple truth to Ron. "Traffic will back up for miles if you picket the entrance to the roundabout. You picket the exit off the roundabout leading to the refinery."

Owing to the number of pilots required for so many duties, only one will invariably be available to create a picket. Elsewhere, Digby Mackworth was conducting a one-person railway picket outside a refinery. It was a long shift as the trains started running at four in the morning. With a little effort and a stroke of genius, he could be alerted to approaching trains from within his caravan parked on a railway embankment, even when resting. It worked like this. Below the embankment, lines connected the signal box to a signal at the entrance to the refinery. He fed string from the line up through the caravan window to a pinch on the front page of the FT. Whenever a train approached, the line jerked the string. The commotion would cause Digby to stir from his bunk, walk down the embankment, and stop the train. And that is how you become a peer of the realm.

Secondary picketing was still legal. The BAH pilots took an unpaid workday to join us during the action. Speaking to them years later, they reflected they had harboured assumptions. The traditional rivalry between BAH and Bristow had set the crews in opposing camps. Some begrudged their loss of pay. Yet when they joined the line, they observed when the dust had settled, "They were crews just like us!" The strike ended six weeks later when a Court of Enquiry in Glasgow was agreed, during which Lord McDonald revealed Bristow had anticipated this strike for 18 months; he had been laying plans to thwart it all that time. There was no going back.

Somehow, Bristow kept their show 'on the road'. Pilots drafted in from overseas operations and reduced schedules to the fields like BP Forties Field from 16 to 4 or 5 flights a day. These cuts were a considerable reduction. Though we must put the original 16 flights a day in context, BP was sitting on an oilfield with a projected yield of 1 billion barrels, later upgraded to 2.5 billion barrels – then the most lucrative field in the UK sector. The number of flights was of no consequence. Even if a single jiffy bag containing an 'o' ring were the only fare onboard, they would point out such a small component could make the difference between continued production and shutdown. Then there was the aviation fuel, trucked in for BHL by unidentified 'white tail' tankers and semi-trailers from as far away as Kent. A specially constructed new fuel farm ensured the operation was independent of the major providers.

Chapter 4. 1977 - 1978

BAH – Hitchhiking on Airlines – On the Seabed – Early Civilian SAR

With Bristow blacking us from employment for 21 years, BALPA helped set up a cooperative registered in Switzerland called OASA (Offshore Aviation SA) to provide contract pilots for Helikopter Service in Norway. Predominantly, foreign nationals opted for OASA, which lasted for six years until the downturn in 1983, and for Groenlandsfly, an established company in Greenland, BAH offered full-time employment for Brits. BAH was an experimental unit of BEA referred to by the Bristow crews as 'Brand X'. We joined BAH on Thursday, the 13th of June and were the first batch of six pilots. Our day began with the Flight Operations Director requesting we "Impart some commercialisation into the company" (Bristow style – though we knew no other), translating into not turning the flight around when only sandwiches from the rig were on offer. Or, if flight ops had not assembled their pre-flight briefing, point out, "If you can't do your job, I can't do mine." And head off for the car park. Offshore, if there was a change of plan or routing, there was never recourse to flight ops for permission or other excuses. We made that call ourselves, took the initiative and got on with it. On the S-61N fleet, this always prevailed. Above all, we should plan a flight to take off rather than plan to keep the hangar doors shut.

*

For BAH, a new era had dawned. In essence, Mike held a view much as Doc Daneeka in Joseph Heller's book Catch-22, who diagnosed (sic).
"Only crazy people fly; sane people don't and, therefore, are the most suitable people to fly."
"That's some catch, Catch-22," observed B-17 Bombardier Yossarian, moved by its simplicity.
"It's the best there is," Doc Daneeka agreed.
Yet hard to believe, Bristow did employ a pilot considered to be crazy, 'Mad Bob'. Concerned about his behaviour, the company sent him to be analysed. Months of tests later, they could find nothing wrong and sent him back to fly the line. Paradoxically, he was the only pilot who ever flew the North Sea with a certificate certifying him as sane. So, where did that leave the rest of us? Talking to divers, they thought helicopter pilots were crazy anyway. From

our standpoint, we reciprocated their sentiments, given their attrition and those with the bends, that we flew back to recover in hyperbaric chambers.
Four days after joining, we were flying the line, having completed our flying checks, and had been to Heathrow to collect our uniforms and have a dental and medical check. The former Bristow captains retained their rank, and, as company policy dictated, they were posted to Sumburgh as all new hires at the time were. There, they remained until senior enough to bid for a vacancy on a mainland base. I bided my time working out of Aberdeen until I accrued seniority for a command.
The folk law tempering our arrival in this new company was to learn we had a credit of three beach landings before demotion kicked in. The reason: on three previous occasions, managers had opted to land on the beach due to low fuel rather than to risk losing the engines waiting their turn to land later at the airport in bad weather. Operating the BAH S-61N was much the same as the Bristow aircraft, although the cockpit layout and cabin trims differed slightly. One key operating difference caused a close call many years later: an instrument departure in poor visibility off the Northerly runway at Aberdeen in an air traffic sequence behind a Bristow S-61N.
The climb out was normal, entering the overcast quite soon after taking off with a clearance to climb to 3,000 feet en route offshore. We broke into a small gap in the cloud shortly before levelling off to find a Bristow S-61N inside it a few yards ahead. With an evasive bank to starboard to avoid disturbing the Bristow passengers aft of the airstair door reading papers and some, we dived back into the cloud for safety with them non-the-wiser until we filed a near-miss. Why? It transpired air traffic control had not appreciated, even after all these years; the BAH climb settings differed from Bristow. BAH S-61N pilots used more power. The theory being a faster climb-out saved fuel en route by arriving earlier in the cruise. We had caught them up. Close. Offshore, where air traffic control was in its infancy, spatial awareness of aircraft in the vicinity would have kicked in much sooner as reliance on a third party for separation was not a given. Overseas is an altogether different matter related later.

Commuting. There are no flight concessions for the first year in any aviation company. Commuting to and from the South Hams in Devonshire was a question of asking the flight captain for a jump seat. One evening, the flight from Heathrow to Aberdeen was cancelled. Aberdeen was snow closed.
Approaching Glasgow, he radioed, requesting I join them night-stopping in their hotel. Upon arrival, a call to the Glasgow Operations Manager assured me that would be fine.

British airways helicopters

British Airways Helicopters began as an experimental helicopter unit within British European Airways in August 1947. Its fleet consisted of three Sikorsky S51s and two Bell 47B-3 aircraft.

In June 1948, the first helicopter-operated public mail service began from Peterborough to various points in East Anglia.

In June 1950, BEA Helicopters began the world's first regular scheduled passenger service between Liverpool and Cardiff using S51s followed a year later by a link from London Airport to Haymill Rotorstation, Birmingham.

In 1954, two Bristol 171 helicopters were used on services between Heathrow and Southampton, and the next year Westland-Sikorsky WS-55s operated an experimental service between Heathrow and Waterloo as well as twice-daily service between Birmingham's Elmdon Airport, Leicester and Nottingham.

In 1964, the first of BEA's Sikorsky S61Ns were delivered and the Penzance to Isles of Scilly route was inaugurated. The route has proved the economic viability of scheduled helicopter operations. It is the only profitable scheduled passenger helicopter service in the world. Previously the Penzance-Isles of Scilly route has been operated by a fixed-wing service, carrying less than 28,000 people a year. It now carries over 90,000 passengers a year.

North Sea Oil support operations started in the same year. British Airways Helicopters now play a vital part in the offshore exploration effort, operating North Sea services from Aberdeen, Sumburgh (Shetlands) and Beccles in East Anglia using 20 S61N helicopters, two Sikorsky S58Ts and one Bell 212 helicopter.

A Search and Rescue service is provided under contract on a 24 hour basis. In 1977, BAH received the major life-saving award of the year from HM Coastguard in recognition of their efforts.

British Airways Helicopters has made several major contributions to world rotary flight. The Company pioneered the ability to fly the helicopter at night and became the first civil operator to obtain clearance for night operations. Subsequently, they developed and obtained IFR clearance, becoming the first operator in the Western world to achieve this. The Company also explored the effects of helicopter flight in icing conditions and achieved another 'first' when they obtained clearance for such flying.
For the future, the company is planning to introduce even larger helicopters seating over 40 passengers for use both in the oil industry and on inter-city services.

Fig 12. BAH Commemorative Communication #110, on the 15th of August 1977. *Author's collection.*

Later in the bar that evening, a plan developed to arrive in Aberdeen before my shift started at 07:00. A BA (internally called 'Mainline') crew offered a lift but would not arrive until 09:00. Then I saw Rhys Perraton. An ex-Bristow pilot, he had diverted his Embraer Bandeirante freighter, originally bound from Stavanger-Sola to Aberdeen, to Glasgow instead. And yes, he had to be there at 07:00. Except there had been overnight snow and a tailback for de-icing. And no. Some snow was not going to interrupt his schedule. Pulling out of the queue of aircraft waiting for de-icing, he received clearance to line up and take off. Away from the apron lights, it was still quite dark. I did not have a headset, so looking at the starboard wing, at Rhys, and back to the wing, he answered the question above the din of the engines at max rpm by mouthing, “Watch this”. Now nicely spooled up, he released the brakes, and we trundled forward. Slowly, at first, then finally, at V1, he raised the nose, and we were momentarily airborne. Aft from the leading edge, you could see where the slipstream was carving furrows in the snow; he throttled right back. We bounced hard onto the runway in a flurry of snow. He repeated this process a couple more times. “To make sure”, he remarked afterwards before we climbed out.

*

A few years later, a neighbour, Prof Chalmers Clapperton, was interested in hearing this story. “That'll be him. I was attached to the Antarctic Survey Team studying glaciers in the region. I wrote a small book about the geology of South Georgia. It came in handy during an engagement to remove an Argentine Navy-supported commercial venture to dismantle the old whaling stations on the island.” Except this was an act of piracy as a British Company, Christian Salverson, a former whaling company, already had the contract. This was the first engagement of the Falklands War, Operation Paraquet, so named because the official name had been Parakeet. This title was a bit tame, and they adopted the weed killer's name instead. After all, this was a force of marines from 42 Commando, a troop of Special Air Service (SAS) and Special Boat Service (SBS). “The action took place three weeks into the declaration of war on the 21st of April 1982 to retake the island; they used my book as a guide. Several times, I had flown in the back of the De-Havilland DHC-6 Twin Otter in the Antarctic. It had been leased from Logan Air, painted red, fitted with skis, and our pilot was Rhys. The runways were built with packed snow, forming an embankment above the permafrost. And this was where he had learned to 'de-snow' the wings. On one occasion, we accelerated down the runway and slid off down the embankment. He managed to climb back up again, straighten out and, to our surprise, took off." Wise after the event.

*

For captains joining BAH from Bristow, the commute was different. BAH policy on your first posting to Shetland was to live on the island. This practice changed when confronted by a bunch of ex-strikers who were happy to work but not to reside there. Unlike Bristow, BAH crews had to find their own accommodation unless on a temporary posting. They commuted on the same charter flights as the offshore workers on a sub-load basis. I.e., if a seat onboard was available. Shell Expro, the main contractor, provided the service, chartering Dan-Air Services Ltd with their BAe HS 748s, otherwise known as 'Budgies'. With the exponential growth of the oil industry, Dan-Air procured as many HS 748s as they could from around the world. There would inevitably be at least one aircraft with a local modification. And their fleet was no exception. Unhappily, the consequences of one mod played out two years later in Sumburgh. I experienced this routine when I had my command.

*

By now, BAH was receiving new S-61Ns as per their original order and the crews to fly them. Again, the aircraft arrived as deck cargo at Southampton. The crewing clerk tasked some of us with delivering them to Gatwick, the main operating base. Onboard, they had no internal panels or floor, just bare spars. When en route with G-BEWL, the engineers reported the doors and windows falling out and into the sea. And now the rear port door had also removed the high-frequency radio aerial fasted along the same side.
(This aircraft was later lost at the *Brent Spar* accident in July 1990 when the tail rotor struck the top of the crane pylon, spun 150°, fell onto the side of the deck and toppled into the sea, as reported later with more detail).
Stopping at Shoreham, West Sussex, on the south coast while the engineers removed the cable from the tail rotor, Dave Creamer commented losing a few windows and a door could have been worse.

*

On the night of the 14th of November 1970, he had been in command of the BEA S-61N, G-ASNM. They were en route from Aberdeen to the drilling rig *Staflo* and flying at 1,250 feet in contact with Scottish Air Traffic Control

Centre (ATCC). Fifteen minutes after midnight, they are 52 miles outbound when the master caution and the main gearbox's low oil pressure lights come on. The main gearbox oil pressure gauge indicates zero, but all other indications are normal. In a descending turn back to Aberdeen, Dave asks his co-pilot Keith Gregson to transmit a MAYDAY "Fifty-two miles from Aberdeen on a track of one-one-eight (degrees from Aberdeen)" and alert their passenger.

Before the controller at Scottish could establish two-way communication, the transmission faded. Heading back, Keith makes further distress calls as they have not received a reply. Levelling at 50 feet, Dave reduces speed to 40 knots to land immediately, if necessary. The landing lights pick out the 9 to 14-foot waves below them. But could these be false indications? A minute later, they hear an unusual mechanical noise from the number one engine and gearbox region. As Dave turned to starboard and into a 30-knot wind, the number one engine accelerated, wound down and stopped. While Keith secured the dead engine, Dave prepared to land. At about 20 feet, the number two engine accelerated, then stopped. Three minutes after the initial warnings, he made a power-off touchdown 30° to the waves as recommended. The landing lights went out as the hull settled among the rough seas; all other lights remained on.

Acting on the original MAYDAY, Scottish informed the Edinburgh Rescue Co-ordination Centre at 00:16, and the search and rescue began. At 00:21, Scottish received a distress message. A United States Air Force C-141 Starlifter relayed they received a MAYDAY at 00:16 over Benbecula. It had been transmitted on the military rescue frequency 243.0 MHz, giving a position 51 miles from Aberdeen on a track of 118°M.

When the rotors stopped, Keith and the passenger launched the 26-man dingy from the emergency exit door on the port side of the rear fuselage. Initially, it blew downwind. They haul it back, load the aircraft's emergency equipment pack and floating emergency radio beacon, and clamber onboard. At this moment, the helicopter yawed to starboard, followed by a large wave, and began slowly rolling over. In doing so, it tore the life raft's upper compartment. Keith cut the dingy free to prevent further damage. Dave jumped into the water as the aircraft capsized and swam across to the raft. Because of the damage, they were unable to raise the canopy. Wet through, it feels much colder in their light clothing than the +2°C in the wind carried on a Northerly polar air steam. When they tried to operate the emergency radio beacon, they found the water in the life raft had activated its water-soluble switch; its aerial had extended. Except the aerial had broken off. While boarding in the dark, a survivor has trodden on it, snapping the aerial ¼" from

the base. Instead, they activated one of their life jacket personal locator beacons.
At 01:00, they saw a light and fired a signal rocket from the emergency pack. The pack contains two rockets and six distress flares. Despite the low trajectory caused by the life raft movement, a Swedish ship, MV *Gripen*, sees it from four miles away.
As she came closer, they fired another rocket. Half an hour after the first sighting, the *Gripen* crew hauled them onboard. The aircraft sank and was never recovered. The likely initial consequence of such a loss of gearbox lubrication would be a mechanical failure of the high-speed input of each engine to the main gearbox. A rapid increase in the power turbine speed of each engine would cause the over-speed shut-off system to stop the engine.

*

The experience of losing and dealing with a high-frequency radio aerial will be useful. It wrapped itself around the tail rotor of G-BEWM a few years later over the South China Sea. I've yet to lose a whole aircraft!

*

Flying the line for a new employer provided new offshore destinations. Two of the many stand out for entirely different reasons. The DSV *Capalonga* began life in 1958 as the MV *Bolton Abbey*. Brooke Marine of Lowestoft built her to plie between railheads at Hull and Rotterdam. She provided the link for packages sent by rail. In 1974, she was sold to a Panamanian company and renamed *Capalonga*. The following year, she was sold on and converted to a diving support vessel by her new Italian owners, Sub Sea Oil Services S.p.a. She soon built up a reputation on contract to Shell Expro for rolling whenever a sea was running. It was not unusual for skid-equipped helicopters, such as the Bell 212, to slide across her helideck net, despite the radio operator insisting she was within limits, 4° pitch and roll. Then, watch the artificial horizon dip up to 20 left and right after landing. To remain current, offshore helicopter pilots must complete a night-deck landing recency check every six months. It involved four landings and take-offs. This time, the check was different as it was the first to be conducted in the right-hand seat as part of my command course. John Baker chose the DSV *Capalonga* to complete mine as the closest offshore helideck to Sumburgh. On an evening in January 1980, the vessel operated on the pipelines leading into Sullom Voe from the ESB. Fortunately, I passed despite the best efforts of the ship to unseat us. In 1983, they sent her for scrap. Another memorable destination was the *MCP-01*. This concrete structure was a manifold compression platform located 108 miles northeast of Aberdeen. Initially, it pumped gas from the Frigg Field to the gas processing plant at St Fergus Gas Terminal near Peterhead. Two 32" pipes fed into the base of the platform, up through the central core, and then, under compression, fed back into one of two exit pipelines to St Fergus. Having two pipelines in parallel gave the operators Total the option to close off one for maintenance.

The *MCP-01* also functioned as an intermediate 'pigging station'. In the seventies, the technology to send 'pigs' hundreds of kilometres without assistance, as through the Nord Stream pipelines under the Baltic, did not exist, and required a midway station. At *MCP-01*, they could receive 'pigs' from the Frigg and change them out for fresh ones to send down the line to St Fergus. These 'pigs' were neoprene-rimmed plugs and, when introduced into the pipeline, used the gas pressure to propel them on their way. There were two designs of pigs. One was an intelligent pig recording the results of checks for corrosion and internal damage; the design of the other was to clean and remove accumulated water and condensates with thick abrasive brushes.

Besides the specially prepared breakfast, including minute steaks held over for when we shut down, the main attraction of the installation was the option to walk them off on the seabed. The platform was initially in ballast with water for the tow out. On location, the outer 102 m diameter circular base, nearly twice the circumference of the topsides, was pumped full of 170,000 tons of sand. More stable than water, it provided the ballast to stand free on the seabed. Within the core of the base was a bottomless shaft just nine metres in diameter. With the water pumped out, there was access to the seabed via connecting stairs and ladders attached to its walls. Walking around the North Sea's sandy floor, you could see where the pipelines came in and exited the platform. Of course, one trip sufficed; there was nothing else to see - just a dark gallery with essential lighting. Walking on the North Sea's seabed without getting dressed for the occasion, besides being a thoughtful experience, was the 400-foot climb back up again. By the time you had reached the helideck, a few more minute-steaks would not go missing.

*

Search and Rescue – SAR. The Department of Trade awarded BEA Helicopters a search and rescue (SAR) contract in 1971. It is the first civil aviation SAR cover for the UK sector of the Northern North Sea. A few S-61Ns are modified to have a temporary winch fitted, but critically, there is no ability to home onto emergency beacon transmissions. The aircraft were not dedicated to SAR operations and only fitted the winch when required. They based the service in Aberdeen. Over the years, at least one helicopter contracted to an oil company ditched annually in the North Sea. On most occasions, all on board will survive. Just.

A typical emergency occurred on the 1st of October 1977. On this occasion, Dave Paul, having planned his flight, happened to be at the window overlooking the airfield in BAH flight ops. "I was anticipating my aircraft taxiing in after the first rotation. Next to me on the windowsill was the HF radio with the volume turned down, as usual, to deaden its incessant carrier wave when," "*MAYDAY, MAYDAY, MAYDAY*". "The ops staff were discussing rosters and had just not heard it. I turned around. "*Bristows have ditched inbound from the Forties*!" Initially, they thought I was winding them up."

Crewed with Pushp Vaid VrC on a commercial in the S-61N, G-ATFM; we had not been long outbound to the southeast when, at 14:15, we had the call from ops: "Return to base, drop off the passengers, we're installing the Lucas Air Hoist. Captain Mike Fermor is planning the callout to an inbound from the Forties Field." A helicopter had ditched with main rotor vibration and significant control problems. It was a Bristow S-61N, G-BBHN, routing to Aberdeen from the rig *Venture II* with an injured passenger; he had two broken fingers and a leg in a splint. A BEAS (British Executive Air Services – later acquired by Bristow) Bell 212, G-BARJ heard their distress call. Four minutes later, they were visual with 'HN', shadowed and stood by them as they ditched in seas described as very rough with wave heights of 20 to 30 feet, 48 miles from Aberdeen at 14:18.

An eyewitness onboard the Bell saw brush the S-61N crest of a passing wave, lift off and touch down gently on the next crest and descend into a trough. When the captain of 'HN', Lee Smith, looked at the wall of water ahead, he realised they had to shut down and evacuate the aircraft. It was now blowing 30 to 35 knots from the northwest. They wear uniform trousers and shirts; their passenger is in overalls. They strap on their life jackets around their waists. The witness saw the helicopter climb the face of this very steep wave, achieving a pitch angle of about 30°, and on reaching the crest, the bow lifted clear. It carried the machine backwards, yawing about 30° to the left under the influence of the wind and waves. The main rotor blades dug into the water as it rolled over to port and capsized almost immediately. Despite having difficulty orienting themselves inside the aircraft (they had released their safety belts before the helicopter had settled inverted), Lee escaped through his broken window as the cockpit submerged. He did not notice his co-pilot, American and Vietnam Vet Harry Spriggs, enter the cabin with the passenger walking along the ceiling towards him. Harry released the buckle of the life raft stowage and tried to move the valise towards the cargo door. The cabin was rapidly filling with water as the aircraft settled. Because the cabin was inverted, the floor spreader boards became detached, and the baggage compartment doors were hanging down. The airspace above them was rapidly diminishing. Next, Harry tried to open the cargo door through which to launch the life raft. Due to the water's pressure, he could not open it.

While Harry was manoeuvring the life raft, Lee was trying to open the cargo door from the outside. Unsuccessful, he had swum back to see if the co-pilot was still in the cockpit. Diving down and ascertaining he was not there; he swam back and tried the cargo door again. Inside, the occupants were neck-deep in water; the breathing space left overhead was reducing. Combining their efforts, they manage to prize it open sufficiently, pushing against it from the inside; at the same time, Lee pulls from the outside, and they squeeze through despite it continually sliding shut under the action of the waves and the pitching hull. Outside, Lee held the passenger against the side of the hull by holding onto the submerged cargo hook release cable.

Meanwhile, Harry dived back into the cabin to retrieve the life raft. The inverted flooring and the baggage locker door had trapped it by its natural buoyancy. The captain of 'RJ', flying as a single pilot, saw that HN's crew had been unsuccessful in launching their dingy. (it later inflated inside the cabin), instructed his passengers to toss their dingy down to them. Before they could prevent him from doing so, a passenger partially opened the life raft pack; it landed ten meters from the survivors and drifted away. By the time Harry reached it, it was now 100 meters away. He swam back through the freezing waves, dragging it by the valise fabric. Then, within three metres of the wreck, the life raft spilt out of the pack. The drag was too great for him to make any progress. The life raft inadvertently inflated as he gathered the fabric into a manageable bundle. The wind rapidly carried it away. Exhausted, he boarded it and tried to paddle back to the others. He could not make any headway against the rough sea and high wind or prevent it from drifting farther downwind.

Lee decides to move the passenger to a more secure location by the landing gear sponson. Using his legs, he wedges the passenger against the landing gear struts whilst holding onto a fuel vent pipe protruding from the bottom of the hull. The wreck is broadside to the waves, continuously rolling the survivors underwater and swamping them in fuel-contaminated water with each passing wave. Nearly 12 years had passed since his crew plucked those three men from the sea when the *Sea Gem* capsized. If they could survive, so could he and his wounded passenger. G-BARJ remained overhead and dropped a floating emergency beacon. A second helicopter arrives, an S-58ET G-BCDE flown single pilot. The captain instructed his passenger to drop their life raft, but it drifted away when it inflated. Leaving 'RJ' at the scene, 'DE' took station on the life raft containing Harry Spriggs. A second Bristow aircraft arrives, the S-61N, G-BBVB, and takes over from 'RJ' running short of fuel.

Not long after taking off, we landed back at Aberdeen. The engineers fastened the Lucas Air Hoist frame to hardpoints inside the cargo door and connected the power source umbilical to a bleed air outlet from one of the engines. They swing the business end of the hoist out of the cargo door and insert a pin into the knuckle joint to lock it. Then, the cable is paid out and back in to check for snags. Now, with the cable fully reeled in, the locking pin removed, the hoist swung back inboard, and the cargo door closed, the hoist is ready and tested for rescue. The winch operator and winchman (the guy who goes down the wire) were now on board, closing the airstair door behind them. The flight departed 26 minutes after we heard the call, and Mike, with his co-pilot Steve Stubbs, intercepted the most direct route from the Forties Field.

Fig 13: Disembarking Captain Lee Smith from G-ATFM. Technical Crew member Ken Jacobs is in attendance. *Photo credit: Dave Paul*

Forty-three minutes after the distress call and 35 minutes after ditching, they spotted the landing lights of G-BBVB. Their crew escorted them to the upturned helicopter. It was not easy to locate and keep in view due to its white hull amongst the seas. Ten minutes later, winchman Ken Jacobs had plucked both survivors from the wreck and Harry from the life raft that had drifted half a mile downwind, just 53 minutes after the ditching. It was a close-run thing as Lee was suffering. His body temperature had fallen below +33° C into the semi-conscious zone, displaying moderate hypothermia symptoms. The medical opinion considered that if there had been a delay to his rescue by even a few minutes, he would have lost consciousness and drowned in the existing sea conditions.

The cause of the vibration was a temporary repair using blade tape to mask a partially raised and disbonded trailing edge pocket. The previous day, the tape had lost adhesion and was flapping loosely. Though there was no record, they replaced the old tape that night. It was a standard procedure permitted by the manufacturer and airworthiness authority. This solution could have been inadequate, as the pocket may have partially delaminated. In the first case, the manual cites *when a chordwise temporary repair tape lifts and partially separates, there is a one-per-revolution vibration and possible feedback through the controls.* Tape wear used to happen frequently without any drama. It was more likely the second case: "When a pocket dis-bonds, it separates at the rear of the spar (the back wall) and peels back into the airflow. This pocket lifting causes a tab effect with one per revolution vibration depending on the extent and location along the blade of the pocket. And it can result in feedback through the controls and noise. Moreover, it can become quite loud and symptomatic of flying with one of the hydraulic systems disengaged." (Agreed. I know from experience!) It was this feedback and noise the crew reported having experienced. With the noise increasing and, as Lee brought 'HN' to a hover, the vibration intensified, making the aircraft increasingly difficult to handle. They dispelled thoughts of keeping it in the air to the extent that ditching was preferable, for they suspected the rotor hub was now under extreme stress. Making an unscheduled arrival later onto land placed the passenger at additional risk if they crashed.

Three days later, the floating wreckage of the aircraft was towed into Peterhead Harbour. According to the report, *examination of the main rotor head and its associated cyclic and collective control systems revealed no evidence of any failure that could have contributed to the conditions described,* fitting in with pocket delamination in flight. They do not recover the main rotor blades.

As a postscript to this incident, Bell 212 G-BARJ, now owned by Bristow, was later ditched in the East Shetland Basin. On the 24th of December 1983, the crew were on a winch training flight to the *Brent 'C'* standby vessel, an ex-Lowestoft trawler, *Huddersfield Town*. Dave Chinn was offloading a drill bit from his S-61N on the *Brent 'C*. "I watched them lower the winch hook with a ballast weight, and it fetched on the stern. As the vessel began to corkscrew in a more significant swell, it allowed two turns of the cable to collect on the deck. The winch operator winched in, and as the stern dropped into a deep trough, the cable swung aft. The hook struck the guard rail, where it and the weight wrapped themselves around the middle rail and immediately pulled taught. This snatch caused the aircraft to roll to the right, pitch approximately 45° nose down and plunge into the sea." Witnesses estimated the elapsed time from snagging to ditching was three to four seconds. "Of course, they had no time to put out a MAYDAY. And much to the displeasure of the crew on the standby vessel, the helicopter blades had severed their radio aerials on the way down. I put out a MAYDAY on their behalf as the 212 disappeared from view below the edge of the *'Charlie'* helideck." The crew survived. Happy Christmas!

Chapter 5. 1978 – 1980

A Rope & Some Paint – Spindles - Distressed Budgie - Grounded

HN was one of at least 24 aircraft to ditch in the UK sector between 1975 and 2012. So frequent were they when asked if the Bristow attrition rate was of concern, a Lloyd's underwriter replied, "On the contrary, they are very reliable. They lose one every 18 months." Unfortunately, there have been a few since then. The Norwegians did not fare much better in their sector.

Following HN's incident, Bristow introduced the first two safety measures: a rope to hang on to around the hull and the white hull painted with dayglow orange chevrons for better visibility. Ditching procedures for helicopters were to take into account the probability of a capsize after splashdown, including locating the emergency exits from where you were sitting (by placing one hand nearest to it; the other on your harness release) and a suitable time to release safety belts (ideally when you judged the aircraft was stable and had stopped rolling [over]); the stowage of inflatable life rafts in helicopters designed to be deployable with the aircraft inverted (meaning at least one could be accessed from outside); auxiliary floatation bags to be fitted to S-61N helicopters to increase their waterborne lateral stability; both crew and passengers in helicopters operating over cold water should wear anti-exposure clothing –(survival suits, formerly only required when flying in polar regions); helicopter pilots, when operating over water, should be required to always wear life jackets; the sea anchor be redesigned to facilitate deployment rather than stowed under the co-pilot's seat and all helicopters assigned to the SAR role should have the capability of homing onto emergency beacon transmitters. It was quite a list when you consider Oil & Gas (O&G) helicopter operations had been operating over the Northern North Sea for ten years without any of these safety modifications and procedures. Apart from the rope and the chevrons BAH now added on the back of them being mandated, it will take a few more years for the other recommendations to be mandatory. Finally, Shetland should have a SAR Helicopter base. Indeed, when Sea King helicopters became stationed at RAF Boulmer and RAF Lossiemouth, British Airways Helicopters relocated SAR from Aberdeen to Sumburgh in 1979.

*

Training and checking. Around this time, BAH had an S-61N Flight Simulation Training Device (FSTD), usually referred to as the 'sim', built at Aberdeen. In 1978, it was to be the first full-motion helicopter simulator ever built. It could demonstrate many emergencies with an accompanying soundtrack from the engines, transmissions, and rotors. At any stage, the flight could be 'frozen' to discuss the next event or bollock/commend the previous one, then resume. Part of the acceptance trials was to calibrate the systems and navaids. From time to time, the calibration team took a pilot offline to assist in this process. When my turn came, it was to calibrate the distance measuring equipment (DME) that calculates the range from a (usually) co-located radio beacon.

Once completed, I asked the Rediffusion engineer if I could simulate flying to an oil rig. On landing, I lowered the collective, expecting the slight rocking motion as the oleos compressed, except it did not. It continued to descend! Briefly, it went pretty dark. Then, just as in an elevator (lift) passing floors going down, the legs of the rig appeared around me and then disappeared. I was heading for the seabed. "Haven't sorted that bit out yet, sir. Can you come back tomorrow?" Luckily for the passengers, my landings were never that heavy. I now had the unique experience of knowing what to expect. Once up and running, the 'sim' changed how the trainers conducted our checks. The usual method among one or two unpopular trainers was to exercise their knowledge on the unfortunate by luring them into areas guaranteeing failure.

That said, the sim enabled the instructor to demonstrate and for us to practice systems and manoeuvres that would otherwise be unsafe to carry out in an aircraft. In the eyes of the instructor, this training meant there was no reason to fail. Of course, we knew better. The following response worked equally well after a poor ground school exam result. When the instructor lamented his student's poor performance, we replied, "It's a shame. You've tried and only have yourself to blame. You may think you know the stuff. It's just that you have a problem imparting it." With the new simulator and an enlightened CAA, by 1980, evolution consigned the trappers to the dustbin if they wanted to continue in the training section. Another benefit of having the sim was the operator and proficiency checks. They already alternated every six months; now, they alternated with one in the sim and the other in the aircraft. Operator proficiency checks in the sim could include abnormal and emergency procedures otherwise considered unsafe to practice in the aircraft. In contrast, a proficiency check is a check ride to demonstrate flying skill and to revalidate aircraft type and instrument ratings or privileges.

Unsurprisingly, the aircraft became an easier venue for some pilots. As a prelude to all check rides, the instructor would brief, "I want you to treat this as a normal flight." I was on an instrument check flight in a Super Puma AS332L1 in the 1990s with Mike Tingle, a type rating examiner. For this check, screens are fitted across and inside the windscreen to simulate flying blind. Air traffic control directs us to join the stack and take up the hold before an instrument approach. After several racetrack patterns, I tapped a cigarette free from its pack,
"May I have a light, please?" Silence.
"Just treating it as a normal flight, Mike."
"Go on then, give me a fag."

*

Unlike most professions, commercial pilots have regular checks to ensure they are suitably proficient to continue their trade. These two checks are backed up with an aircrew medical every six months, an annual technical refresher, and a line check. The latter is a normal commercial flight assessed by a line trainer or an instructor. And it was on a line check a few years later; we had a surprise guest. Along with Iggy Davidson, who was now heading up the Training Department after Dave Humble retired, we set off towards the Piper field on a misty morning.
The Piper and Claymore fields were part of Occidental Petroleum's (OXY) empire owned by Armand Hammer. The passengers will leave the aircraft on the first of five stops; freight is the remaining payload for the other destinations. Arriving in the field, we let down into the fog, and after disembarking the passengers, we dropped off the deck back in sight of the sea again. Then, at a low level and with the aid of the radar and rig radio beacons, we routed to the other destinations. All the sectors were in up to one-mile visibility, and towards the end, Iggy remarked, "I hope you know where you are because I don't and have just been there." Understandably. Trainers spend less time on the line than we did due to their onshore commitments in the office, lecture room and simulator. Nowadays, if the next installation nearby cannot be seen before taking off and you cannot maintain a suitable height, each approach is via an airborne radar approach (ARA). And this involves a time-consuming climb out and let down.
Arriving back in Aberdeen, we shut down. Before we disembarked, Iggy signed me off for another 12 months. Then, a gentleman poked his head into the cockpit and introduced himself. "Hi! I'm Julian Hammer. Thank you for the flight." Our expressions betrayed us as we let that sink in, unaware we

had a passenger onboard and now none other than a Hammer when he continued. "Usually, the pilots are so careful not to alarm the passengers, but that beat anything at Coney Island. Best flight in a helicopter ever." Armand's only son, travelling incognito, wanted to experience a North Sea flight. And he was not disappointed! Somehow, we overlooked him as the offshore manifests do not record any passengers – he is a round-tripper. The ramp staff had loaded freight on spreader boards forward of the airstair door. He had boarded at Aberdeen and sat hidden, unless you checked, by a double, high-backed seat facing backwards in row eight, aft of this door.

*

In June 1978, one word was foremost on the mind of the S-61N fleet in the hangar, tech office, ops, and crew room: spindle - a main rotor-head component plugged into a blade's root. Bolts fastened them together around the rotor-blade cuff. It took time to recede when it was back in the news on the 12th of March 1981. Bristow S-76A, G-BGXY, was on a training flight over South Kirkton, Aberdeenshire. At about 15:12, they were 3,000 feet above farmland when one main rotor blade detached. Two crew and two passengers died. The accident report concluded the blade detached through failure, in fatigue, of the blade root spindle. The cause of the fatigue was wear in a dry-lubricating bearing and a production deburring process that differed from the fatigue test standard.

It had happened before on the 14th of August 1968. The Sikorsky S-61L, N300Y, on Flight 417, operated by Los Angeles Airways from LAX, crashed at Compton en route to Anaheim, California.

Los Angeles Helicopter Control cleared Flight 417 to take off at 10:26. The captain reported to Hawthorne Tower they were departing Los Angeles eastbound along Imperial Boulevard at 1,200 feet. At 10:33, Helicopter Control advised,

"LA, four seventeen, seven miles east, radar service terminated."

The crew acknowledged, "Four seventeen, thank you."

It was the last known radio contact with that flight. Three crew and 18 passengers died when the spindle connecting the main rotor head to the yellow main rotor blade broke. The Safety Board determined the accident's probable cause was the fatigue failure of the yellow blade spindle. The fatigue crack originated in an area of substandard hardness and inadequate shot peening. And more recently, in May 1978, a main rotor head spindle failure to a US Coastguard Sea King.

This time, it was closer to home. Helikopter Service A/S Flight Helibus 165 was operating out of Bergen-Flesland to *Statfjord 'A'* on the morning of the 26th of June 1978. Today's flight time in S-61N, LN-OQS, was filed as 65 minutes. Helibus 165 departed at 10:25 with 16 passengers and two crew and was now working Stavanger Radio. En route at 1,000 feet, they had reported passing waypoint Charlie at 11:06. They estimated waypoint Delta at 11:22. Six minutes after the crew failed to report at Delta, Stavanger Radio tried and could not raise them.

Ten minutes later, the crew of a Bell 212 on the same route reported wreckage in the sea—midway between the two reporting points and 78 nautical miles from Flesland. No one survived. A salvage team recovered the main part of the helicopter from the seabed at 200 metres. They found the main rotor head badly damaged; the main rotor blade No.5 with spindle had separated from the main rotor head. The cause was material fatigue in the spindle. The spindle must accept up to 40 tons of centrifugal forces on large helicopters. The manufacturer had no choice and developed a new reinforced spindle. But this will take time.

Meanwhile, engineers carried out extensive checks on all S-61Ns. At the time, before the Super Pumas arrived, they were the workhorse of the North Sea. The only way to check the integrity of a spindle is to remove each 28-foot rotor blade to access it. Helikopter Service avoided another S-61N crash when they found a spindle with cracks propagating 90% through it.

*

Besides BHL and BAH, there were now two more heavy helicopter operators on the North Sea: British Caledonian Helicopters and North Scottish Helicopters, the latter owned by the Bond Family. In 1979, these two operators began building a fleet of S-61N helicopters. It was usual for most companies to secure new work with a lost leader. And then, when established, jack up the price to ensure a reasonable profit margin. The market share was paramount for the Bond brothers, and any small margin was at their staff's expense. As their Flight Operations Manager related one evening to me, "BAH pilot's terms and conditions were unsustainable." He could have said, "His crews were content to travel by train third class on wooden seats and slip in B&Bs; BAH Union reps will only accept first-class travel and slip in five-star hotels for their members." True. But then he only hired non-union crews. They were predominantly a core of former NCOs who were preconditioned to accepting instructions and would tolerate these third-rate conditions. Their terms were as those crews flying the mail across the

US in the twenties and thirties—no wonder this treatment led to the formation of the Air Line Pilots Association.
British Caledonian Helicopters was part of the fixed-wing company of that name. They built up a fleet of four S-61N and three Bell 214ST. One S-61N was ZS-HDK, owned by Court Line Helicopters, South Africa. BAH leased it in 1978 and registered it as G-BFPF. Unfortunately, it spent time being unserviceable before being moved to BCal in 1981. Their terms and conditions of employment were similar to BAH. They will only operate for seven years before being bought by Bristow. British Airways acquired its parent company a year later.

*

A few seconds after 16:00 on the 31st of July 1979, Dan-Air HS 748, G-BEKF, Shell Expro charter Flight 0034 ran into the sea at the end of runway 09 at Sumburgh. The gust lock selector for the elevator in the cockpit, poorly modified by its former owner, Argentine oil company Yacimientos Petroliferos, inadvertently re-engaged during the take-off run. Unnoticed by the crew, it had locked the elevator in the full, nose-down attitude. The flight never made it airborne. Unable to rotate, they ran out of runway. The aircraft crossed over the airfield perimeter road, breaking off the nose wheel on a half-metre-high step bordering the road and an area eroded by wave action. They plunged at approximately 11° nose down into the sea 20 meters from the shore. The port wing broke off on impact.
The aircraft came to rest a farther 30 meters out into the North Sea. It surged through an open forward cargo door, threatening all 47 persons onboard, tilting the aircraft further. When the air hostess, Elizabeth Cowe, opened the rear cabin door, a heavy swell on the back of a 26-knot Easterly flooded in. Within 30 seconds, the water was up to neck height. She evacuated most of the 44 passengers before being pushed out by a passenger. She was among 30 who managed to swim the 40 meters to the shore, including John Finnie (ex-BHL and flying for BAH). John put his survival down to being asleep at the back of the aircraft. Fifteen others and the flight deck crew drowned. Two well-intentioned S-61N helicopter crews in the area may have contributed to their demise. They flew overhead and dropped two inflatable life rafts. The wind blew them away from the scene. In an attempt to blow them back with downwash from their rotors, they unintentionally drowned some survivors. Divers later found six passengers and the co-pilot in the aircraft. 23-year-old Liz Cowe was awarded the MBE for conducting a calm and orderly evacuation.

Fig 14. Dan-Air Flight 0034. Sumburgh, the 31st of July 1979.
Photo credit: ©Daily Record/Mirrorpix

The accident report noted BAe designed the HS 748 as a rugged DC-3 replacement aircraft. Most operators of this type consist of smaller overseas companies flying in widely varying conditions and often with limited engineering resources, over whose standards the CAA and the manufacturer have little or no control. They concluded that, under these conditions, the rigorous control of all aspects of the maintenance of the gust-lock system that are demonstratively necessary for the aircraft's safety might not be achieved continuously by all HS 748 operators.

*

After 18 months with the company and sufficient seniority, I secured a command vacancy and completed the command course at the end of 1979. It was still a condition for new BAH captains to operate out of Sumburgh. The choice remained: set up residence or commute. In January 1980, knowing the risks, I chose the latter.

There were less frequent, alternative means of travel, including Skyways DC-3 Dakotas. I knew the Skyways Captain, Ray Elliot, who had taught me to fly twins at Air Service Training, Scone, Perthshire. There, he had executed a perfect wheels-up landing on the grass when the gear in the Cessna 310 failed to lock down. Ray invited me to a ride on the jump seat and, once airborne, asked me to tune a non-directional beacon (NDB) frequency using its original 'pepper mill grinder' automatic direction finder tuner in the overhead panel, just for old times' sake. So, turning the handle to the left, too much; a shade to the right, not quite; back a touch; just right! And I thought our kit was ancient.

*

It was usual to spend the first two years on the island until senior enough to bid for a position elsewhere. For one commuter who had successfully secured a position in Aberdeen, departing on his final Friday was not so easy. Inherited from the RAF, he had left his regulation blue holdall in the crew room. When he returned from his last flight, he could not collect it. The culprit explained this prank to me when I went across the apron to the terminal to check in on my flight home. He had been to the company stores and had borrowed a hammer and a handful of galvanised roofing nails, the ones with the large heads for fastening bituminous felt. He had removed the bag's contents, nailed it to the floor, replaced them and zipped it back up. And now the police had been summoned. Even they saw the amusing side and drove off without pursuing it further.

*

In June, with Mike Warren, we conducted an arrival procedure I had never tried before or attempted again. We had left Sumburgh earlier than usual at just after six in the morning, bound for the *Heather 'A'* with overnight freight Union 76 wanted 'yesterday' as usual. The weather brief did not forecast fog for Sumburgh. Except, on the return sector, it beat us to it. Turning west off track, we headed for Scatsta. When two way on the radio, they declared they had been fog-bound for a few days; the approach was still below limits. It was unusual for both airports to be unusable due to fog. We continued on top at 3,000 feet to the overhead, where, to our surprise, we could see the runway below through a continuous break in the cloud. It did not take long to agree; this option was too good to miss so long as we kept the turns tight and remained within this clear hole. It will probably be all right. Circling down through this providential shaft in the weather, it was not long before we touched down. Taxiing over to the apron, we shut down next to some Dan-Air HS 748s. They had been there since the fog arrived. The taxi took us to the nearby small town of Brae, where the driver discharged us across the road from the hotel. He risked losing his car in the deep water-filled ruts in the main road to drive any closer. In fairness, it looked as if horses and wagons had churned it up; it could have been a winter scene out of a Western frontier town. We quickly fitted in with the locals with mud up to our hocks. When checking in, we met up in the hotel lobby with some Dan-Air crew. They mentioned they had the refreshments sorted and that we join them for lunch. Dan-Air had the charter to airlift workers from Glasgow to construct an enormous oil terminal on the northern shore of Sullom Voe.

At any one time between 1975 and 1981, there were 6,000 persons on site. It was one of the largest construction sites in Europe and covered over 1,000 acres. The contractor had moored a car ferry nearby to house them until they had built two construction camps: Firth and Toft. Originally, the drive to the camps passed along the track that took in the shoreline from Gaven, washing the tyres in the sea at high tide and then up to Calbeck before they laid proper roads. At Toft Camp, we had lunch and subsequent meals until we flew out the following afternoon when the weather had cleared. It was a good thing we did not stay longer.

We would have begun to look like our fixed-wing friends. They revealed their condition when we joined the queue in the galley and had not warned us no expense was spared at these camps to keep the contractors well-fed. Picking up a warm plate, I proffered it to the chef forking out steaks – big T Bones. Then, I made the mistake of momentarily looking away. With my arm now sagging, it was too late to realise there were already three onboard, and he was reaching to land a fourth. The term 'bears' was often used to refer to offshore workers. Looking around the dining room on the first day, it became clear they would disappear in the shadow of these men. No. The term 'bear' will need to be redefined.

They later installed a more permanent camp called Stanley. From here, they will conduct the running of the terminal. It had three areas: the power station and a plant separating the gas from the oil piped from the East of Shetland Basin and later from the West of Shetland oilfields shipped by shuttle tanker. The oil fed into a third area, a field of 16 crude oil storage tanks. Each tank can hold 600,000 barrels or potentially store 9.6 million barrels on site. From them, pipework led to the four loading jetties. They could load over 500,000 metric tons an hour when at peak discharge and turn a supertanker around in a 12-hour shift. There was a time when four vessels arrived and left daily to ship Scottish crude worldwide, now reduced to just one sailing a day.

*

There was an occasional break from Sumburgh to work out of Aberdeen. One of these cropped up the following month in July. We had returned from

the drilling rigs *Western Pacesetter II* and *Sedco 701* and had joined the Aberdeen holding pattern. Our licences cleared us to operate to lower limits for landing, but the weather was just below them. We need a 500-metre runway visual range and a 150-foot cloud base. (They calculated this range in the early days by counting runway lights by standing on top of a car – nowadays with an instrument on a 14-foot-high pole above the height of the runway. The lights are usually spaced 30 metres apart. Then multiply the distance between them). There is a possibility of the weather lifting. Inverness, our alternate, was wide open with a suitable terminal area forecast. We elected to go there when we were down to visual landing fuel reserve remaining plus half an hour, as we did. As we passed RAF Lossiemouth down our right-hand side, we called Inverness on the other box. They informed us they were (sea) fog-bound. Preserving fuel for a go-around, we let down with fog in the vicinity at Lossiemouth, already on our weather limits for landing on instruments.
Would we make it? Now, passing the critical 1,000 feet above the threshold when an approach may continue if the runway visual range falls below limits, the controller advised us the visibility was now below 100 metres. Then, Henry Kissinger's observation came to mind: "The absence of alternatives clears the mind marvellously!" Continuing, we touched down with one centreline light (here, they are at 30-metre intervals), just visible in the fog ahead. We declined taxi instructions and waited for an escort/follow me land-rover whose driver admitted he had trouble finding us. Lost, and not only for words.

*

Grounded! It was around 22:30 on an August evening, again operating out of Aberdeen. There was a phone call from the rostering clerk,
"You're grounded."
No explanation, just "You're grounded."
As captains in British Airways, we have a DO3 staff category as Senior Staff Members. I called the Chief Pilot. Emphatically, I told him,
"A clerk has grounded me!"
"He's not a clerk! He's an officer, and you will report to the Flight Ops Director in the morning."
He gave no other explanation. With Dave Hogg, the BALPA Company Council Chairman, we met outside the Flight Operations Director's office the next day. It transpires that George Bain, a former BAH Sumburgh Chief Pilot, now the BP Aviation manager, refused to pay for the flight. We had not got

in. Jock Cameron, the BAH founder and managing director, was furious. When I arrived with Dave, the Flight Operations Manager and the Chief Pilot were already in the Flight Operations Director's office. It did not look good, and Jock wanted a result. Before Dave went in to receive the brief, he asked me: "So what happened?" I explained we had come into work in the afternoon to fly a BP ad hoc flight for Bristow to a drillship some 140 miles west of Stornoway, Outer Hebrides. To save time, before we arrived in ops, the Flight Ops Manager had planned the flight using Decca maps provided by Bristow. As it was outside the coverage of Decca roller maps used by the company, we would hand navigate on the Decca paper maps our position against the decometers. No problem. He had assured me these maps were now on the aircraft.
At 14:00, we took off and headed for Stornoway, our first fuel stop, 144 miles away. Progress was slow as we battled a stiff headwind. After a climb to Flight Level 65 to clear the hills, it was two hours before we left the storm-swept Beasts of Holm on our port side as we coasted in to land on RW 24. In similar conditions, *HM Yacht Iolair* had run aground on the Beasts. It was no ordinary shipwreck. In the early morning of New Year's Day 1919, 205 lives, mainly World War I veterans, are lost, including 175 from Lewis alone. Not since the *Titanic*, on the 15th of April 1912, had so many been lost in peacetime from a British ship.
Now, fuelling, we looked for the maps. They were not on board. Despite the wind, we decided to fly at a height to enable crosscuts to be taken from beacons to plot our position along our bearing from Stornoway VOR. Radio reception from the ship was weak, if non-existent. On arrival in the area, we let down below the broken cloud to the visibility of up to ten miles and stormy seas. No ship. After we had used up the five minutes of loitering fuel searching, we routed back. By now, Stornoway was closed. Inverness was still open until 21:00. There, we refuelled. It will be 21:10 before we shut down in Aberdeen over seven hours and 570 nautical miles later. At this point, Dave mentioned a passenger had seen the ship; we had flown past it! Then, the Flight Operations Director's office door opened, and he went in, leaving me to digest this new and improbable information. A few minutes later, he reappeared. It turns out the manager had returned the maps to Bristow before the flight. And his plot for the drillship was in the wrong position. It was west of the wrong island, not Lewis but Shetland way to the north where the Schiehallion and Foinhaven discoveries lie. Back on the line! And yet there was an irony to where the Flight Operations Manager had plotted it: The petroleum industry now has evidence of a significant oilfield

off the west coast of Lewis dwarfing many of the more important discoveries worldwide.
By coincidence, I will be based offshore some years later on the semi-sub emergency support vessel ESV *Iolair* in the same area where this drillship was working.

Chapter 6. 1980 - 1982

Sumburgh Ops' – Shrapnel - Water Landings – Dambuster Airfield

Bill Ashpole best describes Sumburgh operations up to 1972 in his blog – www.ashpole.org.uk and not much had changed except by 1978, it had become the second busiest airport in the country after Heathrow, peaking at 55,000 movements. By 1980, there was no noticeable decline. Invariably, landing clearances for the lead of four or five helicopters arriving at once receive a block clearance to land; there was no 'airtime' on the tower radio frequency for all to make the regulatory calls. Pete Weller, an air traffic control controller, should be remembered for effortlessly choreographing the show day or night. Seemingly dense skies of traffic morphed into an airborne ballet when he was on shift as he gave unhurried instructions, clearances, and suggestions to keep the flow moving without holding.
The BAH and Bristow hangars are located on the western end of a disused runway 04/22, just past the passenger terminal. (This was before the new one, Wilsness, opened on the eastern side of the airfield in 1979). And helicopters and fixed-wing all parked, in a fashion, together. Space was tight; it was known for the skid-equipped Bell 212s to 'chop' their way onto a spot and take a 'bite' out of a DC-3 vertical stabiliser. The rule was if you had to damage another aircraft when manoeuvring, and it happened, then it was better to impact one not belonging to your company; tight. S-61Ns had a slight advantage as they could reverse out of confined areas. Just a matter of having the tail wheel lock engaged, pulling pitch on the collective to release the weight off the oleos and easing the cyclic back until the ship began to move backwards, just as fixed-wing propellor aircraft when the reverse pitch is applied.

*

Offshore, the Cold War was much in evidence. Every aircraft had a booklet describing Soviet aircraft and warships, including silhouettes for recognition purposes. On the way to the East Shetland Basin, it was not unusual to see a raft of 12 or more Soviet warships, submarines, and auxiliary supply ships moored three abreast. Or the Soviet ocean-going tug bristling with aerials permanently on listening watch 30 miles offshore from Sumburgh under the inbound track 'Mike' from the Brent. On one occasion, we made a slow fly past a new Krivak-II class anti-submarine frigate with the crew lined up on the deck, hats held aloft and waving, providing a warm reception tempered by its signature flat pod of four surface-to-surface anti-submarine (SSM/ASW) missiles on the bow deck. And rap. "Hot dog pack, Smokestack, Guns in the Back – Krivak," according to US Navy silhouette training. Some cold war.

*

It may surprise some that Sumburgh is not east of Edinburgh but a few miles south of 60 degrees north, the nearest railway station being Bergen, not Waverly. This line of latitude stitches its way through the world's best-preserved Iron Age Norse broch. It is on the Island of Mousa, a reporting point just eight miles northeast of the airfield. From this line north, the weather is consistently different. A perfect environment to hone young captains, it takes few prisoners. During the winter, gales ensure there is no litter in Shetland or anything else not battened down, and daylight hours reduce to just six: between 9 and 3 o'clock - farther north, much fewer. The wind rarely drops below 40 knots for more than 24 hours, with gale warnings for Faeroes, Fair Isle and Viking: force 9 to storm force 10, occasionally 11 broadcast three times a week (Beaufort Scale 12 = hurricane).

*

Sitting in the cab and waiting to start up some days would be somewhat unnerving with gusts going through. Leaving one to blink in awe as a rotor blade tip slaps the ground, throwing sparks before bouncing back up, even with the droop stops in, alternatively disappearing out of sight and adopting a vertical position somewhere above. Things that should never, ever happen. When high winds above 40 knots preclude Bristow Bell 212s based offshore on the *Treasure Finder* semi-sub flotel in the East Shetland Basin from engaging the rotors, we will fly their morning and evening shuttle. Usually, a single S-61N was sufficient to cope. Much later, back on land, we waited for the wind to stabilise before shutting down – choosing the best of a wrong time between 90-knot gusts spilling over Fitful Head and down onto the airfield. With both engines stop cocked, you were exposed to a sailing blade striking the tail boom or the cab's roof if a droop stop failed to lock into place. Now, with the rotor brake fully engaged and the disc winding down, the blades slow to a final flap, shudder, and stop before easing back off their dampers. It would be best to time this last bite of the pucks by releasing the brake just enough to ease the pressure, then re-engage it and breathe again.

Fig 15. *Treasure Finder* + Bristow hangar. BAH S-61N on the northern deck. *Brent 'B'* (Condeep platform design) background.
Photo credit: Given to author by the late Campbell Bosanquet.

Even everyday sectors could take some time. On one dark winter evening, the flight inbound from the *Dunlin 'A'*, 120 nautical miles from Sumburgh, with a young Nigerian co-pilot, "Trust the instruments, Robert, we'll get there" (later to become an Airbus A380 captain with Emirates) took four hours. With an average ground speed of barely 30 knots (we topped up with fuel en route at the *Cormorant 'A'* with 90 to go), it was not much faster than a bicycle, though this was the way. To plod through these depressions without a glimmer of sunlight was the norm. Another time, we knew a depression was going through at the flight planning stage. Outbound to the East Shetland Basin with an 80-knot tailwind giving us a ground speed of around 200 knots, the Sumburgh Manager flying with me remarked:
"This is great. Be there soon."
"Don't speak too soon, Alan. It won't last."
Shortly after, we popped out of the turbulent overcast into a 'blue lagoon' of the calm sea below and bright sunlight from an azure sky above; the wind had completely dropped off, the eye of the storm.
Usually viewed by satellite, we rarely entered this oasis of calm. Then, less than ten miles later, we plunged back into the overcast. Back to a 40-knot ground speed, we altered the course to Unst for fuel, where Bristow had set

up an operation in 1979 to service Chevron's Ninian Field. On the same latitude as Anchorage, Alaska, and farther north than St Petersburg, it is the most Northerly airport in the British Isles—next, landfall, the Arctic. A visit to a Skyspace at Tewlwolow near Penzance on a cloudless day may offer a similar experience. Though on a miniature scale. Here, you can enter an elliptical domed chamber designed by the Californian light artist and pilot James Turrell RA. Look up when the skies are blue. Revealed through a large aperture in the white ceiling, the scene mimics the centre of a hurricane surrounded by clouds. He has constructed many skyscapes worldwide. When the weather is suitable, this one best represents that day.

*

This résumé of high winds in the region may initially appear alarming to the passenger; it can paradoxically be the medium enabling the helicopter to perform best, so long as aerodynamic lift is respected, especially during in-field shuttling. Platform evacuations were quite common, with one particularly vicious event being the *Cormorant 'A'*. A gas leak in one of the Condeep concrete legs caused chunks of metal to spew out, including into the flight path and across the helideck. It had to be one of the fastest evacuations of c400 men. Each time a helicopter lands, they sprint across the deck and bound up the airstair door two steps at a time to the relative shelter of the cabin. We board up to 40 at a time. They fill the 19 seats, with as many on the floor, then fly them to a neighbouring helideck. One of the BIH S-61Ns took significant shrapnel aft of the cabin. A bit intimidating to watch, hovering above the formation of helicopters, stepped below, waiting your turn to land, hoping: it'll probably be all right. You will not have read about it in the press. Offshore Oil & Gas was the original 'unreported world'.

*

Sink or Swim. Our engineers conduct 'D' maintenance checks on the aircraft at London Gatwick, the BAH HQ, every 9,000 airframe hours. It was across the railway tracks from Gatwick South Terminal and adjacent to the original London Gatwick terminal, known as the 'Beehive', a monument to early civil aviation. The check primarily involved stripping back to the airframe, inspecting for corrosion, metal fatigue and mislaid cartons of duty-free fags from the rigs, and then reassembling and replacing the time-expired parts for new ones. Being amphibious, part of the S-61N air-testing program to

release the aircraft back into service included landing on freshwater to establish if the hull was watertight.
Lou DeMarco found this was not the case when he had that sinking feeling on a reservoir near Heathrow and became airborne just in time. Ringwood (Hampshire, UK) gravel pits could be just as entertaining. These flooded excavations have islands with well-established scrub obscuring other users of the water from each other, much as former President Trump's golf course on the coast north of Aberdeen. Here, you can play a round, thinking you have the place to yourself, as vast dunes separate each hole. And so, the inevitable happened. Soon after landing, we were surprised to see a speed boat. It appeared from behind one of the islands and raced towards us in the narrows. With a quick presence of mind (call it self-preservation), the driver spun the wheel hard over and retreated in a cloud of spray; the water skier kept going and disappeared up the bank into the bushes. No doubt he lived on that story for some time.
Proficiency checks included water landings and taxiing on the Loch of Skene and Corby Loch near Aberdeen or the West Voe and Virkie Pool at Sumburgh and Quendale Bay, a short distance to the north of the airfield. Still, being amphibious was not much use in the North Sea unless it was calm, a rarity. They were wholly dependent on the hull and sponsons for buoyancy and stability. It did not take much of a sea state for the aircraft to invert due to a high centre of gravity (gearbox & engines). The rationale was they stayed upright long enough in waves no greater than six feet to deploy the sea anchor, launch a life raft, load emergency equipment, and access a brass navigation lamp stowed in the floor locker between the crew. This hatch also contained the lever to pump the gear down when it hung up. After the rotors had stopped, it was just a case of climbing up and fastening the lamp to the pitot 'mast', the rod between the beanie, a fairing over the rotor hub, and the pitots feeding dynamic air pressure to the airspeed indicators and switch it on. Under international maritime law, this white light was to signify you were at anchor. I do not believe anyone ever achieved that, though the intent to comply with the law was there. Before they withdrew the amphibious classification, and long after the lamps had 'disappeared', an event occurred on the 31st of July 1980; the crews in other companies considered a calm day offshore as 'ideal British Airways Helicopters ditching weather'.

Dave Paul was the commander of Speedbird 70G with Ian Recton, the co-pilot. They were on the way back from the rig *Atlantic II* drilling a well in the Clyde field, 180 nautical miles east, southeast of Aberdeen. Thirteen

passengers were on board their S-61N, G-BEID. Cruising at Flight Level 45, the crew noticed a slight fall in the main gearbox oil pressure and a rising oil temperature. With the temperature now at +110ºC, air traffic control cleared them to descend on track. They put out a 'MAYDAY' relayed on Channel 16. Two RAF Sea Kings, Rescue 37 and Rescue 38, scrambled, and a rescue-equipped RAF Shackleton, already in the area, diverted to the scene.
Along with other vessels in the area, the research vessel RV *Correlia* picked up the call on Channel 16. Dyce air traffic control alerted the RNLI lifeboat station in Aberdeen harbour, "There is a helicopter 30 miles east of Girdleness Lighthouse with problems." The shout went out, the crew mustered, and at 12:25 GMT, their 54' Arun class lifeboat *BP Forties* slipped her moorings. The tide had been flooding for two hours in fair, calm weather with a fog. She proceeded at reduced speed in visibility between two miles and nil under the command of Acting Coxswain James Dickson.
Onboard 'ID', the oil temperature continued to rise, and the hot oil temperature warning came on at +140ºC. Fortunately, the fleet engineers had recently fitted an emergency lubrication pump to all the S-61N main rotor transmissions. This system bypassed the oil cooler and fed a direct supply of lubricant to the gearbox. With the pump selected, the pressure rose from 30 to 50 psi and stabilised at 40 psi. The oil temperature continued to rise. When it reached +150ºC, Dave elected to ditch per the company's emergency procedures. They continued the descent through some low stratus into sea fog. The visibility was down to half a mile. Now in sight of the sea, they made a power-on landing in light wind and a sea swell of three to five feet. It was 12.20 GMT and 15 miles from Aberdeen Harbour. After BAH engineers had fitted a winch to S-61N, G-BEDI, she lifted from Aberdeen, and several fishing vessels in the 'Buchan Deeps', just north of the ditching position, began hauling their nets and making way to the ditched aircraft.
Dave attempted to water taxi towards the coast. When an uncomfortable roll crossing a three to five-foot swell set in and the oil temperature continued to rise, they decided to shut down the engines. It was time to deploy the sea anchor and board the aft life raft, remaining tethered to the aircraft to present a better radar return for searching aircraft.
As a smoke haze wafted gently around the transmission casing and mingled with the fog, a voice bleated, "Do you think I could get my attaché case?" Visions of a lot of cash entered Ian's mind. "No. There's enough clutter around here; besides, it's probably safer in the aircraft. It'll be by helicopter when we get picked up, and you'll likely lose it. Anyway, what's so important?" Hesitantly, "Well, it's got my airline ticket in it, and I have a flight

leaving Aberdeen to catch". Silence. Suddenly, the life raft erupted into laughter.

At 11:48, the Shackleton located 'ID' and dropped a flare overhead, but the survivors did not see it. The visibility was down to 100 yards in fog when the BAH G-BEDI crewed by Mike Evans and Dave Bailey arrived at 12:15 with the RV *Corrella* in attendance. George Edge, the duty winchman, was winched down and recovered eight survivors from the life raft. The remaining seven boarded the RV *Corrella*. She later transferred them to the *BP Forties* when she arrived on the scene at 13:33.

By now, the weather had cleared. Some lifeboat crew members went across to 'ID' in their 'daughter' inflatable lifeboat. There, they found a life raft inflated inside the cabin; the pilot's window and the emergency door were open with no water inside. Meanwhile, George Edge had swum across to attach a towing line to the helicopter. At a recommended three knots, *BP Forties* took up the tow with the rig supply vessel *Edith Viking*, acting as escort, when a Bristow S-61N G-BBGS arrived.

Fig 16a. Bristow G-BBGS winchman Colin Larcombe recovering survivors off the RNLI Lifeboat *BP Forties towing* G-BEID at three knots. Ian Recton is in the foreground. *Photo provided by Dave Paul*

Colin Larcombe, their winchman, winched down two BAH engineers and two inflation bags onto the *Edith Viking*, then manoeuvred to winch the seven survivors off the lifeboat before setting course for the Aberdeen Royal Infirmary to join the others - “with due publicity,” as noted in the RNLI log. Other than a case of seasickness, there were no injuries.
The dingy crew transferred the two engineers and equipment to the ditched helicopter, where they attached and inflated the bags. They remained on board and, when 7.5 miles from the harbour, replaced the emergency door.
At 19:20, the tow arrived in Aberdeen Harbour, where a crane hoisted G-BEID onto Atlantic Quay. It took only a short time to find one of the two oil cooler fan belts had broken and dragged the other off its pully. Engineers removed the main rotor blades and, in the wee hours, towed her back to Dyce airport by road and put her to bed in the hangar.

Fig 16b. G-BEID on the way home. *Photo credit: ©Doug Winton*

The subsequent accident report toned down the truth when it revealed the fan belts were obsolete. Jock Cameron was furious with the crew for ditching as Sikorsky had already advised the company the main gearbox temperature would rise and stabilise at around 180°C in the event of a total cooler failure, and the flight could continue to its destination. Critically, the management had not requested an amendment to the emergency checklist to remove the ‘150°C limit- land immediately’ instruction to reflect this advice. It was still sitting in the pending tray.
Sikorsky had also directed that some fan belts they had supplied the company had come into contact with acid during manufacture; they should replace them all immediately. Instead, the BAH engineering department ‘assumed’ this only applied to non-Sikorsky-supplied spares. They did not heed the imperative. After all, the practice was to replace a fan belt only when

necessary after an inspection. If anything was obsolete, it was the temperature gauge; it only indicated up to 155ºC.

Fig 16c. G-BEID is approaching Atlantic Quay.
Photo credit: ©Doug Winton

As luck would have it, G-BEID was the only BAH S-61N aircraft fitted with those acid-damaged belts. Ten days later, she was back operating commercial flights until 1988, when her luck ran out.

*

Nevertheless, the sea anchor would often be used. When launched, it deployed a drogue on the end of a line secured to the aircraft. It was to ensure the 'craft did not broach the waves broadside'; always comforting to know (though it seldom worked in practice). The instructors remind you of this gem during the annual emergency and survival equipment checks; although you may cling to the hull as an amateur, your aircraft will ride the seas as a pro, even if upside down. Knot tying and semaphores were optional. Until recently, there was no budget for helicopter safety. It was not for lack of funds. By 1980, the investment to extract oil from the North Sea far exceeded sending a man to the moon.

The following May 1981, I had the chance to operate out of Ellough Airfield at Beccles, the BAH base in Norfolk. They shared the Southern North Sea contracts with Bristow, working out of North Denes on the coast. Beccles, as it was known, was originally constructed for the USAAF in 1943, though better known for the RAF De-Havilland Mosquitos based there later. These crews trialled the prototype 'bouncing bombs', code name Highball, a weapon to be developed into versions twice the size. Operating Avro Lancasters, the 617 'Dambuster' Squadron initially used them to bomb axis warships, then to rupture the Möhne, Eder and Sorpe dams in the Ruhr in 1943. Today, they are the first RAF squadron to operate the Lockheed Martin F-35B Lightning (JSF), an aircraft I was to be involved. For those who enjoyed golf, the early starts offered the opportunity to be on the course by one o'clock in the afternoon; it was not the base for anyone regularly wanting to rise *that* early and then have the rest of the day ruined looking for balls in the rough.

Chapter 7. 1982

Bergen & Penzance Ops' – Boeing Vertol (Chinook) – OPEC - NSPA

Freedom from Sumburgh (for the moment) came after two years of plodding to and from the East Shetland Basin. A detachment to fly out of Bergen-Flesland began on the 17th of April 1982. Having distance-measuring equipment (DME) to operate within Norwegian airspace was mandatory. Until now, these were in the store at London Gatwick. They deemed if used, the pilots would break them! The Norwegian operation was an exception. They fitted them to the three S-61Ns selected to fly the contract. Not to their replacement aircraft. It was a typical case of force majeure. UK-registered Oil & Gas helicopters usually fitted equipment when it became a mandatory requirement to enhance flight safety. Despite the airlines using DME for years and a legal requirement when nominating Norwegian airfields as alternates, they were a drop in the ocean when we revealed the profits ploughed back into British Airways mainline during this period.

*

It was reminiscent of the early days of mail flights in the USA. This problem culminated after two weeks of accidents on the 22nd of July 1919. Fifteen mail planes had gone down in the fog. Two of the crews did not survive. The others were severely injured. Looking at the fog after loading the mail on that July morning, Leon Smith decided it was too bad to launch. Instead, he sat on the muddy tyre of the former World War I surplus De-Havilland Airco DH-4, lit up a cigarette, and refused to take off. They call in Leon's backup pilot to take the flight. He, too, refused. They were on the first strike in aviation history. They did not have the instruments to fly safely in this weather. Many mail pilots had requested to have the forerunner of the turn and slip indicator, the 'stabilator', fitted. The Post Office flatly refused it. Their advice when flying in the cloud is, "Steer by compass. Turn indicators are too expensive." They cost US$7. Despite growing anger among their fellow pilots, these two did not stand a chance. Without a union to support them, they were both fired.

It was not until the 27th of July 1931, after a series of pilots' associations came and went, that they formed a union. They called it the Air Line Pilots Association (ALPA). Dave Behncke headed it. Eric Lane-Burslem, who founded BALPA six years later in 1937, shared a common experience with him.

Eric was operating an Imperial Airways flight, a forerunner of British Airways, when his De-Havilland DH86 Express lost all four engines over Germany due to icing at 9,000 feet. The DH86 is a four-engined bi-plane - a scaled-up version of the more common DH89 Rapide- seated ten passengers and two crew. Eric restarted the Gypsy Six engines by 5,000 feet, though the last DH86 was written off, landing at Madrid in 1958.

Dave lost both engines on a twin-engine Boeing 247. On the evening of the 20th of December 1934, he operated a mail flight express for United Air Line Inc. They departed Chicago Midway, Illinois, in NC-13328, en route to Omaha, Nebraska. Three crew and a company employee were on board this ten-seater with 1,600 pounds of cargo. The cloud ceiling was at 700 feet, with one-and-a-quarter-mile visibility in light snow. The next waypoint was Waterman, west of Chicago, where the weather was worse. Fifteen minutes into the flight, the starboard engine shut down near Aurora. As they returned to Chicago, the other engine slowed down, despite all the instruments reading normally; Dave forced landed in the dark at Western Springs, Illinois, a residential suburb west of Chicago. The starboard engine tears off on impact, with the aircraft ending 45° nose up against a parkway elm tree. Though injured, both he and his co-pilot survived. The probable cause was carburettor icing. The plane was recovered, rebuilt, and served with the US Army Air Force throughout World War II until late 1944 when it returned to passenger service with United. Dave wrote later, "I do not doubt that if my co-pilot and I had not lived to defend ourselves, 'pilot error' would have been given as the cause of the crash."

These airline pioneers were the prime movers for the two pilots' unions we are familiar with today. They succeeded when others had failed. Their efforts were primarily due to successful lobbying, Dave in Washington, D.C., and Eric in Westminster. They had legislation approved, committing airline operators to comply. This work continues to this day.

*

It is common knowledge most BAH aircraft still need to have DME fitted. The Bergen-Flesland air traffic control is also aware of it. Thus, to arrive in an aircraft to replace one that had gone AOG (aircraft on ground), it was necessary when asked to provide your DME range to the next waypoint, to reply "Standby," then "It has just gone u/s" (Unserviceable). After arriving at Flesland, I confided with the managing engineer, Bob Middleton, he could expect a ramp inspection. I suggested removing the high-frequency radio set we were not using. It was not a requirement for that operation anyway. When asked, explain it was the former location of the distance measuring equipment. Then order the real thing from the Gatwick stores asap.

The Bergen operation was a BAH wet lease to support the Helikopter Service S-61Ns. The flights mainly involved trips to Mobil's Statfjord Field. It is large and covers nearly 600 square km. Andy Spillane headed the lease. He was a former BALPA Company Council Chairman who had enjoyed formidable success over many years. A telephone chain between crews was in operation during his tenure. It was activated the evening before the event whenever he had any negotiating difficulty. The phone rang all too frequently! The crews remained home in the morning until Andy had resolved his dispute, usually by lunchtime. With Bergen, he agreed to run the show on one condition – he did it his way: as Sinatra.

He gave only one instruction: go on or before the scheduled departure time. The incentive not to do so was to 'win' the 'Galtieri Trophy', a large pot plant in the lobby of our hotel. Given that the ten-week Falklands War, which began on the 1st of April, was in progress and General Leopoldo Galtieri was leading the wrong side, it was a prize to avoid.

Helikopter Service (HS) operates as a scheduled 'bus' service. On arrival offshore, we invariably filled all the seats, and HS returned half empty. The Mobil representative explained that the passengers would rather wait for a BAH flight to come through. The reasons given were surprising as they were a modus operandum for us. We enjoyed flying higher, threading through sunlit caves in the clouds and generally out of the worst weather. They preferred our sight picture approaches to land offshore, being more sedate when compared with the military quick-stop technique, a method they still adhered to. The latter involved a flat and fast arrival, followed by a positive flare to slow down before moving across the deck to land.

In comparison, the sight picture method came in higher and slower throughout the final descent, aligning the landing reference point through a selected small section of the cockpit chin plexiglass. In essence, they appreciated a more comfortable ride. We also talked to them over the public address system. Intentionally or otherwise, the ladies reciprocated this goodwill. Unlike in UK waters, Norwegians working offshore comprised a large percentage of Scandi women. For passengers, the warm weather aggravated wearing uncomfortable immersion suits in an aircraft with poor air-conditioning. The first thing they did when we shut down was to unzip to the waist in anticipation of the airstair door opening and fresh air flooding into the cabin. It was only a short time before a mob of engineers responded to an arriving BAH S-61N when only one would do. Dropping the door down would reveal a bevy of tanned females fanning bare chests at the top of the steps. Until then, HS never had any competition. Times change. No doubt their service has, too. Although what they did not have in competition, they made up for with the quality of life and equipment. No scrapping over loose change for them. Their helicopters have whatever kit they desire. Their pilot seats were custom-designed for comfort rather than standard issues. The latter was a source of significant back pain in many crews. They even had human range extenders feeding into a small reservoir, relief for the pilot to plug in without leaving his seat. There were chests in the hangar to dip into, frozen microwave meals. Reindeer pies. Sorted!

*

For a foreigner, Norway is a country where everything is great. But not quite. This sense of well-being is when everything goes better than one's expectations. Then, the unexpected happens. And here is an example. It was an arrival one morning from the north to land at Bergen-Flesland in a Southerly direction; it turned out to be different. There was only one runway, and the weather was on limits – rain and mist. Their radar controller vectored us through the mountains despite being below a sector-safe altitude. It required considerable skill from the controller. We were above the cloud for this part. On intercepting the instrument landing system's vertical localiser and merging onto the glide slope, the controller releases us for the descent. Breaking out of the overcast, we touched down as you do. And this is where the expected quickly morphed into a surprise. Air traffic control orders us to evacuate the runway immediately. No, not ground taxiing to the next turn-off; instead, hover taxi clear – now! As we lifted into the hover, a white light raced out of the mist towards us. The glare from the light is becoming brighter. Then, through a cloud of spray from the reverse thrust, we could discern a Braathen's Douglas DC-9. They were on course to use the entire length of the wet runway, having let down on the same runway from the opposite direction on another radio frequency. Neither knew of the other's traffic, so I sometimes wondered if the controllers knew their intentions. They must have; it's just that we were unfamiliar with it. It seemed such a well-coordinated (Norwegian) procedure. The moral in bad weather was to vacate clear in the hover and not carry out any fancy landings on the active runway,

for it is considerably more active than you think. Hiring cross-country skis on the weekend and launching into the wilderness of pristine snowfields around Voss was much safer.
Before I left Bergen, Head of Training Dave Humble invited me to convert to the Boeing Vertol BV 234LR Chinook (the civil version of the military CH-47A Chinook; LR as in Long Range). BAH took delivery of the first three the previous year in February 1981 and now had a fleet of six helicopters. I declined. You may ask why. Aberdeen to Brent is 280 nautical miles, with fuel for an 880-mile alternate to Paris was impressive for a helicopter. This sort of long-haul helicopter flying did not appeal. And there was another, not fully appreciated when the aircraft first arrived. Traditionally, airborne times operating the military version were short. Even in Vietnam, as a CH-47A driver, Rick Peterson explained. There, they only fuelled them with a 20-minute sector time endurance. Just enough to insert troops and then rapidly return to base. In their role on long North Sea routes, each airframe rapidly built up the hours exceeding any model until now.

Fig 17. Passengers offshore boarding G-BWFC via the ramp.

Photo credit: Commander and one of two survivors when G-BWFC broke up in flight on the 6th of November 1986, Capt. Pushp Vaid VrC.

It soon became apparent to the crews that although the cabin vibrated, the experience in the cockpit was worse. The reason: the company did not want to 'waste' money on bespoke Boeing Vertol rotor blade tracking equipment. Instead, they tracked blades using the age-old hit-and-miss method of holding up a taut tracking flag on a pole to record the coloured chalk pasted on the tips of the rotating blades and then adjust accordingly. Not surprisingly, after nearly six hours of a return flight to the East Shetland Basin, the crews were fairly 'shaken up' - a consequence was to see them resting in the crew room for up to an hour after one of these flights. They were waiting for their livers to stop vibrating. This behaviour was highly unusual. Pilots typically had one foot in the tech office signing in the aircraft or describing defects with the other in the car park, dashing for home or to the pub/golf course/farm.

The aircraft suffered, too. This false economy translated into components wearing out much faster than they should. On reflection, staying on the S-61N was sound despite the crews holding the Chinook in high regard. They could program it to conduct the whole flight on the automatics. Many considered it the best helicopter they had ever flown until a sinister design fault revealed itself four years later.

*

During the summer holiday season, crews from the North Sea help out on the Penzance to Scillies operation. The road leading into town from upcountry passes by the Eastern Green on the right-hand side. Formerly marshy ground used as a rubbish dump was drained and replaced with a heliport. For some reason, dumps make suitable airfields, as with the new Doha airfield. During this process, the smell of seasoned filth, when excavated, is indescribable, particularly in summertime temperatures with the wind blowing the wrong way. Doha was no exception. Ten years after the Penzance to Scillies scheduled service began, an S-61NM, G-BCEB, seating 32 passengers, took over in 1974. It differed from the 'N' models. It had less range and more stowage for baggage and freight. Like the baggage doors of a bus, it had five of them along the lower port side of the fuselage. And, to provide more seating, the airstair door replaced the standard cargo door on 'N' models.

A North Sea S-61N supplemented 'EB' for the summer tourist season. This summer, it was G-ATFM. 'FM' has a history. Assembled in 1965, it was the first helicopter to make a transatlantic crossing. Its destination was Gatwick for BEA Helicopters. And now, it was contracted to an oil company operating the rig *Bideford Dolphin* drilling in the southwest approaches equidistant from the Scillies, Cork, and Brest. This location provided an interesting choice of alternates depending upon the most favourable wind. Besides crew change

days, it involved taking tourists and residents to St Marys and standing by on the beach with a pager for a call out by the oil company.
One evening, we took a freight flight out to the rig and were asked to drop in on St Marys to collect some stranded French tourists on the way back. The weather at Penzance had closed in, and the ferry MS *Scillonian* was not running. We collected the tourists and let down in the prescribed manner using the Decca map and the 125° bearing from the LND VOR (Lands' End VOR) towards St. Mounts Bay, then headed north. You could usually see the streetlamps bordering the airfield at this point. Instead, fog banks obscure them. We plodded on with our landing lights, picking up the sea below. As the harbour lights became visual, we altered course a touch to port and headed towards them like a moth to a lamp.
Then, on reaching, we turned to starboard to skirt the end of the town to the east and continued the descent to the airfield. The following morning, the taxi driver remarked, "Did you hear that one come in last night? You? Nearly lopped our chimney pots off. You." It was nothing personal, just West Country speak. Here, most sentences append with a "You" for unconscious emphasis. I agreed it was disturbing for the locals late at night, leaving him with our shared experience. Years later, in 2012, the S-61 operation was discontinued after 48 years of proper service.

*

In June, Bristow Helicopters conducted a Helicopter Evacuation Trail with the British North Sea Oil Corporation (BNOC). They used an S-61N to make a controlled ditching on Meikle Loch near Aberdeen. The purpose was to produce a flight safety film on helicopter ditching procedures for offshore oil workers.
During this trial, the crew experienced serious difficulties deploying the life raft in the prevailing 15 to 20-knot wind. It began soon after they launched the 18-man life raft from the cargo door on the starboard side. It started to inflate normally when the wind picked up. The windward side of the partly inflated life raft lifted and then rolled in a semi-inverted position over the starboard sponson. The crew entered the water and, with considerable difficulty, righted it. The wind caused it to drift aft, where it encountered the VOR aerial under the tail cone. It ruptured both chambers, and the life raft was rendered unusable. This inconvenient truth will play out when G-ASNL, the BAH S-61N, ditches the following year.

*

By July, the Falklands War had concluded, and thoughts on resupplying strategic enclaves under construction around the islands were imperative; large helicopters were an obvious solution. BAH and Bristow competed for the work using S-61Ns. BAH fielded a strong team supported by a former BAH pilot, Lord Simon Glenarthur, currently a Government Whip. They were well on the way to securing the work when they realised a lady working for them was the wife of a Bristow pilot.
Bristow serviced the contract for 14 years.

*

I had spent much of the year away from home. When asked to cover the Penzance offshore operation again, now flying G-ASNL, the original S-61N that inaugurated the service in 1964, I agreed to extend for a final week. Now, the chief pilot in Aberdeen was renowned for inactivity. Unless leaning back in a chair with your feet halfway up the wall, proofreading the Press and Journal counts? At the end of the week, I was due to travel on leave. With no relief, and with him believing the Penzance crewing problem 'would go away', we did. That evening in the Admiral Benbow, we were ready at closing time, bags packed, to take the night train. Soon after midnight, we were on our way with the rhythmic tagadada of the bogies below us. Swaying from side to side, we clattered over points with a clack, clickety clack as we changed tracks, then tagadada again as we raced through the night. We traced the rails upcountry to Reading for the bus transfer to Heathrow and the Red Eye north.
Long before the call for "All change at St Erth for St Ives," we had forgotten the possible repercussions for my crew. As a former WO_2 Army Air Corps pilot, he had briefly wrestled with second thoughts. Absent without leave. In Aberdeen, nothing phased Flt Ops. Sure enough, as I was going on holiday, they suggested my co-pilot take a week off too. Looking through the door of the chief pilot's office on the way out, he was still on page two, business as usual.
Engines: they never fail? Despite being told the engines, General Electric CT58-140-1, were reliable, over 28 days in Autumn 1982, I had three: two fuel control unit (FCU) failures on approach, one just before committing to land on a rig offshore, and one letting down with the weather on landing limits at Aberdeen. Foreign object debris caused the third with interest. It was with Dave Chinn on an air test at night at Aberdeen after a fuel control unit change on the number one engine. Just after taking off and starting a climbing turn left into the circuit over Dyce at about 450 ft, the number two engine blew up.

Dave had already selected the gear up, as was the practice on reaching VY (best rate of climb speed). Unlike in the simulator, only one or two lights come on with an engine failure. This illumination was a Christmas tree accompanied by an enormous explosion. I elected to land on the extended centreline of the runway, unlike the De-Havilland Mosquito that continued into the circuit during World War II. After the good engine stopped, they crashed into a house in the village. Meanwhile, Dave reselected the gear, recounting, "Among a maze of lights, I was praying for the three green 'down and locked' lights to illuminate before we touched down".
We later determined the culprit was a terry cloth for wiping up oil. It was left behind under the number two engine starter motor, cleverly hidden in the dark by the ice guards. The compressor blades were stripped clean off. The engine failure on finals to land on the rig was only one of two times I failed to land offshore. The other was fog.

Two years into the introduction of Chinook, with four operators competing for fewer contracts, coincides with declining demand for helicopters on the North Sea. The slowdown in oil & gas activity at the end of 1982 can be traced back to an event in 1959 that had come full circle.
It was when Wanda Jablonski secretly convened a meeting for a splinter group attending the first Arab Oil Congress in Cairo. She is the most influential petroleum journalist and power broker of her time. Due to the low season, she chose a quiet venue - a yacht club in Maadi, a city suburb. Five representatives of their respective countries attended. So secret, the Iranian commented afterwards, "We met in a James Bond atmosphere." They came from three Arab countries: Saudi Arabia, Kuwait, and Iraq; the others were from Venezuela and Iran. They reach a gentleman's agreement known as the Maadi Pact. This initiative, in turn, morphed into a new organisation the following year, when, in September 1960, they met in Bagdad. There, they discussed ways to raise the oil price and consolidate their approach to dealing with the major oil companies. They call it OPEC (The Organisation of the Petroleum Exporting Countries). They included the word 'export' to exclude Egypt, not an oil exporting country. The primary reason was to ensure Egypt's President Nassar, who was all-powerful in the region, did not become a controlling authority over their new baby. During the following decade, the organisation was ineffective in controlling the fluctuating oil price, a weakness displayed during the Six-Day War of 1967. In 1973, their fortunes changed because of their inaction six years earlier. Oil prices began to move in leaps and bounds following what became known as the Yom-

Kippur War, then by inertia and a series of events, including the miners' strike in the UK.

The wave broke when oil peaked at over US$35/barrel (US$110/barrel adjusting for inflation in 2020 dollars) at the end of 1980. Over the next five years, the surf will run out of energy. To arrest the decline, Saudi Arabia and Kuwait reduced production. The other OPEC members, including many more petroleum-exporting countries, failed to follow suit. In early 1986, Saudi Arabia, tired of its efforts to support the oil price, increased production. This hike led to an unwelcome combination of helicopter overcapacity on the North Sea and US$10/barrel, less than 24 cents a gallon. The size determining the capacity of a barrel goes back to a statute in 1482 when the fishing industry used various barrel sizes for transporting salted herring, and cheating was rife. The law now regulated the size to 42 gallons, though you will be hard-pressed to find an original barrel other than inside a museum.

*

With work for so many aircraft now scarce, margins were tight to non-existent. Service companies were also grasping at flotsam left over from the tsunami built up over seven exceptional years. When a rig operator objected to an oil major tearing up a new contract for millions of dollars, their response was, "See you in court."

Given that oil companies' total transport costs (aircraft, shipping, and others) were less than 1% of their operating costs, it seemed reasonable they share some of their wealth. More so with a service they were 100% reliant upon. The BALPA model was in jeopardy!

The Sumburgh Club was unusually busy one evening in late 1982. BAH pilots usually migrated there after the third rotation from the Porta pub (Portacabin with beer, bar, and barman) - a veritable BAH institution located next to the hangars and flight ops. This bar was an incentive to discourage pilots from sloping off and not waiting for the regulatory 30 minutes required for the engines to cool down below +100°C before having the sea salt rinsed out and lit up - the drying run. A swift couple of pints, and they were game for anything!

This procedure was carried out every evening for a very good reason. The sulphur content of aviation turbine fuel (AVTUR) can react with the salt-laden air offshore. When sucked through a gas turbine, the mix can erode the blade material. The result is a loss of engine power.

Several Bristow co-pilots had arrived at the Sumburgh Club for the evening. It was their last flight on the line, and they were now redundant - last in, first out. It was the beginning of a downward spiral that lasted until 1986. There was a glut of oil, and industry could no longer absorb these heady prices. It was a bear market. And it included pilots. As good Bristow pilots, they were not too concerned. On the contrary, they were pleased to alleviate the size of the pilot workforce; they were ensuring the company's future. Right! These were the first aircrew redundancies on the North Sea. Sitting down with Dave Chinn a few nights later over a beer, we discussed this new phenomenon and a concept to deal with it. It was one thing for the erosion of their terms and conditions, but pilots? The time had come to stem the tide and develop a safety net.

Somehow, this had to be addressed, ideally in a construct understood by the ultimate paymasters, the oil companies. After all, they would have been familiar with a similar arrangement they had conceived 11 years earlier. During that period, oil-exporting governments shared the petroleum revenues with the exploration companies – 50/50. Then, in 1970, things changed. Dr Armand Hammer, Chairman of Occidental Petroleum, at the time one of the small, independent oil companies, had struck a deal with General Gaddafi of Libya for his company to remain in Libya. For a good reason: he had three billion barrels of recoverable reserves under the sands of the Western desert.

*

Let us put that into perspective. The Norwegian Ekofisk field had yielded three billion barrels since production from this reservoir began in 1971, 50 years since the Phillips Petroleum Company from Bartlesville, Oklahoma, got 'lucky'. It was particularly notable for being the first oil discovered in the North Sea. Production is expected to continue until at least 2050. Yet it nearly didn't happen. The company had already drilled 32 uncommercial wells when the drilling crew received the order to stop. But, their rig, the *Ocean Viking*, was still on contract. They would still have to pay the daily rate whether or not they used it. Rather than release it, they chanced just one more hole. And the rest is history. When a Phillips executive was asked at a technical meeting in London a few months later what methods the company had used, they fully expected something special. Instead, he replied after a pause for thought: "Luck!" It was luck, too; the line dividing the UK and Danish waters from the Norwegian of the North Sea had been drawn by – you guessed - the Norwegians! They recognised the UK was in a hurry to sign anything, and the Danes – well, they did not fully realise what was happening when the signing took place as their minister was invariably hung over in the morning - so the story goes.

In Libya, Hammer named his new venture the Idris Field after the deposed King Idris. The Libyan coup d'état led by a group calling themselves the Free Unionist Officers Movement had overthrown him. The then Colonel Mu'ammar Gaddafi led this group. Paradoxically, Idris was located under a former Mobil Oil base camp using relatively new seismic technology. It was one of the biggest oilfields in the world. So, no. He was not going to relinquish that prize any time soon. He turned to Exxon to enlist support and had the cold shoulder. He was not considered an oilman and one of their ilk, just an art collector and a new boy in the industry. Hammer was always in a hurry, indicative of the size of the flare on his Piper 'A', which was another example, as we will later find out. He could not pump the stuff out fast enough. Now running out of time, Hammer closed the deal- 55/45 – an increase of the profits to the General of another 5%. Not long after this move, the Shah of Iran followed suit.

Then, at the beginning of 1971, greed kicked in, and Gaddafi started renegotiating an even higher take of the profits. At this point, the oil companies could see where this was going. They agreed if any company drew a line in the sand and refused to accept a lower margin and possibly cut off from exporting their crude, the other companies would step in and provide the shortfall. Ironically, this was what Hammer had wanted earlier. They called it 'The Libyan Safety Net'. As pilots, we, too, felt close to the end of the line. We, too, are seeking a safety net.

The concept was to access a fair share of income from the oil companies. This move was to ensure a sustainable future at a reasonable standard. A viable contract rate or daily operating charge (DOC) would need to be agreed upon by the crews of all four Operators (Bristow, Bond, BAH and British Caledonian). Anything less than this, the pilots refuse to fly the line. In essence, the other three companies will decline unviable work already turned down by the fourth. Because each company enjoyed a reasonable profit margin, it would not be in the interest of their managers to intervene. After all, successful organisations enable managers to spend more time on the golf course to 'network'. Here, the fundamental understanding to be put across was once they agree on the terms, the individual pilot bodies can decide how to deliver the spoils. I.e., loss of licence, private health insurance, allowances and more. On one condition: only after the DOC had been agreed upon by all four pilot representatives and the money in the bank. As an

employee action, it would be difficult to construe as a cartel. We called it 'The North Sea Pilots' Association' (NSPA).
Being a union company, we decided one of the other non-union companies delivered the concept, and Roger Old in Bristow agreed to carry it forward. Around a year later, he convened a pilots' meeting for all four companies in the new Skean Dhu Airport Hotel at Aberdeen Airport. After 20 minutes, I looked over at Dave. We walked out. The meeting never took off with the concept we had envisioned.

*

Moreover, it was never even mentioned. Just the same old: scrapping over crumbs. Timing is more important than policy and support. And we were running out of time.
We were not alone in realising a dream, promoting the idea of engaging the other helicopter companies to a common cause; the divers were in a similar situation. With the assistance of the National Union of Rail, Maritime, and Transport Workers (RMT) trade union, they set up the Offshore Diving Industry Agreement (ODIA). This involved divers from six operators. The agreement governed minimum rates of pay and conditions. It was a big step toward realising the value they provided to the oil companies, though this was no giveaway. Too many divers gave their lives to this enormous effort to develop the oilfields. Occasionally, a rig lost two at a time. After taking a Professional Association of Diving Instructors (PADI) course in Aberdeen with Sub Sea Services, I began to understand something about the work of divers, though different, involved in engaging similar disciplines to stay alive as we did.
Though, it did not induce me to become professional and change tack. We could only ruefully look back and acknowledge where we had failed; they had succeeded - in spades. After diving, crane driving was just a little behind in appalling attrition. One rig lost two cranes with their drivers in a week - the usual problem of rushing to unload workboats when heavy swells were going through. BAH never repeated the five-year roll beginning in 1977 and ending in 1982.

*

The week before Xmas, I assisted the return to service of G-ATFM, which had spent the intervening time on a 'D' check. After the engineers signed off the air tests a few days later, we left London Gatwick as it was becoming dark. It was a bitterly cold evening. A cabin full of engineers and a dog returning north for the festive holiday were in the back. Just south of London, the heater broke down. When we shut down at Teesside for fuel, to raise your voice threatened to shatter the night sky and bring it down in shards around us. Over four hours later, we touched down in Aberdeen; we did not feel a thing – frozen to the bone.

Chapter 8. 1983 - 1985

Dinghies float, don't they? – Scillies Lessons – Heathrow Link – Line Training

The new aircraft joining the BAH S-61N fleet in the late seventies significantly contributed to its parent organisation, British Airways. A contribution skilfully ramped up by Brian Lawson, operations controller in Aberdeen, who secured the best ad hoc prices for many of BAH's 30 helicopters – daily. It was not apparent how large it was until years later, checking in for a flight to London at Mexico City.
The flight was full, with no seats available. The check-in supervisor suggested a visit upstairs to flight ops. There, we can review our options. An ops person assisted us when an older man enquired about my position in the company. "BAH, captain." I half expected an answer like "Who?" On the contrary, he insisted he handled the situation with, "You lot saved my butt. I'll never forget!" We went across the room to another computer. Curious to know how this had come to pass, he explained. For five years, between 1977 and 1982, British Airways News published articles on how all 56,000 BA employees worldwide had depended on BAH's profits to secure their jobs and salaries. BA fixed-wing operations had been going through a financially challenging time, primarily because of the buoyant price of oil. The background began with the Arab/Israeli War of 1973. Until then, it was a steady US3/barrel. The 1973 war increased the price fourfold, cutting BA's profit margins. By 1979, following the Iranian Revolution and the Shah's removal, it jumped to US$30/barrel. The Iran-Iraq war consolidated this price the following year. We checked in with upgraded tickets routing through Dallas/Fort Worth, TX.

*

On the 11th of March 1983, we landed back in Aberdeen at 15:00 on a flight from the drilling rigs *Glomar Biscay II* and the *Drillstar*. Upstairs, there was intense activity in the operations room. Ops were coordinating the rescue operations of a helicopter that had ditched. It is G-ASNL, the first of many S-61N to be delivered to BAH 20 years earlier, in December 1963. Crewed by Tony Buckley and Ian Recton, they had gone down 75 miles northeast of the airfield at 14:43. They were on the return from the *Piper 'A'* and *Claymore 'A'* platforms to Aberdeen with 15 passengers. Not long after departure from the *Claymore 'A'* and, just before reaching their cruising altitude of 1,500 feet, they heard a loud bang and experienced a high-frequency vibration and noise from the main rotor gearbox. At the same time, the No.1 engine ran down and stopped. Ian, who was flying the aircraft, established there was still sufficient power to maintain height. When carrying out the emergency checks, they noticed the main transmission oil pressure had dropped from the normal operating pressure of 50 psi down to 30 psi, and the emergency lubrication pump had kicked in.

Unknown to them, passengers could see oil beginning to stream across the cabin windows on the starboard side. After putting out a MAYDAY on Highland Radar, they announced they would make a controlled landing on the water as a precaution. They also inform *Piper 'A'* and a Bristow Tiger (AS332L1) in the vicinity of their decision. Everything went well when they ditched into a calm sea against a long regular swell of six to ten feet with a ten-knot wind from the south. The floatation gear inflated; the sea anchor streamed (eventually after Ian had manually removed its cover), and the undercarriage was selected down. To further enhance their stability, Tony decided to keep the rotors running and the passengers onboard. Then, both engines' fire warning lights illuminated in the 'T' handles located outboard of the speed select levers; the bi-metallic thermocouple sensors outside the engines had detected excess heat in their area.

When the 'T' handles were pulled to stop cock the fuel and arm the fire extinguisher bottles, the remaining engine shut down. There was no response when Tony applied the rotor brake. It was a matter of waiting now for the rotors to coast down. They were still stable in the water, but as a precaution, they decided to launch the rear dinghy using the cockpit release mechanism, except the dinghy attached to the door of the left emergency exit had jammed in the aperture designed to allow it to fall through. Ian went aft, found the securing pins had withdrawn and pushed the door free. He then inflated and secured it to the aircraft cleat to float close hauled. It was not long before a passenger came forward with some bad news: the dingy was deflating. It appeared it had drifted aft on the slack of the mooring line and impaled itself on the tip of the 'V'-shaped VOR aerial mounted under the tail boom.

The second life raft, stowed in row one and across from the cargo door, was launched and inflated. It immediately rolled over and inverted itself against the sponson and could not be righted. They then noticed a small puncture in the lower chamber's footstep where it had encountered the cargo door.

As the raft was inverted, it was difficult to access the leak stoppers stowed in the emergency pack secured to its floor. These screw-threaded, cone-shaped rubber stoppers come in various sizes. While attempting to recover the emergency pack from the aft dinghy, a large wave swept the front raft against the sharp end of the sliding cargo door rail. In doing so, the upper chamber received a six to nine-inch tear in the fabric. Both life rafts were now unusable for normal use, ironically due to the damage sustained by them encountering the aircraft structure.

Fortunately, their deflation did not affect the successful evacuation and rescue.

The crew of the Tiger had been observing the ditching, and 'NL's transponder established its location received by an RAF Nimrod aircraft operating at FL170, having diverted to the scene. This aircraft became the 'On Scene Commander'. It could not descend due to its low fuel state. The Tiger remained in the vicinity and provided a valuable link between the ditched helicopter to the rescue services via the Nimrod. When they made the distress call, an RAF Sea King scrambled from Lossiemouth. At the same time, a BAH and Bristow S-61N left Aberdeen for the scene. Their ETA was 16:00. When these helicopters were en route, a second Nimrod arrived, descended to a lower level, and assumed control.

By the time they came to board the forward life raft, continuous wave-induced impact damage with the cargo door rail had punctured three of the four inflation chambers. As Ian boarded, he slid under the collapsed canopy of the waterlogged dingy. Others piled in after him. When they heard muffled cries for help, they realised they had trapped him beneath them.

The Sea King and the BAH S-61N arrived around the same time. The BAH crew attempted to lower a life raft, but the downwash from the aircraft created problems for the survivors. After a short discussion, the Sea King lowered another on a long line. The passengers and crew boarded this life raft in two batches. The Sea King winched them up and set course for Aberdeen, landing at 17:40.

Later in the day, the oil support vessel *Maersk Retriever* tried to hoist G-ASNL on board. During this attempt, the tail sinks to the sea bed, followed by the rest of the aircraft. Two days later, the diving support vessel DSV *Shearwater Aquamarine* arrived and looked for 'NL' using equipment to locate its underwater location beacon. Due to their high background noise, the thrusters used to position the vessel dynamically interfere with any signals from the beacon. Once the thrusters are shut down, they receive a good signal from below. Initially, they only found minor pieces of wreckage; then, on the 15th of March, they found the main body of the aircraft.

She is recovered and sold to Carson Helicopters in the USA. In September 2022, she was still working, flying from Dallas, Oregon, for Croman Corporation fighting fires.

Fig 18. G-ASNL onboard DSV *Shearwater Aquamarine*.
Photo credit AAIB

It was Ian's second ditching in less than three years. It was time to return to the RAF and resume a drier career.

*

The day after they ditched, there was confirmation at work of how sensitive life rafts were to be damaged, something never registered during the wet dingy drills, probably because it was imprudent to know any different. Otherwise, what was the point of them?!
The accident reporter noted: "Once upon the water, the subsequent attempts to deploy the life rafts met with a total lack of success. This was despite the almost ideal sea state, the undamaged aircraft structure and flotation systems, and the absence of injuries among passengers accustomed to working in a hazardous environment. Due to an actual ditching experience in the North Sea, it has become increasingly clear that the expectation of a successful evacuation into life rafts carried by aircraft is low, even in good conditions."

It transpired the circumstances encountered by the crew of G-ASNL were not dissimilar to those experienced the previous summer by the Bristow crew on Meikle Loch. In no time did the CAA receive a copy of the Bristow/BNOC video. All VOR aerials were subsequently modified by fixing black rubber cuffs over the pointy bits, and the ends of the cargo door rails were coated in silicone.

*

It remained to determine the cause of the bang, followed by the noise and vibration from the main rotor gearbox. The subsequent investigation attributed the failure of the spur gear (the one used to transfer speed/torque/motion from one shaft to another) to a fatigue fracture near a tooth. The fracture had propagated inwards through the rim and web of the wheel. It then bifurcated into radial and circumferential branches and developed into overload fractures, leading to the break-up of the wheel. It caused substantial damage to the input casing and its internal components. A large segment containing some 60% of the total toothed rim of the gear ejects through the input casing. As it passed through the main rotor disc, it damaged one of the main rotor blade pitch arms. The failure of the rotor braking effect was attributed to a fatigue fracture of the hydraulic supply pipe at the disc calliper unit, presumably caused by vibration from the gearbox or shrapnel severing the lines. The aircraft had a history of spurious double fire warnings, another manifestation of this intermittent fault in the fire detection system. It is another example that is too common of curious noises, bangs, vibrations, and warnings experienced by helicopter crews!

*

It should have been a good summer. All such things can come to an end, and quite abruptly, as they did on the 16th of July 1983, during the peak holiday period for the Penzance – Scillies Islands Link. It was before we left for a flight to the rig *Drillstar* out of Aberdeen in the S-61N, G-AWFX. The news came in the company S-61N, G-BEON, on BA Flight 5918 to the Scillies, had ploughed into the sea while descending towards St Marys. The visibility was poor, with fog in the vicinity. Of the 23 passengers and one cabin attendant onboard, only four survived, along with the two pilots.
I was going on holiday that evening, and it was a month before I learned more details on our return from our beach cottage in English Harbour. It appeared they were just 1.5 nautical miles from the coast as the co-pilot was

monitoring the radar and advising the commander of their distance to go. Expecting to see the coastline, the commander looked up. Just as he was doing so, the helicopter struck the sea. The impact rips off the sponsons and the combined inflatable floatation gear; water forcibly enters the damaged cockpit. The disruption of the aircraft's hull causes water to burst open the two freight hatches on the cabin floor. The fuselage rolled over, filled with water, and quickly sank 200 feet to the seabed. 'ON' was later recovered with the remaining 17 victims on board by the diving support and salvage vessel MV *Seaforth Clansman*.

Fig 19. Recovery of G-BEON showing damaged cockpit and hull.
Photo credit: AAIB

Though there are no good accidents, sometimes conclusions are raised in the subsequent report revealing the scope for specific improvements. In the case of this accident, they were significant and many. Implementing most of them reflects how we managed without them for so long. To put them into context, it is worth exploring the principal ones since they became a legacy from those who perished to make flying offshore for hundreds of thousands of oilfield workers much safer. First, to describe the kind of visibility that is so common, though equally not fully understood within the aviation community. The Head of Flight Skills Section of the Royal Air Force Institute of Aviation Medicine provides the best summary. Here, he assesses the problems pilots face when flying by external reference in poor visibility over the sea, particularly concerning this accident. "To summarise, though, it can be said the perception of attitude may be achieved using the horizon and surface texture as clues. Height perception does not depend on the horizon. It does require surface texture and, what is more, requires the observer to be aware of the real size of the texture."

*

The report concluded, "They are deceived into believing adequate cues were available for safe control of the helicopter's flight path – at least for short periods." The pilots' accounts reflect his analysis. When they hit the sea, they were under the illusion they were still at 250 feet. And because the commander had confirmed adequate visual reference, the co-pilot concentrated on his navigation and communication duties. He considered the range from the coast of particular importance because if the helicopter were to reach one mile from the land without it being visible, he had to warn the commander to prepare to carry out an overshoot procedure. Rather than as part of the FMS (Flight Management System) on the instrument panel with modern equipment, he had to lean over to his right to monitor the radar as the display was on the console between the pilots. Then, to see the picture satisfactorily, he had his face within a foot of it as he shielded the tube with one hand from the sunlight.
Likely, they had not monitored the other instruments on the approach as well as they could. As a result, when they approached St Marys, the monitoring pilot was fully concentrated on adjusting the radar to the exclusion of monitoring the other instruments, and the flying pilot was scanning outside for visual clues, all the time reducing power and trimming back to reduce speed from 110 to 90 knots. Again, at the exclusion of monitoring the instruments, using power and attitude together to reduce airspeed can result in an unwanted change in height; unless control is perfectly coordinated, it is the most likely outcome. It was not a good recipe, made worse when the cabin attendant walked through the cabin to check the passengers before landing. A demonstration of the alteration of the centre of gravity by the time he reached the cockpit can tip the aircraft forward by one degree before he returned to his seat just before they impacted the sea. It was not much and discounted in the report as not being significant. Still, early on in flying S-61Ns, the line training captain took delight in jogging up and down an empty cabin during a flight to demonstrate that the centre of gravity can change quite significantly.

*

The accident report also revealed the G-BEON incident was an accident waiting to happen. It considered "The operating procedures left too much to the individual commander's and co-pilot's discretion. Specifically, regarding flight instrument monitoring when flying VFR (when below 3,000 feet to be clear of cloud and in sight of the surface) at a low level in poor visibility, compared with a formally structured method of arranging the crew duties. Such that one pilot would continuously monitor the flight instruments in these conditions, e.g., the concept of a monitored approach. The practice of operating the S-61 (a helicopter with neither autopilot nor height hold on its automatic flight control system) in VFR flight over water, at 250 feet in visibilities down to 900 metres, without a company operating procedure capable of ensuring the flight instruments would be continuously monitored, eroded safety margins. To the extent it allowed catastrophe to be the consequence of a human error of a kind already well-known in aviation. This practice was thus a major contributory factor."
This observation could also apply to other offshore helicopter operations. It brought home to the Civil Aviation Authority changes were overdue; commercial helicopter operational procedures and equipment fit should not differ from those applied to fixed-wing: the flying pilot would remain on instruments until the commander instructed otherwise. The commander (non-flying) would judge when the visibility was suitable to land or, if not, go around. If it were a right-hand seat (commander's) deck landing offshore, the protocol would switch to the co-pilot deciding.
That is not to say some crews have already embedded and applied this concept. This improvement was still a significant step forward for the remainder and has placed them in a more organised, safer place.

*

Next up was the radio altimeter (RADALT). It was not mandatory equipment, so operators had recently fitted only a rudimentary version - one for each pilot. Other than a small yellow light illuminating when the aircraft descended below 250 feet if the gear was not down, there were no audio ground proximity warnings. This light also came on when the aircraft reached the desired 'bugged' height in the descent. If you did not notice it with the gear already down, locked with three greens indicated, and took corrective action, then the descent blithely continued unchecked. And this was easy when you realised where the lights were on the S-61 instrument panel. The co-pilots on the periphery of their instrument scan in the bottom left-hand corner; the

captain's is placed out of view, unless he chanced to look, behind the cyclic stick.
The report did not shy away from commenting. "At the time of the accident, the BAH Operations Manual contained no instructions on using the radio altimeter height alert system but issued them after the accident. The height alert system is unlikely to attract the attention of a pilot not looking at the instrument panel because the radio altimeters are mounted low on the panel, and the warning light is small. Surprisingly, following the requirement taken a decade ago to equip the larger public transport aircraft with a ground proximity warning system (GPWS), no one had taken action to apply this important safety system to helicopters."
To build awareness, the head of the BAH Training Section, Peter Bramley, included this abbreviation in the annual multi-choice technical questionnaire. In the absence of this system, one plausible answer was: 'Geriatric Pilot Willie Stimulator'.
"Had even the simplest audio alert system, such as one operated simultaneously with the RADALT decision warning light, been in use on G-BEON, it could have alerted the crew in ample time to safely arrest the helicopter's descent. Such systems are reliable and have been available for many years. The lack of an audio height alert system capable of warning pilots even if they are not looking at the flight instruments is therefore judged to have contributed to this accident."
The manufacturer later modified the equipment to include an additional audio element to alert the crew when the aircraft had reached the selected bugged height. This recommendation became a mandatory fit two years later.

Once in the water, the type and use of emergency equipment onboard constrained their rescue and survival. There was one emergency position indicating radio beacon (EPIRB) BE 397 stowed alongside the emergency exit rear door, and each crew member (3) had an RFD 5DC Life jacket, each fitted with BE 375 PLB (personal locator beacon). In the event, they deployed none of these beacons. The aircrew life jackets were under their seats. They did not have time to reach them or the EPIRB. Without beacons, locating the survivors clutching suitcases to stay afloat in the water was difficult. Other than the smell of aviation fuel from the ruptured fuel tanks in the hull, there were no means in the fog to guide the rescuers to them. The passengers had airline-type life jackets, also in use on the North Sea. The difference on the Penzance/Scillies run is that the valise is not required around the waist. Instead, one is on each passenger seat for donning if an emergency arises,

as can be standard practice on fixed-wing passenger flights. They never had a chance.
The impracticable fit of these survival aids led to the mandatory fitting from the 1st of March 1986 (three years later) of an automatically deployable emergency locator transmitter (ADELT). In addition, aircrew on public transport helicopters operating offshore are required to wear life jackets with dual frequency (121.5 and 243 MHz) personal locator beacons. However, the life vest in a valise for offshore workers was still used in 1990 when they also began wearing life jackets over their immersion suits before boarding. Never had UK offshore commercial helicopter safety moved forward by so much.

*

From September 1983, opportunities arrived to operate out of two new bases. But only briefly. These included Inverness and Gatwick. Inverness was in response to an air traffic control strike at Aberdeen. On contract to Occidental Petroleum to service the Piper and Claymore fields, it would better serve their crew changes. Then, the first of two tours to fly the Airlink between London Gatwick and Heathrow materialised. This service was a joint venture between the British Airports Authority that owned the S-61N, G-LINK fitted with 28 seats, British Caledonian providing check-in and cabin crew wearing Cameron tartan in deference to Jock Cameron and BAH, the engineering and flight crew. When it was in maintenance, BAH North Sea S-61Ns backed up G-LINK. This arrangement was the case when I arrived to operate G-BDDA. The service began in June 1978. It continued until 1984, when BCal Helicopters, under Chief Pilot Graeme Thomson, took over for the final two years until 1986. Ten return flights a day were scheduled, flown by an early and late crew.
The route northbound was via a dogleg at Epson and Esher, then direct to Heathrow. The return sector backtracked this route. There were no slots allocated. Arrivals and departures had to be slick - 18 minutes from chock to chock. Just 3 minutes were for taxying and holding to take off, with 15 minutes airborne en route. An instrument landing system joined between the middle and inner marker for arrivals in poor visibility to make approaches to runway 27L or 09R at Heathrow was the norm. This procedure did not disrupt the flow of traffic with slots. Then, when established on the glideslope, you sensed the turbulence from the heavy in the cloud ahead; usual rules of separation were not a consideration. The VFR arrival at London Heathrow

often involves a cloud break procedure at 90° to runway 27L/09R, arriving at 500 feet above the airfield just west of Terminal 4.
Then, when cleared, cross the runway and land at one of the exit blocks leading through the outer and inner parallel taxiways to a stand located between Terminals 2 and 3, and park next to the one used by Concorde. It was a matter of time before both services were axed, albeit the fastest and slowest. These stands were marked 'H' and called 'Hotels'.

Fig 20. S-61N G-BDEA is on the way to the 'Hotels,' passing Concorde G-BOAC. London, Heathrow.
Photo credit: ©AirNikon Collection-Pima Air and Space Museum, Tucson, AZ.

Taking off one afternoon, we sensed a thundering roar in the cockpit becoming louder. And it was not the usual din from the rotors and jet turbines above us. Helicopter pilots have a habit of expecting and facing the unusual, then racing through the possible alternatives of what could go wrong. After all, the emergency checklist can only record so much.
We relaxed when we saw a Concorde on a 'Dover' departure climbing through our level and accelerating to its cruise speed of Mach 2.

*

One evening in late November, on the last flight in and out of London Heathrow, we were asked to route directly to the 'Hotels' and land on the inner taxiway leading to them. This section of the outer taxiway and the ground between it and the inner taxiway, including the entry/exit blocks, was under maintenance. It was ring-fenced off with plastic cones and pink plastic tape strung between them. This temporary barrier allowed only the inner available for arrivals and departures off RW 27L/09R; so far, so good. Later, on arrival back at the Beehive, having hopped back over the railway tracks and shut down, ops asked me to take a telephone call. An irate gentleman is on the other end. "You've caused some trouble this evening, captain; you've closed our airport." It was the manager of Heathrow. The cones and tape were not secure. The rotor downwash had blown them into the inner taxiway on our departure. At Aberdeen, the cones are fastened to railway sleepers when similar airfield maintenance is in the proximity of helicopter operations. These measures were not in place here, and taking note of these precautions, he hung up. So, if you had a long wait before pushing back that night – blame me! My last flight on the Link was on the 25th of November.

*

On the 2nd of May 1984, we were on the second flight of the day. With Roger Cookson, we left Aberdeen in the S-61N, G-ATBJ, at 11:25, destination: the drilling rig *Sedco 700*. While we were refuelling on the rig, the HLO informed us there had been an incident with one of the company's Chinooks. On the way back to Aberdeen, more radio chatter confirmed a Chinook had ditched. Chinook G-BISO was on the return sector from the *Polycastle* flotel. The flotel was a semi-submersible accommodation barge and moored alongside the *Magnus* platform 100 nautical miles northeast of Shetland Isles. At 12:20, they felt a violent disturbance ten minutes after take-off while cruising at 2,500ft in good weather conditions. According to the Air Accident Investigation Branch report, the aircraft pitched slightly nose down with a distinctive negative 'g' sensation. Then, immediately followed by a harsh increase in positive 'g' and violent upward movement of the whole aircraft with the nose rising and the sound of decreasing rotor speed. The first officer and handling pilot lowered the collective to reduce the pitch angle on the rotor blades. The rotor speed rapidly increased until he restored it to the cruise setting.
Everything settled down. Then, five minutes later, it began again. They tried troubleshooting the fault(s), particularly the fluctuating No.2 flight control hydraulic boost system. But to no avail, they descended the aircraft to 500 feet, intending to divert to Sumburgh. The second series of disturbances occurred with diminishing control over the collective inputs. On one occasion, a steady application on the collective to arrest the descent of 800 ft/min did not affect the rotor speed or torque of the aircraft. It was as though the collective was disconnected. One disturbance followed another so closely the first officer described it as a continuous series of recoveries from unusual attitudes. These extreme control difficulties were due to two unconnected and serious defects in the flight control system. Unknown to the crew, these violent, un-demanded manoeuvres accompanied by rotor rpm fluctuations

occurred without warning because the System 2 side of the collective lower boost actuator was intermittently deactivating. This response was due to fluid depletion when the System 1 side of the actuator was already in bypass mode, a condition not indicated to the crew on the flight deck. Due to fatigue damage, two of the three cap screws containing the hydraulic fluid had failed. Both had been under-torqued at the last installation.
It became clear the flight could not continue with two flying control malfunctions. It is time to make a precautionary landing on the sea. Thus, 21 minutes into the flight, the call over the pa came: “Brace, Brace, Brace.” The captain made a controlled ditching, and the aircraft settled on the water, riding a two to three-foot swell. They were eight nautical miles north of the *Cormorant ‘A’*.
The disturbance continued to a lesser degree on the water. After a short time, the disturbances ceased when they lost the No.2 hydraulic system pressure completely. They could see the *Cormorant ‘A’* on the horizon and began to water-taxi towards it. Despite a reasonably smooth sea state and a two to three feet swell, the waves were coming halfway up the windscreen. Their attempt to reach the platform had to be abandoned. Fortunately, a Bristow Bell 212 had arrived and hovered nearby, waiting to assist.

Fig 21. G-BISO: Survivors being hoisted aboard Bristow Bell 212.
Photo Credit: ©John Sinclair Morgan. Former member of BHL.

By now, the Chinook had begun shipping water through previously damaged aft ramp door seals. And passengers were reporting flooding in the rear of the cabin. The armrests of the seats were disappearing under the water. The manufacturer had designed the fuel pods to be watertight, providing additional buoyancy and stability. Instead, the aircraft settled deeper into the water as the sea flooded through 3/8-inch diameter holes into the fuel tank pods. Had the fuselage not been taking water through the ramp, the depth in fuel pods would have settled at 3-4 inches. But the pods continued to fill, collapsing the fuel bladders. It would soon start displacing the fuel through vents. The aircraft was sinking. At 13:23, the captain gave the order for evacuation. Brenda Old, the cabin attendant, launches the first life raft through the forward starboard exit, doubling as the airstair door. They no sooner had some passengers boarded when it blew out of reach. Using the rear starboard emergency exit, she realised it was possible to walk back up along the sponson and enter the raft. Its painter had begun to chafe on the sharp edge of the airstair door frame. Then, the mooring broke. There were only nine passengers onboard. The second life raft did not fare any better. Launched through the airstair door, two passengers boarded before that painter sheared through. The remaining 33 passengers evacuated through the aft door into the sea. Surface craft and two more helicopters come to their rescue. Despite these trying circumstances, Brenda managed to execute an orderly evacuation of the oilfield workers.

At this point, the flight crew stopped the engines and rotors that maintained the aircraft's stability and upright on the water. The Auxiliary Power Unit (APU) in the tail was left running. At 14:01, they, along with Brenda, evacuated the aircraft. The Chinook rolled over two critical minutes later, 82 minutes after the touchdown. How critical will shortly be revealed. There was no other damage to the aircraft where it lay inverted. A rig standby boat fetched the first line onto her until the nearest vessel with a suitable crane, the DSV *Seabex I*, arrived from Conoco's Murchison Field.

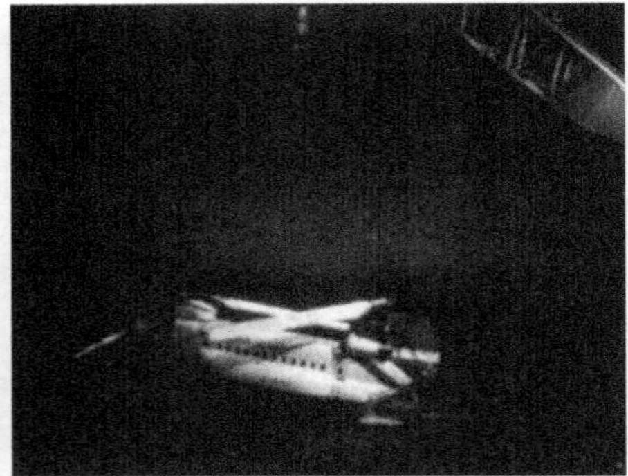

Fig 22. Preparing to and lifting G-BISO onboard DSV *Seabex 1*.
Photo Credit: Dave Anderson.

When the crane driver asked the BAH engineer supervising the lift, “How much does she weigh?” “No problem to lift with a 120-ton crane; it only weighs 35 tons”. “What about the water?” As Dave Anderson, a diver on board, recounted: “The crane alarm was continuous…But we got the salvage dosh.” Nine hours after ditching, using a strop on each rotor head, they crane her onboard close to midnight and, after a voyage, unload her onto a semi-trailer at Aberdeen docks.
Columbia Helicopters in the USA purchase G-BISO. They converted her to a BV 234UT, though she never flew again until the 23rd of May 2018, a few days over 34 years after she ditched. Happy landings, N235CH! It is sobering to think they may have experienced a complete in-flight loss of collective control if the crew had not elected to ditch. And this was just a line training flight, though, in truth, it could happen anytime. I do not think Bruce Morton expected to teach his student Max Bailey such a thorough example of ditching and evacuation so soon into the syllabus.

*

The revelation that the permanent removal of screwed blanking plugs from the holes in the fuel pods was a requirement for CAA validation of the FAA Type Certificate to improve fuel leakage detection from the bladders did not go unnoticed in the crew room. The authority did not seem to appreciate they were compromising floatation and stability on the water.

Within days, the cockpit voice recorder (CVR) became mandatory equipment from June 1984 for helicopters with a maximum total authorised weight of over 2,700 kg or capable of carrying more than nine passengers. The device had to have four channels, one of which was to record rotor rpm. The majority of passengers found their immersion suits leaked in an excessive amount of seawater. There was no statutory requirement to wear them or performance specifications. Military immersion suits specify a leak rate of 50 mg every ten minutes; of the 40 suits worn in this incident and subsequently tested, only one meets this specification.

When the ditching report was published, three years later, it noted the emergency exits exceeded the requirement for ditching and evacuation on the water with a seating capacity of 40 to 59 persons. The minimum requirement was two Type III exits (not less than 20” wide x 36”) on either side. The Chinook had two additional Type IV exits (not less than 19” wide x 26”) on either side. It then revealed that a problem would arise if the aircraft turned over. During underwater escape tests, trained Royal Navy personnel demonstrated only four persons could likely have time to evacuate through one exit, a ratio of 4:1 when, in practice, it was 11:1 with 44 passengers on board. “It would therefore appear that, if a capsize should occur after a controlled ditching in the North Sea, a significant number of passengers would be trapped in the fuselage, and fatalities would be inevitable.” The inconvenient truth only emerged after BAH withdrew the Chinook from service in 1986. Correcting this imbalance by “increasing the window size in the BV 234 to provide additional Type IV exits would require such structural changes as prohibitive.” By the time the AAIB published their report in 1987, the problem had gone away.

The need for more emergency exits was more than just a Chinook problem. The S-61N and the Super Puma were similarly affected to a degree. The solution for these aircraft was to modify the existing cabin windows into ‘push-out’ windows to supplement the emergency exits. Operators incorporated them three years later.

In 1985, my turn arrived to fly on BAH overseas offshore operations.

Part II

Chapter 9. 1985

Bombay High – Towers of Silence – Snakes – 24 Hours - Reported!

India, October 1985. The operation here was based at Juhu (VAJJ), an airfield just up the coast to the north of Mumbai (Bombay) and still within the suburban area. The nearest railway station is Ville Parle. The airfield flooded extensively during the monsoon. At ten feet above sea level, the natural drainage was poor. Founded in 1928, it was India's first civil aviation airport. Farther inland was Santa Cruz (VABB - Chhatrapati Shivaji Maharaj International), the international airport for Mumbai. They controlled our departures via the Juhu control tower to align with their traffic. A request to start could take up to half an hour. It meant waiting in the cab for the magic words "Speedbird G-ATBJ. You are cleared to start motors," an instruction probably harking back to the days of in-line and radial engines. When summertime temperatures nudged +35°C and more under the plexiglass above our heads, we envied the pack of stray dogs sleeping in the shade. Not until the ground crew removed the chocks did they slope off and crash under another parked helicopter.

*

The airfield has two entrances: one on the eastern and the other on the western side. The latter is accessed just off the beach road, where the motorised rickshaw taxi drops us off. On foot, we pass through the gates with a guardhouse on one side and a low pink building on the other. This retreat provided a discrete sanctuary for lovers away from crowded tenements. Walking across to the hangar, one could not miss the instructions in fresh paint on a wooden board signed by a British army captain in 1938, 'No Photographs' and then past a pair of Beech 18s (twin radial engine Beechcraft) on the right, parked in the shade of the trees. Bollywood filmmakers owned them.
In contrast, another world used the other side of the field. Usually twice daily. There appeared to be a 'freedom to roam', not dissimilar to the rights in Scotland. Yet this was on the airfield. So long as entry was not through the main gates or when you wanted an apron pass for a vehicle, authorities overlooked this habit. People entered through holes in the fence clutching a

tin of water to conduct their morning ablutions, women at one end of the field and men at the other, loosely segregated by a disused runway on the way to the tower. When the southwest monsoon arrived in June and flooded these areas, they perched on the edge of the runways.
While there, the Indian Air Force bought some Russian MIL Mi-26 Helicopters. These had two decks in an Airbus A380 configuration. Their base is on the far side of the airfield from our operations. Whenever these powerful aircraft lifted into the hover, they blasted the residue of dried ablutions into billows across the airfield towards our flight line. A 'brown out' every time they flew. Yet paradoxically, when airborne, they made the drone of an Airbus A320. Serene, by comparison.

*

India's Oil and Natural Gas Corporation (ONGC) contracted five operators. They included BAH with an S-61N (G-ATBJ that Chris Twyman, who later headed Shell Aircraft, had ferried over from Zhuhai, China. With the chicken scratch removed, the emergency exits had the corresponding text sign-written with red paint in Sanskrit for the benefit of the indigenous passengers), the French company Héli-Union and Schreiner Airways, a Dutch company, both with Sud Aviation SA 365N Dauphins. The latter was crewed mainly by Portuguese and Argentinians. Then Elitos, an Italian company with a Sud Aviation SA330J and Okanagan with some Bell 212s and an S-61N. Okanagan was the blue-chip Canadian heavy helicopter company with the hummingbird logo Craig Dobbin acquired when he beefed up his fleet of Bell 206s in a company called Sealand. He renamed the lot CHC (derived from Canadian Holding Company) in 1988. Their S-61N was off-contract.
It was indeed a harlequin fleet of helicopters from many nations. They parked on a flight line along the disused runway leading from the hangar to the main runway; from across this flight line, the Indian Air Force and Navy parked their Russian-built Mi-8s. These aircraft were unpopular with Western passengers as they did not have the single-engine performance capability; they could not stay airborne on one engine. If they did arrive on the water in one piece, the emergency exits were just too small to egress through for the average built Western oilfield workers.
The BAH contract included transporting 26 passengers + cargo. The cargo was mainly fruit and veg, hiding a variety of hitchhikers. They revealed themselves flying, hopping, crawling, or just slithering around the cabin during the flight. The main destinations in the Arabian Sea were the Bombay

High, located 90 miles offshore to the west, and the Heera Field, 60 miles to the southwest, then returning with the crew change without refuelling. The fuel offshore was reserved for infield shuttle aircraft only. The route to the Heera field crossed the centre line of westbound flights out of Santa Cruz and required reporting clear with their air traffic control or, when returning to base, requesting onward clearance to cross from a reporting point just offshore from Bandra. This waypoint was easy to find when a large white building came into view - the Russian embassy.

*

It was mandatory to give the Towers of Silence on Malabar Hill a wide berth before continuing offshore. It was not only the carrion, predominantly vultures, attracted to the area to avoid; instead, the five towers in a sacred site of 55 acres where they lay deceased Parsi to rest. This practice continues a 3,000-year-old Zoroastrian tradition. These people began to arrive in India in 900 AD. Their migration was after endless failed attempts to fend off the Arab invasion of Persia, starting 200 years earlier when the invaders spread out across the Middle East, North Africa, and the Iberian Peninsula. Being successful people in business, they could no longer tolerate the invaders and protect their faith from Islam. They began a new life on the subcontinent of Asia, taking their traditions with them. One of these conventions was a method of laying their dead to rest. They considered a corpse could harbour disease and infection; evil spirits could colonise it. To prevent them from contaminating the land or sea after their cremation, they lay them intact outside for the carrion to dispose of them – excarnation or 'sky burial'. To provide privacy for the deceased, they constructed towers to lay them out. They consecrated them on Malabar Hill in 1670, and their ancestors continually used them. Known as dakhma, they are circular, roofless structures with walls 18 feet high and a round plinth within them.
Around this eight-foot-high plinth, a class of people called 'untouchables' lay the corpses out in a pattern, each head to toe with another, resembling the spokes of a wheel. They place the children in the centre around a well, followed by females, then males emanating from the centre. As the plinth sloped in a gradient towards the central well, it allowed the rains to run off and whatever else had been discarded by the raptors. From there, it drained into four pits outside the main building containing sand and charcoal, as depicted in the drawing. Once the bones had been thoroughly pecked clean, usually after three days, the untouchables removed them to make room for others.

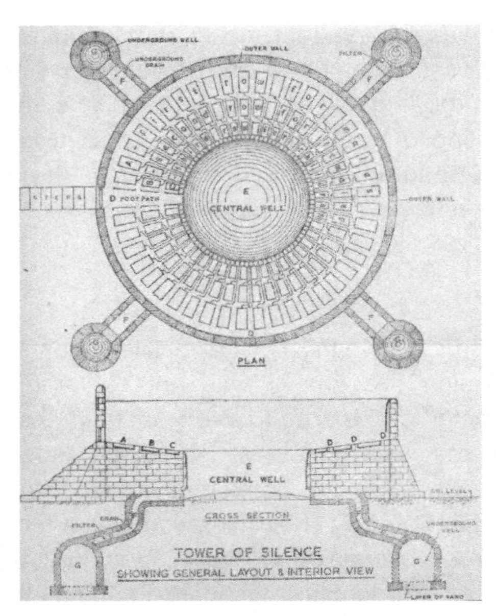

Fig 23. Tower of Silence (Dakhma).
Attributed to Sapur F Desai (1860-1960)

Back in the land of the living, carrying more than the usual North Sea complement of 19 passengers was practicable as the offshore workers here were considerably lighter. Thus, there was a requirement for a cabin attendant, usually an engineer. Performance-wise, two local dispensations enable commercial operations in temperatures up to +36C. One was the WAT (take-off weight factored for Weight, Altitude and Temperature). The CAA allowed the company to reduce this restriction to 500 feet (rather than 1,000 per the Rotorcraft Flight Manual - RFM). The second was the necessity to dump the contents of the centre fuel tank in the event of a flame-out. These enabled the flight to climb up to 500 feet on one engine.

As a commuting base, the managers changed out with the crews. Joe West, one of our managers, felt we should have a balanced diet and not exist on beer or the curried omelette sandwiches provided offshore for breakfast. To achieve this, a five-course meal including a drink for under £1.00 (17 rupees at the time) should be available. (Our meal allowances are £40.00/day – leaving plenty of change for drinks by the hotel pool). If he survived the night, Joe identified his approval of venues by fastening a BAH 'Fly to the Bombay

High' or an 'Offshore in India' sticker to their door/hole in the wall or Hari Krishna temple steps as appropriate.

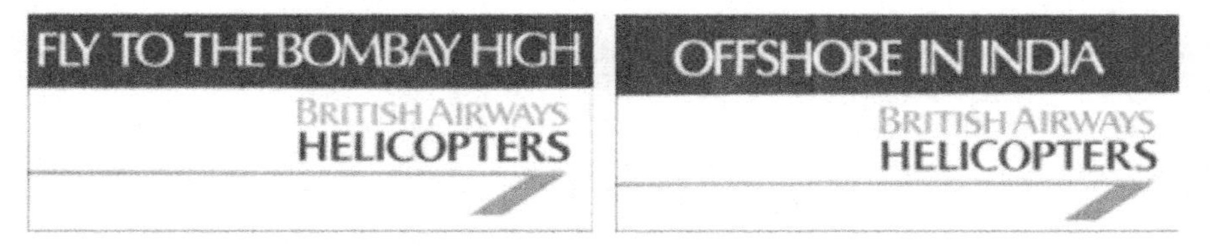

Fig 24. BAH Stickers – *Author's collection*

As a guide, one saw and ate in many places with Joe, where he intently watched you for adverse reactions. The food critic and guinea pig succumb to ice when the hotel's ice-making machine breaks down on a Sunday afternoon. Blocks of ice the size of coffins were dragged through the streets from downtown, broken up and slipped into our drinks. The ever-courteous waiters delivered them to us on the lawn overlooking the sea wall with a smile and roll of the head and varying doses of amoebic dysentery. On subsequent flights offshore for the next week, it was a matter of keeping the curried egg sandwiches down long enough for the result to be bagged and dropped into the Arabian Sea at a slow forward speed before resuming the flight. No wonder the route from the Bombay High attracted huge fish; the manta rays with wingspans extending up to seven meters assembled in the area following the curried egg-flavoured plankton. This feast appeared before the monsoon when these rays, large enough to support a Sikorsky S-76 helicopter footprint, arrived. Most pilots, including those from other operators, attracted poolside by the Swiss Air cabin crews staying on the top floor, were also afflicted. For the Swiss Air chief engineer on the station, who took great care sending samples of swimming pool water back to Zurich every fortnight to be analysed, it must have been depressing to report the water was OK, though the ice was suspect.

*

Swimming in the sea was not an option. Fins could be seen in the shallows, cutting through the muddy water that extended up to 70 miles offshore after the monsoon. Yet this was a peaceful hotel compared to where the Héli-Union detachment stayed farther down the beach, not far from the western entrance of the airfield. Part of a pilot's time off must include eight hours of undisturbed rest. An exploratory night in their hotel determined this could be

a problem for Joe's back-to-back, Chis Rutter and his family. Under each bed was placed a meal tray consisting of a traditional square biscuit tin lid with scraps of food mixed with warfarin surrounded by a sticky substance. During the night, a loud clattering and banging heralded the food tray being dragged around the room and over the bed firmly attached to a large rodent's tail. Forget about the aviation requirement for undisturbed rest. Sleep did not come into it. A tired family returned to the Sun-n-Sand hotel in the morning to join the rest of us in a hotel where the heavy flock wallpaper cascaded down off the walls if you left the windows open during the humid nights leading up to the monsoon. Fumbling your way out of this nocturnal cocoon was a minor inconvenience.
The hotel was next to a more prominent, newer international hotel, the Holiday Inn. It was a natural destination for the Okanagan crews to stay - and a gold smuggler. In India, gold commands a price two-thirds higher than the world market due to its buoyant demand for gold jewellery. It often comes in from East Africa by air. A raid on a flight unloading cargo can expose ground handlers to being caught up in the melee and, according to a friend who owned a handling agency, up to ten years in jail before his employees' case comes to court. On this occasion, the smuggler was making deals in a bustling lobby of the Sun-n-Sand. The police abruptly concluded their arrangements, and our man from the Inn threw himself out of an upstairs window. Across the street from this hotel was a former municipal garden shaded by cabbage palms. Since independence in 1947, it has become overgrown and neglected. Here, a family of black-spotted pigs rooted and squealed in the undergrowth. A young girl around ten years old joined them early one Saturday morning. She lay on her side just off the road on the dry earth bordered by bushes all weekend. On Monday morning, she had gone, carted away on her last journey.

When the tide was out, the beach over the high sea wall provided a highway for commuters on foot from Versova in the north to the bridge, a good walk later leading into Danda Village, with its rocky foreshore. Close to the wall, a tidal-dependant colony would appear. This gathering included horses and camels for hire, harnessed with cracked leather tack that had never seen saddle soap. Street vendor barrows selling pressed sugar cane juice and betel nuts, red evidence of the latter dyed in the sand by the juice spat out, and family fairground troupes. These performers made themselves known to the hotel residents in the gardens above by projecting a baby perched in a small basket on the end of a pole above the parapet of the sea wall.

Local food, though good, a lobster or T bone steak could be enjoyed in a restaurant just up Pali Hill from Pali Market for 17rp (£1.00), did not assuage a yearning for the simple taste of basic British fare, when we found a solution. British Airways crews passing through en route to Hong Kong were already exchanging their cash expenses in rupees for sterling. For this 'service', it was not difficult to persuade one or two crewmembers to purchase cheddar cheese and pork sausages in the UK and San Miguel Beer in Hong Kong. With the components assembled, a barbeque on the hotel roof provided a taste of the West.

*

Snakes. Once the flight planning was complete, a cycle across the airfield was required to retrospectively check the weather (performance flight planning used the outside air temperature gauge and a pressure altimeter setting of the aircraft in the shade and closest to the hangar. It was always worthwhile looking for tell-tale pools of water under the chosen aircraft. A recently washed machine could trick the unwary with the temperature probe now nicely cooled down!) before signing out with air traffic control.
The weather was illustrated in a leatherbound, coffee table-sized manual on a large round table in the lobby. The book had the appropriate page open corresponding to the calendar date. Thus, there were 365 pages - one for each day of the year. The weather, including the monsoons, seemed to repeat itself sufficiently accurately every year. And even that arrived on the same day each year. Right? A cycle ride across to sign out before the monsoon nearly came to grief. I had cleared the main runway when what appeared to be dry reeds cut for fodder, blowing across the disused runway leading to the control tower – were not. They were migrating snakes. En masse, they were leaving the Gents' side of the airfield to surprise the Ladies in the evening. Too late to take avoiding action, and with feet on the handlebars, the bicycle thumped its way across.
Luckily, there was sufficient momentum to clear them. As the wobble set in, even those caught up in the pedals and spokes wriggled free. Not to be outdone, the engineers had their share of snakes to deal with. They placed buckets of water in the grass bordering the flight line. Close by, they were handy to wash the oil and grease off their hands. They were also attractive places to stay cool. Invariably, they included a wriggly hidden in the dirty water waiting to peck the unwary on the nose when bending over to wash.
It was usual for the shuttle aircraft to top up with fuel before flying back onshore in the evening. Generally, it was of good quality. Except one

evening, a returning Okanagan Bell 212 lost an engine soon after taking off. Most of the crews still on duty wandered out of the hangar to see how the pilot managed a single-engine landing. It was twilight now, and the purple-pink evening haze in the west had dimmed. We could hear the approaching signature beat of the main rotor. It was no longer dusk and much louder now when its landing light came on just before coasting in. On the base leg, the other engine flamed out. The descent increased as he lowered the collective to maintain rotor rpm. Now in autorotation, it was soon near the ground when the pilot flared to check his descent, then levelled increasing pitch on the blades to cushion the landing before he touched down, slithering along the runway, shedding sparks from the skids to great applause from the assembly. As the slowing rhythmic wocka-wocka beat of the heavy main rotor wound down, we returned to the hangar, leaving the airfield to the background hum of the Indian night. His engineers trundled off in the opposite direction to recover their bird with ground handling wheels to attach to the skids.

*

Air tests, training, and check flights could, on the one hand, amuse and, on the other, upset the locals. We usually carried them out on weekends, making full use of the runway – as you do. At the eastern end, small children attracted to the sight of a helicopter carrying out systems checks would briefly congregate, then disappear in a cloud of dust when the aircraft lifted into the hover. The threshold at the western end was a popular place for picnics. It had easy access, close to the coastal road and still in the shade of the palms bordering it. Watching an arrival over the trees, we saw the downdraft initially dislodge picnic hampers, tablecloths, babies, and stray dogs on the periphery lurking for morsels, then disappear into a maelstrom of food, tiffin tins, dead leaves and dust until the helicopter landed.

*

For a week, Joe left me in charge of the operations when he went off for a break on a houseboat in Srinagar. Well, it always happens when the manager is away. First up, a jack-up rig under tow had broken off its seawater pump. The rig was in transit to a new location in the Gulf of Cambay, where the tidal range can be up to 38 feet. With the legs jacked up, they flood the seawater holds to provide ballast and stability in transit. These legs can reach over 400 feet above the vessel and up to 700 on newer rigs. Then, when on location, they use electric motors to crank the legs down and a pump to empty the seawater of the holds - relatively straightforward, except the last time the surveyors charted the seawater depth was in March, before the monsoon. By September, the mud from the rivers feeding into the gulf had migrated much farther offshore. The workboat had unexpectedly run aground, and the rig had kept going under its momentum, mounted the vessel and broken the pump. A replacement arrived at the airfield on the back of a ubiquitous Leyland Comet truck with a gaily painted, wooden cab. I request an apron pass to enable the lorry with its 1,500 kg load to access the helicopter. Since 1980, the Bombay mafia had been growing with the economy's demise, and the airfield security demanded an outrageous sum to proceed – or have us wait a few weeks. One option was to move the cargo by hand. When I asked the American manager of the oilfield base if we could use some of his men, he paraphrased a former Viceroy of India, Lord Curzon. In 1900, Curzon noted, "All the millions I have to manage are less than schoolchildren." The manager replied: "I've hundreds of them down at the yard, but no. They will just get in the way!" So, not much change there, then. It did not take long to unpack the pump and break it down into manageable components, and with the aid of a forklift truck from Héli-Union to transport, reassemble and repack it inside the helicopter. On arrival at the rig, we shut down beside a leg encrusted with sea life. I cautioned the crew before we started. My main concern was if the 1.5 tonnes of kit came to rest on the lip of the cargo door, the aircraft would tip onto its nose. The vision of the donkey suspended in the air by the shafts of its overloaded cart kept crossing my mind. It stated the obvious and had to be said. We agreed a few men in the back of the aircraft would counter the impending alteration of the centre of gravity.

The crew originated from Louisiana, home to a language and dialect only they could understand. It then transpired the barnacles and limpets marooned hundreds of feet up in the sky had a far better view of the helideck than the rig crane operator. He could not see the helicopter cargo door entrance from where he operated his console in a well just below the helideck. A roustabout on the deck above relayed instructions to him from the HLO by the cargo door. We set to work using hand signals; the noise from turbine generators powering the rig drowned out verbal communication over any distance.

Thus, communicating with flicks of the fingers and twists of the wrist, they delicately threaded the 1,500 kg pump in its 14-foot wooden box out of the cargo door; not even a shimmy from the tail wheel indicating a lift-off was imminent. On reflection, they probably also used hand signals a lot with foreigners. Returning to Juhu, knowing the limpets would soon have a fresh food supply was satisfying. By now, they only had rusted steel for their unique teeth to gnaw. Their gnashers have a reputation for being the toughest material in the biological world. And without expensive implants, as I found out later, they are refreshed by a conveyor line of new ones every two days. Lucky them!

*

The second event came close to putting us in the penalty zone. To be grounded with an aircraft on the ground (AOG) meant incurring charges to the customer for not providing the service.
During a daily maintenance check in the evening, the engineering manager, Don Robertson, informed me two brackets above the tail rotor drive shaft were shearing off. Even one frame out of line presented a problem. The cables linking the cockpit controls to the pitch change rods of the tail rotor blades thread through holes in these brackets. There was a chance, with two out of line, the cables would chafe against the misaligned walls of the holes and fray. We could lose tail rotor control. Still, he had a solution. Back in Aberdeen, they used a rigging tool template when constructing new brackets so these holes, when correctly placed, all lined up when reassembled.
In the meantime, we began with aluminium from Air India and contracted a local artisan with a drill to make the holes. The first effort could have been much better. Was the drill powered by our man pumping the treadle with his feet to rotate the bit the problem? He went off to try again. As no one had located the template, Don volunteered to fly back to Aberdeen and return with it, despite efforts to express our predicament by fax for the spare parts. Instead, we received faxes to supply our immersion suits' size and expiry date. These bags were safe in their lockers in Aberdeen, far away from the +36ºC outside on the apron. Just 24 hours later, Don returned with the template perfectly matching the second attempt. We were back in the air! We also realised a tail rotor control malfunction was possible if this was a trend and other brackets followed suit. It was time to practice.
Loss of tail rotor control or a yaw control malfunction is not a problem so long as the collective pitch to the main rotors is carefully applied along with a decent amount of airspeed, say 80 knots, to control directional stability. To achieve this, we can explore the optimum settings of power and airspeed in flight before making a low approach without disturbing this newfound configuration. Ideally, a crosswind can come in handy when space to land is limited, and anticipation of power is required to arrest the descent. Wind from

the left for American aircraft with their main rotors spinning anticlockwise in the proper direction and from the right for our French friends with their rotors spinning in a direction God never intended. Conversely, you can reverse the wind direction when you have the luxury of a long runway and no need to arrest the descent. This crosswind helps to stop you from veering off the pavement and disappearing into the bushes when you lower the collective.
Therefore, we took it upon ourselves to hone our run-on landing skills. Running on is not a problem in an S-61N when the tail wheel locking pin is engaged to prevent shimmying. It has a published max normal run-on speed of 40 knots. The effect of touching down at 80 knots is much the same, with even better directional control, except when you come to apply the brakes. They heat up quickly, especially if you are running out of runway! The result is a cabin full of dense smoke, and best to try this procedure without occupants in the back and with the cockpit windows closed to prevent the smoke from venting past your eyes. Just as a fuel leak in the cabin smarts them, but not so bad. Now reasonably proficient, a fax arrived from the Chief Engineer in the UK. We could only operate if the components had a Sikorsky part number. Maybe he knew something as the parts came on the next BA flight. It was now a small matter of springing them from Santa Cruz customs over the weekend.

*

Finally, I lost the ONGC contract! Drilling for oil had heavily exploited the area, and water injection was necessary to retain well pressure. This activity contributed to a fragile sea floor, much as onshore parts of Texas today. It required the distribution of weight evenly to avoid any mishaps. A jack-up rig with a mattress footprint was the solution. And ONGC had contracted three from Reading and Bates in Singapore. The helideck area and loading are approved to accept the S-61N, except the plans did not illustrate the superstructure surrounding it on two sides and the anchor winch just off-centre on the helideck. We discovered these omissions on the first flight to the *J.W Mclean*. The rig lay near the Heera Field, some 50 miles to the southwest and off the Coast of Malabar. We routed past the rocky foreshore of Bandra Point, with white dhobi quilting the rocks to dry in the sun, much as on the suburban station platforms of Andheri and Ville Parle in between the rush hours. No Blue; no starch, please! (These were the boxes to check on the hotel laundry list unless you wanted to wear an armour plate).
Then, avoiding the raptors that included black kites, referred to by the crews as 'shitehawks', working the Towers of Silence on Malabar Hill, we headed

out to sea over shipping in the roads; some were waiting to unload and take on cargo, others to stay. Run ashore on a high tide, and they will be dismantled and broken up for scrap. Offshore, the visibility never exceeded five miles in the haze, and often, it was only half that. After clearing this shipping, there was little to see besides skinny inshore fishing boats drifting in rafts on a café cortado-coloured sea. Listless. We aborted the first approach to the rig.

Above the building fronting onto two sides of the helideck are pennants and other maritime signals and warnings. Downwash from the main rotor had finally caused them to chafe through their salt-encrusted, threadbare halyards. They detach from their mooring anchor points on the roof. Then, moving in closer, the rotors began to suck these unruly 'piñatas' from the top of their poles over the helideck towards us. We backed off; they tidied up their signals, and we prepared to make another approach. On arrival a second time, there was just room to place the tail wheel onboard with the main rotor blade tips a safe distance from the building ahead and the starboard sponson nudging the anchor winch protruding from the deck.

The *J.W Mclean* Offshore Installation Manager was on leave. Instead, we advised the bemused ship's captain with the same recommendation we gave to ONGC operations when back onshore: the actual deck size possibly matched their published dimensions, but the encumbered layout did not meet our expectations. We would not operate a commercial flight there again, though maybe for a rescue. Not to be put off by a mere voyage report, a few days later, ONGC tasked Chris Twyman to fly there and, when advised by me, agreed not to do so. What happened next was a surprise: an order to remove all the staff from the country on the next BA flight. The aircraft and spares are to follow within 24 hours. Chris then requested a meeting. Here, we explained again the information was inaccurate. We had written a report and handed it over to their operations manager. The wing commander in charge of aviation matters for ONGC was not satisfied. He insisted it was entirely feasible. The nose wheel placed well forward on the deck provided plenty of room……. "Wait a minute. Did you say nose wheel?" With his team, we trooped into the hangar and inspected the undercarriage layout of the Okanagan S-61N, a tail dragger, as all '61s are—round one to BAH.

The brochure, with Sikorsky's approval, then appeared. It was a perfect picture of a helideck, just a mystery of where all the buildings and anchor winch had gone.

It now seemed a good idea to bring the Italian company Elitos captain with a nose-wheeled helicopter into the fray. They said Elitos had an aircraft on the contract due to grace and favour. Rajiv Gandhi, the Indian Prime Minister's wife, Sonia, was Italian. Their usual work was heli-slinging construction materials up into the mountains around Sestrière rather than flying offshore for Oil & Gas companies. Would Carlos fly out to this rig in his Puma? Without asking for a briefing, he exclaimed: "No problem!" They did not admit it was not the real deal; there may be obstructions. Then, their doubts started creeping in. They were sliding into their trap. We waited for an opportunity to help Carlos out. Overtaken by events, they mused it was now too dangerous. Only. Even though his aircraft was smaller, it did have this fabled nosewheel - round two to BAH.

Finally, the Chief Pilot of Schreiner, Francisco Martins, flew us out in the smallest aircraft type on the ONGC contract, an SA 365N Dauphin, after we had briefed him on the layout inconsistencies. On approach, he naturally asked over the intercom, "Where do you land?" We duly landed; they retreated down to the galley for tea and cakes as we surveyed the deck: size conformed, but buildings, anchor winch and other limitations – no way! They restored the contract with round three in the bag—a fitting end to an eventful week.

*

Towards the end of October, the No. 2 engine's low-pressure valve began to cause a problem. It had failed when flying offshore. As a precaution, we shut down on the jack-up rig *Uxmal* next to one of its three 300' high legs. Our engineer, who doubled as cabin crew, attended to the problem. With assistance from the rig workshops, he judiciously braised over the ruptured valve and stopped the leak. We followed up his success with ice cream on the helideck. Unfortunately, this was a short-term solution until they could replace the part. And the customs people were notorious for not clearing imported parts. So, we had to wait until a new valve could be prized out of their bond by fair means and foul.

It coincided with Santa Cruz International Airport deciding they wanted a control zone. They designed a trial to begin on the 31st to initiate the process. The distribution of various entry reporting points was 40 miles from the airport. The procedure was to advise their radar controller when you were leaving the zone and the estimated time to re-enter it on the return from offshore. The point of entry for helicopters inbound from Bombay High was on the north-western edge of the boundary at a point up the coast. Creating an organised traffic flow seemed sound until the No. 2 engine's low-pressure fuel valve failed again. The repair on the *Uxmal* turned out to have been temporary. This time, it was more significant as fuel from the broken valve burst into the cabin. Being in the cabin roof above row three, it quickly flooded the floor and flowed into the main hold under rows 1 and 2. Though the hold took care of the waste fuel for the moment, a bigger problem was developing: high octane paraffin vaporising in the +36°C heat. Because we had removed the cockpit windows and heater along with the ventilation motor to save weight, there was only one way for the cabin air to exit the aircraft: through our windows. And the route to the windows from the cabin passed across our eyes.

As the fumes began to smart and burn, they restricted our sight. A PAN (French for broken down – en panne) call was made, and a request for an immediate return to Juhu. Of course, re-entering the zone so soon and retracing our track through an outbound reporting point was inevitably denied; they just had to go through with their dress rehearsal. No. We had to enter through an official reporting point, a round trip time of some 30 minutes. Instead, we decided to act on the premise it would probably be all right. We descended to a low level. Chris agreed with my intention to come in under their radar, feigning we could not receive their radio calls and make a beeline for the field. They knew or thought they did. "You have infringed our rules and have been reported. Only. The colonel will summon you to explain your disobedience only! **You have infringed**........, only!" Of course, our radio silence did not respond to any of this chatter. And each time he repeated this mantra, it 'only' became more hysterical. Until we shut down at Juhu, then it went quiet. 'Radio failure' can pay. They never raised the subject again.

Paradoxically, this trial control zone did have rewards. The inbound route could take a long northeast loop to reach the coast, farther than needed if you had the fuel. If you were lucky, the purpose was to formate with flamingos and return with them at a low level, following the deserted, coconut palm-fringed beaches, broken in places by fishing nets laid out on the sand for repair, to the designated boundary re-entry point.

Chapter 10. 1985 - 1986

Chicken Scratch – Glomar Java Sea – Ratting – No Escape

In January 1986, I arrived in China. This operation was initially a dry lease crewed by the Civil Aviation Administration of China (CAAC) pilots trained by BAH in Scotland in 1982. It will provide three S-61N helicopters, G-BEOO, G-BEWM and, for a time, G-ATBJ. They have a new colour radar and Litton Omega Navigation, enabling the entry of nine waypoints. On arrival, they had 'chicken scratch' applied aft the cabin and down the tail, denoting them as a CAAC aircraft. The reference to 'chicken scratch' originated from work by the Japanese artist Katsushika Hokusai. He had coated the feet of a chicken with red paint, then had coaxed it to walk along a sheet of paper painted dark blue. Titled 'Tatsuta River with floating maple leaves', its resemblance to Chinese writing is not lost on the Western crews. The contract was with a joint venture company, PROOC (Pearl River Oil Operating Company): BP and Occidental Petroleum.

The company shipped the aircraft by sea to the Kwai Chung Container Port, Hong Kong, where Captains Tony Buckley and Jim Blain received them in October 1983. The engineers fitted the main and tail rotor blades before being flown to Kai Tak Airfield for a full engineering inspection. Initially, the operation was out of Baiyun, the international airport for Guangzhou (ZGGG) (formerly Canton), before moving to Zhuhai, just over the border from Macau, to be closer to PROOCs offshore exploration blocks. The contracted rig did not have fuel onboard and was 175 miles out in the Pearl River Mouth Basin of the South China Sea. They were near the operational limits of an S-61N for a round trip from Guangzhou until the heliport at Zhuhai was constructed. Each outbound sector was a point of no return (PNR) exercise; success depended on the winds. Although some refer to the area as 'typhoon alley', the area is no more vulnerable to tropical storms than other South China Sea areas. It is subject to severe weather conditions virtually year-round.

*

Later in the month, BP received a request from the Global Marine base in Zhanjiang, a city on the mainland peninsular north of Hainan Island. Around midnight on the 25th of October, they lost contact with their drillship, the *Glomar Java Sea*. Could BP release one of their S-61Ns to look for it?

Crewed by a mix of English and Chinese-speaking crew, this 400-foot long vessel was built in 1975 in the USA on hire to Atlantic Richfield (ARCO) China. It was drilling in an area known as the Qiongdongnan Basin in water 317 feet deep, 63 nautical miles south of Hainan Island. On the 14th of October, meteorologists had detected a tropical disturbance over the Marshall Islands and, moving west, had filled. By the time it had reached south of Hainan Island, it had become a tropical storm, Lex.

The *Glomar Java Sea* crew had prepared for the storm's arrival, even though it may pass them to the north. On the 22nd, they decided since they planned to change the drill bit, they would not wholly lower the drill string (the drill pipe with the bit attached) to the bottom of the well. Instead, they lowered the drill string only as far as there was casing in place, at about 6,300 feet. They then used the rams in the blowout preventer to 'hang off' the drill string in the well. They then disconnected the drill pipe above the blowout preventer on the sea floor and brought that portion back on board the drill ship. At that time, they disconnected the marine riser and brought it back on board. When severe weather was forecast, these standard precautions left the drillship free other than light guide wires. The vessel remained facing northwest and into the wind, held by four bow anchors and five stern anchors deployed in a spread pattern. They still have a spare bow anchor if they have to sever their moorings.

At 10:30 on the morning of the 25th, Lex is 145 nautical miles away and moving northwest at seven knots. Half an hour later, at 11:00, the assistant manager of the Nanhai West Shipping Company, a state-owned subsidiary of China National Offshore Oil Corporation (CNOOC), calls ARCO China, voicing concern for their workboat, the *Nanhai 205*. It is disappointing news. The storm is still not classified as a typhoon. The rig remains on location, and the supply ship must stay with it, acting as a safety vessel. There was nowhere to run and seek shelter from the predicted path of the storm, now altering course southwards towards them: shoals to the south, shallow waters to the northwest in the lee of Hainan and, for political reasons, The Socialist Republic of Vietnam to the southwest. The storm centre of Lex is less than 100 miles away, travelling at eight knots, increasing to ten towards the drill site with winds of 60 knots, gusting 75.

Both vessels are rolling and heaving heavily. To such an extent, by 13:00, the supply ship is having trouble with its cargo. The cables and chains securing the casing have parted. One stick of casing has already gone overboard, and there is no chance of tying down the remaining cargo, lose on a deck rolling 30° to 40°.

Later in the afternoon, the seas have risen. Waves approaching 40 feet are now going through. The *Nanhai 205* has trouble maintaining her position. A refrigeration unit has broken free and lodges under the anchor handling winch cable — the storm upgrades to a severe tropical storm. The conditions are becoming worse than forecast.
At 21:00, the *Glomar Java Sea's* radio operator tells the ARCO China radio operator in Zhanjiang the drillship was experiencing waves of 37-39 feet and winds of 50 gusting 60 knots from the northwest, a 30-foot swell from the northeast. Just over an hour later, he returns the call for an update. "The winds and waves are heavier now; the ship is rocking, rolling, and pitching. The waves are beating on the deck; sounds like thundering."
At 22:50, the *Nanhai 205* receives a 'No. 16 Typhoon emergency warning' from the Hainan Weather Station. Lex has been upgraded and will pass directly overhead.
At 23:00, the drillship reported to TianDu, the military airfield where their two CAAC Bell 212 helicopters are based, "Wind and waves are too heavy now, listing very much, and the foreigners have asked us to put on our life jackets."
At 23:15, *Nanhai 205* passed the weather warning to the drillship and advised them they planned to sail away against the wind.

The last call from the *Glomar Java Sea* was made by satellite phone at 23:48 by the assistant rig manager to the Global Marine Drilling Group Vice President in Houston, Texas. He reports they have an unaccountable 15° list to starboard. Waves driven by 75-knot winds are piling onboard over the exposed seaward beam, and despite trying to pump drilling mud overboard from the deck silos to reduce the centre of gravity, there is not much else they can do. They are prepared for the worst and have donned life jackets. After two to three minutes, the line goes dead. The seas have overloaded and broken three of the four bow anchor chains, causing the ship to roll and lose satellite connection.
At midnight, the *Nanhai 205* tries to contact the *Glomar Java Sea*. There is no reply. During the night, the shore bases fail to contact either of their vessels.
Less than five hours after the last communication with the drillship, a distress signal transmitting on 121.5 MHz. is picked up by two airliners, Lufthansa and Cathay Pacific. They pass the information on to Kai Tak Airport, Hong Kong. It will be late evening before it is confirmed and relayed to Arco China in Zhanjiang.

*

At 03:30, after failing to re-establish contact with the drillship, Global Marine's office notified the US Coast Guard. Forty-five minutes later, the Department of the Air Force, Western Pacific Rescue Coordination Center (WESTPAC RCC), Kadena, Okinawa, assumed control of the search. They issue an urgent marine broadcast seeking information on the drillship and attempt to contact it through a United States Air Force C-130 within 300 miles of the well site.
At 06:20 in the morning, the *Nanhai 205* eventually established radio contact with Arco China. Returning to the drill site, they report, "Sea condition is abnormal, no way to determine ship location. Far from the drillship, 12 scale wind force." It will not be until 11:10 before she arrives back at the drill site.
ARCO China alerts Chinese sea and airborne assets. Their two Bell 212 helicopters on contract to them prepare to take off as soon as the wind drops. Then B.P. phoned Tony and requested he take an S-61N to look for the *Glomar Java Sea* and any survivors.

*

With Ian Stone, a B.P. interpreter and co-pilot Captain Ye, Tony departed for Zhuhai to collect Dave Clucas, a BAH engineer setting up this new base, and sufficient consumables, oil, and grease to last a week. From here, he planned to route on a direct course to the military base at TianDu to refuel and then head south 63 nautical miles to the scene of the search. Air traffic control cautioned him and recommended they route via Zhanjiang on the mainland. By taking a direct route, there was a good chance the air defence forces on Hainan would launch missiles to shoot down any intruder entering their airspace from this direction. Point taken! He also had to have a military minder onboard. At that time, he will be entering the military zone encompassing the whole of Hainan Island.
The flight to Zhanjiang leaves with a shaky start after air traffic instructs them to climb to 3,000 m (9,842 feet), a height bordering the rattling limits for an S-61N. After Zhanjiang, Ye insists they descend to 3,000 feet, despite mountains over 4,000 feet on Hainan Island hidden in the clouds below.
You can imagine this argument to remain clear of the hard stuff with Ian translating on the jump seat.
When they finally arrived overhead, at the last known position of the drilling rig, all that remained at the scene were the original nine yellow anchor buoys. Still in position. An eerie reminder of where the vessel had been before it had capsized and sank in the storm.

They return to Hainan and set up a local coordination centre at Sanya. Sanya is a civilian airfield on the southern shore of Hainan Island and a few miles to the west of the inshore base at TianDu.
Here, Tony briefs the search teams, with Ian translating, on how to search by allocating sector grids and expanding search patterns within them.
Late evening, Global Marine informed WESTPAC RCC that two airliners had reported receiving a distress signal. They alert the U.S. Navy Forces at Cubi Point, the Philippines. An hour later, a US Navy P-3 Orian aircraft is airborne to investigate the source of the distress signal.
Over the next two days, radios receive signals from locator beacons. On the first day at 13:07, the freighter, MS *Willine Toyo,* picks up a distress signal with the *Glomar Java Sea* callsign, 'WFDS', from an emergency beacon on a lifeboat broadcasting on 500kHz.
At 08:10 on the 28th, a Chinese helicopter reported a capsized lifeboat with its propellor showing. But was not seen again by any other party. Later in the day, at 18:16, a tug recovers an empty life raft. They positively identify it as one of three missing by its serial number and service markings, having come from the *Glomar Java Sea*.
The air search draws a blank despite flying seven hours a day and searching in visibility down to 1 mile under a 2 to 300-foot cloud base. Maritime assets recovered and identified 31 bodies. The others are missing. They estimate the *Glomar Java Sea* capsized to starboard at 23:51 and sank within minutes.

After five days, Tony and his crew returned to Zhuhai. He recalled when Ian started taking pictures on the way back, their minder became quite agitated and assumed they might be MI5 agents. So, no more photos.
They called off the search for survivors after a week. All 81 persons onboard perished, comprising the ship's crew and oilfield workers. It was one of the worst oilfield disasters on record. It was the first time a US-flagged drillship had sunk. In hindsight, the drillship could have put its stern to the wind and run slowly away from the storm track into the 'navigable semicircle', where the wind and seas are less severe. After all, ships of similar design had survived worse conditions. A later survey of the wreck indicates they deliberately released the starboard lifeboat from its stowed position, boarded it by an unknown number of persons and launched it. They had brought the lifeboat's portable emergency radio with them. They used it to transmit at least one distress signal the MS Willine Toyo picked up several hundred miles away, probably due to freak atmospheric conditions. Unfounded speculation: survivors had reached the shore of Vietnam.

Under Chairman Mao Zedong's regime, the cadre moved China's people around. The administration orders them to perform duties irrespective of their background, skill sets or aptitude. In many cases, they must relocate. And they could wear clothes of any colour so long as they were blue. Therefore, the fashion-conscious supported a lucrative market of blue denim smuggled into the country. Though he died in 1976, the wheels of change were slow, and the non-alignment of aptitude selection to the labour skills required persisted. Not long after the PROOC operation had started with an all-Chinese crew, the mainly Western passengers expressed disquiet. The oil companies requested a Western instructor pilot in the cockpit to alleviate this fear. Communication necessitated an interpreter on the jump seat. And BAH did not have sufficient instructors. Within 18 months, they had exhausted their supply of instructors willing to go. Iggy Davidson explained this deficit to me.

Until then, I had only conducted occasional line checks. And then, at the most, only once a month. To work more was not viable as the training supplement for line trainers was just £80.00 per month. Despite not being an instructor, never-the-less, could I help out? Armed with a telephone number given to me by Al Prentice, who had recently returned, I night-stopped in Bahrein, arriving in Macau on the Boeing 929-100 hydrofoil from Hong Kong at the beginning of January 1986. After a night on Coloane Island, I called the number. Instructions from Bob Middleton, the chief engineer on the other end of the line, suggested I apply for a visa from an office above a bank and wait for a white minibus outside a café at 3 o'clock that afternoon to take me into China, the hotel bus.

Once onboard, we drove north and through the border arch into the economic zone to the hotel. It backed onto the weather-worn terracotta earth hills bordering the Pearl River delta where pine trees grew, their green foliage stunted by the salt spray carried on the winds from the South China Sea. From a distance, they resembled bonsai. Like all other Zhuhai construction investments, the hotel was Hong Kong Chinese. This particular investor was determined to build according to traditional architecture: a reconstruction of the village over the walls from the Joseon dynasty Gyeongbokgung Palace in Seoul constructed in 1395: low buildings with curved wooden eves covered with glazed green clay tiles; a shallow stream meandering through paved with slates cut to resemble fish scales and crossed by small arched bridges resembling those that traverse the canals in the back streets of Venice; the water stocked with small fish to attract kingfishers and the gardens planted with azaleas, willow and iris. It was a blue willow pattern reincarnated.

*

En route to the rig the following day, PROOC requested we recover a casualty (CASEVAC) and drop him off on the way back at Kai Tak, Hong Kong. I had given our agent my passport for the border police to enter a multi-entry visa. Of course, having arrived from a foreign state when landing back in China, the guards, each with a musket slung over his shoulder, requested this document. After what seemed a long 40 minutes of palming them off with flight paperwork, including flight log sheets (English format; chicken scratch headings – you had to remember which box applied) and load sheets, all the while feigning a misunderstanding, when my passport arrived; slipped into my back pocket by the agent. Freedom!

*

The work mainly involved line flying to the rig *Transocean Sedco 600* in the South China Sea, to Guangzhou and then to Kai Tak, Kowloon, for the Chinese crews to practice procedural flying on instruments. The latter we started after 09:00 when the airport was quiet and again in the evening. The procedures included holding at the non-directional beacon (NDB) and letting down on the instrument guidance system (IGS). The IGS route led you in from the west over Stonecutters Island, then a right turn short of the chequerboard painted on the cliff above the town before landing on the Southerly runway. Then, go around and climb southbound to the Tat Hong Point (TP) NDB, practice a hold, and repeat the process from the opposite direction, this time letting down from the south.
The trip usually took onboard CAAC workers and some of our engineers. After parking on the cargo apron outside the Hong Kong Aircraft Engineering Company (HAECO) hangars, they would go on a shopping spree. Arriving at security one evening with an engineer and his wife, the three of us elected to go through the crew security airside rather than join the queue for passengers. They are dressed smartly, both wearing leather jackets and blue jeans. Not too scruffy! As the British Airways 747 crew led by their captain came around the corner, the security man asked me from across his desk:
"What airline?"
"British Airways."
"And those two?"
"Oh, they're my crew."

Looking back, before we disappeared down the stairs to the apron, the BA crew looked non-plussed and thinking. Really?

In the evening, I was sitting in the cab on the ramp at Kai Tak and preparing our second training sortie when a tug hauling a string of baggage trailers loaded with large cardboard boxes teamed with an elevator vehicle appeared. I expected them to drive past and onto the RAF C-130 Hercules transport aircraft next down the flight line. Not so. The elevator drove over and parked against the cargo door – it was the CAAC shopping. This cargo included TVs, cookers, microwaves, fridges, and deep freezers.

G-BEOO Kai Tak, Hong Kong

Fig 25. G-BEOO, US Navy P-3 Orion and Miss Szu, Chief Interpreter, RAF C-130 Hercules – Kai Tak *Photos: Author's collection*

I asked the baggage handlers to load the cargo forward of the air stair door with one provision. To unpack the freezers and stack them on top, leaving their doors open. The remaining seats aft are for shoppers - those unlucky to secure a seat, so take Hobson's choice. By the time they tied everything down, it was dark. Rather than spend 45 minutes as planned for training, I stretched it much longer by flying the IGS and then route all the way around to reshoot it. And again, for good measure. Then, landed to refuel for the 45-mile sector back to Zhuhai. Their preferred choice on subsequent trips was Sony Walkman and cameras.

They had constructed the heliport at Zhuhai with a concrete runway, apron and hangars, control tower, passenger handling area and rats (most likely cane rats – Rhizomys Sinensis). The animals were migrants from the cane fields and rice paddy razed for this vast building site springing up around the heliport, an economic zone celebrated by firecrackers on completing every new floor. Rodents were everywhere, mainly on the tower's ground floor, lurking in and around the drains; outside in the storm drains, they'd pop out and dash into the hangar. And they did not stop there.

Ratting Chair and 'Mk II' tug

"Arjen tse" ! (Rotate) @ 80 feet. Oblique Take-off

Figs 26. G-BEWM is fuelling from a CAAC ZIS-150, Zhuhai Heliport.
Photos: Author's collection
Photo top right. The pace of construction around the heliport demanded we alter our oblique take-off profile when they site a Ferris wheel at the end of the runway, rotating at 80 rather than 40 feet. (Capt. Forbes Ramage I/C)

The soundproofing material in the S-61N's panels below the engines and gearbox was a choice place to raise a family. Warm, with plenty of free travel and inflight food (cable insulation), except for the pups, dining on the latter was not conducive to having a full house of electrical services. They are essential for some aircraft, though Sikorsky are happy to fly without an electrical supply once the engines have started, whether from generators or batteries. So, to improve serviceability and reduce en route passenger-induced breakdowns, the air stair doors were closed whenever not in use. These intrusions called for a visit to the local Friendship Store, a mini market for foreigners and supplier of the 'first defence'. Except for some hardware, the shelves were mostly bare, though it did have a couple of .22 rifles for sale. I selected the one with the least tight trigger. And a bargain for the equivalent of £5.00 in FEC and a box of ammo.

FEC (Foreign Exchange Certificates) were illegal for use by the Chinese; hence, FEC could only be used in hotels and Friendship stores. They cost 10% more than the national currency to buy. Conversely, for Gweilos (derived from the Chinese 'gwailou', meaning 'ghostly man', more usually termed 'Foreign Devil), it was illegal to have the Chinese currency, the renminbi (RMB). They overlooked these rules during the Chinese New Year when we received traditional little red envelopes containing gifts of the renminbi in denominations of 1, 2, and 5 Fen (Fen-Tien). This regulation was to discourage foreigners from travelling out of the economic zones into the Middle Kingdom and vying with the iron buffalo (wheeled rotavator/trailer combinations), bicycles or just farmers herding flocks of waddling ducks on the empty dirt roads strewn in places with corn in expectation of being winnowed by a cadre's speeding BMW.

Figs 27. 1 Fen (£0.0011) 2 Fen

Currency: Author's collection

The 1 Fen (100th of a yuan) depicted the ubiquitous Soviet ZIS-150, a 4-tonne truck built between 1947 and 1957 with a top speed of 40mph, one of which was used as a bowser to refuel our helicopters; the 2 Fen, a Soviet Glazunov Li-2 aircraft; a Douglas DC-3 'variant' built under licence between

1940 and 1954 designated PS84, they constructed nearly 5,000. A variant, as all the component measurements and manufacturing processes, some 1,300, had to be converted to metric before construction could begin.
The 5 Fen, a cargo vessel of the same period, is not depicted here because it is, well, just another freighter. A staple often held these notes together in blocks of the same denomination and, being relatively small, 43 x 90 mm, ceased to be legal tender in 2007. The 1 Fen above is uncirculated; the 2 Fen shows its age (Block XII), including time in my pocket.
The red Roman numerals, a hangover from the Sino-Roman relationship beginning around AD 1 between the Roman and Han Empires, identify the block number.
Thus, tooled up and settled into a director's chair, it was a question of shooting four-legged boarders approaching the hangar and not difficult. No. Not due to the lack of security but because the targets were as big as rabbits.
Flight planning involved cycling across to the tower to read the weather on a blackboard. Blackboards, protected by an awning from the weather, also doubled as newspapers to record the news in villages. And the weather was metric - wind speed in metres/second, height in metres, anything other than imperial.
I did not own a pocket calculator before, but now seemed like a good time to take a trip to Macau to buy one. There, I found a small store selling a Casio MC-801S. Just the job, he smiled as he rattled the price from his abacas. Watching this ancient display, I offered to buy him one too. "Unreliable!" was the reply. Having seen better days, it was still up to making the monthly VAT calculations until SAGE software took over.

*

Macau has a Las Vegas-type reputation for hosting gambling casinos; instead, it is an attractive provincial town with architecture dating back to the 16th century.
As the harbour slowly silts up, it can still allow shallow-draught vessels to enter. During the Chinese New Year, it was packed full of wooden junks. Their owners festooned them with bunting. On the stern, each had a traditional miniature orange tree. I asked an old lady with a sampan to take me around to look at this armada better. It did not take long for the ever-vigilant harbour security to catch up. Their patrol boat appeared out of nowhere. Speeding our way with a heavy machine gun trained at the lady and her screaming at me, I jumped ship. I made my way across the vessels moored in rafts, taking care not to trip over the pots of orange trees calling

"Gong hei fat choy!" the seasonal greeting used in these parts meaning, "Wishing you great happiness and prosperity!" on the way back to the wharf. Otherwise, this was a quiet, tree-shaded haven, not changed much since the time of a former resident, Luís de Camões, who was considered Portugal's greatest poet and comparable to Shakespeare. He would have recognised the small restaurants set back from the harbour with menus held in small tanks, cages, and baskets on the pavement outside. They would include mud turtles, racoons, snakes, and owls. Slung up in the tree branches above, songbirds in cages attracted others to the table. Elsewhere, you could hear the slap of Ma Jong tiles breaking the silence from dimly lit rooms looking onto the street. My kind of 'day centre'!

Entertainment also included golf. Beyond the economic zone of Zhuhai and in the Middle Kingdom on the road to Guangzhou, Arnold Palmer had recently designed a golf course with a vast clubhouse. Chung Shan. Not since the 1930s had a golf course been built in China. Better still, on the same scale, the car park could accommodate an S-61N. Thus, with these facilities, we either drove in the Mk II tug or flew, depending on aircraft availability, to play golf (Mk II, as the original Suzuki, had disappeared into the silty Pearl River. The hook attached to the sling below the S-61N had tripped en route from the Hong Kong dealership). To drive out of the economic zone into the Middle Kingdom required a statement to the border guards your destination was Guangzhou and the production of a driving licence. Each Western staff member used the same photo on their licence application. For reciprocal reasons, we all look alike. Being dependent on wealthy Japanese tour groups, who rarely came, we invariably had the course to ourselves.

*

Our co-pilots sat in the right-hand seat to balance the cockpit gradient. We were required to have a rudimentary knowledge of the emergency checklist – written in chicken scratch. In practice, it was easier to say, "Wo you kongzhi quan" or "I have control." Otherwise, everything else routes through the interpreter, a student learning English sitting on the jump seat. An incident flying out to the *Sedco 600* occurred when the high-frequency radio aerial broke off and wrapped itself around the tail rotor. Sound familiar? I called up the rig and requested shears and steps on arrival. Now, every pilot knows having an electrical engineer attend to a problem during the day is unrealistic. There are so few; they mainly work the night shift to repair the broken birds when they come in offline.

We shut down across the wind to steady the tail rotors and were met on the helideck by a man with steps and shears in one hand and a CAA licence in the other; hard to believe, but true. He introduced himself as an ex-Bristow greenie (or B2, the term for avionics engineers) and is now receiving better pay with Sedco. So that is where they all go! When back on the beach, we restored the radio to function again as it was an integral part of the comms. Not only when beyond VHF range for 'ops normal' calls or by the Chinese crew to jabber with the other one billion but as a telephone too. The call had to be routed through Portishead Radio near Bristol at a specific time window during the day. This window ensured the radio wave accurately skipped off the ionosphere to the selected radio receiver back on Earth. These times were published for different places in the world in the Aerad international editions. When two-way with the radio controller, he connected you to your party via the telephone exchange; as a reverse charge call (or collect call), billing to your friend/recipient's account is by their agreement.

*

Occasionally, there would be 'banquets' with CAAC managers. Everything was available to make up for the famines under their late Chairman. This variety contrasted with the monotonous diet of the principal inhabitants of Zhuhai, the construction workers. They lived in a large, two-storied attap building and fed on rice from huge steaming cauldrons delivered on the back of a truck.

It is an ancient Chinese tradition to leave some food on the salvers decked in tiers on the dumb waiter for the kitchen. This custom indicates you are satisfied and ready for the next course or have just had enough. Seeing some rather special prawns on the way back to the kitchen, our illustrious chief pilot, fortified by many toasts of rice wine, took the initiative. Leaving his place, he executed a tremendous rugger tackle from behind on the unsuspecting waiter holding the salver aloft with the prawns. Leaving both men struggling on the floor, the prawns, now airborne, successfully made a home run through the kitchen door. Defeated, he returned to the table with effuse apologies to the stunned hosts and a toast to the waiter. It then begged the question: "What does the Cantonese not eat?" Through the interpreter to the Mongolian pilot handling the aircraft on the way to the rig, his reply, after considering most birds, fish, reptiles, and vegetables known to man, came back 24 minutes and some miles later, "Stones."

Before my return to India, we transported some CAAC workers boarding at Guangzhou. On this occasion, we had dropped off the PROOC passengers and were joined on the flight deck by the Bell helicopter rep. He was on his way, routing southbound from Beijing. He asked us for a lift to Zhuhai. Except unknown to us, others were also looking for a lift. It began when we tried to exit the cockpit. Bicycles, bed rolls and buckets of fish heads impede our way out. After clearing a path, we exited through the cargo door. Then, taking a company car, we drove past three rows of biplanes. They were coated in khaki and adorned with a large red star on the fuselage and wings. These were Antonov An-2. First built in 1947, they are single-engine taildraggers around 40 feet long. Their ranks stretched as far as the eye could see. On arrival at the remote office on the edge of the airfield, I advised the CAAC agent I required a manifest to construct the load sheet and suitable access to the cockpit and emergency exits. Only then will we continue the journey with their employees and baggage. We decided to give them time to sort this out. The Bell rep suggested we take a taxi downtown and have lunch.

On entering the city, we confront shoals of sit-up-and-beg bicycles spewing from side streets into main thoroughfares, handlebars almost and probably touching. There was not an automobile in sight; a city mayor's dream transport solution was it not for the coal fires fuelling the factories and buildings and creating smog. You cannot have it all. Because of the seemingly organised flow of these machines, there were no holdups on the way to a suitable restaurant he knew. A few hours later, after an extended meal, we returned to have the paperwork presented – in chicken scratch. The numbers were confirmed to me by the Chinese co-pilot as being close to the truth.

By now, spring had arrived with my last flight over the South China Sea. After a short break operating out of Aberdeen over the North Sea, I was flying the line back in India over the Arabian Sea by May of this year.

Besides the S-61N based at Juhu, BAH also had an S-76A on contract. Porbandar, on the coast of Gujarat, is the usual base for this aircraft. To move alcohol into this state required a pilot to be registered as an alcoholic. With that affirmation stamped in his passport before he became airborne, he could cross the border with the supply.

This was supplemented with steaks and Coca-Cola from the American rig. The latter is in direct competition with the national cola, Thumbs Up and illegal to import.

Yet when the four SA 365N aircraft based at Juhu operated by Schreiner Airways and Héli-Union were grounded for a fault in their Turbomeca engines, the BAH S-76A was brought down to cover them. The shuttle involved flying the work crews from the mother platforms to normally unattended installations (NUI) with risers; at midday, the tiffin run with stacked aluminium lunch containers, and a third shuttle to return the workers to their mother platforms in the evening before flying back to the beach. Except it is to be with one aircraft instead of the usual four, with additional support from the Okanagan Bell 212. As the S-76A has the original Allison engines, it could still operate rather than the Turbomeca power plants fitted to later models. Now, 80 sectors a day is quite a few, so rather than flying as a single pilot as was the norm, an additional pilot made up the crew. Every other day, from flying the S-61N, I assisted. Between shuttles, we rested on aluminium pallets in the sickbay of a jack-up rig built on the Clyde without air conditioning. Anyone needing sickbay services would have opted to take an early way out rather than convalesce in a puddle of sweat. The one mitigating factor was a bountiful supply of fresh lobster tails prepared for us in the galley and washed down with iced tea drunk out of catering-size Maxwell House jars.

Working the Bombay High towards the end of this tour, we overheard a pilot approaching a rig with its cranes and flare booms extended, leaving nowhere to go around in the event, for example, of an engine failure. "There's no escape!" Another piped up, "There is no escape from the Bombay High!"

At the end of September 1986, and just after leaving India for the last time, the sale of BAH went through to Mirror Group Newspapers and the birth of a new name: BIH (British International Helicopters). The callsign and logo changed from 'Speedbird' to 'Lion' – the Mirror Group logo. The aircraft colour schemes changed, too. These were only cosmetic. We had entered the lion's den.

Fig 28. British Airways Helicopters (BAH) renamed British International Helicopters (BIH) foreground.

The photo was given to the author by Capt. Archie D'Mello.

Part III

Chapter 11. 1986

A KGB (FSB) Agent – Chinook Down – Hindi in Hospital

Robert Maxwell, the owner of Mirror Group newspapers and a reputed FSB agent, acquired BAH through a company registered in the Cayman Islands. Despite other contenders being considered entirely unsuitable and vigorously fought off, somehow, albeit reluctantly, it was all right to approve Maxwell. He proved to top them all in the unsuitability stakes by a wide margin. It was a 'fire sale'. British Airways wanted to offload the company and quickly. They planned to privatise the following year and perceived BAH as no longer fitting into their company portfolio. It was unappealing to squeamish shareholders and too high risk due to the number of hull losses they had absorbed over the years. Then, maybe they were on to something as the next accident, a few weeks after the sale had gone through, would dwarf all previous ones. The net book value of BAH at the time of purchase was £99 million. Maxwell paid British Airways just £7 million for all the assets. This transaction included a valuable pension scheme as part of the transfer conditions; he will abandon the purchase without it. Hindsight is wonderful, but why emphasise the pension fund when he already had a good deal? We will find out later. The debt assumed included the remaining five Boeing Vertol 234LR Chinooks.

*

On arrival back in Aberdeen from India, fate extended a short detachment to Sumburgh until October 1995.
No one in BIH envisioned this extension. It was simply not on the cards.
Soon after I arrived on the base, Pushp Vaid VrC had positioned a company Chinook, G-BWFC, from Aberdeen to supplement the S-61N we were operating to the East Shetland Basin oilfields. One evening in the Sumburgh Club bar, I asked him how he had earned the VrC. "The Vir Chakra is the equivalent of your Distinguished Flying Cross. It was during the 14-day war between India and Pakistan in December 1971. West Pakistan intended to destroy a liberation army called the Mukti Bahini. The latter formed in East Pakistan to free their country, comprised ethnically, culturally, philosophically, and linguistically different from the Punjabi-dominated West Pakistan and become independent. And India supported the independence movement. The war began when Pakistan bombed 11 Indian air bases."

Numerous massacres, later classified as genocide, caused millions to flee their homes, including many who crossed the border into India. In response to the deteriorating situation and now being attacked, India declared war on West Pakistan. During the ensuing conflict, epic numbers developed: 25,000 injured Pakistanis and 12,000 casualties with some 90,000 prisoners of war, a more significant number than in World War II; India had 8,000 wounded and 3,000 killed.

"Among the many actions, including air strikes by the Indian Air Force, were a battalion of Indian troops detached to the eastern border of East Pakistan along with eight Mi-4 helicopters. And I was the Flight Commander/Operations Manager of the Mi-4s. The objective was to insert the troops and their supplies into a landing zone 20 miles over the border near Sylhet. It was late in the day when we began the lift. We managed to fly three sorties. During the last sortie, we came under fire, and our Group Captain, Chandan Singh, considered it unsafe to continue in the darkness. Unfortunately, the logistics did not match the troops with their supplies. And now they were cut off without food, water, and ammunition.

The brigadier commanding the operation and the Group Captain discussed the situation with more senior staff officers for five hours. The latter was adamant the supply went ahead. The Group Captain requested I provide a volunteer crew to recce the route to see if it was feasible. He did not expect the flight to return, reasoning – a helicopter flying slowly at 1,000 feet would be shot down. Rather than loading my crews with a decision, I volunteered to take the flight and asked for a co-pilot to accompany me. Well, they all wanted to come! The flight went well despite lighting a bonfire to identify the landing zone, encouraging intense incoming fire. Though it assisted us in locating it, it also distracted the enemy. So, we landed a little way off, where it was dark, without attracting too much attention. Other than a rain of small-arms fire, we did not take any hits. On the return sector, I radioed for the resupply to continue. On the third flight, I knew the aircraft had taken a round when the fuel gauge went to zero; the engine kept running. We flew all night and the following day, and despite their best attempts to shoot us down, we did not lose a single aircraft. Besides supplies, we inserted an additional 1,000 troops. The position was secure.

After Sylhet, we moved towards Dhaka and the 4,000-yard-wide Meghna River bordered by marshes. Pak sappers had blown up the Ashuganj Bridge. To continue the advance, four more Mi-4s join us. We airlifted the troops using the running take-off technique, carrying 23 onboard instead of the helicopter performance maximum of 14.

Fig 29. Indian Air Force (IAF) Mi-4 medium helicopter.
Photo credit: Bharat Rakshak, Indian Armed Forces site run by veterans and volunteers.

Over eight days, flying day and night with only short breaks, we airlifted 8,000 troops and 2,002 tons of their equipment. The operation became known as the Meghna Heli Bridge. By the 15th of December, nearly 10,000 Indian soldiers supported by Mukti Bhani troops were outside Dhaka. If the Pakistani General Naizi did not surrender, the Mukti Bhani would come in and slaughter everybody. He capitulated, and The People's Republic of Bangladesh was born. We helped a bit to bring an end to that war."
He had used up many of his lives, and I jokingly suggested he make good use of those remaining. Two days later, he did.

*

Our flight routing on Thursday, the 6th of November, was via Unst, then offshore to the *Cormorant 'A'*, the *Stadrill*, *Cormorant 'A'*, *Heather 'A'* and back to Sumburgh, followed by a flight in the evening to the *Cormorant 'A'*, *Brent 'Delta'* and *'Charlie'*. Robbie Skyring was the only other S-61N pilot on the base, and we were operating G-BEIC. Our first flight taxied at 11:25 for the Northerly runway and positioned behind the Bristow SAR S-61N, G-BDOC. They were on a delayed training flight under the command of Gordon Mitchell that had been due off at 09:30 and were now finally ready. We were waiting, in turn, to take off from the runway after 'OC'.

Fig 30. Right base RW 33 LSI in summer and winter with Fitful Head & Virkie Pool north of RW 09/27

Photos© kindly provided by Kieran Murray Snr, SAR Crewman. Sumburgh, LSI.

The wind was 25 knots, gusting 38 with 20 kilometres of visibility. We heard Pushp in G-BWFC, inbound with 44 passengers and three crew, give Sumburgh tower their range from the field as 4.5 miles. He received clearance to land on heli strip 24. On company frequency, we heard him call, "FC is just coming in." He will be landing in two minutes. It was to notify the ground handlers to meet him on the ramp. Moments later, a falling, orange-coloured object caught the eye of a Marconi engineer working outside on the aerials at the summit of Compass Head, 1,000 meters southeast of helicopter runway 24/06. Looking out to sea, he observed this object weaving from side to side and descending through 400 to 300 feet. The lower set of rotor blades flew off to the right. It then hit the sea, making a large splash seen from the airport and by the crew of some fishing boats in the immediate vicinity.

With 'OC' climbing out farther down the runway, we receive clearance to take off. Now airborne, we could see a stern trawler lying off Virkie pool. Suddenly, its engines fired up with grey diesel smoke belching out of its twin funnels near the stern. Strange. Then, almost immediately, it was underway and making its way into the bay to the southeast of the field; just another typical day in Sumburgh, or so we thought. Being clear and sunny on the climb out, we turned to starboard over Virkie Pool, expecting to see 'FC' from where I was sitting in the right-hand seat. It was not to be.

Looking over my shoulder, some orange flotsam in the water drew my attention. Then 'OC' came on the radio and reported two inflated life rafts floating in the sea to the east of the airport. Shortly afterwards, aircraft wreckage appeared floating on the sea and a survivor clinging to a part of it.

Fig 31. *Photo© kindly provided by Kieran Murray Snr, SAR Crewman. LSI*

As they began winching him aboard, they could see other bodies floating on the sea; all appeared lifeless, except one man clinging to the side of one of the life rafts. After rescuing him, they searched in vain for other survivors. But Dave Ellis, the winchman who later became Technical Crew Manager of UK SAR, realised the condition of the two survivors on board was rapidly deteriorating. Captain Gordon Mitchell called off their search and took them to a hospital 18 miles away in Lerwick.
An intensive air and sea search failed to find any more survivors, but the bodies that remained afloat were recovered by fishing vessels and taken to the airport.

*

It transpired 'FC' had broken up in flight. The aircraft had struck the sea in a tail-down attitude with considerable force. They were just over a mile to land. And these were the orange immersion suits worn by the passengers. It happened so quickly. With the earlier Dan-Air disaster in mind and with sea and airborne assets deployed to a scene with little evidence of significant wreckage, we agreed, without hoist capability, to continue with the schedule. Of the 47 persons onboard, only Pushp and a passenger in row 1 facing aft were winched aboard 'OC' alive. For Pushp, the ordeal was not over. Though his injuries were not yet apparent from the crash, hypothermia nearly did him in as he slipped in and out of consciousness. His immersion suit had filled with water; his body temperature was now +33°C. Later, he remembers

coming around with a doctor speaking Hindi in the Gilbert Bain Hospital in Lerwick. Some dreams come true!
Following the debacle three years earlier when G-BEON crashed into the sea off the Scillies, a group of BIH pilots from Aberdeen flew north to prevent a similar scene when a manager tried to remonstrate with the crew physically. After landing in Sumburgh, some pilots, including Peter Jackson, arrived by road at the hospital to ensure the press and management did not force the survivors into making statements under duress. Pushp later recounted how he tried to save the aircraft. "At 3.5 nautical miles from the runway, the whining noise we first heard half an hour ago was becoming much louder." Also described as a roaring noise. "Just then, our cabin attendant, Mike Walton, came through the door and told us he had checked the cabin for landing. After closing the door, we heard a very loud bang." The tandem rotor blades had collided. "Suddenly, the helicopter pitched vertically up. There was no time to give a MAYDAY call; we were falling backwards at over 100 miles an hour towards the North Sea."

At the hospital, the surviving passenger, Eric Morrans, asked Peter. "Do you really want to know what happened? When I boarded the helicopter on *Brent 'C'*, another passenger had taken my seat at 2D. Only a seat in row one, facing backwards, was left. After strapping in, I zipped up my survival suit most of the way. I was deadbeat and fell asleep after putting on my headphones. I was out for the count. The next thing I remember was the 'bing' over the intercom and someone telling us we would be landing soon at Sumburgh. Then, there was an enormous bang. It was like an explosion, a very, very loud bang. I couldn't tell where it was coming from; it was all around me." His view down the cabin was horrific. "The cabin windows shattered, glass flying and bits of metal flying everywhere. Some men had not tightened their seat belts and were floating out of their seats like astronauts. Bodies, glass, and shrapnel filled the cabin. Things moving about the cabin were hitting people. I could see they had no fear on their faces – just a look of shock, no panic. That was the strange thing." At the end of the cabin, a large void had appeared where the aft section supporting the gearbox and rotors had broken away. "Before we hit the water, my survival training kicked in. I wrenched my survival suit zip up to my neck and braced myself." At this point, he lost consciousness.
Pushp takes up the story: "When I pushed the cyclic stick all the way forward, the front rotor blades that were still responding to the controls flipped the cockpit section of the helicopter forward. My view changed from looking up into the sky to the waves below. The cockpit floor was still attached to the

main part of the helicopter and seemed to be going straight towards the sea. The cockpit broke off from the main fuselage on impact with the sea.

After sinking about ten metres, the buoyancy of the passenger's survival suit ejected him up through the void left by the cockpit. On the surface, 20-year-old Eric spots an inflated life raft that bobbed up nearby among bodies surfacing in their immersion suits. "I kicked out to reach it and managed to hook my right arm (my left arm was broken) in the tie rope around the life raft. Then I heard the whirr of a helicopter and saw it going over my head and away from me. The first thing I thought was: the bastard has not seen me. I remember seeing a body being winched out of the water 50 yards away when I blacked out again and came to in the helicopter."

In the cockpit, the starboard door on Pushp's side had fallen away. "I later realised the cuts on my face and broken nose were when the forward rotor chopped off the part of the windscreen in front of the co-pilot." He did not mention his swollen neck, broken nose, three fractured metatarsals in his left foot and his back was blue from bruising. "The cockpit must have gone down at least 30 feet (10 metres) below the surface before it stopped moving. I could see the sunlight and knew which way I had to swim. I reached the surface and saw what looked like a fuel tank cover. I managed to climb into it before a wave tipped me out. I was not worried; in the back of my mind, I knew the rescue helicopter would be overhead in a few minutes."
Back at the airport, the press descended. Jim Miles lets one lady working for the BBC know how we felt. A former army sniper in Aden and Scottish Champion at clay pigeon shooting told her she was not welcome on this island; her aggressive behaviour was particularly disrespectful. She took the hint for a good reason. Pushp was due to hand over the aircraft to Jim to fly the next rotation.

*

The Chinook has a tandem 3-bladed rotor of 60 feet in diameter that overlaps by about 80% of the disc radius over the fuselage centreline. Two engines provide power, one on either side of the tail pylon, via right angle gearboxes, to the combining transmission. Synchronising shafts then transmit the drive from the combining transmission to the forward and aft transmissions and maintain the correct phase relationship between the rotors. The forward transmission receives drive where the synchronising drive shaft mates with the spiral bevel gear.

Note: Radial severance of gear rim and the gap between rim and shaft flange.

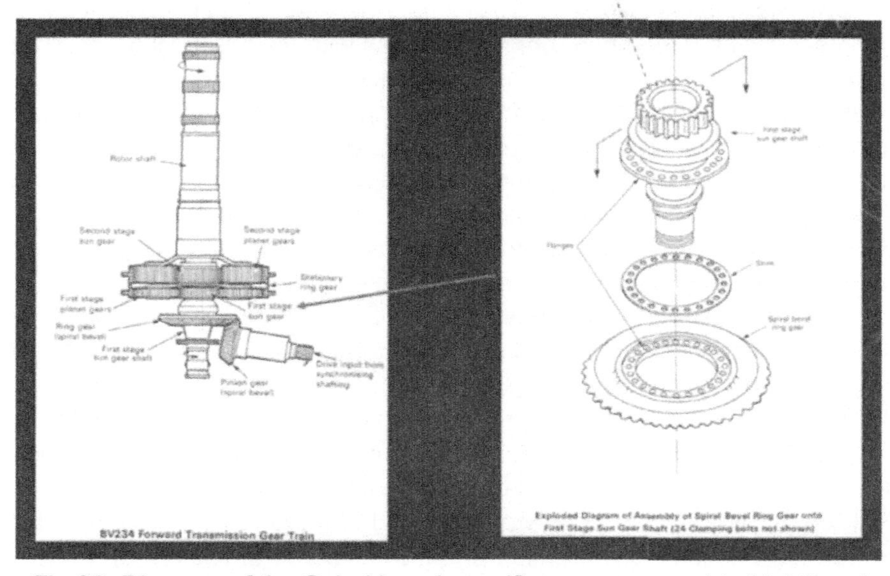

Fig 32. Diagram of the Spiral bevel gear/Sun gear assembly (right) and where the synchronising shaft input engages it (left). *Capt. P. Vaid VrC collection.*

Torque loss in the forward transmission had led to modifying the spiral bevel ring gear. The spiral bevel gear is clamped to the sun gear, driving the rotor head mast with 24 bolts. To increase the torque, they used larger bolts. For them to fit, they drilled larger holes in the gears to accept them. The forward transmission mounted on G-BWFC had this modification.

Some say this process weakened the gears, and the modification did not test for saltwater ingress. The official report cites the cause of the accident was attributed to the spiral bevel ring gear in the forward transmission fracturing due to corrosion. Synchronisation is lost between the rotors. The tip of an aft rotor blade struck the root end of a forward rotor blade, and the resultant forces tore the complete aft rotor assembly from the aircraft. Following an enquiry launched by relatives of the victims, worse was to follow.

*

It is that recurring story afflicting aviation on the North Sea: money. But first, the discovery of an article by two Boeing engineers written in 1981. They pointed out the unreliability of the transmission system installed in the ten Chinooks due for delivery that year to two operators on the North Sea: British Airways Helicopters (6) and Helikopter Service of Norway (4). The manufacturer had been here before and dealt with the same torque loss on military CH-47A Chinooks to be experienced by the civilian Chinooks. Except, this modification (bigger bolts and increased torque settings) did not address the problem. Documents at Boeing and the US Army overhaul depot at Corpus Christie, Texas, recorded hundreds of transmissions being returned with problems and failing, just like the one on G-BWFC. In 1979, two years before they delivered the civilian Chinooks, Boeing found a solution. Instead of bolting the gears together, they designed a one-piece bevel gear and shaft - seven years before the Sumburgh gear failure. The stunned investigation team realised the manufacturer knew it could fail before the point of delivery.

Notifying the Federal Aviation Administration of modifications and failures is a regulatory requirement. The FAA official who approved the modification that caused the Sumburgh disaster testified at the Fatal Accident Inquiry (FAI) there was no record of documents filed with the FAA or seen by them concerning the same modification and the hundreds of failures on military Chinooks. This one-piece bevel gear and shaft should have been mentioned in the Inquiry or the AAIB report. If Boeing had filed these reports with the FAA, the Administration would have insisted on an entire certification procedure before approval for use by civilian operators, a process not worthwhile for only ten helicopters, involving time and expense.

*

Over the following days, being the only BIH S-61N on the station, we maintained the daily schedule to the East Shetland Basin and other flights with a police escort in the back. The flights were initially to the multi-service vessel MSV *Deepwater 1* and later to the semi-sub and multi-function service vessel MSV *Stadive*. These were both diving support vessels tasked with the recovery operation. The police were responsible for ensuring numerous black plastic bags, some larger than others packed with remains recovered by divers, arrived at one of two assembly points sealed off from the public: covered walkways extending from either end of the Wilsness Terminal.

Fig 33. BV 234LR Chinook cabin looking aft. Forward half of the cabin after the tail had parted in flight & the airstair door section & cockpit had broken off when it struck the sea.

Photo credits: Capt. P. Vaid VrC.

These cold, unheated corridors leading to the aircraft parking stands furthest from the building are converted into morgues. A former policeman related how "We had to assemble sandbags in large, circled areas two or three high, to be able to put the individual bodies when they arrived with us. It was the nature of their injuries – the rotor blades came through the helicopter and the impact with the sea. So, we needed to keep the bodies segregated so that no individual parts would become mixed up with others. We had to take the bodies out of the bags and go through their survival suits to find their photographic IDs to identify them. Most of them were in such a condition it was physically impossible to marry up the photo to what was there, but they all had their photo IDs with them, so we assumed that that was the person we had. A few days later, I took a van up to Broonies Taing, Sandness, on the Island's east coast. Fishermen had recovered three more bodies, eight miles from where they entered the sea."

Back on shore, Mike Stanley was still coming to terms with a decision to let Neville Nixon take his place. Mike had been crewed with Pushp for the first two of three round trips out of Sumburgh to the East Shetland Basin. They had swapped shifts because Neville wanted to build up flying hours after a break for three years, helping his wife Pauline set up a pharmacy in York. He was the handling pilot on that last sector, unlike Pushp, who suffered non-life-threatening whiplash sitting hard up against the back of his seat; Neville was leaning forward a little, controlling the aircraft, as you do.

*

The official report cited the death of the passengers, and Neville was due to whiplash and the impact when they hit the sea. Flown in to assist, it took many weeks for the forensic anthropologists to complete their work, reconciling the remains within the sandbag enclosures aided by Deoxyribonucleic Acid (DNA).

Chapter 12. 1986 - 1988

A Flying Club – Det 1 on Sea Float

Following the ditching and with the Chinooks withdrawn from passenger services, their crews converted back onto the remaining S-61Ns. Ironically, the rest of the fleet is in storage at the eastern end of the Bristow hangar in Sumburgh. It was before they were either part exchanged or sold. Some go to the combined Royal, US and Canadian Navy Atlantic Undersea Test and Evaluation Centre (AUTEC) based on Andros Island, Bahamas. Here, they recover submarine-launched torpedoes in The Tongue of the Ocean. Others go to Carson Helicopters to convert into Shortsky (they remove the plug extending the S-61 fuselage), or new Aérospatiale Super Pumas/Tigers are part exchanged for them. The former Chinook crews, now newly re-converted, joined us flying out of Sumburgh.

The Chief Pilot was Peter Boor, who, on leaving the Royal Navy, was hired as Chief Pilot on one of Big Al's earlier operations: Kharg Island, Iran, in 1966. Peter's 'mobile' office consisted of a few sheets of A4 in a folder. He could ensure the world went around for all the flight crew under his wing. And some who were not. When Dave Paris' American wife fell ill while he was flying the helicopter on the film set 'Cliffhanger' in the summer of 1992, he had to leave the set and rush her to a hospital in Paris, France. Peter took the next flight to Cortina, Italy. He resumed the camera flying sequences shot in the Dolomites that doubled for Durango, Colorado, until Dave returned. His leadership and crew telepathy to judge when to go out onto the flight line and fire up the engines was the key to its success. Flights departed every ten minutes. It was just a question of knowing who was crewing the flight preceding yours and mentally adding ten minutes before boarding your aircraft. It was not amusing to abuse Peter's trust. Non-compliance was rare. Any variance to this give and take would be 'noted' as I was to find out later.

In 1979, my friend Bill Roy left the OASA operation in Norway and spent the intervening time flying HEMS (Hospital Emergency Medical Services) in the USA. The appalling death rate among pilots flying single pilot crashing at night made him realise the North Sea was not so bad! When he joined the Sumburgh operation in 1988, it dawned upon him this was, as he put it to me, "The finest flying club in the world." And he should know.

Fig 34. BIH S-61Ns. 'The finest Flying Club in the World'
Sumburgh, Shetland Isles.
Photo© kindly provided by Kieran Murray Snr, SAR Crewman. LSI

During the war in Vietnam, Bill volunteered for an all-volunteer squadron. As the US Navy did not have a helicopter attack squadron, HA(L)-3 (Helicopter Attack Squadron Light), known as the Seawolves, was formed. HA(L)-3 had nine detachments (Dets), all based in the Mekong Delta, a Viet Cong stronghold. Bob Britts and Jim Church were also volunteers.

The Delta is a vast, forested swamp of more than 2,500 miles of waterways in the southern quarter of the country. "I was attached to Det 1 and based on a Mobile Advanced Tactical Support Base (MATSB) called *Sea Float* anchored in the middle of the Bo De on the southern tip of the Ca Mau peninsular (175 miles southwest of Saigon (Ho Chi Minh City). A six to eight-knot tide fed into it from the South China Sea in the east and the Gulf of Thailand in the west.

We supported the Naval Special Warfare operations and Mobile Riverine Forces in the Can Lon River and Southern Mekong Delta, Vietnam. These were principally SEAL (Sea, Air and Land) platoons and River Patrol Boats (RPBs) often crewed by South Vietnamese Marines." Their mission was part of an effort to establish for the first time in many years the government of South Vietnam in this area. Eleven modified barges were moored in a raft to form the base, including the facilities to accommodate and support 700 men. *Sea Float* survived despite numerous attempts to destroy it. Part of the defence was a patrol made up of four marines. Among other duties, they were responsible for dropping concussion grenades every minute or so into the water, particularly at night when it was difficult to spot the swimmer sappers, known as 'zappers', leaving the mangrove swamp bordering the river. "I saw how one Marine Sergeant picked them off with his Colt .45. I oversaw 12 pilots, and as many door gunners and, being a self-sufficient unit, they doubled as aircraft engineers. We worked a 24-hour shift with 24 hours off ashore. This arrangement enabled us to provide helicopter cover at night.

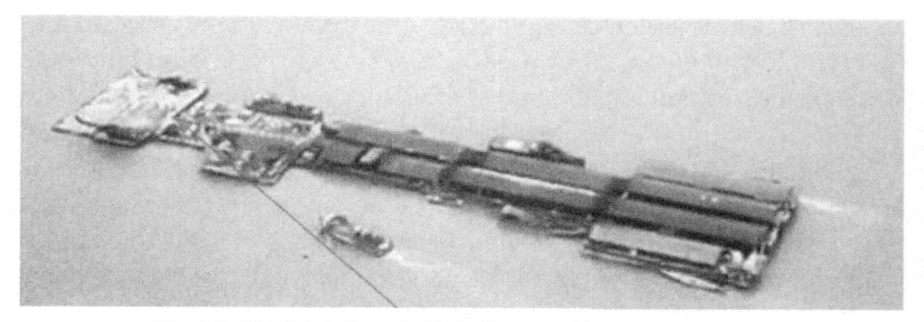

Fig 35. HA(L)-3 Det 1. UH-1Bs on *Sea Float.* 1970.
Photo credit: Ed Lefebvre.

Because we were so active, on the 16th of June, we were assigned three aircraft instead of the usual two. They were primarily worn-out Bell Iroquois (Huey) UH-1B gunship helicopters, hand-me-downs from the army; we never did get around to repaint them." The helicopters were the most heavily armed gunships ever used in the war. Besides door gunners with M-60 machine guns that could fire 500 to 650 rounds a minute, there were two M-21 miniguns, one mounted on either side. "These had six electrically operated rotating barrels (like a Gatling gun). We usually fired 2,400 rounds of 7.62mm a minute, aiming and operating them from a module between us in the cockpit, taking care not to take out our people on the ground. I determined that the miniguns were responsible for a lot of the brassing of the tail rotor. Inboard the miniguns were rocket pods containing seven missiles; the captain had the fire control for these 2.75" folding fin rockets."
During the year, HQ determined that the M-60 door guns be attached to sugami vertical hard mounts – rather than hand-held. To prevent brassing the synchronised elevator and tail rotor from the left door gun's spent brass, they developed the Odom Mount to deflect it. They then realised that with brass deflectors, they could mount two M-60s, one on either side of each sugami. Thus, doubling the cabin's firepower and providing continuous protection should one gun go down, a concept unpopular in practice for three reasons: sitting in the doorway attached to a safety restraint with their legs

hanging down outside enabled door gunners far greater freedom and accuracy to fire being much easier to allow for the ship's forward speed when firing their hand-held M-60s from the shoulder; removing a gun for greasing took much longer, and the sugami mount in the doorway obstructed access.
“My pilots were fresh out of the Navy training school at Pensacola, FLA, the ‘Cradle of Naval Aviation’, and didn’t give any trouble. They knew if they stepped out of line, I would send them up to HQ at Binh Thuy as sandbag officers, some 85 miles southwest of Saigon. Yet they enjoyed the work so much they wanted to do a second, 12-month tour averaging 600 combat missions. Something unheard of in Vietnam.” HA(L)-3 operated between the end of July 1967 and March 1972. They suffered a high casualty rate, including 44 men killed and over 200 wounded. It became the most decorated Squadron in the Vietnam War, with 5 Navy Crosses awarded, 31 Silver Stars, 219 Distinguished Flying Crosses, 15,964 Air Medals, many other medals, and multiple Presidential Unit Citations. To give some idea of the intensity of HA(L)-3 flying ops: during 1970, when Bill was with them, the Seawolves logged 33,973 hours and expended 18,909,490 rounds of 7.62mm; 108,297 – 2.75-inch rockets; 41,718 rounds of 40 mm grenades and 1,951,956 rounds of .50 calibre machine gun ammunition.
Over one week, two aircraft could launch 1,000 rockets and fire one million rounds of ammo with expelled M-60 brass building up in the cabin to six inches deep after a single mission. Some flying club!

To make the time off on Shetland more enjoyable, along with Roger Cookson, we had acquired funds from British Airways Clubs to form a windsurfing club; now was a suitable time to spend them.
We stored the second-hand equipment in the hangar across the road and dunes from the West Voe. Sailing was mainly in the afternoon and late into the long evenings during the summer after the second and third rotations. With the hangar so close to the beach, sailing between the first and third rotations was possible, though a bit of a scamper to jump back into uniform in time for the third! We provided instruction with Bristow SAR on hand, though never used, to rescue surfers needing help tacking back to the beach or caught in the tide race around the southern tip of the island. Sadly, Roger passed away in February 2015, some 1,460 feet from the summit of Mount Aconcagua in Argentina, the highest mountain in the Western Hemisphere at 22,835 feet. As a lead training captain on introducing the Sikorsky S-92A onto the North Sea for CHC, he spent many hours at the Flight Safety Simulator Learning Centre in West Palm Beach, FL, teaching crews to convert to this new type. We all miss him.

Chapter 13. 1988

Queen of the Seas – A Ditching in Calm and Rough Seas

Though one aircraft could claim to be 'Queen of the Seas'. The clue was in the registration: G-BEID or 'ID' (I Ditch). The first time was eight years earlier when an RNLI lifeboat towed her back to Aberdeen Harbour. The second time, there was less to recover.
The UK CAA Strategic Review of Offshore Helicopter Operations succinctly records under Mandatory Occurrence Report (MOR) No.198802141: 'Engine fire warning. A/C ditched, burnt, and sank'. Ian Sutherland was the captain, with Malcolm McDougal co-pilot. Malcolm later recorded the incident with extracts from the Aircraft Accident Report No. 3/90.

*

On Shell flight 13, at the front of the third rotation out of Sumburgh on the 13th of July 1988, we departed from the Safe Felicia, *attached to the* Eider Platform, *taking a work team commissioning this new Shell platform. I was the handling pilot on our second trip that day.*

The aircraft was cruising on track JULIET at 1,500 feet altitude in instrument meteorological conditions (IMC). At 14:23 and 40 miles from Sumburgh, they established two-way with Sumburgh Approach Air Traffic Control. They identify the aircraft on radar and pass an inbound visual flight rule (VFR) clearance.

*

We had talked for a while and now returned to a companionable silence, each concentrating on our appointed tasks. As we reached thirty-five miles to land at Sumburgh, I had a strange sensation of having felt or heard something but was unsure exactly what it was. I turned to Ian Sutherland, the captain of this flight, and asked, what was that? Bringing the almost inevitable reply, "What was what?"

Several passengers hear it, particularly the occupant of seat No. 4B, as a loud bang from above, from the area of the No. 2 engine drive train. They then heard several abnormal noises, with the passenger in seat No. 4B hearing a grinding, mechanical noise from almost directly above.

It emerged when Ian and I attended the technical/scientific debrief at the Royal Aircraft Establishment (RAE) Farnborough. I had sensed the half of one per cent fall in main rotor speed caused by the engine malfunction. The No. 5 bearing had disintegrated, causing severe friction in the area, and with the bearing gone, oil was pumping out under pressure over red/white-hot metal. This blow-torch effect was not in the engine compartment but playing back on the magnesium alloy gearbox, igniting into a searingly hot magnesium fire.

Back in time, with the flight in the cabin, an engineer in row three, more or less underneath the gearbox, heard a sharp cracking sound. Our first positive sign in the cockpit was a No. 2. engine fire-warning light. After our brief conversation, we were both fully alert and discussed the unusual engine indications, in that both engines were matched and normal.

After the fire warning, the co-pilot descended to level off at 500 feet and continued VFR.

*

Therefore, a further twenty seconds after I had looked over my right shoulder and reported white smoke was swirling down from the cabin roof, we responded to the electrical indication of engine fire and completed the shut-down drills on No. 2.

Perhaps thirty seconds later, I called, "Fire-Warning No. 1." I was turning right towards the land and descending, as we were only about twelve miles east of the Out Skerries Islands. Further discussion produced the agreement that we would not shut down this engine, as while it was running, it gave us through-shaft protection and allowed us to make a controlled ditching. Also, like in the first emergency, the engine instruments gave no corroborating indications.

At about this time, passengers saw oil coming from the cabin ceiling, streaking down trim panels and inside the left (port) window adjacent to seats 4A and 5A, dripping almost continuously onto the occupants. Oil covered the outside of the right (starboard) windows in rows No. 4 and 6. Then smoke began to issue from a joint in the ceiling panels in the central part of the cabin.

*

During this second minute of the emergency, we thought we were doomed. The manifestations of our problems were quite unlike any drills we had simulated in training. Time seemed to drag; an acrid smell of burning wafted from the cabin. It was a smell that stayed with me for many years. Whenever a fault brought a smell of hot equipment into the cockpit, it bathed me in sweat for a second or two.
We were pretty heavy, and the remaining engine was up to its limit. Ian took control at this point, and I was free to open the port cockpit window and put my head out, holding onto my headphones to prevent them from being pulled off by the slipstream. The strange thing is I have no memory of what I saw. At RAE Farnborough, I heard my voice from the cockpit voice recorder reporting, "We are seriously on fire." This condition is called stress-related memory loss. I was so appalled at the sight of smoke and flames billowing back in a trail behind the aircraft my mind immediately irradicated this vision from my memory.
We began to prepare for the ditching with a radio call, a passenger brief, and a run through the checklist. I pulled off my shoes, threw them clear back over the step into the cabin, shook out my immersion suit from beneath the document box and laid it fully extended beside me. We had a few seconds left when we asked each other if we had covered everything. Ian said, "We could have the gear down," and took his hand off the collective lever and selected the undercarriage down. I had experience with water landing training in Bristows and said, "No, we won't," and re-selected U/C up, and Ian accepted. He then ordered me to inflate the sponson floats, and I did.

As Ian requested, the correct procedure at BIH was to select the gear down to help stabilise the aircraft in the event of a landing on water with no realistic chance of taking off again. Training procedures for water landing practice to leave the gear up is also correct, as the intention will be to take off again. (Author).

Upon receiving the distress message at 14:28, Sumburgh Approach Control immediately vectored a nearby S-61N, G-BFFK, towards the scene. At 14:31, when Sumburgh Approach lost contact with 'ID', the crew of 'FK' reported they had just heard a ditching call. At 14:33, Shetland Maritime Rescue Sub-centre (MRSC) scrambled the HM Coastguard S-61N SAR helicopter Rescue 117 and requested the Aberdeen Maritime Rescue Co-ordination Centre (MRCC) scramble the Bell 212 SAR helicopter Rescue 145 from the Cormorant Field. (Bristow operates both of these helicopters.) In addition, at 14:45, Lerwick launches their lifeboat with an estimated time of arrival at the ditching position an hour later.

*

We were below one hundred feet, flying at sixty-seven knots and slowly descending as Ian brought up the nose for the final commitment to the sea.

They made a gentle power-on ditching 11 nautical miles off Shetland Island coast at 14:31, some 30 seconds after visual confirmation of the fire and 3 minutes after the initial abnormal noise.

*

We were probably crosswind and around forty-five knots when we made contact, though recollection is a little hazy. This touchdown is slightly faster than ideal, and the result was a positive nose-in, with the attitude going to twenty degrees, maybe more, as I saw the sea green on the forward windscreen. The aircraft settled back nicely to a stable rolling, bobbing motion. That fatal cracking noise signalled this whole sequence of events until the remaining engine shutdown took only three minutes and eight seconds! We later learned the hydraulic lines had burnt through as Ian found the rotor brake ineffective thirty seconds later. It is a chilling inference that we would have lost main rotor control after a further short interval, and anyway, these three minutes seemed like a lifetime.
Besides all the actions described, we had experienced various personal thoughts on the dire nature of our emergency and the inference that, with the progressive worsening of the situation, we may lose control altogether and perish. They frequently say one has no time to worry in such a situation, but Ian and I were a couple of sensitive and intelligent chaps whose thoughts were racing in these seconds dragging like hours. I began feeling more optimistic with the helicopter intact in the water.
Ian ordered me to jettison the rear port door. He had to direct my finger to the switch, a further psychological block discussed later with the Air Accident Investigation Branch; apparently, items that are 'touched' regularly remain within immediate memory, whereas others you discard under stress.
I left my seat immediately and stepped into my suit. The passengers were sitting at the edges of their seats, looking very tense, and I was concerned they might panic and run around, impeding my disembarkation drills. I told

them to remain seated while I organised the dinghy, then unclipped it and dragged it to the door. Because the life raft installation was upside-down, once, outside the cargo door, it inflated; I tried to hold it close to the door, but the thin nylon cord of the long lanyard skinned some flesh off my hand.
Happily for us, these nineteen passengers were a single company team. They were all known to each other, most of whom were seasoned travellers; they behaved like a disciplined ship's crew. On my call, they filed into the forward dinghy. There was a wall of smoke beyond row 3. I tried to run through it to see how the passengers at the rear were coping. I got only six feet and staggered back, choking. Ian had tidied up in the cockpit, joined me in the cabin and said he would have a go. He was back, spluttering and shaking his head as quickly as I had been.

Some four minutes after ditching, the forward life raft was still attached to the aircraft by its painter. Its passengers, who had initially seen small flames around the No. 2 engine exhaust, could now see signs of a growing fire at the right side of the main gearbox housing.

*

Ian joined the passengers in the dinghy, and I paused to lean back out of the door, looking up at the engine area, intrigued that the fire had subsided considerably. But, later, it resumed in earnest. I was reflecting on the remaining drills: to take a first aid kit, torch and so forth, when a hysterical shriek emitted from one of the passengers coping less well than the others. Ian motioned me to join them in the life raft, and we cast off, found the paddles, and one of the guys, now in his element, organised a paddling team. The crew had completed their task successfully, and we were happy to let them get on with it.
We exerted considerable effort to move the dinghy. After perhaps ten minutes, we paused about a hundred metres from the scene and watched in awe as a raging fire gradually engulfed the hull. The gearbox fell to the hull floor with a mighty crash, and then the fuel tanks exploded in three distinct events of a white ball of flames and sparks, the great rotor blades melting and crumbling like wax until only the tail section was left recognisable.
As we reached this position, we were elated to see the other dinghy paddling from the other side of the burning hull. We now confirmed all souls onboard were safe. The rear port door electrical jettison had failed, as did an attempt by one of the passengers from the inside. Instead, they popped out a window and went through it to activate the release from the outside. We closed with

the other dinghy and, in the approved manner, used the lanyards to lash the two crafts together.

At 14:35, 'FK' obtained a radar contact at three nautical miles range, and shortly afterwards, the crew sighted a plume of smoke. A minute later, they were overhead and reported the helicopter was floating upright with life rafts deployed from the front and rear. Then, some five to nine minutes after ditching, they saw blue paint above the rotor brake area behind the gearbox turn to a greyish white, with flames around the main rotor mast but no sign of fire in the engine bay areas. They described the fire as spreading forwards and rearwards through the engine and main gearbox bays before entering the cabin and progressively destroying the fuselage structure above the floor line. Then, 15 minutes after touchdown, the main rotor head and main transmission were seen to subside into the cabin.

*

A great morale booster was Dave Anderton turning up and giving us the stirring view of an S-61N circling overhead, keeping us company until the rescue helicopter arrived. Sadly, a year or so later, he perished in his accident.

We had been very fortunate in the weather. Because of limited visibility, we do not succumb to the temptation of flying a few miles to the shore with an imminent control failure. Sea-state three provided a straightforward challenge for Ian's ditching procedure. The sea temperature, unusually warm so early in the summer, at fifteen degrees Celsius and light winds presented us with no exposure problems.

Twenty minutes later, once again seeming like all afternoon, the Bristows Coastguard helicopter arrived. The winching began, the winchman organising most of us into the second dinghy while he took guys up two at a time. The exercise took an hour and was chilly, the rotor down-draught lashing us with cold, stinging spray. Ian bravely and traditionally demanded to be the last man up to the helicopter. Still, unlike me, he had not changed to don his immersion suit as he left and was beginning to look very uncomfortable and distant. One of the more vocal passengers, possibly a diver, made representations to the winchman and me to get Ian away before the remaining three or four men. The winchman agreed and organised it thus. I was the last up. I will never forget the final scene as I dangled on the end of the winch-wire and saw the tail section reaching up at an awkward angle, stark against the grey skies, a dark skein of smoke trailing away, undisturbed, in the gentle breeze, towards the horizon.

When Rescue 117 arrived at 14:59, they released 'FK' to return to Sumburgh and commenced winching operations. After lifting 14 of the life raft's occupants, it was necessary to dump fuel before lifting the remaining 7, arriving back in Sumburgh with 'ID's occupants at 15:49.
Approximately one hour after the ditching, when the fire had destroyed most of the fuselage structure above floor level, the remnants of the aircraft capsized and floated with only the tail boom above the surface. After an unknown floatation period in this configuration, with the tail boom sustaining damage from a surface-borne fire, the fuselage remains parted at the position close to the attachment points of the main landing gear sponsons, and the forward portion of the fuselage sank to the seabed. The aft portion of the fuselage continued drifting, supported by the right sponson and associated floatation bag. The Lerwick lifeboat had now arrived on the scene, sighted the bag, and commenced towing the sponson. It was not initially apparent a substantial portion of the aircraft was suspended beneath it. After a short distance, the remains of the aft fuselage broke away and sank. After being towed for about a mile, the sponson also sank approximately three hours after the ditching. They found the sea depth over the area of the wreckage site was between 90 and 110 metres.

*

We both had our moments of emotional trauma since then. There have been one or two sleepless nights! The bad dreams stopped after a couple of years. I stopped wanting to fly at low cruising levels and always thought about ditching. Even today, I would rather not do simulated ditching in the simulator. Ian and I remember how disturbing it had been a week after the incident, sitting in a darkened room at RAE Farnborough, side by side, listening to the tape of our flight, all the mechanical sounds, and conversations. We imagined we were back there and had to request time out to get ourselves back together before resuming the debrief.

The report concluded the cause of the accident was an uncontrollable fire in the main gearbox bay, probably resulting from a failure of the No. 5 bearing cage in the No. 2 engine caused by a defect in the bearing cage or excessive imbalance forces on the bearing. An underlying factor was the lack of fire detection or suppression capability within the main gearbox bay. After a fierce fire had consumed much of the floating aircraft, the remains broke up and sank.

In a safety meeting later in the year, they altered the SOP (Standard Operating Procedure) to reflect our intuitive interpretation of the checklist.

*

Calm seas for ditching are rare in the North Sea, as these conditions occur fewer than 2% of or seven days a year. For the Sikorsky S-61N G-BDES crew, the 10th of November 1988 was not one of them. Steve Martin, a former greeny (avionics engineer), was in command with the Flight Operations Manager Steve Stubbs as his co-pilot. This time, the cause was attributed to a catastrophic failure of the helical combiner gear within the main transmission input gear train. The gear has the same function as a spur gear, except it can accept larger loads with less noise and vibration; unlike spur gears with teeth in a parallel line of contact, helical gears' teeth line of contact is diagonal. One of the gear teeth had fractured due to fatigue.
Since manufacture, progressive damage to this helical combining gear had gone undetected. The origin of the fatigue was associated with aluminium oxide inclusions being a by-product of the steel production process. The steel to make the gearbox was subject to just one cleanliness inspection based on a single sample when poured into the ingot stage. And now the time had come for the fatigue to cause the gear to break up. Sometimes, helicopter pilots must wonder what is going on above them!

This flight leaves Aberdeen with three stops offshore: the semi-sub rig *Sedco 707,* the diving vessel semi-sub DV *Smit Semi 2* and the semi-sub rig *Sedco 703*. All three turnarounds were normal, with no fluid leaks observed from the helideck or when walking through the cabin. At 08:25, they lifted off the *Sedco 703* with 11 passengers and headed back to Aberdeen. When passing 1,500 feet, the commander became aware of a slight buzzing noise. He was not unduly worried, handing control to the co-pilot so he could tuck into his breakfast. The co-pilot then began to hear the same noise. It was 16 minutes into the flight, and the commander was well into his eggs and bacon when a passenger came forward and asked to speak to him. The noise became much more apparent when he removed his headset to listen to what he had to say. And it was coming from the cabin. Worse, it was of a significant volume – and becoming louder. The passenger had come to report a 'thump' and 'a bearing-like sound'.

Below them, a 25 to 30-knot Southerly wind gusting 40 knots was whipping the sea into waves 15 feet high. Rain showers were reducing the visibility to six kilometres. The crew decided the best course of action was to descend and head off downwind to the nearest helideck. The *Claymore 'A'* oil production platform was not far, some 18 miles away. There were still no indications of a problem other than the increasing noise level. The commander requested a priority landing. Then, the flight Information liaison officer (FILO) on *Claymore 'A'* realised this was no ordinary diversion. To try and troubleshoot the problem, the co-pilot moved the speed select levers (SSL) forward and increased the 100%NR setting to 102%NR (Main Rotor Speed). The noise level just became worse. They reduced the NR back to 100%. By now, they were down to 500 feet and travelling at 110 knots when the main transmission emergency lube pump kicked in with just eight miles to run. The main oil pressure pump had failed. They continued the descent down to 250 feet, with the situation deteriorating. Rather than climb back up to land on the platform, the commander decided to land on the adjacent semi-sub *Uncle John* drilling rig. It was just 170 metres northeast of the *Claymore 'A'*. The lower helideck height would be a better option. With just six miles to run, the crew had doubts about making *Uncle John* and armed the floats in preparation for ditching. Then, at a range of three miles, there was a sudden and substantial increase in noise and vibration levels. Rapid fluctuations of both torque and engine speed on both engines accompany this increase. They were fast running out of time; there was just insufficient warning of an impending transmission failure to avoid ditching, much less to consider an attempt to land into the wind. The commander announced his decision to ditch and reduce speed to 20 knots. When he felt he was losing yaw control with a tailwind component, he cushioned the ditching using collective control. In a slightly nose-up attitude, the aircraft contacted the water in a trough between two huge waves. On impact, he lowered the collective, shut down the engines and attempted to deploy the floatation system.

Immediately, the front of the aircraft was engulfed by a wave, rolled over to starboard and inverted two and a half miles from the rig *Uncle John*. Fortunately, the passengers were experienced oil field workers. They were well trained in the helicopter underwater escape trainer (HUET), known as the 'dunker' for this sort of event, including the drills for evacuation from an inverted aircraft rapidly filling with water. The dunker had one weakness that soon became apparent. It did not have pushout windows, just ready-cut apertures in the cabin wall. In addition to the emergency exits, including two amidship windows on the S-61N, you could also push out 7 of the 11 windows. With the aircraft now relatively stable, they grabbed the red fabric tab connected to the rip-out beading surrounding the window nearest them, pulled the seals free, and punched out some of the windows. One passenger on the port side jettisoned the amidship emergency exit window beside him and made his way out. Four passengers exited the port side, seven out of the starboard. Later, there was confirmation one passenger had broken a bone in his hand – they had not appreciated the force needed to push the windows against the pressure of the water outside.

For the crew, their difficulties were just beginning. The co-pilot had managed to open his sliding window with the aircraft inverted. Because of the location of the collective lever between him and the emergency window release handle, he could not reach this handle. Even with the window slid open, it only has an aperture of 29" high, 10" wide at the top and 11" at the bottom. Despite his size, he managed to wriggle through; the commander could neither reach the window release handle nor even open his window. He, too, was suspended upside down in his seat some two crucial inches away from his window release handle. His next option was to enter the cabin and exit the large cargo door on the starboard side. Moving back into the cabin, he realised it was still closed. There were now just two feet of air between the cabin floor above him and the rising water level. The passengers had evacuated through the windows. To open it, he needed to pull back the release handle, push the door out and slide it back on its rails. He had not reckoned on the weight of the water on the outside. It forced the door closed. He was never going to open that door. After this failed attempt, he 'resurfaced' except the airspace, previously there, had gone. Despite being an excellent swimmer, he felt he was on the point of drowning. Then, diving down again, he located one of the forward cabin windows on the port side and tried to push it out. Initially, his efforts just eased him back into the cabin. On the second attempt, he managed to punch out the window, heave himself through, and, with a final kick, surfaced alongside the hull. He could breathe again.
Here, he joined the co-pilot and the four passengers. They had either managed to climb onto or cling to the hull. The waves wash some of them off. They swim back and hold on to the sponsons, the high-frequency radio aerial support pylon on the port side or the safety rope surrounding the hull. From here, the commander activated his search and rescue beacon (SARBE) and directed an approaching helicopter to their position with the speech mode. There were two life rafts onboard. They did not deploy the raft opposite in row one because the cargo door would not open. It remained in

its harness; the remaining one was still attached to the aft door on the port side. The co-pilot instructs the passenger nearest it to release the door from the outside. The wire-locked handle was still above water, and it was easy to locate and break this wire-locking when turning the handle. It falls free, and the life raft inflates. The four passengers boarded first; then, the two pilots made their way aft and boarded too. The short painter connected to the aircraft was still attached to the life raft, bumping against the V-shaped VOR aerial and the aft end of the port sponson. There was a danger it may puncture and deflate. Quickly, they cut both the short and long painters. In doing so, they mistakenly cut the cord to the raft's sea anchor. They were free.

The life raft then drifted past the tail pylon and clear of the hull. The other seven passengers had drifted away and had now formed a group. The survivors in the dingy could see them and attempted to make their way over. Paddling was futile. The wind was too strong, and the sea was too rough to progress. Help was on the way. The FILO had heard the brief MAYDAY from the co-pilot at 08:52 and had now lost contact with G-BDES. A minute later, he informed Aberdeen Coastguard by telephone that G-BDES had transmitted a MAYDAY. They, in turn, informed the Rescue and Co-ordination Centre (RCC) at Edinburgh, who stated they would act as co-ordinators. They dispatched three units to the ditching area: a Nimrod from RAF Kinloss, a Sea King from RAF Lossiemouth, and a Coastguard S-61N from Sumburgh, Rescue 117. The FILO then scrambled the S-76A+ based on the safety vessel MV *Tharos* and despatched the rig support vessel *Nautica* to the presumed ditching position. An S-61N, callsign 53C, en route to the *Claymore 'A'* with 20 miles to run, also heard the MAYDAY, as did another helicopter, 98P, just 11 miles from the platform. They both routed to the search area. That was all they could do as none of the helicopters was rescue winch equipped.

The Forties Field SA 365N Dauphin helicopter, engaged in a local shuttle, was recalled, and prepared for SAR duties. It then made its way to the scene of the search. At 08:59, *Claymore 'A'* and Flight 98P heard a distress beacon operating on 121.5 MHz. '98P' then proceeded to home in on the beacon using its onboard VHF homer and, at 09:04, reported overhead. A minute later, they spot seven survivors in the water and six in a life raft. Their position was 1.6 miles from *Claymore 'A'*.
At 09:13, the *Ocean Victory* rig's standby vessel, *Grampian King,* advised Claymore Radio, "We are three miles from the datum and proceeding." The

S-76A+ assisted her to a position ½ a mile away from the survivors. When at 09:26, she launched her fast rescue boat. Two minutes later, the SA 365N arrived. It was now using the Callsign Rescue 143 and commenced winching the six survivors out of the life raft and flew them to the *Claymore 'A'*.
Just four minutes after they launched the FRC, the crew had located and recovered all seven survivors. The last one had been in the water for 42 minutes and was suffering from hypothermia. The FRC crew transferred them to an offshore supply ship, the *Maersk Cutter*, now positioned half a mile away. These survivors chose to return to Aberdeen by sea. Those now on the *Claymore 'A'* were flown back – in an S-61N. As they reported, it was another unnerving experience. The rescue was completed entirely by North Sea-based assets. The shore-based assets were too late for active participation.
Five days later, the aircraft was recovered. She had floated for a few hours before sinking in a position 13 nautical miles east, northeast from where they had ditched. The automatically deployable emergency locator transmitter was still attached to the aircraft.

Chapter 14. 1989 - 1990

Standby - US$10/barrel – A Sad Day at Brent Spar

Warm winds moving up from the Continent over a relatively cold North Sea can generate fog in late July and August over the Sumburgh peninsular. When money was no object in the seventies, the helicopter operation decamped to Bergen and operated from there. On one of those occasions, the famous lift party, the brainchild of Pete Jackson, was given in a downtown hotel. The components included a card table and cloth, glasses, minibar contents, and Pete dressed as a sommelier. Despite being popular with the hotel guests, it did not meet the management's strict service code. For this reason, the ensemble had to be moved from lift to lift to avoid them; probably more fun than serving drinks anyway!
Though, those were memories. Until a clearance in the weather came through, the oil companies were content for a backlog of flights to build up. Then, it was a rush to clear it. Recovering the program sometimes meant flying three trips a day or all three rotations. Invariably, it would be a weekend. With most crews being Monday to Friday commuters, there was a crew shortage for these occasions.
With a commuting roster, 14 days a year were set aside for sickness. On the other hand, if you did not go sick, you could effectively use them for vacation, on one provision: you were available when in the country to assist with flight backlogs on your day(s) off. And this coincided with a Saturday yacht race during West Highland Week.

It is an annual regatta held at the end of July. And sometimes, Ron Young invited me to help him to crew. It is thanks to him he taught me to sail. Ron joined Bristow just after me and became a member of a local club at Stonehaven to learn how to sail. They recommended he buy a Mirror dinghy and follow them on race days. He was selected within a brief period to represent Scotland at the next summer Olympics in Australia. Call it bad luck; it was not sufficiently funded for their team to enter.
Ron knew the rules and how to trim to perfection. He also learned how to take advantage of a spinnaker downwind, quite unafraid to hoist it, blowing 40 knots when others were still in their bags below. So much so he was in demand by owners to skipper their yachts; Ron always won, whatever the venue or the vessel's design, class, and size.

For this race, we had a crew of five. The first buoy to round was about two miles away and five points off the wind. At the start, Ron positioned us on the windward side of the start line and behind the vessel in a pole position to enjoy the cleanest air. As the start klaxon sounded, the fleet took off on a starboard tack. They intended to put in a port tack later and beat back to the buoy. Not Ron. Close-hauled, we slowly fetched the buoy as the fleet raced away on its own. It seemed ages before the marker grew larger. Meanwhile, the fleet had tacked and was closing rapidly. And this was when the rules came into play. We had the right of way. As we reached the buoy and filled the sail on a port tack to round it, the tightly packed fleet had to give way. But could they? Then the phone rang. It was Peter Boor, our Chief Pilot.

“We have a few days’ backlogs, and the weather forecast is to clear up. We need you this afternoon.”
“Of course, Peter. Though now’s not a good time to discuss how. May I call you back?” as I held the phone up to convey the sound effects of screaming winches and flapping sails. The din was indescribable. Expensive vessels collided and barged into each other. GRP bruised, and splinters of wood shed; to avoid us. Their skippers were incandescent, shouting at everyone and everything. Except for Ron, he never did. Instead, we sailed away, Ron puffing his pipe and smiling. Around the remaining markers, we sped to win by a comfortable margin. When we were mooring up, I explained the brief content of the phone call to Ron. Peter had asked if I would be available on the weekend to clear a backlog of flights in case the weather cleared. I agreed to help out. Not thinking it would, I left for the West Coast with Ron. In short, I had broken a gentleman’s agreement. And Peter was understandably not happy. Come the evening, Ron offered to drive me back across Scotland to Aberdeen.
He never appeared in a hurry on the flight deck or the crew room, just a man with a heart of gold. Yet, with his signature laid-back posture, he raced the big car smoothly through the glens. When I commented on this skill, he admitted, “In the REME (Royal Electrical and Mechanical Engineers) in Cyprus, we raced cars. These were Mini Coopers. We competed on dirt tracks, and when there, I won a few, the Champion driver.” You would never have known. Warming to his prowess in yachts and now cars, I asked him if he was good at anything else. “Well, one year, I was the Champion glider pilot in the army.” And this from a pilot using the call sign of the previous flight for the current one, who after a flight and on reaching the crew room invariably muttered, “Bother, left my pipe in the aircraft” or some other suitable comment as he headed back down the stairs to the apron.

And if that was not all. We were heading northbound to the drilling rig *Santa Fe 135G* one December morning back in 1976. The weather was seasonable, and storms were eating into the fuel margins. After lighting his pipe for the nth time at some point during this sector, Ron mused, "It'll probably be all right." Apart from "Make it a double," it was probably the most useful phrase you could ever learn.

*

1989 and the previous year had been challenging times in the oil industry. Brent crude had slumped and hovered just above US$10 / barrel. It was the lowest it had ever traded since listing in the mid-seventies when it first came ashore. Until 1988, there had been a shortage of drilling rigs. They commanded a charter rate of US$250,000 a day. Oil companies paid this sum to secure the rig, even in maintenance. Then everything changed. They tore up the contracts. If a rig operator complained, the response from the oil companies was to see them in court. On shore, complete suburbs of towns were for sale in the northeast of Scotland that had been developed to meet the needs of the industry. For helicopter operators, the pickings were particularly thin. In the fixed-wing world, wage hikes were soaring due to the low cost of aviation fuel, and cheap Oil & Gas buoyed the economy.
Whereas wage parity with fixed-wing for helicopter pilots working for companies with oil & gas contracts was futile. The employer pleaded business was on the rocks, and no money was available. Paradoxically, the reverse was confirmed when the oil price was high. Then, they maintained wage hikes should track fixed-wing. And guess what? Under these circumstances, operators froze airline pay. It happened every time – over the proverbial barrel! Naturally, most crews believed you could never win – or could you? Well, not unless you negotiate differently. What does this mean?

*

October 1989, BIH pay talks had stalled at 6%. It did not meet the Pilots Local Council (PLC) expectations. There had been meagre wage increases for years; mortgage interest rates had now reached 17%, a fact not lost on the crews in Sumburgh. Moreover, the pay differential with narrow-body jet pilots had significantly widened under the Maxwell tenure.
By March 1990, last October's failed pay negotiations were still at an impasse. To move them forward, the crews in Sumburgh took the initiative. They withdrew goodwill. This action reduced the program from the airport to

the East Shetland Basin from three to two rotations a day, simply by not rotors-running into the next rotation. Instead, we shut down on return to Sumburgh after the first and second rotations to plan the next flight, observe the time allowed for wearing immersion suits regulated by the CAA and take meal breaks on the ground. It meant you could only complete a partial program of flights within the airport opening hours. And this action was compatible with our pilot's service agreement. But we added a further twist.

*

Both were reminiscent of the Arab oil embargo of 1973 when some major Arab oil exporters supported the Egyptian and Syrian forces during and after the war. The groundwork was to increase oil prices by 70% and a total oil embargo on the USA, including The Netherlands, Canada, Japan, and the UK, as they were perceived to influence the USA and its policies towards Israel. The embargo then extended to Portugal, Rhodesia, and South Africa as a signal from the Arabs they were expressing solidarity with the nations of Black Africa. It took the form of specific measures to maintain the oil supply to the brotherly African countries. Then, to ensure the screw bit, oil production was cut by 5% every month and planned to continue until production reached 12.5% of the 1972 level. This squeeze was when annual consumption was up by 7.5% per annum, and there were no reserves – anywhere. At the beginning of the war, Iranian crude was selling for US$5.40/barrel. Two months later, in December 1973, there was a rumour a Japanese consumer was bidding Nigerian for US$22.20/barrel. These figures had an uncanny resemblance to what happened next.

*

For us, the days progressed into weeks. As we maintained the reduced routine, we informed the Chairman of the BALPA Company PLC, Mike Tingle, the rate had changed. We increased it - much as the Arabs had done to bring pressure to bear on the USA. As the days went by, we increased the rate in increments from the original 6%. And this will continue until talks resume. And should they be successful, we will restore the original three rotations. Mike duly passed these new rates to Oxford, the Mirror Group HQ. Then, an unusual conversation took place.

We had travelled back on the oil company charter flight to Aberdeen on a Friday evening when Captain Dave Anderton stopped me in the terminal. "Could we chat in a pub on the way home?" He lived in the area and chose

the Garlogie Inn. Now, he did not frequent bars and appeared to seek a more peaceful, non-confrontational existence. With the pints ordered up, he let it all out. As with many former military pilots, their discipline kicked in whenever industrial matters arose, and they abstained from too much action. Not this time.
On the contrary, he assured me he highly supported what we were doing and asked how he could assist. I had known him for years, or so I thought. He was one to keep his powder dry. As it was such a simple action, there was nothing I could offer other than to carry on as usual with the withdrawal of goodwill. Sadly, four months later, we attended his funeral in Banchory after he went down with his aircraft when it struck the crane on the *Brent Spar*, a permanently moored semi-submersible offshore storage and tanker loading unit. The loss of someone of firm convictions and so well-meaning, not seeking the limelight, would not be forgotten.

*

By the end of the month, we had arrived at 22%! At this point, the PLC have an invitation to discuss the situation at Oxford. Just off a flight from Sumburgh for nine days off, I happened on a BALPA briefing in progress to crews in the Aberdeen crew room. In fairness to the Council, they had no representation in Shetland. So, when they accepted the remains on the table, it was well below our expectations in Sumburgh. There was no mention of the 100% solidarity behind the action by the Sumburgh crews.
Instead, the Company Council deemed it a significant result. Had even one of them been in Sumburgh then, they would have known first-hand a result much closer to the 22%, particularly for co-pilots, could have been achieved. In theory, we had provided them with a loaded gun. We also had the tacit support of the principal client, providing around 70% of the company's revenues; Shell Expro wanted an early resolution. The advantage we had provided was lost too quickly, too easily. On arrival at Oxford, the Council emptied the chambers before negotiations had begun. And then watched the rounds roll off the table until there was just 15% for captains and 11% for co-pilots. We thought that would be the end of it.

Following time off skiing in the Swiss mountains, this second winter break in the sun above the clouds ended with a rapid descent back to earth. Indeed, down to sea level. A message was waiting to call Mark Young, General Secretary of BALPA at Heathrow.

"Maxwell has fired you twice, Andy," then a pause for effect, "and I've reinstated you twice." "Thanks, Mark!" He then said it included three others: the Flight Operations Manager Stewart Birt, Mike Tingle and 'The General', a name acquired by Mark Lacy in Bristow and now flying the line for BIH operating out of Sumburgh. It seemed a suitable time to visit Stuart to restore his credibility with Oxford. "Stuart, I have a suggestion. For £250,000, I'll quit." It was a long shot. You had to ask. His response reminded me of a scene from a William Goldman screenplay. They are spoken by Woodcock responding to Butch Cassidy. "Butch, you know, if it were my money, there is nobody I would rather have to steal it than you. But you see, I am still in the employment of E.H. Harriman of the Union Pacific Railroad." And so, it was with Stuart.

"If I could receive that amount myself, I would ask for you too. But I can't as they employ me." Little would we know Stuart will be in a better position to say "Yes" in a couple of years. Back to working normally, the head of Shell Aircraft, Howard Hollingsby, observed the rotations were running smoothly again. On a visit to Sumburgh, he tried to fathom what had happened. As a former BAH pilot, we had often crewed together. He could not believe they did not want to talk, causing so much disruption. Nonplussed, "Was that really the reason?" "Afraid so, Howard." And that was that - for the time being.

*

On a lighter note, I determined through crew room gossip being a North Sea Helicopter pilot waived the need for a master's certificate to bareboat charter sailing. It was time to test this theory. I called an international yacht charter company, and they affirmed it was true. They would provide a staff member on the first sector/hour of the first charter to ensure we were safe and observe our yacht handling. Before the hurricane season, we took a week for two successive years, starting in July. The first out of Road Town, Tortola BVI, in a 37-foot catamaran when we dropped off our minder on the dock of Grand Harbour, Peter Island, after a five-mile sector across Drake Channel; the second year out of Oyster Pond (French) St Martin with a 42-foot Beneteau monohull owned by a cement company in Ohio. Brand new, this was her first charter, plus no minder this time as we set sail for Anguilla.

There was only one caveat to chartering: to sail during daylight hours and moor up before the green flash (sunset). This advice is for two reasons. The pre-sailing briefing informs us this is due to some of the islands' locations. Their sat nav position indicates they are 2½ miles from their charted position. The second was because many schooners trading between the islands are underway at night, and few use running lights. The last evening, we arrived off Oyster Pond from St Barts with a high sea and big surf. The way into the harbour required manoeuvring through reefs, losing their red and green marker buoys during the last hurricane; no American convention 'red, right returning' this time. We requested a pilot, and soon, an RIB appeared; well, only occasionally, as its hull crested each wave on the way out. With the main up and the motor ticking over, we followed it in, just as the North Sea, except this time from the workboat skipper's perspective. I still don't have a sailing certificate, inshore, offshore or any other. Just memories of an amazing experience!

*

After returning from a flight out of Sumburgh, unwelcome news came into ops. There had been an incident offshore, and we had lost another aircraft. It would be the last time I signed for G-BEWL. The day before, on the 24th of July, I had flown it on a crew change to the *North Cormorant* and *Eider* platforms. It took some time for the details to trickle in. Before I took off again in the evening on a flight to the East Shetland Basin, it became clear that of the 11 passengers and two crew onboard, only seven passengers had survived when the aircraft fell off the deck of the *Brent Spar* into the sea. To lose passengers overboard in a strong wind was one thing; to lose a whole aircraft overboard on a calm day was something else. Those surviving the ordeal were on their way to the Aberdeen Royal Infirmary. *Brent Spar.* This vessel was a permanently moored semi-submersible offshore storage and tanker loading unit located not far to the northwest of the *Brent 'A'*. And that morning, the shuttle oil tanker MV *Drupa* was moored to it.

*

After we had landed, shut down at 22:10, and handed in the paperwork at flight ops, the story began to unravel. Now, the deck on the *Brent Spar* is smaller than most and was designed to accommodate helicopters with a 'D' value up to a maximum diameter of 19.8 metres; the S-61N has a 'D' value of 22.2 metres. A 'D' (Diameter) value is the helicopter type's overall length, including rotors. They paint this value on the helideck – in this case, 'D 19.8'. For this reason, the CAA imposed restrictions on S-61Ns operating to this deck as it was 11% smaller than prescribed for this helicopter size. They also included a maximum operating weight of 19,000 lbs, 1,500 lbs under the maximum landing weight. Because the whole of the *Brent Spar* can move rapidly and unpredictably in high winds and rough seas, causing the helideck to move laterally over a considerable distance, the helideck's maximum permitted pitch and roll has a restriction of 1° for the S-61N. The usual limit for an S-61N landing on mobile structures is 3° to either side of the pitch and roll axis. The *Brent Spar* helideck, including the crane, is mounted on castors, and can be rotated mechanically through 360° by the installation. This ability ensures the product hoses are not unduly loaded during loading operations. With a tanker moored but not loading, the structure rotated under the influence of the vessel. For example, during the morning, the MV *Drupa's* heading at 11:00 was 132° true. Her engines provided propulsion slowly astern to maintain a slight pull on the mooring hawser. This effort is to counter the tidal drift of a 0.4-knot current from the southwest. Maintaining this position was causing the helideck to rotate. Though not much under these weather conditions.

Dunlin 'A', just ten miles to the north, recorded the weather where the wind was calm; visibility 400 metres in fog; 6 oktas of stratus at 100 feet with full cloud cover at 800; both temperature and dewpoint +13°C and a QNH of 1022 Mb. The conditions in the *Brent Spar* area were not much better. On these days, the sea dissolves into the sky. There is no horizon other than one defined by the artificial horizon on the instrument panel in the cockpit. And then only horizontal when you're in level flight.

*

G-BEWL departed Sumburgh on the first rotation with 16 passengers on Shell Flight 1. Its planned route was to the *Polycastle* (a semi-sub flotel connected with a walkway to the *Brent 'A'*), then to *Brent Spar*, *Polycastle* and back to Sumburgh. With the weather in the Brent Field not great, they conducted a standard en route let down with a rig Radio beacon/Radar approach to *Polycastle* and landed facing 060°M. They took on some fuel and reboarded the 11 passengers for the *Brent Spar*. It was only a short 1.6 nautical miles sector across to the *Spar*, where the deck crew were waiting to receive them. As another BIH S-61N, G-BEWM, called landing on *Brent 'B's* deck, Brent Approach radio operator clears 'WL' to lift from the *Polycastle.* Once airborne, they made a sharp left turn to maintain visual with the *Spar*. They established two-way with its HLO, who gave them clearance to land from his position at the top of stairs leading to the helideck. Up on the *Brent 'A'* helideck, BIH S-61N G-BEDI was closing the doors and preparing for take-off with a clearance to climb to 2,500 feet on Track Mike back to Sumburgh.

It was not long before the *Spar* crew change aircraft appeared out of the drizzle and flew around it on a right-hand circuit at a low level before turning onto finals down the port side of the MV *Drupa*. They could hear G-BEDI calling on the radio as they passed the stern of the vessel,
"Eh, Brent, Approach eh Golf Delta India ready for take-off."
"Roger Delta India. Break. Whiskey Lima, are you visual with the *Spar*?"
"Whiskey Lima, roger, we're turning finals."
"Thank you. Delta India, just to be on the safe side, can you hold for thirty seconds and let him land on the *Spar* first?"
"Eh, roger, Delta India holding."

By now, 'WL' had passed alongside the MV *Drupa* and was slowing to a 50-foot hover abeam the *Spar*. The Captain, Dave Anderton, "Going across now." The co-pilot responded, "'Kay." From this high hover, they began to move over the helideck. Meanwhile, the oilfield installation manager joined the HLO. It appeared to them the aircraft started to drift slightly rearwards and was yawing to the left. On the flight deck, Dave would have sensed the crane was behind him and realised he no longer had any forward reference. Being too high as they moved across, he would have begun to lose sight of the small helideck as it slipped from view under the aircraft.
Now, on the edge of losing spatial awareness, they slowly drifted backwards and yawed left. To restore his sight of the deck below them and develop a reference point to land safely? And was there some pressure to land? Let the merry-go-round of helicopters feeding into and out of the oilfield resume. Rather than go around and set up a fresh approach. Who knows? Some of the helicopter's passengers were becoming concerned about its position relative to the installation. They could sense they were abnormally close to the crane and not in the normal landing position. Some reported the helicopter's tail swinging to the right just before impact.
At the same time, it became apparent to eyewitnesses on the *Spar* there was imminent danger of the tail striking the crane structure. The HLO could see this, too. It was not his job to transmit a warning. If he could, it was already too late. He only had time to duck from the debris raining down as the tail rotor tips struck the handrail surrounding the anemometer mast attached to the 'A' frame of the crane.
The crew lost directional control as the blade tips shattered on impact; the aircraft spun through 150° to starboard and, still turning, crashed down onto the edge of the deck, where it teetered.

*

The safety net frame around the deck supported it for a few seconds. The option to evacuate the aircraft evaporated when it gave way. The aircraft slid off and plunged 105 feet down into the sea below. It was later estimated they impacted at around 50 mph with a peak load of 20 to 25 g. Already severely damaged from the fall onto the deck and made worse when the front of the aircraft hit the sea, the distorted cockpit and cabin rapidly filled with seawater. In no condition to float, it sank almost immediately. Enough time, though, for seven passengers to escape from their collapsed and structurally damaged seats, out and through the shattered windows, and surface alive. It was 09:43.

Given the time of their last call, Brent Approach judged they had landed and sought confirmation so he could release 'DI'.

"Whiskey Lima Brent." Then again.

"Whiskey Lima Brent." And again,

"Golf Whiskey Lima Brent, do you read?"

Then 'DI' came on the radio.

"Delta India Brent. Yeah, we hear you loud and clear. We can't pick him up."

It was now 09:45 when Brent Approach replied,

"Roger, we appear to have a Sixty-One in the water alongside the *Brent Spar*. Could you disgorge passengers, please and eh, advise on the *Alpha* deck when you're ready to lift."

*

The survivors had difficulty donning their life jackets in the water close to the Spar. In those days, passengers strapped a valise containing it around the waist. In normal ditching, there would have been time to open it and place it over the head before exiting the aircraft. Then, when outside, inflate it by pulling on a toggle to release air from a small gas cylinder into the chambers. It was proving much harder to go through this procedure in the water. Fortunately, they did not have long to wait. *Brent Spar* had already put out a Red Alert and launched their lifeboat. The alert had galvanised vessels and aircraft close by into action. It included two rig standby boats in the vicinity: *Seaboard Support* was one mile away between *Brent 'A'* and *'Bravo'*; *Seaboard Sentry* was just 400 metres northwest of the *Spar*. Their fast rescue craft (FRC) were soon racing toward the scene. Brent Approach requested *Brent 'B'* to release its supply vessel *Far Sleipner* and the Maritime Rescue and Coordination Centre in Aberdeen to scramble the SAR helicopter from Sumburgh, Rescue 117.

Fig 36. *Brent Spar* 09:50 View of *Brent Spar's* deck

Note: prohibited landing direction red lines on the yellow landing circle across from the crane. *Both Photo Credits: AAIB*

The accommodation semi-submersible *Safe Gothia*, now hangaring the offshore Bell 212 shuttle helicopters in place of the *Treasure Finder*, receives instructions to prepare to launch their Search and Rescue Bell 212. G-BEWM, still turning around on the *Brent 'B'*, became airborne as soon as possible and flew towards the *Spar*, where the co-pilot photographed the immediate scene.

Two other vessels, both semi-submersibles, also in the field, would soon play a large part. The MSV *Stadive* was five miles west of the *Brent 'A'*, and the MSV *Rockwater Smit Semi 2* was just two miles away. Both vessels prepared their diving bells and set course for the search area, and the crew of the MV *Drupa* brought their lifeboats to standby. Only an infield incident could summon up such a plethora of assets. Going down in a rough sea, alone en route, on a dark winter evening would have been an entirely different matter. It's hard for those staying onshore to appreciate every flight, year in and year out, exposing one to the possibility this could be your turn.
The *Spar's* lifeboat recovers the first survivor within four minutes of ditching. He had been lying face down in the water about 40 metres from the installation. He did not inflate his life jacket, and his immersion suit leaked. One of the lifeboat crewmembers had jumped into the water. Together with the rest of the crew, they heaved the semi-conscious person onboard. When the *Seaboard Sentry* FRC arrived, they recovered five survivors. The first was bleeding from a head wound and appeared to have a broken leg. At the same time, the second was drifting away from the scene. The remaining three were clinging onto one of the detached helicopter's sponsons. One of

them had a back injury. By 09:51, they were all transferred to *Seaboard Sentry*. The FRC returned to the scene.

The FRC from the *Seaboard Support* had arrived and picked up a survivor floating quite some distance from the others with a cut on his head. *Brent Spar* determined all their personnel aboard were accounted for, though four passengers and the two crew of the helicopter were still missing. When the SAR Bell 212 from the *Safe Gothia* arrived at 09:55, after removing the rescue boats from the scene, they initially searched the area using their forward-looking infrared camera. With no results from the search, they began winching operations to transfer the survivors to the *Safe Gothia*. They completed the task by 11:47. Here, they received medical treatment, and in just under two hours, all seven were airborne on their way to Aberdeen Royal Infirmary. At the same time as the winching operations proceeded, the MSV *Rockwater Smit Semi 2* arrived and launched an ROV. They located the wreckage 35 minutes later at 11:22.

Fig 37. G-BEWL onboard *MSV Stadive* - *Photo Credit: AAIB*

MSV *Stadive* also moved in and immediately launched another ROV, quickly accounting for the remaining six occupants. They were still in the wreckage lying on the seabed. At 15:20, they officially ended the search. By 03:00 the following day, the MSV *Stadive* recovered the wreck onboard.

The investigators could only conclude when arriving at the Spar; it was customary to have the crane behind them whenever a tanker was attached, even if there was no wind. When moored to the installation, the heading of the vessel, 'indicating' the 'wind direction datum', had historically implied the direction to land.

The accident was an unfortunate watershed moment for the offshore community. There are two ways to arrive on the water. One is to ditch, the other to crash. Up to this point, eight S-61Ns had ditched in the UK sector of the North Sea. All on board had survived. This was different; it had crashed. People had died. When surveys ask offshore workers to identify their worst fears, both hazardous and stressful to working offshore, traditionally, 80% replied it was the flight in the helicopter to and from work. By the time of this accident, a more recent survey reported this had improved to just over 50% feeling unsafe. It's still a lot. It did not take much to realise these fears more tangibly when reports of wildcat strikes throughout the oilfields and union leaders voiced their concerns to politicians about the perennial issue of offshore safety, specifically life jackets.

Chapter 15. 1991 - 1992

An Evacuation – Chapter XI - A Night time at Cormorant 'A.'

For years, the Oil & Gas companies had ensured incidents that drew attention to themselves went unreported. There was a press blackout to keep up the myth 'all's well' offshore. On the rare occasions news leaked out, they blacked the culprit from employment. No wonder, by the end of 1990, hundreds were prohibited from going offshore. Since North Sea operations had begun, the death toll had reached 400. Unfortunately, it was not going to stop there.

Fig 38. BIH Flight Line, Sumburgh, Shetland.
Photos© kindly provided by Kieran Murray Snr, SAR Crewman. LSI

At lunchtime on the 9th of January 1991, a sign that news blackouts were finally lifting was when radio stations reported the flotel, *Safe Gothia,* with some 400 persons onboard, had lost two of her eight anchors in a storm. Now, how many times have rigs and flotels had that happen? And how many times had both BAH/BIH and Bristows evacuated or reduced the workforce on them along with the platforms with gas leaks, explosions and other conditions making them unsafe to stay? Mark Lacy, who had operated in command out of Unst for Bristow, reckoned all the platforms in the East Shetland Basin had been down-manned at least once. The oil companies knew how to control unwelcome news and ensure it went unreported!

With its hangarage for Bristow 212 shuttle aircraft, the *Safe Gothia* also provided accommodation for workers on the *Brent 'C'*, which had been closed down for maintenance. Early in the morning, an anchor cable snapped. The connecting bridge had disconnected itself, luckily, with no one onboard. This matters. On a previous occasion, a bridge connected to the *Piper 'A'* collapsed, losing three men as it fell 70 feet into the sea. We had already flown one rotation when the flotel lost another anchor in the afternoon. A busy day ahead. It was newsworthy! The Coastguard believed if the vessel began to drift, as others had in crowded oilfields, it could collide with installations. By the close of play, we had flown another two rotations. The day included over nine hours of flying as part of a fleet of 14 aircraft involved '*operating in storm force winds and darkness'* as the papers report the next day: weather par for the course at that time of year. Of 400 oilfield workers, we fly 136 to the semi-sub *Safe Support* flotel, leaving the ship's crew onboard. Helicopters brought the remainder into Sumburgh. We were in luck. They kept the bar in the Sumburgh Club open for the last flight crew to arrive.

*

Life is always exciting. It was a phoney peace. Then things began to disappear.

Unknown to us, our pensions in the Mirror Group, like the US$2 billion Bulgarian state assets and the House of Commons wine cellar, were being plundered by a man appropriately named 'the dud cheque' - Robert Maxwell. Then, early in the morning on the 5th of November 1991, off the Canary Islands, where his yacht, *Lady Ghislaine*, was cruising, he disappeared. Later that day, the crew of a search helicopter found him floating in the sea, dead for no apparent reason. His skin condition suggested he had not been in the water that long. So, where had he been? Only then was it discovered the pension funds he had used to support his failing business empire had also gone missing. BIH went into administration to protect itself from creditors (US Chapter 11) on the 12th of December.

With a new topic of conversation in the cockpit discussing the loss of our pensions and how to recover them, we would buffet our way through another stormy night over the North Sea. Lights dimmed in the back, and the automatic direction finder tuned to an American Forces Network station somewhere in Western Germany transmitting a Neil Diamond number, "Aw, Cracklin' Rosie, get onboard. We're gonna ride, 'till there ain't no more to go" –breaking through the racket above. Pause to make the ops normal call; then establish two-way with the rig on the other box, pass them our ETA and check out their weather, return load and request some fuel in tanks fore and aft, two packs of fags and the evening menu. "Cus we got all night to set the world right."

*

Just a few miles north of Sumburgh, we packed into the chapel at Dunrossness. Family and friends of the co-pilot filled the ground floor with aircrew in uniform ushered upstairs to a narrow wooden gallery partly extending along both sides of the chapel. It was a standing room only. We had come to pay our last respects to another popular pilot, Ian Hooker, who had nearly survived the accident on Bristow Flight 709 on Saturday evening, the 14th of March 1992. He had not long been married to the daughter of the long-serving British Airways Station Manager at Sumburgh, Jimmy Burgess. His son-in-law, a former Bristow Ops controller, had recently embarked on a new career as a North Sea helicopter pilot and was posted to Sumburgh on the 12th of January 1991.

*

Being a weekend, the Sumburgh base was usually down-manned as most of the flying was on weekdays with crews commuting. Most pilots worked five days on, five off, five days on, and nine off, cycling every 21 days. Then, leave a smaller staff working a different shift pattern on the Island to fly the line to cover weekends. This Saturday was no exception. Because of the severity of the winds and sea state in the East Shetland Basin, some of the flotel accommodation vessels, typically connected to platforms by a gangway, had been moved away to their stand-off positions. The overnight wind still showed no signs of dropping. The Bristow Bell 212s, housed in a hangar on the semi-sub MV *Safe Gothia* flotel, would be out of limits to engage rotors and start the morning shuttle. They had to organise other arrangements.
Around 08:00, the Shell UK Expro Air Transport Controller asked British International if they could supply a fourth S-61N to support the three already engaged for the morning shuttle. In addition, they requested Bristow to provide their Tiger, G-TIGH based in Sumburgh, to help. The Bristow ops controller then phoned their Sumburgh chief pilot, on the mainland for the weekend, and asked if they could accept the task. Ops also explained the aircraft was unserviceable and required an air test; the duty crew would be

available at 14:00. The chief pilot agreed to travel up and carry out the test and fly the shuttle himself. Before he left Aberdeen airport on the ferry flight north, they advised him there was no longer a need for the aircraft on the morning shuttle, but it still might be on for the evening. He arrived in Sumburgh and completed the air test by noon.

When the British International duty crew came in to plan the evening shuttle, it was clear they would not be taking that flight. The weather forecast was against them; no positive air temperature band below 500 feet - essential to clear any airframe ice encountered higher up. Offshore in the ESB, it was shaping up to be the coldest night in six years. They declined the flight.
Shell then asked the Bristow chief pilot if he could take some freight offshore to the *Brent 'A'* and route via Unst to collect spare parts for the Bell 212s before beginning the evening shuttle, now confirmed. When the freight arrived in Sumburgh and was loaded onto 'GH' operating Flight 709, a heavy snowstorm had passed through. They delayed the departure to clean the aircraft. At 16:04, it was already becoming dark when they departed for Unst. That night, they will be the only aircraft operating in the field. Not unusual. The crew's original task on arrival offshore after dropping off the freight on *Brent 'A'* and the spares on *Safe Gothia* is to route *Brent 'D' – Brent 'B' – Safe Gothia – Brent 'C' – Cormorant 'A' – Safe Support – Cormorant 'A' – North Cormorant* then ideally back to Sumburgh, but could they? The temperature on the deck subsequently found on the aircraft flight recorder was -1°C. The absence of a 500-foot height band of positive air temperature for the helicopter to descend to remove ice meant there was little possibility of accomplishing the planned return flight to Sumburgh within the regulations.

Four minutes after leaving *Brent 'C'* at 19:28 en route westbound across the East Shetland Basin, the air traffic control 'Viking Approach' based on the *Cormorant 'A'* informed Flight 709 the platform was in a snow shower with a cloud base of 500 feet. Then, ten minutes later, they reported, "The forty to fifty-knot wind is now from two-nine-five (degrees), fifty to fifty-three knots. A snow shower is passing through, with the wind gusting a bit."
In the departure lounge, they were preparing for the men due to board the helicopter to stay overnight on the platform. They thought their flight would be cancelled.
At the last stop, the crew had asked the HLO to carry out the external checks and loading as the wind made it extremely difficult to disembark through the cockpit doors. Before landing, they requested the *Cormorant 'A'* to also do

the external checks and loading. At 19:41, the crew of Flight 709 set up the approach for the deck towering 183 feet above sea level. On deck, they discussed an area of considerable turbulence downwind of this structure in the path of their next stop, the *Safe Support* flotel. The chief pilot, acting as commander, had twice mentioned visiting the heads when they arrived on the flotel. All sorts of pressure, then? After a seven-minute turnaround, with 15 passengers on board and the port sliding door closed, the HLO gave them the thumbs up, indicating the deck was clear to lift. And this is where the tragedy began to unfold. The crew agreed it would be quicker if the commander handled the take-off, flew a right-hand circuit, and handed over the controls to the co-pilot to land on the *Safe Support*. "To do it – to save a big, long loop round."

At 19:48, the deck crew saw the helicopter move forward in the hover just beyond the edge of the deck, heading 300° and virtually straight into the wind. Then, and this is where the commander's briefing played out, he began a climbing right turn, an acceptable manoeuvre with little or no wind. But over 50 knots? If he kept this up, it would be no time before the aircraft became aerodynamically unstable; he did not seem to recognise the rapidly changing relationship between airspeed and ground speed, a fundamental problem associated with turning downwind in significant wind strengths. He was also distracted from a proper flight instrument scan by visually searching for the *Safe Support* over his right shoulder. It was holding position some 206 metres away from the *Cormorant 'A'* on a bearing of 075°M.
As the co-pilot requested deck clearance to land on *Safe Support,* the automatic voice alerting device (AVAD) chimed, **"Check height!"** The HLO responded to the co-pilot's request, "Good evening. The deck is clear. Just for information, the pitch is four degrees; the roll is five degrees; heave is up to four metres."

The pitch and roll were out of limits to land for a category 'A' aircraft, though that became irrelevant. From an observer's point of view, the wind was causing the helicopter to drift rapidly to its right as it turned, passing directly north of the platform, tracking in a North-Easterly direction (about 045°M) whilst still heading north. The helicopter continued the climb up to 250 feet for another few seconds while turning downwind. At this point, the commander reduced power and raised the nose of the helicopter. The airspeed washed off to zero. Witnesses see the aircraft enter an increasingly steep descent. Once he was aware of the descent, confirmed by the co-pilot shouting, "Watch the height! Watch the height! Watch the height! Watch the

height! Watch the height!" simultaneously with the AVAD chiming, **"One hundred feet,"** he applied full power.
He could not arrest the descent. At 19:50, slightly nose up and in a shallow bank to the left before impact, they struck the sea some 500 meters east, northeast of the *Cormorant 'A'* at 25 feet/second.
The flight lasted 50 seconds. Down draughts and an incipient vortex ring state, as recorded in the accident report, may have exacerbated the situation. The HLO on the *Safe Support*, seeing the helicopter begin to arc down towards the rough seas, immediately ran to the edge of the helideck and, realising Flight 709 was now in the water, transmitted a MAYDAY distress message heard by the Viking Approach Air Traffic Control Officer. He re-transmitted the message and initiated the appropriate emergency procedures. The helicopter initially rolled over onto its right side, then inverted, where it floated for less than two minutes before sinking another two minutes later.

*

From where he was standing, the HLO could now see the lights of life jackets in the water and could initially identify several survivors. Twelve occupants, including the crew, escaped before the helicopter sank. Only six were recovered alive. They included one crewmember – the chief pilot; the others had perished in the hostile sea. Some survived for a considerable time in a sea temperature of +7°C. The rescue operation, using ships and helicopters, began at once. Their efforts were severely hampered in the dark by the conditions. They included 13 vessels and three helicopters: a Bell 212 Rescue 145 from *Safe Gothia*, Norwegian Bell 214 Rescue 146 from the Statfjord Field and the Bristow Coastguard S-61N Rescue 117 from Sumburgh.
When the standby vessel *Seaboard Support* arrived from where she was 'dodging' the weather about 1.5 nautical miles northwest of *Cormorant 'A'*, she sighted three persons in the water. It was too dangerous to launch her FRC into these seas. She manoeuvred through waves, some 14.80 metres high, into a position to attempt a rescue. They recovered one survivor over the starboard rescue zone at about 20:30. Two crewmembers held a second person alongside. But the extreme sea conditions caused them to lose grip; his life jacket tore in this action. They throw lines to the third person in the water. He cannot help himself. It proved impossible to recover him.
At 20:28, the oilrig supply vessel *Edda Fram* manoeuvred alongside two men linked together and threw them three lines. Both were conscious at the time

but could not help themselves. The crew had great difficulty reaching them. The two survivors then split up. One was eventually brought alongside and recovered via the pilot access area at 20:50. Then, a crewmember with a rope tied around his waist jumped into the sea. He swam through nine-meter waves to reach the second survivor and pulled him towards the pilot access area, where other crewmembers lifted them onboard. The survivor lost consciousness and, at 21:00, was found to be dead.

Rescue 145 had also arrived on the scene at 20:28 and a minute later sighted the life raft from the stricken Tiger. A passenger had been able to release it from its stowage from the right cabin door; it had begun to inflate, probably initiated by the short painter. Outside, it suffered significant damage, particularly the floor, due to contact with parts of the aircraft. Conditions were challenging. Besides the damage, it was pretty unstable; it repeatedly overturned. Initially, four survivors had managed to hold onto it: two passengers and the crew. As they were being swept up and down 40-foot waves, George Watson, a passenger, recalls Ian tried to cheer them up. After nearly an hour in the sea, Rescue 145 found only two men still clinging to it. The winchman could not engage the rescue strop on one of the survivors on the first attempt. He tried again. The life raft overturned, and the gas inflation bottle struck him on the head. He was recovered, semi-conscious, to the helicopter. A second winchman is lowered and recovers George. The next time he went down, he recovered the second survivor - the commander. It was 20:51 when they winched him onboard. Rescue 145 flew across to the *Cormorant 'A'*, where the Tiger commander, the passenger and the winchman offloaded and refuelled. They returned to the area of the life raft. Another survivor was winched aboard at 21:15. During this period, Rescue 145 failed to recover another body. His suit was unzipped and full of water; the winchman could not identify him. He appeared dead. Rescue 145 returned to the *Cormorant 'A'* landing at 21:18 and unloaded their survivor. He had been in the frigid water for 1hr 25 minutes.

At this point, Rescue 146 from the Statfjord Field had arrived and nine minutes later, at 21:08, recovered a survivor and then positioned above another person in the water 100 metres away. The winchman goes down and notes the man's life jacket is over his head, and his face is under the water. He found no sign of life and concluded the person was dead. Attempts made to recover the body are unsuccessful. Instead, they wait for Rescue 145 to refuel and return to the scene. There, Rescue 146 kept its spotlight on the body until Rescue 145 had made contact. The Norwegians then took their survivor to the *Cormorant 'A'* landing at 21:25. Rescue 145 was more

successful; they managed to recover the body. It was the first officer. It was 21:32.
The four remaining survivors, who escaped the Tiger before it sank, also had their bodies recovered. The first by the standby vessel *Grampian Monarch* at 21:15. The Coastguard S-61N Rescue 117 winched a body onboard at 21:18 and laid a smoke/flame float near a second, to be recovered by the *Grampian Monarch* at 21:42. The supply vessel, *Far Sleipner*, found and recovered the last body three minutes later.
The search and rescue team recovered six survivors and six bodies.

The four survivors, waiting on the *Cormorant 'A'*, fly to the Gilbert Bain Hospital in Lerwick. They considered the conditions too dangerous to winch the survivors off the *Edda Fram* and *Seaboard Support*. So, they remained onboard as both vessels sailed to Lerwick. The air search terminated at 02:55; the sea search continued until 09:00 the next day.
Divers found the five remaining passengers who did not escape with unfastened seat belts. They were still in the cabin lying on the seabed and later recovered. And the wreck was hoisted onboard the MSV *Stadive*.
The report concluded several human factors, including fatigue. The commander had been on duty for 10 hours and 20 minutes. Frustration led to a rushed and hazardous flight manoeuvre, exacerbated by a demanding flying programme for which he was managerially responsible. These impediments may have degraded the crew's performance to the extent the normal safeguards of a two-crew operation failed.

*

It also acknowledged, "Helicopter operations conducted over the North Sea are in some of the most extreme conditions encountered anywhere. Winter weather can combine the hazards of strong and gusting winds, rough seas, severe turbulence, and icing at low levels with poor visibility in precipitation. The development of successful passenger and freight charter operations in such conditions is a tribute to the design of the helicopters and the crew's method of operating them. It was the first North Sea accident involving a collision with the sea by a Super Puma/Tiger helicopter since its introduction in 1983 and after 370,000 hours of operation. For the record, since 1976, accidents involving controlled flight into the sea indicate such a hazard is ever present in offshore operations."

Chapter 16. 1992

An Aggressive Airliner – Weasels in the City

The year began with the highest wind recorded in the British Isles. At 01:00 in the morning of the 1st of January, 197-mph winds broke the anemometer at RAF Saxa Vord, a reporting post for the UK Air Surveillance and Control System on the top of a 950-foot hill 5 miles north of the airfield on Unst. Twenty-three miles southwest of Unst and 15 north of Lerwick lies Scatsta airfield.

A day in Scatsta. It was August 1992, with the wind in the southeast and days of fog at Sumburgh. Though the visibility was sufficient for the helicopters to take off, it was below limits for the oil company crew-change fixed-wing to land. An airfield farther up the Island on the east bank of Sullom Voe was chosen to operate today. Scatsta. The small, though important, airfield was built during World War II to support and defend the adjoining flying boat base at RAF Sullom Voe from Axis bombers.

*

Originally, the site for RAF Scatsta was a peat bog. During the first four months of 1940, engineers completed the first runway with a ramp leading off to recover flying boats from the voe. A longer runway was begun in July 1941 and completed in April 1942. It was better suited to supply and for fighter aircraft to protect it. Pipe mines were laid under the runways in preparation for detonation to sabotage them in the event of an invasion. For its size, it proved to be one of the costliest airfields ever built. Events well justified the expense. The survival of the United Kingdom depended upon operations out into the Atlantic to protect the inbound convoys from North America. The British economy could have collapsed, and the country capitulated. At least that was the Axis plan - the Atlantic War.

*

Sullom Voe was already no secret to the Luftwaffe. On the 13th of November 1939, the first bombs to be dropped on the British Isles by the Axis during World War II landed in a field nearby - killing a rabbit. The sheltered voe had

22 moorings, some dispersed in nearby Garth's and Voxter Voes. From here, Coastal Command initially operated Saunders-Roe A.27 Londons, soon supported in early 1940 by some German-built He115 Norwegian Naval Air Service floatplanes flown in by their crews when their country fell. The He115s subsequently flew covert operations. Then, the long-range Consolidated PBY Catalina (PB: Patrol Bomber; Y: manufacturer designation) and Short Sunderland flying boats arrived. These flying boats primarily patrol and hunt for U-boats and graceful airliners, Focke-Wulf 200 Kondors.

*

At this point, it would be understandable if the reader wishes to skip this digression. Though, fixed-wing crews might find a summary of an aggressive airliner a break from O&G heliops. Initially designed for long-haul flights, this was an unpressurised airliner with a cruising speed of 190 knots. In 1938, D-ACON made the first non-seaplane Atlantic crossing. The flight took off from Berlin-Staaken. Cruising against strong headwinds below 10,000 feet for 3,438 nautical miles non-stop, 'ON' landed at Floyd Bennett Field, New York, after 24 hours and 36 minutes. The return trip was a less nail-biting, 19 hours and 55 minutes. It was built of light materials to give it its range, later exposing its shortcomings in combat. A daring crew flew a Danish-owned FW 200, OY-DAM, to Shoreham in England on the fall of Denmark in April 1940, where BOAC operated it as G-AGAY. A year later, a landing at White Waltham wrote it off. The usual causes were structural: either the tail braking off, the wing's rear spar snapping off at the root, or the forward retracting main undercarriage collapsing due to its unusual, forward retracting design. This, and its vulnerability to attack, was why they constructed only 276. The military conversion of the FW 200 had a ventral cupola with a forward-facing cannon and a bomb bay. In addition, it carried up to five 250 kg bombs with two machine guns mounted in dorsal positions. The bombs, mounted on reinforced wing pylons, were later relocated in the slipstream behind the engines to reduce drag. These modified airliners formed the Fernaufklarungstaffel (long-range reconnaissance squadron) and redesignated KG 40 to harass allied shipping. They initially operated out of Bordeaux-Merignac with considerable success in the North Atlantic. They send patrols beyond the Azores to 20° west and as far north as Iceland. The outbound patrols intercepted vessels inbound from West Africa, then routed west of Ireland and north into the shipping lanes with convoys inbound from the USA and Canada, finally landing in Norway, usually Trondheim-Vaernes

or Stavanger-Sola and Oslo-Gardermoen. They would be turned around and head south on a reciprocal course two weeks later.
From June 1940 to September 1943, KG 40 sank 93 ships with a combined 433,447 tons and crippled a further 70 of 353,752 tons. Winston Churchill later commented, “To the U-boat scourge, was now added air attack far out in the oceans by long-range aircraft. Of these, the Focke-Wulf 200, known as the Condor, was the most formidable,” and by others ‘The Condor Menace’.
Without a proper bombsight, the crews used a procedure they called ‘the Swedish Turnip’. This method was to come in at a low level - Tiefangriff - at 155 knots and just 150 feet above the waves. Then, with 250 m to run, released up to four bombs, straddling the vessel just above and below the waterline. Even near misses could disable a ship by tearing the plates open to let in the sea. Accidents destroyed 21, and anti-aircraft (AA) fire shot down a further 14. Of the remaining 25 to 30 aircraft, only 6 to 8 were serviceable at any time. They redeployed in March 1941 to preserve them from further attrition.
With the increase in convoys from the USA and the frequency of Arctic convoys to Murmansk and Arkhangelsk, they began operations out of Trondheim-Vaernes, Norway, into the North Atlantic to assist the U-boats on convoy reconnaissance missions. That was the intention. Except, the U-boats were now targeting individual unarmed shipping off the East Coast of the USA and were not interested in coordinating their efforts with the Condors.
By 1941, the long-range Boeing B-24 Liberators of the USAAF 480th Anti-submarine Group were also on predatory missions after Condors. President Roosevelt provided them with his pledge to support “The safe arrival at their destination of all material furnished by the United States to nations whose security is essential to the defence of the United States” without officially declaring war. During the year, eight were downed by the Allies, with a further 24 missing in action or lost through accidents.

The following year, 1942, 18 were claimed by the allies, with another 34 lost by other causes, an increase partially attributed to losing nine of the 18 aircraft sent on the Stalingrad airlift: resupply missions and the subsequent withdrawal of troops from the area. With this attrition rate, it would be some time before production brought their numbers back to strength. And indeed, in sufficient numbers to resume operations out of Bordeaux. On the 25th of October, a detachment relocated to operate out of Lecce in Southern Italy. The second battle of El Alamein had begun two days earlier, and the Afrika

Korps, led by General Erwin Rommel, were desperate for fuel. They stayed for four months, flying this and other materials into the Western Desert, principally to Tunisia and Tripoli, Libya. It was not enough. Their support was part of a hopeless attempt to prevent Rommel's army from retreating and ultimately surrendering. By December 16th, his remaining 153 Panzers, starved of fuel, clattered to a halt, and were abandoned. Before their arrival back in France in the spring of 1943, engineers had incorporated technical improvements.

These included the low Ultra High Frequency (UHF) FuG 200 Hohentweil ASV sea search radar, significantly improving their detection of shipping and the Carl Zeiss Lotfernrohr 7D (abbreviated to Lotfe 7) bombsights. The latter technology had been stolen from the Carl L. Norden Corporation of the USA by a German Duquesne Spy Ring member. When discovered in 1941 by the FBI, US FBI Director J. Edgar Hoover considered this espionage network of 33 members 'the greatest spy roundup in US history.' Among the ring members was Herman W. Lang, a Norden employee since 1938 who had become an assembly inspector. An accomplice had already forwarded the design drawing carried inside a hollowed-out umbrella stick when the German Abwehr invited Lang to explain how it worked. On arrival, he divulged the remainder of the plans he had committed to memory. With this new information, they were able to reconstruct a similar bombsight.
They improved the product and made it much simpler to operate and maintain. It now consisted of only three knurled knobs. The bombardier turned them to adjust the bombsight until he fixed the target in the eyepiece. Then, it calculated ground speed using windspeed and adjusted for drift. On the final approach, the autopilot would be engaged, and the bombsight took control of the flightpath, though the bombardier could still make last-minute changes. The bomb(s) would then be automatically released. With greater accuracy, this enabled crews to release their bombload at a safer, medium altitude (up to 2,790 feet even when the bomb aimer altitude was non-synchronised). They also deployed an alternative method. These were Henschel Hs 293 self-propelled bombs. They could also be dropped from a safe distance and guided by radio control to the target. Except an electric razor could easily throw them off course as the HMSO Instructions booklet described: *The radio guidance of flying bombs may easily be confused by a small sparking station. A simple method is to set an electric razor in motion.* Only sometimes.

On the 14th of March 1943, convoy KMS 11 set sail from the Clyde bound for the port of Bone, Algeria, with 64 merchantmen and 20 escorts, including the Free French sloop *Savorgnan de Brazza*. Abeam the Portuguese coast on the 19th, crews noticed an aircraft shadowing them. They initially suspected, by the noise of its four engines, it was a Boeing B-17 Flying Fortress. Had it come to escort them? It was usual for a pair to be in the vicinity seeking out U-boats. But alone? They needed to find out its identity. The noise overhead had woken the commander of the sloop, Commandant André Jubelin. Arriving on deck, he takes up the story as related in his book *The Flying Sailor*.
"Emerging from cloud cover just sufficiently to take a bearing, a superb four-engine bomber was coming straight for us."
"Range 2,000 (m), 1,800 (m)," announced the telemeter operator.
"When facing the machine, it was impossible to make out its markings. We may easily have mistaken it for a Flying Fortress."
"Fire! 37 guns of all calibres spat flame. A sheet of red tracer converged on the aircraft. In less than ten seconds, an incandescent sphere appeared at the root of the right wing, expanded, burst, caught fire, and the machine dived out of control. At an altitude of 150 feet, a man sprang out. Before his parachute could open, he crashed into the water; simultaneously, the huge plane followed in a vast fountain of spray. A tremendous cheer broke out aboard. Except on the bridge."
Until they recovered a body from the wreckage, some sailors were convinced they had shot down a Flying Fortress. Rather than an allied airman as expected, they quickly identify him as one of the five Luftwaffe crew members, the Condor's co-pilot.
Today, a reconstructed example of an FW 200 is on display in the Deutsches Technikmuseum at the former Berlin Tempelhof Airport.
In a fitting end to Sullom Voe operations, a Catalina crew depth-charged and severely damaged the U-320 off Bergen on the 9th of May 1945. Unable to effect repairs, the vessel sank two days later. It was the last attack of the war on a German submarine.

*

We arrived at Scatsta with the pipes under the runways still in situ. They finally removed them in 1996. In due course, the Shell passengers landed. In the absence of any managers on-site, it was a tradition the pilot with the longest service took command of operations. Today, there was also an absence of operations staff, passenger, baggage and freight handlers,

engineers, ramp staff and all the other ingredients ensuring an operation runs smoothly. And I was the senior pilot entrusted to organise three rotations with eight S-61Ns and their crews. First, feeding the pilots was the most important consideration. A crew were dispatched to the Busta House Hotel (famous during World War II for its involvement in those operating the 'Shetland Bus', a fleet of Norwegian trawlers ferrying agents into and out of Norway) to buy bacon rolls – as many as possible. Other crews organised passengers, baggage, freight, immersion suits, fuel, and the ramp. We allocate the passengers to aircraft with one rather than two or three destinations to simplify the process. Scheduled aircraft, such as British Airways, diverting from Sumburgh for the same reason and had no return passengers were requested to take passengers to their next stop on the mainland to clear the limited seating area in the terminal. This arrangement suited many passengers routing to Glasgow, a popular destination; unlike Aberdeen, their intermediate stop on the provision, they did not lose the schedule.
We had to complete the processing and boarding in 15 minutes; it was not a problem with people going home. Working telepathically as usual and with a fuel supply trucking in for the day, we completed three rotations, landing back in Sumburgh in the evening just as the fog had cleared with an invoice for an ample supply of bacon rolls to be settled by the management. Maybe Shell took note of this day? The next time Scatsta became this busy was when Bristow relinquished their base at Unst and set up operations here in 1998 with their new contract for Shell.

Fig 39. 1st 10,000 hours on the S-61N. *Author's collection.*

By mid-1992, with the first 10,000 hours on the S-61N tucked away, I was unaware Sikorsky recognised these things until five years later when I received a framed notification etched on aluminium.

In the late summer of 1992, we realised the BIH and other pension funds he had stolen amounted to more than US$1.6 billion. The BIH pension fund invested in the Mirror Group fund alone lost £460 million. Maxwell had used these pension funds to shore up his business empire – and lost the lot. He transferred some funds from pensions to two investment banks, Goldman Sachs and Shearson Leman, as collateral. They and the British Government (public funds set aside) restored just half the value of the pensions stolen. Given some members had over £500,000 invested, worth over £1 million today (2022), they would have received just £250,000. How could this happen to a pension fund? During its first term in office in 1980, Margaret Thatcher's Government approved Euro Directive 80/987. This directive centred on the Francovich v Italy case. The European Court had determined pension funds are, in effect, salary deferred and ring-fenced for the employees. The directive was never adopted. And this encouraged companies to continue plundering their employees' funds. Following the Mirror Group pension collapse, there was retrospective pressure to implement the directive; 80% solvency was the best you could expect. That was on a good day. Except for Aberdeen, there was a recession in 1991 throughout the United Kingdom. Corporations put pressure on the government to defer the implementation of the legislation. They needed their employee pension funds to support the share price. And so, it goes on – with no further attempt to enact the directive as was pledged over 40 years ago. The corporations and the City had a vested interest. Not least the shareholders, but to protect the crazy bonuses handed out to those folk in the City. True to a verse from the nursery rhyme ending: 'That's the way the money goes / pop goes the weasel!'

Chapter 17. 1992 - 1994

HLO Down – Buyout – Triggered Lightning - Wreck of MV Braer

Unless deck crews follow guidelines to ensure their safety, operating helidecks invariably exposes them to danger. Yet during the year, two helideck crew members lost their lives in separate accidents involving helicopter blades. The first was during a rotor running turnaround on the bow helideck of the DSV *Mayo*, a diving support and supply vessel. On the 4th of April 1992, she was operating near *Heather 'A'*. Now, the safest place inside the disc of an S-76 when moving around was within touching distance of the nose. And to only approach the aircraft from the abeam. After escorting a passenger to the port sliding door, the HLO was on the return through the safe zone already described. A witness said the vessel was rolling and pitching like a corkscrew. A passenger onboard noted: "Quite a large wave hit the boat, and it rocked to the port side, and, when the boat went to an angle, the chopper moved with it. It jumped the ropes (of the helideck net), sliding backwards when there was a thud. He had his back to us, and when the blades hit, he spun around and just fell" - deck motion is attributed to the cause of the accident. Then, on the 22nd of September, a helideck crewmember was fatally struck by the main rotor blade of an SA 365N Dauphin. It was in the Southern North Sea on the Viking 'B' gas rig this time.

*

The administrators wanted a buyer for BIH. All year, the other operators on the airfield, Bristow and Bond Helicopters, attempted to purchase it. The management looked elsewhere to support a management buyout. They presented a solid case to the monopolies and mergers commission to block the sale to these predators. That did not stop KLM/ERA, Evergreen International and Lloyd Helicopters of Australia from having a look.
On the 1st of December 1992, just under a year into administration, we were informed a consortium buyout of the company had succeeded in fending off the competition. Then, on the 27th of January, the company finally came out of administration. The new company was now 80% owned by the CHC, with the remainder in the hands of the management and a venture capital team comprised mainly of staff members. Stewart Birt was nominated managing

director, and CHC was on the way to acquiring another top-drawer helicopter company.

*

Lightning strikes are relatively common on the North Sea. Where the charge exits, it usually causes 'pin prick' damage near the tips of rotor blades. They are difficult to detect and require tapping on all the sections and pockets of each blade every evening with a coin or similar to register an unusual return that may identify a strike. We now know of a lightning variant, helicopter-triggered lightning. It poses a risk five times higher to helicopters operating in the North Sea than assumed during their certification process, as was found out by the crew of a Tiger in 1995, described in the next chapter.
There is little warning of this kind of strike as triggered lightning in the area is seldom seen until you've activated it. By then, it is too late. The most likely reason for this is triggered lightning strikes occur early in the development of a storm without any previous discharges in the cloud system and before a well-defined cumuliform cloud develops.

*

Over the North Sea, this lightning phenomenon is most prevalent during the last two weeks of February. Though, it can happen during any of the winter months, October through to April, and centred mainly around latitude 60° north. Paradoxically, this is when the incidence of thunderstorms and natural lightning activity is at its lowest. It indicates helicopters have no small part to play in flying through or near clouds, triggering strikes by their presence in the cloud's electrical field.
Though strikes of this kind do not often occur, on average two a winter, it was sufficient for the Met Office to develop algorithms over the past 20 years to predict their likelihood and assist operators and crews in considering alternative routing. Particularly when a low-pressure 'bomb' bringing dry, cold weather from the polar latitudes rapidly arrives over the North Sea's relatively warmer waters at the tail end of the Gulf Stream. Ideally, when the new sea/air temperature differential is above 6°C.

This confluence of conditions creates the ideal potential for atmospheric instability: an electrically charged positive air mass only needs a different precursor to ignite it. And since the positive polarity of lightning strikes during winter is much stronger, the severity of damage is much greater. And guess what? The rotational velocity of helicopter rotor blades generates an equally powerful negative charge due to their frictional contact with the air. Static wicks do not shed this charge to the extent they will continuously dissipate it. Unlike fixed-wing aircraft, it stays with a helicopter while the rotors turn until it has landed. So long as this combination of positive and negative charges is strong enough, then there is an excellent chance, when they collide, of the helicopter triggering lightning.

Helicopters spend much of the time cruising within the 1,000 to 3,000-foot band during winter to keep clear of icing conditions. Coincidentally, this is when the arrival of cold air outbreaks is most common. They bring atmospheric conditions, providing the ideal environment for the aircraft to trigger lightning. Not all the following general parameters must apply for a successful strike, though outside air temperature near the freezing level (0 ± 2°C) is a good start. They may also include frozen precipitation in the form of snow, snow grains, hail, or ice crystals, in clouds or immediately below them and within five miles of a cumulonimbus cloud. The general rule is to give the latter a ten-mile berth.

*

On the 18th of February 1993, we had a hit. We are heading to the semi-sub rig *Sedco 700*, anchored next to the *Dunlin 'A'* platform 120 miles from Sumburgh in the ESB. It became a series of sagas, illustrating a triggered event quite well. They began at around ten past five in the evening on the third rotation, about 15 nautical miles short of latitude 61°N on track 'Lima' at 3,000 feet. We had 40 nautical miles to go, ETA *Sedco 700* in twenty minutes at 17:30. The radar onboard, our S-61N G-BDKI, was set at a range scale of 50 miles with no weather returns.

As we cruised between thin layers of stratus, the air seemed stable with no turbulence. We had reasonable visibility and were not picking up ice, though the landing lights reflected minute crystals as we beat through their tracer. In hindsight, we should have checked the radar at 150 miles from time to time – but then, who knows what fast-moving weather system is coming to zap you when everything is sublime for 50 miles around. At the time, the co-pilot, Steve Martin, was the handling pilot. He was dividing the scan of his instruments with segments of sky through the port cockpit window for traffic: helicopters leaving the East Shetland Basin routing back to Aberdeen or other aircraft coming out of Unst to the rigs that could conflict. So good was his concentration that, amazingly, he did not witness what happened next.

Virtually out of the blue, a silent, bright orange lightning ball with ragged white edges, about 40cm in diameter, burst into the cockpit through the centre windscreen window. It momentarily obscured my view of Steve as it passed between us and into the cabin. We had triggered an impressive lightning strike. Besides the cockpit BIM warning indicating we had lost pressure in at least one of our main rotor blade spars, we did not realise it had also damaged all five tail rotor blades. Then, a passenger came forward to report what they had seen. And to relay the other bad news.

They had seen it streak down the aisle and strike the passenger seated in row 11. Now, row 11 was the last seat in the cabin, against the aft bulkhead and in line with the centre cockpit window. During the BAH days, this row accommodated a 'ship's head' with a curtain to screen it. Occupied, it could have been worse; the aircraft continued flying without anything else untoward. After all, it was an S-61N, a most resilient aircraft to fly through any weather. It's no idle jest; the definition of an airworthy helicopter is over 10,000 parts flying in formation. Despite having, in our case, ten, as we later found out, of those components damaged – they were holding up – for now, and with luck, it will probably be all right. For us, the nearest place to land, and large enough to accommodate a CASEVAC (Casualty Evacuation) aircraft, was coincidently our destination.

On arrival and shut down, and after we had towed the aircraft into the run-off area amongst shipping containers using a rig crane, we were soon joined by a Bristow Bell 212. This aircraft was one of five based offshore on the semi-sub *Safe Gothia* in the Brent field. It had broken its evening shuttle routine to assist. With the passenger evacuating to the hospital in Lerwick, tip socks fitted to tie down the main blades and a 'spider' to clamp the tail rotor, we settled down for the night. Though only for a short time.

A fresh 80-knot wind had sprung up from the northwest, conveying cold weather. The parked aircraft was in danger. Neighbouring shipping containers were liable to slide into it and the helicopter into them. The composite rubber wheel chocks were not holding. The solution was to weld steel chocks in the form of short sections of RSJs (Rigid Steel Joists) to the deck, and ratchet strops clipped onto the undercarriage tie-down rings are fastened to 'D' shackles welded to the deck. The welder places more RSJ sections around the containers to arrest their movement.
A BIH S-61N arrived the following morning with a fresh set of tail rotor blades and two main blades. They did not have a replacement for the other three

damaged blades in the stores. Though there were the usual exit holes where the charge had passed through, the BIM checks on these indicated their spars were sound. But when the leading spar is affected, it can be dire. The spars are pumped full of nitrogen. Tell-tale rings in the clear-sided pods attached to the root of each blade indicate when the pressure falls below ten psi - the BIMs (Blade Inspection Method). These pods contain either a white/black or yellow/red combination. When the red or black rings become visible, their transducer triggers a warning light in the cockpit, indicating the blade is unsafe.

*

Some lightning strikes can be harder to detect. As described later, a catastrophic lightning strike on Bristow S-76A+, G-BJVX would be revealed in July 2002. Had I known the consequence of strikes on the blade, other than the pockets not part of the BIM system, I may have reconsidered returning the aircraft to the beach. It was just part of the culture: not knowing the unknown and living in the wings of enlightenment. And now the experience of triggering lightning. Except in those days, we did not call it that, just another lightning strike.
Back onboard the *Sedco 700*. The blades fitted; the rig ballasted with seawater to form a downward slope towards the helideck; we pushed the aircraft back onto the net. The uneventful flight empty to Sumburgh to have the remaining blades replaced was an anti-climax. This incident probably marked the first time a passenger was injured aboard a North Sea Helicopter - by lightning. And still on the subject of blades.

*

On another occasion, we realised one of the blades was breaking up. Though not what was causing it. Each time this advancing blade passed by my window, it tugged at the cyclic. It sounded like a steam locomotive starting to move out – a rapid ***Chufff*** every rotation at 203 rpm, ***Chufff***. Noisy! We mused the Bristow S-61N 'HN' had experienced similar symptoms when Lee decided to ditch. It was bad, but not *that* bad. Besides, the aircraft was still manageable. Instead, we called up a rig not far off our route, asked permission to land and shut down to find out what was causing this noise.
It was where the lower panels of the blade pockets bond to the trailing edge of the main spar. Two pockets towards the tip of one main rotor blade had ripped open. They were sagging and dragging, un-aerodynamically below

the aerofoil. We had an engineer fly in and make room for his lift, an S-76A+. Now aware the blade had only re-configured itself and was unlikely to have caused any damage to the rotor blade pitch links, we started up. Lifting into a hover, we manoeuvred ungainly to the edge of the deck to shut down. More noise! On arrival, he checked out the main rotor hub and cut off the drooping half of the pockets. He wrapped up the void using blade tape. We started up again, and everything was fine. I raised the collective to pull power to take off. And guess what? The tape merely ripped off. The flight home for some 140 miles without the passengers was much easier to control and, oh, so much quieter. We didn't use tape again.

*

New Year's Eve 1993. It was a packed bar in the Sumburgh Club. Behind it, Moira and her husband Fred had been pulling pints for hours, and their son Phil, who was on leave, had, with a shy smile, given me an insight into his job: "Had the bridge windows trashed again this week." He was an oilfield supply workboat skipper, and this was the third time a rogue wave in heavy seas had swamped his vessel. It came crashing into the wheelhouse, knocking the watch down and leaving them battered and drenched. From then on, whenever the boat crested a wave and slammed down, shuddering like a wet dog shaking, they'd duck as the heavy spray headed their way. They remained soaked and chilled to the bone for the rest of the trip and whenever on duty; not even their oilskins could alleviate their predicament.
Moira had called last orders, and Hogmanay's first footers were setting off with a bottle of whiskey poking out of one pocket, a lump of peat bulging from the other; across the North Sea, the most significant environmental disaster in Scotland's history was in the making. And it was on its way, possibly arriving within a few hundred yards of the club.

*

The MV *Braer* was a single-skinned-hull tanker 241.51 metres long and weighing 44,989 gross tons. A 9-cylinder Sulzer 20,300 hp engine powered her. The Sulzer operates on high viscosity, heavy fuel oil at sea or lighter and much more expensive diesel for manoeuvring in confined areas. It was crucial to heat the heavy fuel oil to reduce its viscosity. The procedure was to extract heat from the main engine exhaust economiser, backed up with steam from a diesel-fired auxiliary boiler.

The saga began after a voyage in ballast from New York when the vessel docked at Statoil's Mongstad Jetty 1 in Norway. Just before midnight on New Year's Eve, they started to pump out the ballast water in her tanks in preparation for loading 84,500 tonnes of Gullfaks crude oil. Destination: Ultramar's St Romouauld refinery in Québec, Canada. Minutes into the new year, the steam-driven pump broke down. The main steam pipe between the boilers and the manifold had burst. Rather than fitting a new pipe, they weld the old one together. It took time, and it was 19 hours before loading could begin. Other vessels backed up waiting to access the jetty; agents put sailing schedules back, and the jetty operator wanted the *Braer* away - but the steam plant, also used to heat the heavy oil for the voyage, was rotten - saltwater corrosion.

Though they depended on using light diesel for navigating inshore waters and mooring, there was insufficient for an ocean crossing. Ideally, it would be necessary to replace the plant before leaving. That would not be possible. The weather was too rough to tow the vessel to a safe mooring, and the fjord was too deep to drop anchor. Under these conditions, the ship cast off on the 3rd of January at 23:40 local into a severe Southerly gale. The barometer was reading 1031mbs. Initially making only three knots, they slowly headed out across the North Sea on a course to enter the Atlantic via the Northerly Fair Isle Strait, heading 243° true. By midnight, the barometer was reading 1018mbs and falling, a drop of 13mbs since leaving the jetty.

At ten o'clock the following morning, with the *Braer* heaving and listing in the seas breaking against her port beam, the Chief Officer and Chief Engineer thought it prudent to check on their deck cargo, four spare steel pipes welded to the aft port deck. They consisted of 250 mm and 450 mm diameter sections about 5 meters long. To put it mildly, what they saw on the aft deck below them was unsettling.
The pipes were no longer neatly secured together. They had broken free. Battering rams, they took off across the deck each time the ship rolled. The men agreed now was not the time to go out on the deck to secure them. It was just too dangerous. The tanker was rolling 22° on either side of the datum, just short of the pitch on a bungalow roof (22.5°). Incoming waves engulfed the deck with seawater 20 feet deep whenever the ship listed to port. It was not long before a 450 mm pipe crashed into one of the aft air pipes venting the port diesel tank. These vents, extending 600 mm above the deck, have a float seal design head 160 mm high. It was significantly damaged. From their vantage point, it wasn't easy to assess by how much.

Sometime later, a 250 mm pipe made its way onto the starboard deck. It was a matter of time before it collided with the aft diesel tank vent on that side, too. For now, it rolled clear.

The engineering watch that evening made routine adjustments to the auxiliary boiler that heated the heavy oil. With the adjustments made, they then tried to light the boiler - nothing. They then noticed seawater was mixing with its diesel supply. All attempts to drain it proved hopeless. The vessel's movement was now causing the mixture to emulsify. And now, the heat from the engine alone was becoming insufficient to preheat the heavy oil. It would have been sufficient in tropical climates to reduce the oil's viscosity but quite inadequate in January in the North Sea. They needed to fire up the auxiliary boiler.

Three hours later, they considered reverting to diesel to power the engine, a temporary solution until they could light the auxiliary boiler. They then discovered seawater contaminating the direct diesel oil supply to the main engine and generator. The vessel's movement frustrated their efforts to drain the seawater from this supply. To continue en route was no longer an option. Turning to port, they set course for sheltered water in the Moray Firth 100 miles to the south, where they could anchor and sort things out. Four minutes later, the engine and generator failed. It was 04:40 in the morning on the 5th of January. They were adrift, wallowing in pounding seas with only battery power. Now just ten miles south of Shetland, the current and winds slowly carried them in the dark at two knots towards Sumburgh Head.

It was not a good time to lose power in a vessel now known as unfit to sail. Into a force 10 to 11 South-Westerly gale and 30-foot seas, the tanker had not only to contend with the prevailing weather; another even more significant storm was on its way. And the current was edging her ever closer to the mainland; landfall predicted on the beach of the West Voe below the Sumburgh Club.

At 05:15, the Master advises the Coastguard his vessel has broken down – he does not require assistance. Eleven minutes later, the Coastguard asks for his intentions. He requests a tug despite not receiving permission for a tow from the ship manager at his home in Stamford, USA. Vital minutes are lost as the request goes unheeded. He makes a second call to the USA.

He turns down an offer of a helicopter. The Coastguard alerted Rescue 117 anyway, the Bristow SAR S-61N based at Sumburgh, just five minutes away. The Coastguard then advised Lerwick Port Control (LPC) they may require the assistance of a tug as soon as they receive clearance from the owners

in the USA. By now, the Lerwick Harbour Master has determined the weather conditions were too bad to send the Lerwick tug *Kebister* to sea. The Lerwick lifeboat crew prepared their boat for service.
At the Rescue Co-ordination Centre (RCC) in Edinburgh, a request is made for the RAF to scramble a Sea King from Lossiemouth, Rescue 137. At this point, the fishing vessel, *Treasure*, reports radar contact with a ship "Dead in the water six miles from Sumburgh Head." Though five hours sailing away, the RCC notify the two Shetland Towage tugs, *Swaabie* and *Tirrick*, at Sullom Voe to make themselves available. Another 43 minutes after the first call to the Braer's owners, they finally authorised the Coastguard to arrange a tug. Fortunately, an oilfield anchor handling tug/supply vessel could be made available in the harbour, the *Star Sirius*. At 06:40, Rescue 117 positions overhead, where they found the *Braer* rolling heavily in heavy seas and winds gusting 65 knots. She is joined 45 minutes later by Rescue 137, having raced to the scene on the back of a strong tailwind. Clearance then arrives for the *Star Sirius* to be prepared for sea. She makes way for Sumburgh Head at 07:05. As soon as she enters the roads inshore Bressay, she faces the enormous seas. Her bridge is engulfed in a wall of water each time her bow plunges under the waves. It will be a rough ride, taking her at least two and a half hours to reach the stricken vessel.

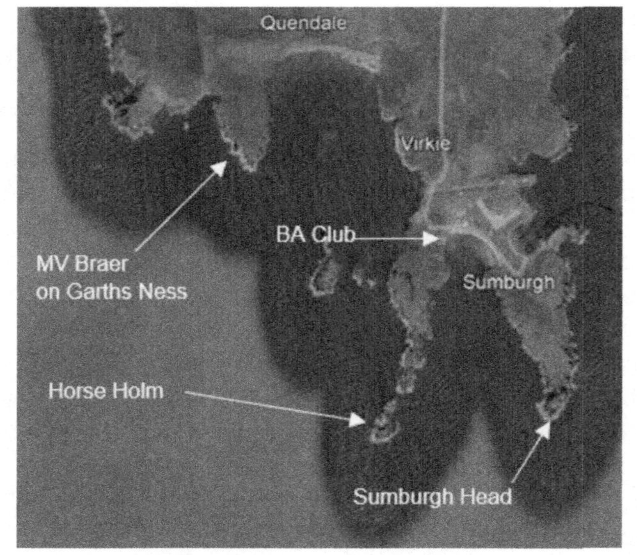

Fig 40. Significant landmarks South Shetland Mainland.
Credit: Google Maps.

Following a distress message, the captain suggests taking non-essential crew members ashore. The *Philorth*, a fishing vessel in the vicinity, picks up the message. Closing in, the crew noticed the two red masthead lights, one mounted above the other – the light signals the vessel is no longer under the command and is underway. *Braer* asks her to stand by if a man is lost overboard should they attempt to release the anchors to steady the wayward drift of the tanker. Of the 34 crew, 16 are winched up in the dark by Rescue 117 from an area near the starboard stern. (It is too dangerous for the crew to make their way forward to the usual helicopter landing area on the foredeck. It is frequently underwater). By 08:07, all were onboard, having scrambled through the cargo door entrance. The helicopter drops them off at Sumburgh.

On a previous occasion, another oil tanker, the *Aegean Sea*, had burst into flames shortly after grounding on rocks. This experience led the Coastguard to convince the captain to abandon the ship. Twenty minutes after they rescued the first batch of survivors, Rescue 137 moved in and began recovering the remaining 18. The *Braer* was just half a mile southeast of Horse Holm. At 08:50, she entered the southwest entrance of the West Voe, and four minutes later, Rescue 137 had completed its lift. The lifeboat stands down. Then, the unexpected happened. Instead of continuing as predicted toward the beach, the current emptying the water out of Voe took over. It slowly spun the vessel in a clockwise orbit before carrying her back into the churning tide race, travelling past Sumburgh Head.
It was just becoming daylight. In the half-light and poor visibility, it was unclear from onshore if the tanker would ground on Horse Holm. It would have created an additional environmental hazard if she had. The remains of two groups of buildings constructed by Neolithic settlers 5,000 years ago were close by: the Jarlshof at the eastern end of the Voe and the Ness of Burgi at the southeastern tip of the mainland. They would have been exposed.
She was now in the grip of the southeast current. Because of her low freeboard, the stream is sufficient to move her against the prevailing wind. She skirts around the Holm – only just. This island (holm) is Shetland's most Southerly point between the West Voe and Quendale Bay, another beautiful beach around the corner. Despite West Voe's reprieve, it did not look good for Quendale. With sheer luck, the stricken vessel slowly cleared this bay as well. Though, in the days ahead, this luck changed.

Fig 41. Rescue 117 and *MV Braer.*
Complements of UK SAR & Artist Mo Jones

Then, the *Star Sirius* arrived on the scene. They decided to establish a tow. Back at the airfield, Rescue 117 boarded a team comprising the Master, the Chief Officer, the Bosun and the Superintendent of the *Braer*, along with the Port Safety Manager (PSM) of Shetland Islands Council and a Marine Pilot. On arrival over the tanker, the winch operator lowered the winchman first, followed by the PSM and Superintendent. Rescue 117 stood off as the *Star Sirius* fired a rocket line to them, missed the stern and fell into the sea. Rescue 117 lowered the Chief Officer to the deck and stood off again. The *Star Sirius* fired a second rocket line. The hulk is now so close to the mainland the inevitable happened. The current swung her around the western end of the bay. A few minutes later, the vessel broached and, with a final heave of the sea, grounded on the rocks below the cliffs at Garths Ness.

It was 19 minutes past 11 a.m. The deck party were winched to safety by Rescue 117. The painting reproduced here courtesy of the former Bristow pilot and artist Mo Jones depicts this action. She produced prints sold in aid of the rescue centre set up to deal with the sea birds affected by the oil, and by chance, the time of year coincided with many species of sea birds spending the winter in rafts offshore, far from the coastline. The original resides at the UK SAR HQ, Aberdeen, where it hangs in the Billy Deacon room, a conference room named after the heroic winchman who died in the *Green Lily* disaster on the 19th of November 1997. RIP Billy.

*

We all expected a catastrophe. At first, it appeared significantly worse than the *Torrey Canyon* or *Exxon Valdez*, for *Braer* had twice as much crude oil onboard. Unlike the *Braer*, these vessels were shipping heavy crude; North Sea crude was light, and Gullfaks was even lighter. For this reason, the North Sea, called 'Brent Crude', commands a higher price than most heavy crude oil quoted as West Texas Intermediate (WTI).

Fig 42. Sumburgh, the 7th of January 1993. DC-6 and DC-3s are on standby—photo *credit: ©atchistory (UK).*

Some 1,000 sea birds succumbed to the oil, and the authorities imposed a fisheries exclusion zone until April; there was no significant oil slick beyond Scalloway on the west coast and the Island of Mousa on the east. The wind blew much of it inland, coating the local area and properties in a film of oil. In contrast, the land benefited from an unexpected dose of fertiliser. Nevertheless, they prepared to disperse the oil. By the 7th, six Douglas DC-3 spray-equipped aircraft and a DC-6 with supplies from Coventry and Aberdeen had arrived to wait out the storm for a suitable time to go to work. On the same day, the marine salvage personnel requested a helicopter take them up to take photographs. Fine, it was me! Except, they wanted to take pictures from the cargo door to give them shots of the bow in the foreground. The vessel was lying with the bow facing west. This required positioning with a 60-knot tailwind. Slow enough to take pictures, fast enough not to aerodynamically stall and enter a vortex ring state (VRS), an undesirable aerodynamic condition, resulting in a significant loss of height before restoring airspeed to exit this condition. And we needed the height.

*

Many years later, I was to learn a Swiss Helicopter Pilot Examiner had resolved this problem of height loss. His name: Paul Vuichard. He put a crop sprayer into a vortex ring state and observed how the spray vortices behaved when he applied his Vuichard recovery technique (VRT). This manoeuvre involved keeping the aircraft straight with the rudder pedals while applying collective pitch and inclining the cyclic 10° to 20° laterally into the direction of the advancing blade. This procedure disturbed the vortex ring to such an extent you could achieve recovery with a loss of only 20 feet.

If only I'd known that. Many takes later, and they called it a day. The waves pounding in against the hull generated so much spray it obscured their view of the wreck. At the time of writing, the European Aviation Safety Agency (EASA) has not approved VRT as a suitable technique.

Three days later, the forecasted storm arrived. Even if seaworthy, the tanker would have sailed into the most intense extratropical cyclone ever recorded in the North Atlantic. It was also quoted as the worst January storm in a century and, for a good reason, was subsequently named the Braer Storm when it passed over South Shetland on the 10th of January 1994. It lasted 12 days and ensured the total destruction of the crippled tanker.

Two years later, the folk-rock band Fairport Convention released their album 'Jewel in the Crown'. It included the track 'The Islands' by Ralph McTell and Maartin Allcock. The song commemorates the wreck of *Braer*, personifying the sea as the protector of Shetland Islands.

Chapter 18. 1995 - 1997

Two Notable Incidents – Turbulence Offshore

Fig 43. BIH (with the Mirror Group 'Lion' logo) S-61Ns offshore

Photo Credit. Captain Archie D'Mello

In 1995, the CAA published a 'Report of the Review of Helicopter Offshore Safety and Survival' for the period 1976 and 1992. In it, Dr Anton of the Aviation Study Group provided a breakdown of the warning time for an impending crash or ditching. Of the 15 survivable accidents in his analysis, "In five cases there were more than five-minutes warning, in three cases one to five minutes and in seven cases there was less than one minute. It clearly had a bearing on the preparatory actions the crew and the passengers can perform between the first indication of trouble and the moment of impact." It was sobering to know 47% had less than one minute. The following two incidents illustrate this theme.

The helicopter, G-TIGK, was operating under charter to Marathon, flying 16 maintenance engineers from Aberdeen to the *Brae 'A'* oil production platform. Before landing at *Brae 'A'*, the flight was to land at the *East Brae* platform to uplift two more engineers.

Ced Roberts was the commander of the Tiger. He had joined Bristows in July 1974 on a fixed-wing conversion course to helicopters at Redhill after being laid off by British European Airways (BEA). His conversion course preceded mine by two months. With his co-pilot, Senior First Officer Lionel Sole, they had completed a return flight in G-TIGK to the Forties oilfield before taking Flight 56C. The helicopter remained

serviceable, and the Technical Log recorded no 'Carried Forward Defects'.
The forecast weather for the flight to Brae Field on the 19th of January 1995 was: Scattered or broken cloud between 2,000 and 6,000 feet above mean sea level, with isolated towering cumulus or cumulus-nimbus, giving occasional showers of rain, hail, sleet or snow, and some isolated thunderstorms.

*

G-TIGK, callsign 'Bristow 56C', was scheduled to depart at 11:30 and, following a slight administrative delay, took off at 11:38 with Lionel as the handling pilot. Leaving the Aberdeen VOR on the 062° radial, they climbed to and levelled at Flight Level 70, where they thought they might be out of icing conditions. They could see several clouds building up around and on their planned route. Although there were comments on the cockpit voice recorder about the cumulus clouds, they later stated they did not see anything particularly significant on the radar. Nevertheless, they decided to descend to warmer air at 3,000. However, the cockpit voice recorder did record one comment concerning the large size of a cloud build-up to the north of the Brae oilfield and another about an accumulation of soft ice pellets on the ice detector.

The flight continued along the planned route, leaving Aberdeen Radar coverage at a range of 80 nautical miles at 12:17 when the Ced changed frequency to the Aberdeen Flight Information Service. Whilst remaining in radio contact with Aberdeen, Ced then established initial contact, on their second radio, with Brae Traffic Watch ('Brae'). At 12:33, Ced informed Aberdeen they were at the reporting point 'Gate in,' 120 nautical miles on the 062°M radial from the Aberdeen VOR and two-way with 'Brae'. At about 12:36, whilst initiating the normal let down to the *East Brae* platform, and as they passed through a patch of cloud at about 3,000 feet, they experienced a 'bang' accompanied by a 'flash'. The helicopter began to vibrate severely.

Lionel briefed the passengers and continued to do so as the flight progressed; some of these messages were heard over the radio. Some passengers heard a bang, others just heard a noise, and a few said they saw a flash but did not know whether it was inside or outside the fuselage. One passenger reported a "Sort of pulsing vibration in the air." All felt the

physical vibration but thought the helicopter was under control. None, however, heard any passenger address announcements.
Assuming an imminent need to ditch, Lionel initiated an autorotative descent and transmitted a MAYDAY call on the 'Brae' frequency, stating they had a lightning strike, had severe vibration, and we were going to ditch. As the helicopter descended through 1,500 feet, both pilots realised although the helicopter was still vibrating severely, it was responding normally to the controls. Therefore, they decided to level off and try to reach the *Brae 'A'* platform, the nearest diversion. Ced informed 'Brae' of this decision and began the approach checks by selecting the landing gear DOWN to complete the necessary checks expeditiously. The decision to land on *Brae 'A'* or to ditch beside it still needed to be made.
The crew of another company helicopter callsign 'Bristow 56B', loading passengers on the *Brae 'B'* platform, also heard the initial MAYDAY message. They unloaded their passengers and, by 12:39, had taken off to assist '56C' if necessary.

Meanwhile, Lionel was unsure whether the apparent directional stability of the helicopter was being maintained by the tail rotor or by the 'weathercock' effect of the airspeed, so he gently deflected the yaw pedals to see if there was a response. He had just commented to Ced that everything was in order when there was a 'crack' and the helicopter gave a violent lurch to the left, rolled right, and pitched down steeply. Realising a ditching was now imminent, Lionel transmitted another MAYDAY informing 'Brae' of his decision to ditch, and Ced carried out the TAIL ROTOR DRIVE FAILURE checks, including shutting down the engines to contain the yaw and then arming and inflating the floats. '56B' relayed their second MAYDAY message to Aberdeen Flight Information Service at 12:41 and set course towards the assumed position of '56C'.
The passengers of '56C' now realised ditching was inevitable. They prepared themselves for it in the manner detailed by the video briefing given to all passengers before boarding. The crew gave another public address announcement at this time, but although it was heard by 'Brae' on the radio, the passengers did not hear it. (The radio and PA are independent systems. It is not unusual for aircrew to select the wrong one, much to the amusement of other aviators and atcos listening out).

*

Lionel accomplished a gentle touchdown on the sea despite six to seven-metre waves and a 30-knot Southerly wind gusting 40 knots; the helicopter alighted with the wind in its one o'clock position. When Ced applied the rotor brake, the aircraft yawed the left-hand side into the wind; both pilots activated the emergency release of their doors. At about 12:42, Ced made a radio transmission to say they had alighted safely.

Fig 44. AS33L1 'Tiger' G-TIGK Flight No. Bristow '56C'.
Without tail rotor gearbox and blades. *Photo credit: AAIB.*

Leaving the Ced to complete the cockpit drills, Lionel went aft to help the passengers evacuate into the heli-rafts. Two of the passengers deployed the left heli-raft. It blew onto its side, with its floor against the side of the fuselage. The wind and the swell combination made it exceedingly difficult to use. On entering the cabin, Lionel decided all occupants should board the already deployed right (starboard) heli-raft to keep everyone together. All the passengers boarded it without any difficulty. Then, the crew joined them and awaited rescue. Soon after boarding, they discovered a buoyancy chamber had punctured below the boarding ramp. Despite this damage and overloading, the '14 man' heli-raft remained afloat. Once aboard the partly swamped life raft, many occupants suffered from seasickness in the crowded conditions and heavy swell.
At 12:43, '56B' relayed to Aberdeen the final message from '56C' and continued with its attempt to locate the ditched helicopter. At 13:00, they saw some surface smoke from one of the two flares set off by the crew

in the heli-raft and found them six minutes later. '56B' then remained in the hover by the heli-raft and assumed the duties of 'On Scene Commander', assisting with coordinating the other helicopters and guiding the surface vessels to the scene. The total assets alerted were: one Norwegian SA 365N Dauphin helicopter, one RAF Sea King and the Sumburgh Coastguard S-61 Rescue 117, all equipped with winches; three Tiger helicopters and one Dauphin, which were not winch equipped; two oil platform safety vessels and one RAF Nimrod aircraft.

*

At 13:35, two oil platform safety vessels, *Grampian Freedom* from the Brae/Miller oil field and *St Patrick* from the Tiffany oil field, were at a suitable range from the heli-raft to launch their FRCs, and, despite the high sea state, their coxswains were able to manoeuvre alongside the heli-raft. By 13:40, they had taken aboard all 18 survivors, some feeling extremely cold, and by 14:06, had transferred them to the *Grampian Freedom.* Of the 18 survivors, helicopters winched 15 onboard. They were transferred to the *Brae 'A'* platform before being flown back to Aberdeen that evening. Nonetheless, three passengers did not wish to be winched and remained aboard the *Grampian Freedom*. She sailed into Aberdeen the following morning.

By 13:55, the *Highland Pride*, another safety vessel, had arrived on the scene. Having recovered one of the heli-rafts, they attempt to salvage the helicopter. The crew brought it alongside at 16:09. While secured to the vessel, the helicopter's flotation bags punctured, and the helicopter sank later at 18:03 after being released. Three of the four main rotor blades had been cut off and lost before the helicopter sank, although they subsequently recovered one. The semi-submersible MSV *Stadive* located the aircraft on the seabed two days later, on the 21st of January. She retrieved the main wreckage and the tail rotor/tail rotor gearbox assembly two days later.

An inspection revealed one main rotor blade and one tail rotor blade had suffered high-energy lightning strike damage; however, the main rotor continued to operate satisfactorily.

Each rotor blade can be identified by a tape of a different colour around its root. The lightning strike sufficiently damaged the 'White' tail rotor blade to induce severe vibration. Cyclic overstressing of the gearbox attachments later caused the complete detachment of the tail rotor, associated gearbox, and pitch servo assembly within 3½ minutes of the

strike.
The detached mass of these components was fortuitously restrained from complete separation from the tail boom pylon by two of the four stainless steel hydraulic pipes connected to the pitch servo. The mass remained suspended alongside the right side of the pylon. In effect, the helicopter's longitudinal pitch control was retained until they ditched.

*

The lightning protection was certificated per Transport Supersonique (TSS) Standards (SST standards in the UK). This was an internationally agreed set of criteria originally for the supersonic transport (SST) aircraft certification proposed and under development between 1962 and 1975. Except for the nose radome, composite structural elements were not used in designing the only SST to enter service in the West (Concorde); the external structure was metallic.
The design of the carbon composite tail rotor blade on the AS332 Mark 1 was not subjected to lightning testing during the helicopter's certification. In 1981, it was considered merely a development of an earlier fibreglass blade fitted to the Sud Aviation SA 350 Ecureuil that had been satisfactorily certificated to the lightning test criteria of TSS8.6.
Advisory Circulars superseded the associated TSS8.6 standard document on the 6th of October 1967 and again on the 4th of December 1985. Frustratingly, manufacturers still used the last criteria to achieve lightning certification two years after the accident.
This circular was only advisory and, even then, only focused on preventing the ignition of fuel vapours by lightning. Nor was there a provision for the differences in behaviour between static structures and rapidly revolving rotor blades. Indeed, it does not mention helicopters anywhere in the text.

*

This accident demonstrated the potential for critical damage sustained by helicopters due to high-energy lightning strikes—particularly those equipped with carbon composite tail rotor blades.
Given Cedric and Lionel had done such an excellent job under trying circumstances, it focused the mind on tail rotor malfunctions. To have a yaw control malfunction followed by a tail rotor drive malfunction must be up there with the best emergency checklist procedures! Later in the year, the crew received the Offshore Safety Award.

Current certification required a much higher current to be applied to an individual test blade than at the time of the AS332 certification. In those days, they widely assumed two or more consecutive blades divided the energy between them.

*

On the 18th of August 1995, at 10:56 in the morning, an incident occurred some 95 miles east, northeast of Aberdeen. It highlighted the need for the CAA and the Health and Safety Executive (HSE) to reassess the environmental hazard to helicopters operating close to offshore installations. The CHC Occidental Petroleum S-61N flight in G-AYOM was working that day out of Aberdeen to destinations in the Piper/Claymore/Saltire oilfields. Fog offshore had delayed the flight, originally scheduled to route to the *Piper 'B'* platform, *Saltire 'A'* platform, and then to the *Claymore 'A'* accommodation platform (CAP). The latter was a new installation and had only been in operation for a few days. Despite this, Peter Boor, the commander of the S-61N, had already been there and was familiar with the layout. It was located west of the *Claymore 'A'* and connected to it by a 95-metre walkway. At 182 feet above the sea, the *CAP* helideck serves the Claymore installations; the *Claymore* 'A' deck was now designated for emergency use only. As the weather had further improved en route, the OXY controller redirected the crew to land on the *CAP* first. The crew descended through 400 feet and broke cloud with two miles to run. They were visual with the *CAP*, with an Easterly three to five-knot wind over the deck; this direction meant the landing arrived immediately downwind of the *Claymore 'A'* platform. *'Alpha'* has two flare booms mounted horizontally. They suspended 50 meters over the sea on the eastern quarter: the northern boom points to the east, the other to the south, and both critically below helideck height. And in the void between the *'Alpha'* and *CAP* helidecks were the production platform's two power turbine exhausts.
A combination of light airs with negligible mixing of the flare from the northern boom and the two turbine exhaust plumes produced a warmer local environment. Most insidiously, it was devoid of the usual elements required to burn Jet A1 fuel efficiently. There needed to be a mechanism to measure the effect of these elements in combination around the helideck, where the most critical flight path segments for landing and taking off take place. The helicopter was heading into the known unknown.
Peter has over 19,000 hours of experience and over 12,000 hours on the S-61Ns. There were 14 passengers onboard. With the little wind available in

the east and the helideck on the northern quarter of the *CAP*, he took control for the landing as it offered, on balance, the best overshoot to the northeast. He reduced the initial rate descent to 350ft/minute and 200ft/minute at two miles as they closed with the deck. With 40 seconds to run and the smell of the flare burning off sour gases entering the cabin, Peter requested the co-pilot to call out all (engine) torques above 60%.

Fig 45. *Claymore 'A'* Turbine exhausts.
Claymore CAP with helideck in the foreground.
Photo credit: ©Sembmarine SLP

They are now into the sight picture landing profile, where the approach angle remains constant relative to the helideck landing circle. With ten seconds to run, he flew the final part of the approach. He planned to arrive in a ten-foot hover before touching down. With no additional control inputs, the rate of descent suddenly shot up to 440 feet per minute. And with that awful sinking feeling, they plummeted towards the deck as the co-pilot called out, "80%! 90%!".

Crossing the deck edge, Peter smoothly pulled even more pitch. He hoped to combine it with the fast-approaching ground cushion effect to arrest the descent. He pulled all the remaining torque at one to three feet above the deck as the co-pilot called, "Over Torque!" Nothing happened. It was too late. With the final increased collective input, the main rotor speed drooped from the normal 102% to 97%. Initially, the landing was straight ahead. So far, so good.

Immediately after Peter lowered the collective, he heard a thud, and the aircraft slewed five degrees to the right. He had a split-second awareness the drive train was damaged, followed immediately by a call on the radio from the HLO. "The tail rotor drive shaft is out!" They shut down the engines and, five seconds later, apply the rotor brake. There were no signs of fire, and the passengers disembarked normally. This aircraft was going nowhere for some time. By now, the crew were also out on the helideck. Here, they could see the main rotor blades had severed the fourth section of the drive shaft from the main gearbox to the intermediate gearbox at the base of the tail pylon. Each blade had a crease where they had struck; the broken, flailing ends of the drive shaft had entered the airframe. Both engines had effectively stalled on finals, and a heavy landing ensued. It was attributed to the helicopter engines ingesting the turbine exhaust plume emitted from the adjoining *Claymore 'A'* production platform.

*

Despite routine helideck surveys being terminated by the CAA five months earlier, they had surveyed the *CAP* at the manufacturer's request. Except the survey had taken place on a barge at Lowestoft, Suffolk, where it was under construction. Not at its final location less than 100 meters from the *Claymore 'A'*. It now became apparent all future surveys had to consider the relationship between platform locations and the siting of the flare and turbine exhaust infrastructure. When you think you have done everything right and the profile and power settings are as nearly perfect as possible, those 'sinking feelings' are not uncommon. How common is further explored when it came to a head two years later.

*

1995. 'The day you think you know everything is the same day you stop learning'. Now, to become triple rated and licenced to fly three different types of helicopters stands one in good stead for future employment. With over 14,000 hours in 21 years on the S-61N, it had been an excellent aircraft to fly and probably the best of all violent weather helicopters ever built; we had looked after each other. And time again, it was reported as too old and was to be replaced. Yet, as I write, many built during the sixties and seventies are still flying for operators worldwide today.
In contrast, the Super Puma (otherwise known in Bristows as the 'Tiger') did not compete. Cheaper and marginally faster, with a slightly lower fuel burn

and better single-engine performance, everything else was in a far lower league. It was developed from the AS332B Puma. The French military specification required squeezing it inside a twin-engine Transall C-160 cargo aircraft, the French and German solution to the Lockheed C-130 Hercules. It was cramped for crews and passengers alike. Another drawback was the main undercarriage. To fit the Puma into the Transall, it had to be narrow. So narrow that when under tow on a windy day, it was pretty unstable; unless both port and starboard sliding doors were open. This void allowed the wind to pass through and prevent it from being blown over.
For the same reason, you could only park it into the wind. A handicap that did not endear it offshore when landing on moving decks and in an environment where the wind in a squall can change direction 180° during a ten-minute turnaround. Then, there were the fragile cockpit doors. They had to be held open on windy days for the pilot to enter and exit the cockpit. Otherwise, they broke off. One even came off in flight and snagged itself onto the co-pilot's collective lever. Did I leave out the cabin doors? They came off the rails if you were too hasty sliding them open. It was so good that Big Al ordered 35 Tigers with a 10% discount on spare parts. Tigers came with a sting in the tail. Replacement parts were a rip-off. You could find their windscreen wipers off a Ford truck in any auto factor. Instead, Aérospatiale charged up to ten times as much. Small bulbs illuminated the cockpit instruments and equipment. They are sealed inside the device, and changing a failed bulb was not viable. Avionics only replaced the unit when all of them had failed and were no longer of any use at night. Despite all these shortcomings, Bristow had the honour of giving the Bristow-configured Super Puma the name 'Tiger'.

In October 1995, I took the plunge and became a Super Puma driver working out of Aberdeen. During the conversion course, we learned the construction of the main rotor hydraulic system. Early in the design stage, Sikorsky realised the French were cloning their hydraulic systems. By then, they had already copied 80% when they had to make up the shortfall with printed circuit boards (PCBs). The folly of this shortcut revealed itself later when operating into turbulence around decks offshore.

To be dual rated on this and the S-61N, it soon became apparent a future flying the Super Puma with its stiff main rotor blades and uncomfortable ride in bad weather was not for me. The passengers and a goose shared my disenchantment with this aircraft. Mine began in the Helikopter Service Super Puma simulator in Stavanger, Norway. Pete Benson, our instructor, a former

Cold War doomsday Vulcan RAF pilot, demonstrated a take-off, circuit and landing. Nausea swept over me before we were even downwind. Pleased with his demo, Pete then invited me to have a go. I explained my predicament when he recommended I go and ask for some Scopoderm TTS patches from the simulator engineer. "A prevalent problem in the Super Puma," he assured me. "Place one behind each ear." He did not tell me these small plasters contained Scopolamine. They could make you drowsy, confused, and dizzy and may affect your vision. Therefore, do NOT drive, operate machinery, or pilot an aircraft or other forms of transport. It transpired Scopolia carniolica, the active ingredient of Scopolamine, could produce such a profound and long-lasting sleep; Shakespeare described it as being "Like death". In short, it helped one to be slightly anaesthetised to fly this aircraft.

*

Back in Aberdeen, the instrument check-out ended with an instrument landing system (ILS) approach to land. The aircraft is not a good instrument platform and tends to 'crab' when you lower the collective. It must be corrected with rudder input to alter the pitch on the tail rotor to keep on the centre line of the localiser. Again, with Pete as the instructor, he kept quiet during the first attempt and asked me to do it again. After a second, ILS, I had to ask him what the problem was with the first attempt. "Nothing," he replied, "Just never seen anyone do that (stay on the localiser/glide slope) before in a Super Puma and thought it was a fluke. When you did it again, I knew it was for real!" The passengers were quick to register displeasure. After travelling for years in a 19-seat configuration S-61N capable of seating 32, they are packed as sardines in a helicopter with just room for 19, the optimum number of seats without the requirement for a cabin attendant.
For the Canadian goose, it was the occupation of what it had considered its helideck. We had landed and were rotors running, refuelling on an installation some 100 miles southeast of Aberdeen, when the goose formated abeam the aircraft. Then, with great care, it glided sideways toward the rotating disc and removed a couple of outboard feathers before inching clear to hold its position until we left. This behaviour was unlike an unfortunate flock of seagulls I flew into one night. It was on the climb out of Sumburgh in an S-61N from the Southerly runway. As we turned east to avoid the high ground of Compass Head and join the outbound heli-lanes, they appeared immediately before us in the landing lights. Terrified, they wheeled in a confusion of white wings before our eyes. We heard a loud rattling noise like

gravel being hurled down the sides of the aircraft as the carnage disappeared aft into the night.

*

In May 1996, six months in on the Super Puma, I was invited to operate on the S-61N again. Relief! And two months later, a third type became possible: the S-76A+. But how?
Steve Stubbs, the Flight Operations Director, assisted by loaning me his copy of an American Airlines technical manual for the S-76A+. With this aid, I completed the Air Registration Board type technical exam at Gatwick. And now for the expensive bit: sufficient overtime had been completed, though not claimed. He intonated this would fund a conversion if not paid, thus avoiding the relevant taxes. Warming to his idea, Steve will notify me when he has the daily operating charge down to around £400/hour. The day came in September when John Baker, a type rating examiner from the southern base Beccles, was visiting Aberdeen. On a Sunday, he taught me to fly G-CHCD and complete the day and night 1179 flight tests, all in under three hours. I duly submitted the overtime claim to cover the daily operating charge and, fully expecting it to settle the account, was rewarded in the next pay packet with payment of the claim in full—an example of what the Flight Operations Director called "An insurmountable opportunity" achieved. The S-76A+ on the licence stood me in good stead, not just now but later when flying for another company. For now, it provided the means to visit some pleasant and not-so-agreeable destinations. The former took clients to golf clubs to play or watch competitions, and some of the latter included the *Beatrice 'B'* in the Moray Firth.

*

This platform was a normally unattended installation (NUI). We would collect a team from the neighbouring *Beatrice 'A'* and shut down for a few hours on the *Beatrice 'B'* for them to carry out their checks and inspections. The arrival at *'Bravo'* would first involve dispersing the resident gulls from the helideck where they roosted during the summer and autumn. All offshore installations have a 500-metre fishing exclusion zone; the waters around the *Alpha and Bravo* teemed with fish. These seagulls took advantage of this well-stocked-larder and processed their meals on the helideck. To such an extent, guano, fish bones, and offal built up to one inch deep over four to five weeks. To remain on deck for more than five minutes, some crews complained of feeling nauseated. Given a choice, watching golf and looking for lost balls was the preferred option. There was no choice.

*

Now, the S-76 was the best aircraft for landing on the armada of floating vessels working offshore: diving support and seismic survey vessels, tankers, drill-ships, SBMs (Single Point Mooring buoys), FSUs (Floating Storage Units), FPSOs (Floating Production Storage and Offloading) and of course semi-submersible rigs, flotels, and crane barges. It had a low centre of gravity and flight stability, enabling 'landing on a dime'. Its star characteristic was the rear undercarriage. Both struts came together under the fuselage. The wheel touching down first on the uphill side of a moving deck compressed its strut to force the opposite strut to extend. This extension enabled the opposing wheel to touch the downhill side of the deck a split second later. All other aircraft had independent, as in the previous sense being dependant undercarriages. These relied on the oleo compression and the pilot inclining the main rotor disc to correct lateral instability.
No wonder the S-76 is our Monarch's preference for the Royal Flight, and an S-61 variant is the President's choice in the USA.
With faultless timing, a crew vacancy for the S-76A+ came up. That was the good news. The bad meant I was predominantly required to fly the Super Puma with occasional relief operating S-61Ns and S-76s. In January 1998, I dropped the Super Puma and reverted to dual-rated on the Sikorsky aircraft.

*

As autumn set in, I began to experience more Super Puma habits. We were operating out of Aberdeen, routing through Sumburgh to the *Brent 'C'* and then back via Sumburgh to refuel. At around eight o'clock on a snowy evening, it was still busy with aircraft queuing to enter the apron. We joined a procession on a taxiway leading off the Southerly runway. We crawled forward in the dark, following the white taillight of the aircraft ahead. The ramp leading up to the terminal had a slight incline. Progress was stop go, stop go, waiting for an aircraft to vacate a stand and make way for another. Our turn came to move forward another few meters. I pulled the collective up a bit and tilted the disc to move forward. Nothing happens. We appeared to have slid into a rut in the snow and ice. I pulled some more pitch. In the blink of an eye, we faced the aircraft behind us - much to the amusement of its crew. We had spun around on the ice within our axis - a perfect ground loop. It's those pesky Super Pumas again!

*

Wintertime taxying on snow and ice on the CHC apron at Aberdeen could also offer excitement with the wind in the west. It would pile down off Brimmond Hill, funnelling between the hangars and out across the apron. On these occasions, you sensed a sideways drift downwind into the chain link fence separating the parking spots from the control tower. With a risk of hitting the curb sideways and rolling over or tangling with the fence, lifting into the hover and moving clear was the only solution.

*

During this time, CHC acquired Veritair, a small company operating a police contract out of Cardiff, Wales. The background to this outfit began with a former BAH pilot, Julian Verity. In the late seventies, he was the only crewmember to own a new Range Rover. It put the rest of our bangers in the car park to shame. Then he left and set up Veritair. This company, along with other onshore operations, was sold off by CHC 20 years later in 2000, believing Oil & Gas contracts were the only parties in town—the new owner: a resurrected British International Helicopters.

*

Around this time, rigs were entering the North Sea with clad derricks. The modification enclosed the lower part of the drilling rig to protect the men working on the drill floor from the elements. Fine, except when the derrick was upwind of the helideck when the wind was howling. The effect of the cladding caused considerable 'mechanical' turbulence when the winds on the approach to the helideck barrelled out into the flight path. And these reverse currents of air were aerodynamically unstable. It was good practice to offset the approach to avoid much of this wind shear and provide an escape, but once committed to land, it was necessary to enter these currents. Losing lift as the blades stalled, the aircraft sinks rapidly towards the deck.

You could experience similar conditions when accommodation semi-submersibles, known as flotels, were anchored downwind of the production platform. These vessels, connected to the installation by a removable gangway, could accommodate up to 400 shift workers carrying out maintenance on the mother platform. Lying much lower in the water than the fixed installation towering above them, they were ideal venues for exceptional wind shear. Once down on the deck, the next problem was lifting off again without running out of torque. Leaving some folk behind for the next chopper was never a popular option.

*

Crews adopted different methods to deal with wind shear. Mine was to correct that wind-generated uncontrolled sink towards the deck by deferring the best part of the collective input. Then, combine it with the ground cushion. On the S-6IN, this is ten feet above the deck. Rather than apply power early at the onset of sinking, plenty of power will be in hand to arrest the descent later at the top of the cushion. Some pundits used to say the S-61N was underpowered. But this was not the case. So long as you stayed within the performance envelope and flew the profiles accurately, it behaved as a lady. No wonder crews and passengers referred to it as 'The Queen of the Skies'. On the other hand, the Super Puma had an additional habit you had to deal with in offshore turbulence around installations and rigs. Because computers provided 20% of the rotor hydraulic system, they never seemed to keep up in these conditions. After committing to land, the best method I found to counter the turbulence was to make small, rapid cyclic movements in random directions. This unorthodox action confused the automatics comprising the remaining part of the hydraulic system, fooling it every time.
Another of the causes of reported turbulence in helicopter pilot terminology is non-steady temperature effects. A pilot approaching too close to a hot gas turbine exhaust plume can produce changes in lift and speed (turbulence) already described by the crew of G-AYOM. This is easier said than done. Despite the guidance, those who design platforms do not appreciate the hazards they create for helicopters by siting turbine exhausts near helidecks – in their view, the closer to the deck, the better. Finally, the flares burn off excess gas. Most flare booms and stacks are usually away from the helidecks, though they can create significant turbulence on approaching to land when lit.
But first up, some insight into the turbine exhausts. Usually, at least two large gas turbine engines are involved. The Rolls Royce RB 211, designed for aircraft similar to the Lockheed Martin L-1011 TriStar and the Boeing 747, is a popular engine to generate the power required to run offshore installations. Their power is enormous. When aircraft with large jet engines run up on the

ground during maintenance, they usually direct their exhaust into a safety wall to protect anyone nearby. Offshore, there is no such precaution.
This oversight is part of the design of these offshore installations; siting the exhaust from these turbines is an afterthought; indeed, so far *after,* it broaches thoughtlessness: their pole position is usually next to the helideck. And it is into this environment we flew. Though it may make sense to those on the drawing board, they are a source of wonder to the helicopter pilot: wonder what will happen next. By now, the helicopter is on short finals and the cusp of the committal point to land or go around. The most common problem is the considerable turbulence they generate, though there is another.

*

Helicopter gas turbine engines are merely smaller examples; they, too, burn oxygen. Burning fuel depleted of oxygen and the local temperature gradient can result in engine power fluctuations, engine surging, compressors stalling and flameout. Coupled with the local turbulence, impaired lift, increased power margin and directional stability, you now have the ingredients for an interesting arrival. There is usually sufficient wind to mix the ambient air and the exhaust. On still-air or light wind days, this is less likely to happen and coincides with when helicopter performance is already inherently poor. Wind tunnel tests demonstrate the problem. Take a standard offshore gas turbine with an exhaust temperature of +500°C and 50 to 100 kg/second flow rates. Using a Gaussian dispersion model, the minimum distance required before the temperature returns to within +2°C above ambient requires 130-190 metres. Often, more than one exhaust is clustered together, proportionally increasing this distance. And there may be others in the vicinity to consider, too. But no. This dispersion model used a Rolls-Royce Spey Mk 202 engine, half the horsepower of a single offshore turbine. You will not find multiple turbines fired up together at a provincial or international airport.

*

When the report (often up to two years in gestation) of the incident was published concerning the approach and heavy landing by the S-61N G-AYOM on the *Claymore CAP* in 1995, regulators could no longer ignore the whole issue of helideck environments. The introduction of restrictions published in the Installation/Vessels Limitations List, formerly HLL, was already available. But it did not account for all eventualities, as this crew found out when the music stopped. The authorities did not terminate their findings with an accident report this time. Instead, a joint CAA/HSE working group went on a fact-finding mission in 1997 to ask pilots their principal concerns when operating offshore. It was a first!

*

They commissioned the Defence Evaluation Research Agency (DERA) Centre for Human Sciences to establish whether, and under what circumstances, the workload on pilots imposed by in-flight paperwork was excessive. Instead, the study surveyed pilot responses to an extensive series of questions regarding the sources and significance of various forms of workload way beyond in-flight paperwork. It asked pilots to rate how often a particular aspect of their operational duties contributed to a safety hazard. Of the 13 key topics listed, 'filling in the paperwork' was only rated as the third most hazardous. This question was behind 'weather conditions' at number two, with 'turbulence within the wake region downwind of an installation' topping the list. In a roundabout way so as not to expose the helideck issue and instead put the emphasis on paperwork, the eventual result after the survey results were in was in the title: 'Research on Offshore Helideck Environmental Issues' – as was the original objective anyway. It was published three years later. In response to the question: 'Does turbulence around platforms cause you a high workload or a safety hazard?', some of the replies are recorded here:
"Be aware!"

"One often wonders who allowed the turbines/flares/clad derricks and other obstructions to be placed in positions adjacent to the helideck."

"New, smaller decks closer to the centre of platforms have increased turbulence problems, e.g., *Piper 'B'* has the covered stairwell projecting above deck level, turbine exhausts, and structure directly adjacent to the deck. I'm led to believe, whilst wind tunnel tests were carried out, they did not simulate turbine exhaust; one cannot simulate common sense!"

"There are some structures, both platforms and rigs, that can be dangerous in certain winds. Turbulence at a strange rig at night is no fun."

"It can be downright dangerous, but it is unusual for the experienced to be caught."

"Some approaches, although the wind speed/direction within limits are precarious."

"Can be a real problem, especially with semi-sub flotels in the lee of platforms. Down-draughting is a severe problem. The combination of down-draughting, reverse wind flow, pitch, roll, and heave can make things very difficult. We tread a fine line here. Very easy to damage an aircraft on landing. I believe our limitations do not take proper consideration of these factors. Only our experience and judgement keep us out of trouble."

"Some turbulence can be particularly bad on certain platforms. Most platforms create turbulence when the wind comes through derricks and cranes."

"Clad drilling derricks seem to cause a lot of turbulence even when landing/taking off in accordance with the IVLL."

"In my opinion, the most hazardous part of our offshore operation is landing on floating decks in the lee of platforms at night."

"Even a powerful aircraft such as the Super Puma can be difficult to control in severe turbulence."

"If turbulence is present, you will have a high workload, often running out of power on take-off and sometimes landing."

"Can be very exciting – local knowledge is vital here – would like to be involved with the take-off certification pilots when a new machine enters service."

"Part of the life on the North Sea, I guess, though helideck location does help a lot, as does the location of turbine exhaust and flare stacks. Something I guess designers should be more aware of."

"Especially flotels in the lee of platforms, a downdraught can be a real problem."

"Depends on the day, depends on the wind. Some rigs are OK, and some are pretty bad. I'd love to meet the guy who designed some of these helidecks."

The report concluded, "Overall, turbulence was found to contribute to high workload and safety hazards more frequently than any other aspect of offshore operations."
In addition, "the high-power production capability of offshore Oil & Gas installations inevitably gives rise to releases of gaseous material either in the form of exhaust from gas turbine plant or hydrocarbon mixtures resulting from some malfunction in the production system. For a helicopter operating in close proximity to such an installation, there is a risk ingestion of such gaseous material will have a detrimental effect on engine performance. The effects of these disturbances are largely transient. Though they pose a potentially serious hazard to safe flight in situations where the scope for recovery may be limited."

*

When the working group reviewed the available incident reports and causes identified, it concluded: "The operability of offshore helidecks has been consistently overlooked. The IVLL, with its many references to non-compliances and operating restrictions, is further evidence helideck operability has not featured very highly during the installation/helideck design stage." So, no surprise there.
"Moreover, the helideck designers do not generally have sufficient knowledge of offshore helicopter flight operations and rarely understand the essential needs of a helicopter pilot when landing on and taking off from offshore installations." Ditto.
Yet, as a survey respondent pointed out, "Nothing has changed. Indeed, consideration for the helicopter pilot has become worse."
With all this feedback, the authorities could no longer wait for their survey to be published. Towards the end of 1998, they devised a study into the extent of the problem. They called it HOMP (Helicopter Operations Monitoring Programme). They used five Bristow Tiger helicopters. These aircraft had their existing Flight Data Recorder (FDR) adapted to link with a BAe Systems PCMCIA Card Quick Access Recorder (CQAR) to extract and download the flight data. The commissioning period began the following year, in September 1999 and by September 2000, was ready to collect flight data.

The trial ran for a year, ending on the 31st of August 2001. At the end of each day, after removing the PCMCIA card, its contents are downloaded in the tech office on helicopter flight data replay and analysis software provided by British Airways BASIS (BA Safety Information System) flight data modules. 'Mapping the helideck environment' provides some of the most significant new information recorded. And turbine turbulence and temperature played a large part. These were Event No. 26A, 'To detect turbulence encountered on helideck landing through changes in collective pitch,' and Event No. 28A, 'Flight through a hot gas plume during take-off and landing by detecting changes in outside air temperature.' With this new knowledge, they could apply limitations. But here's the thing.

*

These five helicopters probably only visited the installations Bristow provided a service, unless on an ad hoc flight for another operator. It excluded over 60% served by the other two North Sea helicopter companies in the UK Sector. The other operators fitted PCMCIA CQARs to acquire the whole picture to remedy this. Now, they could use all this new information to amend existing material in the IVLL. By 2007, 12 years after the *Claymore 'CAP'* incident, of the 70 offshore platforms with sufficient HOMP data available, 18 included in their IVLL entry some element of hot gas hazard or mention of turbulence related to turbine exhausts. That's 1:4 or 25% of offshore installations had not considered helicopters operating to them during the design stage. Despite all this evaluation, it was also well known the temperature could be halved on all turbine exhausts if waste heat recovery systems were in place. Remember, this is O&G offshore, an initiative viewed as an unnecessary expense. The heat given off from flaring was much greater back in the day. Sitting on the helideck, it was sometimes necessary to shield your face from the heat of the flames until they legislated to pipe all the marketable gas ashore and burn only the sour gas.

*

By the end of 1997, the daily number of helicopter movements on the North Sea during the year equalled those for the fixed-wing at Heathrow. And Aberdeen had become the world's busiest heliport, peaking at 480,000 helicopter passenger movements.

Chapter 19. 1998

Offshore in the Atlantic

The summer of 1998 and the next are offshore, based West of Shetland in the East Atlantic on the ESV *Iolair.* She is working in the Schiehallion and Foinhaven oil fields. In winter, they withdraw the vessel from these waters as it is too rough to operate. The work schedule was 14 days on/14 days off and an intro for an offshore allowance.

Fig 46. CHC G-BVCX S-76A+. *Photo credit: CHC*

We did not have one. I arranged a meeting with a former Bristow manager who joined CHC as a line pilot and rapidly rose to Base Manager. A man with negotiating skills. He also tended to react to the third element of a fire triangle, and it fell to me, as a BALPA Council member, to provide it. "We don't have an offshore allowance" was the cue to ignite. Avoiding the expletive responses following me across the room, I opened the window to let them out. Taking care not to look his way, I sat down at the table next to the window and lit up. (He was a non-smoker). A cigarette later, the room became calm. Then a question came from his desk's direction:
"How much?" was proffered. Turning around and honestly not expecting a result,
"£40.00 a day will do, tax-free."
"That's fine, but sort out the tax bit with payroll." It set a new benchmark for helicopter pilot offshore allowances in the UK Sector. A 'David' moment? Though offshore, helicopter pilots remained at the bottom of a pecking order determined by financial income.

The ESV *Iolair* was formerly a BP emergency firefighting semi-sub and was initially based in the Forties field. She was now employed as a construction support vessel and operated six ROVs (Remotely Operated Vehicles) on the seabed at the edge of the continental shelf, 1,500 feet below. They were hooking up the wellheads to two FPSOs. From them, shuttle tankers will take the crude to Sullom Voe. It had also assumed the role of a flotel, with accommodation for 220. These were primarily engineers commissioning the FPSO *Schiehallion*, constructed to a design with the appearance of a large skip. In a rush to start pumping oil, she sailed with tens of thousands of hours of work outstanding. On arrival offshore, she moored over the principal wellhead that others, when connected, will feed into. To keep her facing into the waves, a tug hauled on her aft beam to manoeuvre her into position.
The seas and weather in the Eastern Atlantic are a product of systems allowed to build up without interruption. They are more extreme than the relatively sheltered North Sea. It is known as a very harsh metocean environment where a combination of high waves, strong winds and currents prevail most of the year. Unsurprisingly, the first significant storm significantly altered the 'skip' bow.
In contrast, the neighbouring FPSO, *Petrojarl Foinhaven*, rode out the storms without incident. She had been converted from the five-year-old *Anadyr*, formerly a Russian submarine tender, to an FPSO and retained the sweeping bow typical of their warship designs. The conversion involved removing the centre section of the vessel and replacing it with one wider and 25 meters longer.

*

Days could be long between shuttles, and many crews found time dragged. The bridge doubles as a flight planning room; instead, I requested an alternative place to work. With a bit of encouragement, they provided a cabin. By the end of the day, the radio operator had connected it with their offshore satellite communications—the CHC office. Here, the hours flew by as I worked with my business partner in Ankara, Turkey, to develop a range of environmentally friendly high-performance aerospace coatings and resolve outstanding problems with the traditional ones.

*

Exploration. The research vessel RV *Ramform Explorer* conducted hydrographic surveys west of the Hebrides and Shetland. She towed the latest seismic arrays behind her. She was one of many that could tow 12

streamers up to 3,600m long and survey in high definition 100 sq. km a day. We shut down on the helideck above the array pens below. Over lunch, the captain described that by firing a gun and injecting water into the sea at regular intervals, the acoustic vibrations produced seismic pulses off the boundaries separating the rock layers. Provided the sea state is reasonable and noise does not corrupt the signals, the hydrophones attached along the array detect these reflected pulses and transmit them for analysis. "So, how good was it?" He then divulged over 300 known oilfields West of Shetland were out there, the problem being the tar sands.
In most cases, they were so old the oil was beyond recovery. With a new methodology, this view is about to change. According to the head of the Institute of Petroleum Engineering at Heriot-Watt University, the sedimentary basins here are much like the North Sea, where over 3,000 wells have been drilled compared to just 20 (2014) in this 'fantastic location for Oil & Gas.'

Fig 47. BIH/CHC G-CHCD S-76A+ in the run-off area next to a yellow fuel pod. Offshore based on the ESV *Iolair*, West of Shetland.
Author's collection

It was now August, at the beginning of the hurricane season; I had collected the ship's hand-held anemometer from the bridge and was standing on the edge of the helideck, focused on reading the numbers. Well, quite intently. On returning the instrument to the bridge, the crew was sure they had lost me. (For the reader, probably a godsend!) They had been watching me take the readings when a colossal wave reared up from below the edge of the helideck, engulfed me in its maw, broke, and landed behind on the S-76A+ parked in the run-off area adjacent to the helideck. I had, to their brief consternation, disappeared under the sea. I was unaware of the event, except for the evidence around the helicopter; I was dry. Situational awareness didn't come into it! In other ways, we felt the impending signs of stormy weather, already shredding palm trees far away in the southwest. On the ESV *Iolair*, the North Atlantic fetches are becoming longer, and the swell is building up, no more noticeably than by the violent thump of the waves against the flat hull separating the sea from the floor of my cabin. Rollers increasing in size and whomping crescendo until, around the seventh, boom, the vessel would momentarily shudder, regain her composure, skid back down the lee side, and briefly settle before riding the next onslaught. The play ends for the day when dynamic positing becomes too difficult. She would recover the ROVs and 'go with the flow', ending miles from her original location, with an extended motor back, albeit at 12 knots, being fast for a semi-sub, usually motoring at up to six. And the shuttle went on, each sector shorter than the last as we closed with the oilfields; beneath us, the sea still rolling away over the horizon to the east.

Chapter 20. 1998 - 1999

PLC Chair – Meltdown & Fight Back – Beer on the Frigg

For 31 years, Shell Expro had been the principal oil company BEA/BAH/BIH, and now CHC has provided helicopter services. Since the oil price declined from the heady days before 1983, Shell Expro had become a 'milk cheque' (cash flow) with ever-decreasing profit margins. The dependence on this huge contractor ensured smaller operators could only sup off the hind tit when providing a service. In the pecking order, they were just minnows; Shell Expro came first every time. In late March 1998, CHC lost their Shell Expro contract. Bristow won the work in the Northern North Sea and secured the Shell contract off KLM/ERA in the Southern North Sea.
A somewhat stunned response from CHC Management in St Johns follows this upheaval. The finance director of CHC resigned, and the people at Aberdeen HQ and the unions appeared in denial. It had yet to be part of their management training. It was time to close the doors of CHC UK. A view shared by many in the industry, and the free press fell over themselves, declaring the end was nigh. In the crew room, it was apparent the company had effectively no interest in saving itself. It left them only a 15% market share of the North Sea helicopter oil support. When the inflation-adjusted price for a barrel of oil had plunged to a historic all-time low, it seemed a good time to sell up.

*

Then, there was a glimmer of hope. CHC had won the Ministry of Defence (MOD) Falklands resupply contract off Bristow. On the plus side, it was good news. Conversely, it released Bristow crews from that operation to assist with their new Shell contract. They would never be enough. In all, they needed to employ another 50 pilots. And it will not include several blacked pilots forming that picket line 20 years ago. Four Days in May.
During the first week of May, everything changed. On Monday, the BALPA Company Council chair resigned from the post due to a fist-induced eye injury. This accident precluded him from flying the line and carrying out other duties. As deputy, it was now a case of assuming the role of chairman, though unaware I needed to hit the ground running until the next day. And how! Day one began when the Flight Operations Director requested a

meeting – with coffee. He outlined to me all the 20 contract pilots would go on the 1st of July when Bristow began the work, and 70% of the crews would also have to leave in September. He proffered a list with names earmarked to go in September. As this news was cascading down, it became clear there were only two options with room to spare on the back of a fag packet. And as the pilot's representative, it did not include one of them - pilots leaving. After all, with only a tiny market share in the Central and Northern parts of the North Sea, there will not be enough crew left after September to fly and generate sufficient income to support the rest of the organisation (around 400 staff) in the UK. A quote often used by the Flight Operations Director on these occasions represented another 'insurmountable opportunity'. Though for whom, the following weeks would decide.
On day two, the management held a company meeting for all staff. Here, they presented their plans. The following day, day three, another meeting was held by the Deputy Flight Operations Director. And the crack in their plan revealed itself.
When the music stops. Four days in, we convened a meeting for the pilots and other staff members to join in. We gave them unpalatable information based on the original list and a second provided by the Deputy Flight Ops Director. The aircrew list of names to be released in September did not match. Someone had made a 'deal'. I explained this to the crews. With the unwelcome analysis, they could all be on the final list when the music stopped. Above all, consider this: if we deny Bristow of pilots, they cannot crew the contract. Well, not for a few months. The ad hoc work will buy time before winning new, profitable contracts. Besides, oil companies prefer to have more than two operators to ensure bidding wars prevail.

*

Traditionally, pilots migrated with contracts to ensure they stayed with the work. It was the case on CHC's southern base. When KLM/ERA won the Shell Expro contract three years earlier, it absorbed these pilots under a mechanism called TUPE. This arrangement protected their previous terms of employment.
BALPA at Heathrow supported these arrangements. And this was no exception. When I put their case to a former long-term council chairman in his farmyard on leave, he echoed the union's position. This time, it was different. Because of the sheer scale of migration, it undermined anything left. Besides, Bristow only wanted some of these pilots. We held further meetings with the pilots, and after the dust had settled, the critical issue was

holding together and explaining the strategy to our wives and partners. Moreover, they should make the final decision rather than the pilots. For example, when you ask ten pilots in a crew room a question, you receive 11 different answers.

It was not easy to provide a seamless service to the members when flying the line based offshore on the ESV *Iolair*. For this, the Council Deputy Chairman, Andy Foster, did a sterling job and preserved the strategy, a lesson learned from the North Sea Pilots' Association failure in 1982/83. Some pilots were angry. They are under the impression employment with Bristow was being denied to them by the new chairman. They were few. It was evident they had yet to consider others who would no longer be employed on the North Sea in September if they continued to hold this view.

*

It was also apparent to the crew room the management had shown no leadership or direction other than awaiting the company's implosion.

Despite his being in that post for two years, many pilots did not know what the Managing Director looked like, and in mid-June, I requested a meeting with him and presented their case. Casually:

"So let me get this right: you're the Managing Director?"

"Well, yes. Of course, I am!" Pause for doubt.

"Fine, but can you prove it?"

By the end of the month, he, too, had resigned.

Next was to secure the 20 contractor positions most vulnerable in the short term. Extensions to their contracts had been offered earlier in the year, albeit under revised and less advantageous terms. They did not return them; instead, they tore up the offers except one. We photocopied the surviving document 20 times and delivered them to the Flight Operations Director with the signature of approval by each contractor. He was obliged to honour them with none rejected.

So far, 20 pilots were in the fold, together with those on the new MOD contract to crew three S-61Ns. Even at this early stage, it seemed possible. Yes, we can do this. Providing the crews with the information was imperative, as you might plan a flight. Suitably briefed, it enabled pilots and their wives or partners to make sound medium-term decisions. Yet BALPA disagreed again. They reasoned too much information was dangerous. There was no alternative. Not taking this risk would have been worse. Then the 1st of July dawned. All was not lost. Remember, we still had until September before the doors shut.

The following week, I took an S-76A+ freighter up to the *Magnus*. This BP platform is 99 miles northeast of Shetland, the most Northerly of the UK oilfields, less than 300 miles from the Arctic Circle. Leaving at 18:50, routing through Wick for fuel with Bergen-Flesland as an alternate as elsewhere was shut, I arrived 2½ hours later. Overnight offshore, I flew back in the morning. I was in an S-61N ground school refresher in the afternoon before a stint working offshore on the Frigg Field when the Base Manager, Tony Jones, popped his head around the door. "Great job last night. Thank you very much."
Frequently, when it was freight only, we flew the S-76 alone, single pilot. To be thanked by a manager for flying the line, indeed for anything, was unusual. First, an offshore allowance, and now this. Surely, he meant something else? As related, Tony had a recent history. The experience had undoubtedly taught him aircrew is only human versions of dogs and need a pat from time to time, a cherry. The real icing on the cake was about to unfold—a reward for the crews who had held their nerve.

*

The detachment to the Frigg oilfield in the Norwegian sector of the North Sea provided an amusing story of a small vessel arriving one evening from the nearby Beryl Field in the UK sector. Someone had sent the crew on a mission. They had heard beer was freely available on Frigg, and they had come to acquire some. Well satisfied, they appeared again the following evening with tales of the riotous time had by all. At some stage, it dawned on them the brew was 'alkoholfri'. They did not come again!

*

Returning to Scotland, our gamble on ad hoc work and new contracts was about to succeed. It was followed by a trickle, turning into a flood as work flowed in. Suddenly, loyal oil companies, Bristow's bread and butter for years, share the hind teat. And they didn't like it. In the short term, CHC made more money from Shell in the first six months, with lucrative ad hoc work Bristow could not manage, than they had made during the previous five years. Curiously, the Engineering Manager, who had expressed a close interest in the proceedings to me and with whom he sensed a positive outcome, became the new Managing Director. To top it all, we secured a 6% wage hike at the end of the year, and the oil companies, disenchanted with the new pecking order at Bristow, signed new contracts with CHC. Four

former CHC pilots also signed contracts. They left just before the 1st of July to fly the line for Bristow on the promise of an early command.
Though the command did not immediately work out, two carried the CHC crew room ethos forward. They became longstanding and successful BALPA Company Council Chairman with Paul Cook in North Denes, covering the Southern North Sea and Colin Milne in Aberdeen. We did not plan to plant cuckoos in the Bristow nest, and Bristow did not see them coming. Ho Hum!
Our actions and efforts in Sumburgh during the spring of 1990 demonstrated something: when a group of people come together for a common cause, with some homework and a clear strategy, they become more effective. Had the North Sea Pilots' Association applied these simple concepts in 1983 and the 'hands-off' management techniques exercised in Bergen in 1982 and Sumburgh after 1986, today's North Sea would be a different place. Is a case of hindsight rueing foresight?

*

The Sumburgh S-61N crews on the original Shell contract took the opportunity to move onto the new MOD contract in the Falklands. (Bristow had provided the service since the end of the war in 1982). As Council Chairman, I was approached by Ron Walker the night before they took off from RAF Brize Norton in an RAF VC-10.
"We don't have a 'Pilot's Service Agreement' for the Falklands!"
"No problem. Just write into it what you want, and I'll do the rest."
At 9 a.m., it was ready to submit to the Flight Operations Director. With the clock ticking and hardly a glance, the agreement was approved and has since served them well. Force majeure!

*

At the beginning of 1999, CHC bought a controlling stake in Helikopter Service, the Norwegian operator and the third jewel in the crown; the other two already in its stable were the Canadian operator Okanagan Helicopter Services and BIH; so much for wanting to pack up and leave the North Sea. For their terms and conditions, Okanagan had been one of the three best heavy helicopter operators of its era worldwide when CHC acquired them in 1987, a year after Mirror Group bought BAH. CHC tend to trace their roots back to Okanagan, though strangely, with no mention of BEA/BAH/BIH Helicopters. Yet these two companies were both formed in 1947. Helikopter Service already owned Lloyd Helicopters of Australia, Court Line Helicopters of South Africa, and some additional baggage: Bond Helicopters with their helicopters in red livery. They only checked their purchase of the latter after six months. By then, it was too late to be disappointed.

CHC owns all three major operators now, and life would never eclipse the time when they were independent. A genuine case of those were the days abruptly brought home when the former BIH (read ex-BAH) 'Blue crews' and Bond 'Red crews' in the UK combined their operations under one Air Operator Certificate (AOC). CHC, now trading as CHC Scotia, insisted they cherry-picked the best of the former operations. Unsurprisingly, they chose the cheapest option after the bean counters had trawled through the terms and conditions, standards, and procedures. They went with the one with the least, and there were no guesses about which one.

With the acquisition of Bond Helicopters, they required new premises to accommodate both companies under one roof. To do this, CHC Scotia knocked down the old BAH check-in and operations building and replaced it with an enormous shed. When asked what it was for, the management explained it would be a new terminal with flight ops in a small area upstairs. This unimaginative construction made the old British Airways Helicopters Boeing Chinook hangar look like a palace. The vast check-in area, with steel beams far up in the gods supporting the roof, did not compare with the gemutlich Bristow terminal. Clearly, they only had freight in mind when they approved the plans – the self-loading variety, as they say. When this barn was under construction, we worked out of the Bond buildings on the north side of the airfield, formerly the original Aberdeen Airport Terminal.

The fallout from the 'merger' of Helikopter Service with CHC, as some preferred to term the buyout, was when they re-named the Norwegian entity the following year CHC Helikopter Service.

With only two helicopter operators now serving the UK offshore helicopter market, the Bond brothers, Peter and Stephen, reinstated the third to coincide with a buoyant oil price. They formed a subsidiary of their onshore operations and re-entered the fray in 2001 with a new company, Bond Offshore Helicopters. A large part of this fleet would include the AS332 L2.

These two companies would later be in the headlights after two catastrophic accidents attributed to the failure of the main rotor gearbox installed in the AS332 L2 and its successor, the EC225 LP. Following a petition by 26,000 oil workers and their families, the oil companies refused to contract these aircraft and, with support from the Norwegian CAA and the UK CAA, ensured their removal from the North Sea, irrespective of the European Safety Agency grounding these aircraft for 'precautionary measures' on the 4th of June 2016, and until further notice.

Chapter 21. 1999 - 2003

Denmark - Glass Cockpit – Provence Pink - An Old Strike – Fired!

In 1999, CHC Scotia signed a five-year contract with an optional three-year extension with the Danish company Maersk Olie og Gas, A.S. It will operate out of Esbjerg, Denmark, with two Super Pumas based onshore and an S-76A+ based offshore. It effectively put the Danish helicopter operating division of Maersk Air, with a fleet of SA 365N Dauphin helicopters, out to pasture. The Canadians initially absorbed most of their crews and imported their inferior CHC working conditions. Many former Maersk crews left to work for DanCopter. One was Susanne Hessellund, who had been running a small company called Bel Air Aviation A/S in her spare time. As co-owner of DanCopter, she built up experience in management and, by 2009, had fully developed Bel Air to break away and launch offshore operations with an Agusta AW139. By the following year, she secured an offshore shuttle operation for Maersk. Not bad! So, what's an offshore shuttle operation like in the Danish Sector of the North Sea?

*

Beginning in October 1999, the following two winters, broken by summer months on the *ESV Iolair*, were based in the Tyra Field on the *Tyra East* platform in the Danish sector of the North Sea. We operated the 'OY' registered S-76A+ aircraft for Danish International, a new CHC company to service the Maersk contract. We flew under the new JAR Ops 3 rules for helicopters (the forerunner of the European Aviation Safety Agency - EASA - Regulations), with my licence endorsed accordingly. Our co-pilots were Danes, who formerly worked for Bristow at Den Helder in the Netherlands, flying the S-76A++. The offshore working routine was 7/7, defined by the Danish SLV (CAA). This rule allowed us, and we consistently achieved it, to fly up to 45 hours every seven days. Usually on a shift beginning at 05:00 and ending at 22:30. This contrasted with the UK Flight Time Limitations. The UK never adopted the European JAR Ops 3 Sub Part Q Flight Time Limitations. Instead, the CAA preserved the CAP 371 Bader Flight Time Limitations (constructed initially by Douglas Bader of World War II fame).
Early and late shuttles in the fields, particularly during the winter months off Denmark, converted the day pilot to a night one; we rarely flew during the daytime. Paradoxically, the latter became a more comfortable environment

for flying. Yes, it could replace flying in daylight over water, though it never replaces it over land with its geology and countryside with changing seasons to absorb one.

*

Operating the S-76A+ offshore in winter without a hangar did pose serviceability problems. Finishing a shuttle on standby instruments was not unusual; the gyros had failed again. Located under panels in the nose just forward of the windscreen, it was challenging for our engineer Brian Ruddiforth to dry out, particularly at night in bad weather with snowstorms freezing his hands. Away from a main operating base, there is an allowance for the serviceability of instruments and systems. One of our co-pilots was a former Danish kickboxing champion. To tell him, "It'll probably be all right", from a safe distance did not always work – the first time. More importantly, he knew of Esbjerg's best rib restaurants where each carcass was 18" long.

*

The galley on *Tyra East* matched some of the better restaurants in Copenhagen and, when closed, provided an endless supply of hot Danish cookies and other delights. And at nine every evening, a variety of freshly baked bread and a good selection of cheese appeared. Their famous smorrebrod was considered insufficient sustenance on 12-hour shifts seven days a week. After the galley had officially closed, the chefs indulged us with specialities twice a week: choices of pizza one night, a variety of hot dogs on another.

Since 1986, *Tyra East* and its sister platform, *Tyra West*, have been sinking into the limestone seabed at one meter every six years. By the end of my second winter, the superstructure was already more than two metres closer to the waves. It was most noticeable during storms when they pounded through the walkways between installations. With access by foot too dangerous, the shuttle S-76A+ proved its worth. At Esbjerg, one storm blasted the hangar doors off their rails. It travelled through the building, ending up against the aft wall, crushing a light aircraft on the way. By 2022, these platforms had sunk a further three meters and were replaced by seven new installations. The primary one is *Tyra II*. The Hereema company barge, the SSCV *Sleipnir* (Semi-Sub Crane Vessel), lifted the topside onto *Tyra II*. *Sleipner*, named after Odin's eight-legged horse in Norse mythology, has two cranes, each with a lift capacity of 11,000 short tons. In October 2022, *Sleipnir* hoisted a record marine lift of 17,000 tons: the *Tyra II TEG* module. Still, things continued to go missing. Most former British Airways Helicopters employees had topped up their pensions using additional voluntary contributions (AVCs); these contributions invariably continued when employed by BIH. The principal vehicle used was the oldest insurance company in the world, Equitable Life, established in 1762 and now with over £26 billion under management. What could go wrong? If it was careless to lose a pension, the rumour of losing additional contributions was not much better. Just nine years after the Maxwell debacle, Equitable Life closed for business in 2000; it had accumulated huge un-hedged liabilities. These obligations guaranteed fixed returns for investors with no provision for adverse market conditions. The so-called fixed return for investors was no longer viable, resulting in the value of the funds invested falling to a small percentage of the original. It was a case of losing some and then you lose some more. Just as a casino. And those chips? It'll be your pension fund. Over time, AVC holders received a cheque – for 20% of the value of their investment. It could have been worse.

*

Timing? Coincident with a looming need for diversification, a new Flight Ops Director with only a background in Oil & Gas divested CHC Scotia's non-Oil & Gas-related UK onshore operations. They included the Falkland MOD contract, the former Veritair operations and the Penzance-Scillies link to a new company, British International Helicopters (BIH). As happened to many crews and engineers, you'll go full circle if you stay in one place long enough. His focus on offshore helicopter support did not account for a decline in North Sea gas production. During 2000, it peaked at 60,000 million cubic feet/day and equated to the combined output from Algeria, Libya, and Nigeria.
Despite so much effort and lives lost over the horizon, the government could have invested its revenue in a sovereign wealth fund like Norway. Instead, it funded tax breaks and unemployment benefits rather than investing in retraining for a generation of workers laid off from traditional industries having closed: mining, shipbuilding, and steel production. Scotland was particularly badly hit; it was the catalyst for today's drug problem. Today (2022), the Norwegian fund is worth US$1.4 trillion, US$244,000 for every citizen and growing.

Fig 48. CHC AS332 L2 CHC AS332 L1

Author's collection

In January 2001, I began flying the Super Puma again and stayed on the fleet until the 9th of November 2001, when I started an AS332 L2 conversion. The following day, a company Super Puma, G-BKZE, rolled over on the drillship *West Navion* 80 nautical miles West of Shetland. The aircraft landed, heading 295° magnetic with a 2.5° list to starboard relative to the helideck. The captain had remained on board the aircraft with the rotors running whilst the passengers disembarked. The co-pilot was assisting with the refuelling when the drillship's dynamic positioning system lost heading control and reverted to manual. The helicopter captain and the crew on the bridge were unaware the drillship's heading was drifting clockwise, slowly to the right—a list of approximately one degree to starboard and a crosswind developed. When the aircraft heading reached 030° magnetic, they had turned through 95 degrees. The helicopter toppled onto its starboard side, blown over by a 32-knot Westerly gusting 42. As the main rotors impacted the deck, they broke up, and the co-pilot received a severe leg injury from flying debris. The move to the AS332 L2 did not come a day too soon!

*

Unlike the 'L1' (Super Puma and Tiger), the name they gave to the civil version of the military Cougar was always referred to as the 'L2'. Among many differences, it has an Airbus A320 glass cockpit electronic flight information system (EFIS) with primary flight, navigation, and mission displays (PFD, NMD). It was a significant improvement on analogue instruments and less cramped than its predecessor, the 'L1'. It came with essentials largely automated, including navigation, approach, and go-around procedures. It was just a matter of pressing the right buttons. Like a lady, it was capable of quite impressive results if you selected the right ones. One

wondered how we had managed to manually ‘pole’ the approaches before; it was a forerunner for installing fly-by-wire systems and remained one of the best in its class. From a training point of view, I could trade the Scopoderm patches for Provence Pink. The ‘L2’ simulator was based at Marignane in the South of France. Nearby was the Eurocopter factory, now the helicopter division of Airbus. Our instructions from the training office in Aberdeen were to ensure we had spare capacity in our carry-on and nav bags – the latter needed dusting down.
Introducing immersion suits for pilots in the 1980s superseded the need for one. With copious pockets, there was sufficient space for a spare knife, fork, and an aluminium Felsenthal E-6B Computer or, if posh, a modern Dalton model. Open an O&G helicopter pilot’s nav bag, and what do you find: condiments to make rig meals more palatable and documents as an aide memoir. Except for the latter being uncontrolled, it could dump the owner in quite a pickle when referring to them again at the subsequent inquiry. Now in Provence, we spent time between slots in the sim touring vineyards our instructor/guide/oenophile Iggy had already shortlisted. There, we tasted the best of the region for the least. Twelve bottles in creaking cases with change from 20 euros seemed a worthwhile incentive to stay on the fleet.

*

A sad tale emerged of a lightning strike going undetected. It was the cause for a Bristow S-76A+ to go down on the 16th of July 2002. Operating out of Norwich, the flight was on a six-sector sortie between offshore installations in the Sole Pit and Leman gas fields, 28 miles northeast of Cromer, Norfolk. During the fourth sector, the aircraft was transiting between the *Clipper* platform and the *Global Santa Fe Monarch* drilling rig attached to the normally unattended *Leman ‘F’* platform. This sector was to transfer one passenger from the *Clipper* before returning to Norwich with the remaining eight passengers. At 18:44, witnesses reported hearing a muffled bang or a boom and seeing the aircraft dive steeply into the sea. One witness described seeing the main rotor head with the blades attached falling into the sea after the remainder of the aircraft had already impacted the surface. The fuselage disintegrated on impact, and the majority of the structure sank.
G-BJVX had suffered a catastrophic structural failure about 0.8 nautical miles northwest of the *Global Santa Fe Monarch*. Despite the fast rescue craft launched from the multipurpose standby vessel *Putford Achilles* being quick on the scene, there were no survivors among the nine passengers and two crew.

When divers from the DSV *Mayo* recovered the wreckage, two items were of major significance. Evidence indicated the main rotor gearbox casing had fractured and, together with the rotor head, had broken away from the fuselage in flight. Also, one of the main rotor blades had snapped approximately 76.75" from the root. They did not recover the remaining outer section.

QinetiQ's material laboratories found approximately half the circumference of the blade's titanium spar had failed in fatigue before the outer portion separated. The blade had been in service for 21 years and had accumulated 8,261 hours of usage.

Their investigation revealed a manufacturing anomaly: reduced insulation between the main rotor blade spar and a small area of its two-piece titanium leading edge erosion strip. Each strip finishes at one end in a wedge, mating together to form a scarf joint. The tip of the inboard end of the outboard erosion strip was bent and folded under the outboard end of the inboard erosion strip. The additional strip thickness in this joint caused microscopic damage to the titanium spar where they came into contact.

They also found microscopic evidence of a lightning strike reported three years earlier, in 1999. It had the appearance and discolouration of intense thermal damage similar to an electrical spot weld. The strike had exploited this manufacturing anomaly. When Bristows returned the blade to the manufacturer for assessment, they did not detect this microstructural damage. It was turned around and returned to service. Unfortunately, a fatigue crack developed in the spar originating from the earlier microstructural damage, now hidden by an opaque protective patch applied to the erosion strip's scarf joint. A thoughtful day for all concerned with North Sea heliops, but not something to dwell upon - I would be flying these aircraft the following year for Bristow International Business Unit (IBU).

*

The successful effort to save CHC's UK operations in 1998 was unknown to some junior managers and the Flight Ops Director and long forgotten by those who had assumed the vacant positions on the top floor. Maybe their behaviour had let them down and required memory erasure. In January 2003, the company notified four pilots they would not need them in the financial year beginning on the 1st of May; they were too old to keep on after 26 years of service, in seniority terms, meaning too expensive. With a statutory government payoff, and at 56 (a year older than the BAH retirement age in the seventies) and three others, Keith Dawson, Steve Martin, and

Roger Holloway, we were made redundant a few months before government legislation prohibited employers from removing staff on account of their age. My last flight was with Mike Irvine to the semi-sub drilling rig *Paul B. Loyd Junior* (some say she was a gift from his benevolent uncle) on the 30th of April. After we landed, I went to CHC House to collect the P45 employment discharge document. Coming out of the board room surrounded by his executive guests on the second floor, the Managing Director spotted me. Breaking ranks, he came across and enquired,

"How's it going, Andy?"

In the day, we knew each other well. As an engineering supervisor in Sumburgh, and more so when he enquired how I saw the future without the Shell contract in the car park before going home. How should one reply to the boss who has just terminated your employment; after his instant promotion to Managing Director had been secured by our efforts four years earlier? So, loud enough for others to hear,

"Well, you should know; you fired me. How does that feel!"

Speechless, his shocked clients closed in around him. Then, as one, they wheeled him off to safety behind the closing doors of the lift.

Since I started flying on the North Sea, there have been seven fatal helicopter accidents from 1975 to the end of 2002. These had claimed the lives of 88 offshore workers and flight crew whilst travelling to work. Catastrophic component failure was the primary cause of four accidents, the remainder being pilot error. Yet during the same period, over 48 million passengers have been carried over 6 million sectors, with pilots collectively logging 2.45 million flying hours; data covering 1992 to 2001 indicates the average fatality rate per billion passenger kilometres for UK offshore helicopter transport was similar to travel by car.

Part IV

Chapter 22. 2003

Caspian Tales – H_2S in the Air - Stamukhas

Norwich, England, September. It began with a checkout on the S-76A++ G-BIEJ with Bristow Helicopters. Entering their flight ops building, the first person to meet me was a good friend, Graham Church – ex-BAH. He was now working for Bristow, having been absorbed by them when they acquired the CHC Shell Expro contract from KLM/ERA. He signed off the checks when I reverted to flying on analogue instruments. A week later, I'd be airborne on a line check (three sectors were sufficient) to a rig on the Aktoty field and a small town called Bautino. I had been posted to Atyrau in Kazakhstan to work for a Bristow International joint venture with Atyrau Aue Zholy, a local airline. Routing through Budapest, the final 3 hours and 45-minute sector was in their ancient Tupolev TU-134 (well, even the new ones look ancient). They are too noisy and NOx (Nitrous Oxide) polluting to operate deeper into European airspace. Leaving Europe behind, we rattled across the width of Ukraine and the panhandle of Russia, where it reaches down to Azerbaijan to our destination a few miles inland from the Northern Caspian Sea.

*

And so, the journey began to demonstrate I was employable. It culminated the following year in flying three aircraft types, two were conversions, on three licences, in three countries and with two operators and operations based above and below sea level in temperatures ranging from -40°C to +56°C. And if you've read this far and Part IV is the last, it means a few more pages via four more countries before this entry concludes - back on the North Sea.

*

At the head of the Caspian Sea, Atyrau lies 20 miles inland through the reed marshes. These were pockmarked where wild boar had slept the night, mute swan and pelican nests and parts of spacecraft: recovery capsules and jettisoned fuel tanks launched on space missions from the Baikonur Cosmodrome in the north. Atyrau also straddles the Ural River that empties into the Caspian, with unusual geography for a town: Europe on the right bank and Asia on the left. Dairy camels grazed the margins between where the reeds left off and the outskirts of the town began. They say camel milk can prolong the gestation period in humans by up to 11 months to facilitate, if necessary, spring births. Apropos of camels, there is something the Kazaks, Native North Americans and other indigenous peoples have in common: the descriptive application of forenames. For example, the forename of the lady in charge of passenger handling, when translated, was 'Little White Camel' despite her dark hair.

*

When part of the former USSR, the town had been a traditional dumping ground for prisoners captured by the Russians or farmers displaced by Stalin to requisition their land and Chechens. The prisoners included Koreans, Germans, Italians, Poles, Turks, and other European nations who found themselves on the wrong side. And many had remained. It explained why the Soviet-style apartment blocks were poorly built, with reinforcing bars protruding into the rooms. As is common in the former Soviet Union, most buildings front on the spacious intervening ground of baked mud in the summer, providing a useful hard standing for cars and trucks. But when it rains, they, along with the streets and pavements, disappear under slurry three to four inches deep. With nowhere to drain to, the traffic is a similar colour. A bucket of muddy water and brush left outside domestic properties hint at a less offensive entry.
It was an unruly town. At the time, it was one of the few still controlled by the police; the mafia waited in the wings to take over. The latter provided subtle protection from the former, including our local, more of a dive with room for just 25 customers. They served only beer and vodka, though they could provide an excellent ragout, safe in the knowledge there were patrols in the frozen shadows outside, tramping their feet to keep warm in frost -30°C and below. The meat was easily on a par with reestit mutton, a speciality of Shetland. As silver darlings were, it was preserved in salt and stored in barrels.

*

This local cold war between these local factions of police and mafia is why flights transiting Kazakhstan only diverted to Atyrau with a severe emergency. Speaking to their crews on the radio as they flew overhead, they made this abundantly clear. Others thought we were just mad. Reports of Chechen rebels added fission in a small way to the experience. At first, I attributed the bulletproof door of our apartment to their presence, a veritable fortress with triple locks, one above the other. Scratched paint around the badly dented door frame was a clue of an unwanted visitor. If your flatmate was in town, access was by phoning him. But not in a clear view of the police as cell phones were harder to come by than guns in this country. They were liable to be 'confiscated'. If he was at home, it was to assure them this was not a raid.

Though by Chechens? Since the beginning of the second Chechen war, stoked back into life by the death of 293 persons in Russia blown up in their apartments, nowhere seemed safe. The Kremlin was determined to depose Dzhokhar Dudayev, a Chechen politician and former Soviet Air Force General who had established this anti-Russian country in 1991. Looking deeper into these bombings, there was reason to believe it was merely a pretext to resume hostilities. Then blame them on the Chechens, somewhat difficult to swallow when citizens caught Russian security services planting a bomb in a block of flats.

Then, before the security service had time to detonate it, the Duma announced an explosion. Finally, it was all explained away as a training exercise. Right! No, these people claimed Kazakhstan as their 'second home' and welcomed, despite Stalin deporting them there en masse on the flimsy charge of collaborating with the Nazis. Times change. A new influx of refugees, mainly women and children, had arrived. They generated unfavourable press reports, mainly by Russian correspondents frequenting bars in the town. Their presence helped to pile on the rhetoric of 'Chechen terrorists', 'Illegal armed Chechen immigrants in Kazakhstan' and 'Reinforcing the Western border of Kazakhstan and its Caspian Sea Coast. The towns of Atyrau and Aktau are most affected by this incursion'. Their articles appeared to be on behalf of the government in Almaty. Namely to ensure they aligned their support for neighbouring Russia and its foreign policy pretext to wrestle back control of the oil-rich miscreant state of Chechnya.

Though, it did generate an industry in constructing armoured apartment doors. Then, inside ours, complete the locking-in procedure to frustrate an unwanted entry, but not from mosquitos. They came out at night in the depths of winter to feed, smearing the bedroom walls with my DNA when swatted. Later, I found this battery of locks on doors of city apartments quite common in Kyiv and Moscow. Could there be that many Chechen invaders? Still, the effort was worth it. You could relax, break open a green tin of succulent starred sturgeon washed down with a beer, and wait for the cassoulet or kaiserschmarren to reheat on their fifth or sixth and final evening musing why cookbooks predicate all recipes on even numbers of helpings rather than odd.

I may have needed to stay longer in this town. At the time, I was the only member of staff the police had not arrested. And spend the night in jail. It was a common police ploy to elicit funds from the joint venture company to secure their release. Another tactic was to waylay us on the ride to and from work in the UAZ jeep or 4x4 Bukhanka minibus. It could occur at roundabouts, traffic lights, or anywhere else we stopped on the way. A policeman would appear at the driver's door, take him around the back, and ask him to explain the broken taillights he had just 'interfered with'. In exchange for a few hundred tenges the driver had ready, we would proceed; you paid to stop or stopped to pay. Either way, you fuelled corruption. Before leaving Asia on the way to the airport in Europe, a new building complex fronting the river could be seen upstream on the left bank. An impenetrably high wire and steel fence surrounded it. Within this barricade lay the Chagala Hotel. Not wanting to risk staying elsewhere, it is host to visiting Westerners and the only fortified accommodation in town. Owned by a Brit, you could drink Newcastle Brown and Guinness on tap while watching the rugby and other sporting events on a huge screen—a veritable Western oasis. And if leaving late in the evening to trek through the slush and slurry back to the apartment, there was always a welcome pit stop en route: a rotisserie chicken street vendor. These fowls were as good as those Costco is famous for. So, taking one bird was never enough, as two at one sitting to soak up the beer were so much better!

Now, over the bridge crossing the Ural into Europe, the driver would turn right, leave the tarmac, and enter another world. Here, the road turned into narrow, rutted tracks where he threaded the vehicle between a colony of connecting hutments shielded by corrugated iron and covered in black tarps. No danger of being stopped here. He had come to collect one or two more Kazak employees. It was a welcome respite for them to go to work from the appalling conditions at home.

Heading west on the highway out of town, the vista opened up, the Steppe. So flat the earth's curvature disappeared over the horizon as on a calm sea. Guards inspected our passes on arrival at the heavily armed gates giving entry to the airside of Khivaz Dospanova Airport. Inside, we'd drive down a lane bordered on one side by a jumble of discarded crates and packing cases; their Siberian pine panels weathered black by the sun. Then, turning right, our transport halted outside a long three-storey building. Its whitewashed walls had seen better days. The duty crew peeled off from the engineers who drove on down the side of the building, then left into a yard with a Ural 365 6x6 truck parked against the wall. A few metres past the chipped paint collage of the old truck, through a pedestrian door giving access to the rear of the hangar. To the right and across the way from the hangar, a forlorn sight of abandoned Air Kazakhstan Antonov An-24 high-wing turboprops caught the eye. And when you looked closer, it was clear these 44-seaters were slowly merging into the long grass around them. Indeed, the company collapsed like its aircraft in February of the following year.

*

The aircrew entered the long building and started the shift by visiting the airport workers' clinic on the ground floor. An unsmiling nurse checks your fitness to fly the aircraft for another day by administering a 20-minute check-over and recording your samples and tests. This medical was mandatory – every day. After the check-up, it was a long walk, tracing the route the engineers had taken, but down dimly lit Soviet-era corridors; the walls, as everywhere else inside, reflect a dirty pale blue. They led you past rooms revealing rows of triple-deck wooden bunk beds and, if your eyes had time to adjust to the half-light, exposed still more tiers of bunks hidden in the gloom. A few other rooms contained only a table and chair, where an airport official quietly worked under a weak, unshaded light bulb suspended on a long cord from the ceiling. Other than these few people, the place appeared deserted. Long ago, during the time of the USSR, a building of this size must have been humming and have made a good set sequel to the Ipcress File. Before reaching the airside, there was access through a door to the stairs leading up to flight ops on the first floor. Here, we planned the flights with our former Soviet Air Force and Kazak co-pilots.

*

The airport elevation is the lowest for any international airport at 72 feet below ocean sea level. One had to adjust to a QFE (atmospheric pressure at airport level) greater than the QNH (atmospheric pressure at mean sea level). It is unlike most everywhere in the world, where the reverse is the norm. With upside-down performance calculations sorted using these unusual parameters and load figures passed it was down to the gate to collect the manifests and onwards to the hangar. There, the three aircraft on contract waited. Usually, one of the two S-76A++ (G-BHBF and G-BJFL) alternated daily and a Bell 212 with a winch. The latter remained on standby to recover any flight that had gone tech; fitted with skids, it was ideal for landing on the ice. When it was suitably thick enough to support its weight, Canadian scientists arrived and flew out to measure pollution by taking core samples of Caspian ice and recording the annual change. The flying primarily involved crew changes to rigs drilling wells in the Northern Caspian Sea, the surface being 89 feet (27 m) below sea level. Elf and Shell Expro ran the Offshore Kazakhstan International Oil Consortium when I was there.

*

They constructed the drilling rigs on artificial berms graded flat with motorway-type construction equipment. After completion, the massive bulldozers were kept on to protect the installations from the encroaching winter ice. No sooner had this sea ice been pushed into the sea than the wind shifted it back up again, threatening the destruction of the rig and supporting infrastructure. Marine engineers sited additional steel caissons and smaller berms nearby to divert the ice and protect the mother berm. At the time, four rigs were drilling. Two were on the Aktoty and Kiaran fields; the others were the *KCA Deutag T-47* on East Kashagan and the Parker Drilling International *Rig 257* working West Kashagan and Kalamkas Fields. *Rig 257* was locally christened *Sunkar* after a Kazak poet and politician.

The *T-47* had formerly been on contract at Wytch Farm in Dorset. It had a significant upgrade to deal with this much harsher climate. *Sunkar*, once a Nigerian swamp barge, became the largest rig barge of its time. Initially, it had been heavily modified in Louisiana, shipped back and then prepared for sea ice defence in Astrakhan, Russia, at the mouth of the Volga. This US$100m engineering exercise included installing two four-meter-high deflection tanks to protect it. *Sunkar* sits on a one-meter-high limestone berm protected by 24 ice-resistant piles; each 70-ton pile is 1.6 m in diameter and 30 m high.

Every rig had its means of escaping from a serious incident. Three Canadian-built Arktos vehicles provide the means. Up to 50 personnel at a time could board these tracked orange monsters with pressurised cabins. Two travelled in tandem, connected by a universal joint. They could move through the water and over ice. From these ‘islands’, the drilling crews sent their drill bits down between four and five kilometres before breaking into an oil column under enormous pressure, 783 bar (11,356 psi). Economic production is forecast until 2076.

A fifth installation a mile or so west of *T-47* was also under construction called Island 'D'. At the time, it was a considerable expanse of crushed rock shipped in by barge and graded flat, with just the risers connecting the wellheads below protruding vertically out of this pale yellow, barren landscape. Before they piped the oil ashore, it would become the site for its production and separation. Later, two enormous compressors, mounted on two barges, moored alongside. One was 'The Widow Maker', the other 'The Rotating Bomb', so named due to the complexity of their operations. Their role was to pump sour gas, including H_2S, at 800 bar back into the wells to dispose of it and to maintain production pressure. The final result of Island 'D' is the one most photographed to represent Kashagan with its crescent-shaped, ice-diverting satellite berms surrounding it.

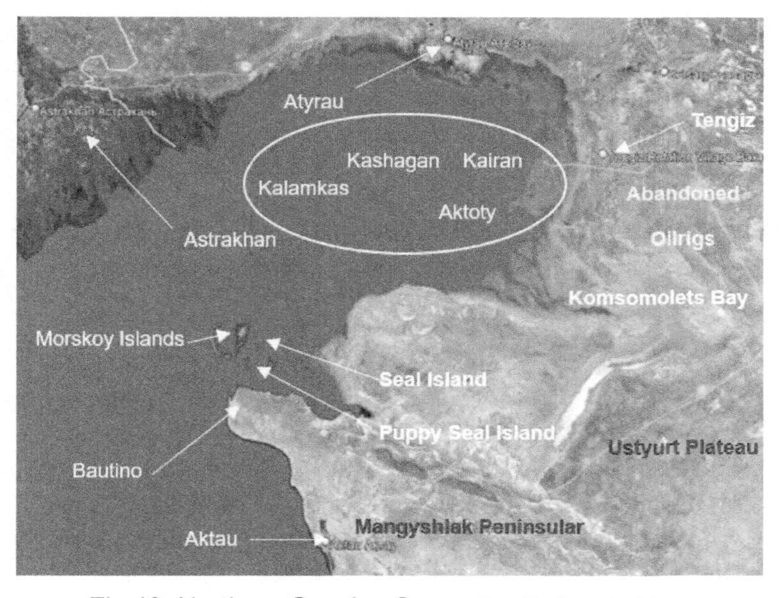

Fig 49. Northern Caspian Sea – *Credit: Google Maps*

Flights to the towns of Bautino and Aktau (formerly Shevchenko) on the eastern shoreline for freight were different as the sector between the two was overland. East of Bautino, the Steppe formed the Ustyurt Plateau between the Caspian and the Aral Sea. The latter is growing ever closer thanks to the 13-mile-long Zhanaozen dam completed in 2011. This was before a crazy agricultural policy drained it in the 1960s to support cotton fields in place of its thriving fishing industry with an international export market. Flight over this

arid, temperate land supporting grazing for herds of horses – is devoid of rivers, buildings, vehicles or people, no doubt a consequence of the policy under Stalin to requisition the stock, mainly cattle, from the nomadic Kazaks. This madness drove them and millions of others all over the USSR off the land and caused famine, spawning the phrase 'Serp i molot – smert I golod' (Hammer and sickle – death and hunger).
Better looking than the Caspian horse, they had the attributes of a Standardbred and were, on average, 15 to 16 hands high. When approached from above, they break into a gallop. On one occasion, we were returning from Aktau with freight when we saw some. Thinking my earlier comments of appreciation had been picked up by Yevgeny, my former Soviet Air Force co-pilot and probably a descendant of white Russian parentage, he asked to let down. We landed quite close by, hoping not to spook them when I began shutting down the engines. At this point, he said, "Don't worry," and jumped out. He returned quickly and closed the door. After refuelling at Aktau, he could not remember whether he had replaced the fuel cap. He wanted to check. How often has that be-devilled a pilot's mind as he settled into the cruise? Unlike cattle, the animals were not curious and galloped away, then stopped and stared back at us from a safe distance. With the fuel cap confirmed secure, we took off. Leaving the horses to seek grazing, we coasted out from the Mangyshlak Peninsular towards Kashagan. His diligence came unstuck the week before Christmas.

*

It is a condition worldwide; every pilot must have a current aircrew medical, renewed annually and bi-annually in the UK when over 40 years old. It is also a legal requirement to sign the medical certificate on completion. This time, Yevgeny had completed his medical and had submitted the certificate to his manager. He had not signed it. Now, most managers draw attention to the omission and ask the pilot to redress the situation with a signature. Not in Yevgeny's case. He was grounded without pay and had to re-sit all his commercial aviation exams. (There can be over ten of them); this is on top of supporting a young family, one probably disturbing his sleep as they do, but in mid-winter in one of the more inhospitable places on earth. It made us all pause, as I suspect others would, too.

*

A boat with no name. Three days during the first tour in the autumn stand out from the usual offshore crew changes. The first two occurred when the oil company consortium tasked us to assist a team of ornithologists from Moscow State University. It was part of the ecological effort conducted by the oil companies to preserve wildlife and the environment. The requirement was to fly the team quite slowly, maintaining 500 feet just offshore the coast of the Northern Caspian. It was a wader bird census before their migration (flying, not wading) south. Along these shores is a rich diversity of 280 species. They migrate through or spend the summer here before leaving like pensioners for winter in Southern Africa. To enable the count, the noise of the approaching helicopter disturbs them into flight. They tallied the birds in 'blocks' of 20, 100 or more, depending upon the flock size; a single flock could add up to thousands of birds. We flew west to the Russian border short of Astrakhan on the first day. Of note was the discovery of an open boat drawn out of the water into the reed beds. Well camouflaged, but not from the air.

We could not identify it. It was not any old boat: filling it from stem to stern was a giant sturgeon estimated by the Russians to be nearly four meters long. At that immense size, they agreed it could only have been beluga. We traced the coastline towards Turkmenistan in the southeast on the second day. This sector took us up into the northeastern part of the Caspian over the clear, barely flooded, shallow water of Komsomolets Bay. We put up hundreds of flamingos, an awe-inspiring sight as they lifted off for counting. Working down towards the Turkmen border, we stopped for lunch and fuel at Aktau, the principal oil supply base for the Northern Caspian. Waiting for a crew car, the team leader remarked: "Just love the smell of the Steppe," as we lined up on the edge of the tarmac to water it. Not much higher than heather, this vast quilt of wildflowers covering thousands of square miles turns to autumn colours, not unlike the woodlands in Scotland and the states of New England.

Nowhere in the region are these colours more vivid than a little farther north and onshore, the northeast neck of the Caspian and not far from Tengiz, the sixth largest oilfield in the world, producing 570,000 barrels a day from a column of oil 1.6 kilometres deep. It rivals the Gulf of Mexico. The first thing striking one landing here was the dunes of bright yellow sulphur. These stockpiles were a by-product of cleaning the crude oil of sour gas. The process separated the LPG with a ready market from the sulphur. No one wants all of it; there is too much. More recently, there has been a move to combine it with aluminium to make batteries or convert sulphur flakes into fertiliser. We could see even more oilfields on the north-western hinterland of Komsomolets Bay. Over 1,500 derricks protrude from the marshlands. Long abandoned from earlier exploration projects dating back to the late 19th century, these structures rotted and rusted away. Many had subsided under water due to fluctuating sea levels. It did not stop them from oozing the black stuff, giving their locations away. After all, oil is not a new phenomenon in the region. Though the Northern Caspian first produced oil in 1911, Marco Polo heard during his travels farther south on the way from Tabriz to Saveh near the Caspian, “There is a fountain from which oil springs in great abundance.” He recommended it: “For burning and as a salve for men and camels affected with itch or scab.”

The third day of interest was also in October. It began as a routine callout and then deteriorated into an unforgivable event. A rig in the Kashagan field had reported a leak. Kashagan is the second-largest oilfield in the world. Saudi Arabia has the largest. Now, a leak in any oilfield is a notifiable issue, but one estimated to have the fifth largest reserves in the world could turn into a big one. Oil wells are usually a combination of Oil & Gas. Here, the gas contains between 15% and 19% hydrogen sulphide (H_2S). These are some of the highest concentrations of sour gas anywhere on the planet. The enormous pressure it is under only added to the problems the explorers must contend with as H_2S corrodes metal, making leaks a constant nightmare. Though accidents happen, it is usually burnt off by the rig flare, converting it to sulphur dioxide (SO_2), smelling of rotting eggs. Its exposure to humans, even in small amounts, at more than 150 parts/million, causes paralysis of the olfactory senses. Concentrations between 300–500 ppm make it harder to fly an aircraft as you begin to lose consciousness. Because of the paralysis, you can’t understand why.

*

Our instructions were to position some 20 miles downwind to the west of the rig and then, looking for signs of an oil slick, to fly towards the source. After scanning the sea and seeing nothing untoward, we arrived at the rig and observed a strange sight. The area surrounding it, the entire berm, was covered in a layer of what looked like heaps of woodland bark chips, much as you see at a sawmill. There was no activity around the rig, so we descended for a closer look. We realised this was no bark but small brown birds: dead sparrows. Using the rig as a waypoint, they must have been en route to the south for the winter, yet this was no Icarus event; they had been unaware of some hidden danger. How did they die? We called the rig, advised the radio operator we had drawn a blank and began discussing the birds when he requested we clear the area and return to base. No explanation. After returning to the beach, we soon learned we could have joined the sparrows. It was not an oil leak. Just as the sparrows had formerly entertained us with their birdsong and chattering around eves of the hangars, we would never have known. Yet we were lucky.

*

H_2S is heavier than air; it can be carried in the wind. Flying into the wind as instructed to trace a leak, assumed by the agent to be of the usual material, oil was an unfortunate call. Sensitive though that may have been, had it been reported as an H_2S leak, they would not have requested us to fly. At more than 1,000 parts/million, the result is instantaneous loss of consciousness with slowed and stopped breathing = death. It is why oilfield workers in the Caspian, Persian Gulf (3%) and other regions where H_2S prevails are not permitted to grow facial hair. The masks associated with the emergency breathing apparatus will not fit snugly and could cause the gas to penetrate inside. And the rig worker who reported the avian carnage on social media? NRB (Not Required Back – blacklisted).

*

With a rotation cycle of six weeks on, four off in the winter and moving to a stone age of two months on and off in the spring, it was time to hand in my notice. I'd terminate my employment after the second tour. This move was after taking the precaution to call Andy Redfern, Chief Pilot at Gulf Helicopters based at Doha Airport, Qatar. Gulf operated the Bell twin-engine, two-bladed 212 and the four-bladed 412s. We had never met, though Andy appeared to judge a suitable candidate when you heard one; having come from South Devon and he from North Devon, it was a deal. Best of all, the work cycle was one month on/off. I'd be on the move again in the New Year. As an example of the legs doing the walking, Bristow adopted this routine within 12 months.

*

And the second tour was cold. So cold, on the 10th of December, the Ural River still allowed fibreglass boats to cruise down it; after a couple of hard frosts, it supported locals cutting holes to fish and driving motorbikes across it on the 12th. And offshore, the Caspian was freezing, too. It eventually reached as far south as the Morskoy Islands near Bautino on the east coast, usually ice-free. Rusting hulks of abandoned trawlers and navy patrol boats beached on the northern shore of the town could be seen from the landing area for helicopters. A flat gravel area towards the end of the land spit reached out to the northwest of town towards Seal Island, loosely connected to the smaller Puppy Seal Island, both part of the Morskoy group of Islands. These appropriately named islands provide the best freeboard for the remaining 111,000 Caspian seals to spend their summer months. Today, a virus, canine distemper, is taking its toll on their dwindling numbers. There was a time not long ago when they exceeded one million.

Fig 50. Rig *T-47* surrounded by sea ice; dock (behind helipad), East Kashagan Field, Northern Caspian. *Author's collection.*

Routing to the rigs, the seascape below changed on every flight. The kaleidoscope of cracks in the ice 'twist' continuously, daily revealing new patterns. Seals gathered on the edge of the larger fissures with their pups. It was here they gave birth on the ice twice a year. For this reason, a dedicated advisor is carried on the icebreakers to ensure they are not disturbed. Where the wind had gathered smaller floes, it forced them upon each other, creating small icebergs. Stamukhas. They could build up quite quickly and are known to reach six metres in 24 hours and, over time, reach up to 500 metres at the base. They could travel up to five knots and reach 100 feet high if they had not already grounded in the shallows. The shallow draft, blunt-nosed icebreakers were the only vessels capable of operating year-round. They

had positioned from the Baltic to the Caspian through European waterways to tow ballast barges for the berms and move freight to the rigs.
The S-76A++ was at the other end of the supply spectrum. The aircraft does not have ice guards or an icing clearance; it was not ideal to operate in winter temperatures below -30°C or below anything else. Besides, the engine and gearbox temperature gauges took an age to indicate they were even connected. A hint the needles were reaching the green was a good time to taxi. On a previous occasion in Aberdeen, a snowstorm had gone through when waiting at the holding point to take off. With permission from the control tower and much to the amusement of the crews waiting in the queue, I climbed out to remove the snow under the beating main rotor head before lining up. It had packed up on the upwind side against the gearbox panels and in front of the port engine intake. There it lay, waiting to be ingested as soon as we pulled in power and who knows what else.
And then there was the runway to contend. It was much like any other in the former USSR provinces. Being tarmac, it became heavily rutted during the warm summer months - ruts filled with ice in the winter. A Ural 365 6x6 heavy truck with two jet engines mounted at 45°on the front fender was the answer to improve the braking action. The vehicle moved at a walking pace. With engines roaring, it blasted thick slabs of ice into the air. It was acceptable for landing fixed-wing aircraft with their bulbous, all-terrain tyres. Not-so-good for the poor (2 crew and 12 passengers) little S-76A++. When waddling onto the active to line up, the exposed ruts posed potential traps for its small wheels to fall in and damage the low-slung undercarriage knuckles. Less serious impediments have ripped them off. Then, in-flight freezing rain on a supercooled aircraft without icing protection could be an issue. It struck out of nowhere.
A thick layer will envelop the aircraft in seconds, coinciding with a significant jump on the torque-meter needles—time to return to base. A Muslim necropolis with its lilliput-sized white buildings sited southeast of the airfield on the Steppe provided a helpful landmark to find our way back. The hangar had no heating and poorly fitting doors, allowing the wind to blow the snow through. Eddies formed snowdrifts inside. Now grounded, the aircraft took time to thaw out - lots of time. It was not all bad. We had a spare aircraft to go out and try again!

*

'Ad hoc' work could be unusually rewarded. Any knowledge of how far the ice had migrated south at this time of year was valuable information. And not only for the rig supply company icebreakers. The Kazak boss explained this when he called me into his office on the top floor. His uncles wanted a briefing to determine when to launch their motorcycle sidecar combinations for fishing forays across the sea ice. Not only could it save lives and equipment lost falling through it, but it also indicated when the deeper, more productive water became accessible. Local knowledge is everything and not a condition for flying for Bristow. Still, starting the day with the smell of fresh roe loaded on blinis and cream in the morning is as good as it gets in this forsaken part of the world. More so when the going rate was an 'eyewatering' US$20/100 gm for sevruga in the local market. A certificate for export was required, the latter acquired after a long wait outside an office upstairs, though not so long as the time these fish and their cousins, the spiny and beluga sturgeon, took to maturity or the distance they had travelled with their eggs. A round trip of 1,400 to 1,600 km up to the headwaters of the dam-free Ural, a river they needed to navigate before they could spawn. Their smolt then made their way downstream to the Caspian to mature over seven years before making the journey themselves, provided they could escape the poachers bagging 95% of the annual catch.

Chapter 23. 2003 - 2004

A Cemetery with Lights – Kish Island – Flying with Angels

We had worked together in the early days. Martin Bull, the base manager, had qualified to fly helicopters out of Aberdeen on a course soon after mine. With a smile, he quipped on my leaving, "You're welcome back any time." A kind touch of forgiveness, given the last time the parting was accompanied by being blacklisted from working with Bristow for 21 years. And so, part one ended with my last day on the base operating to the *T-47* on the 20th of January, with the next phase beginning in Qatar two weeks later. Specifically, Doha – the fabled 'Cemetery with Lights' where Big Al Bristow had set up his first Persian Gulf operation in 1955.

Here, I put a Bell 412 conversion and Qatar Air Transport Pilots Licence - Helicopters together. I collected the latter from the Qatar Civil Aviation Authority Flight Operations Inspector downtown. Seated opposite him, he leaned across his desk to indicate where the signatures should go when his halo detached. Bouncing off his desk, it landed on the floor behind me. Perfectly balanced, it cartwheeled across the room and through the open doorway into the corridor. Retrieving it for him, we both had to smile. Operating out of Doha could always provide something new. On some occasions, the airport shuts with no advance notice or Notice to Airmen; invariably, an incoming or departing sheikh with priority over all other movements in the zone. Rather than run out of fuel, we shut down on Banana Island, so named on account of its shape; this spit of shingle and white pebbles is about 200 metres from tip to tip. At times, and if need be, it could accommodate a small colony of helicopters awaiting onward clearance. Sat just a mile offshore from the mainland with a view of the airport, it was home for the residents: terns and little gulls. When disturbed, they lifted off and, screeching in annoyance, swarmed around us. It has been significantly enlarged and turned into a holiday resort with a helipad and marina. Like the terns, I preferred the sanctity of the original.

The time came to stay in Doha and operate in the oil and predominantly gas fields; the North Field is the largest, or to move abroad. The other choices at the time were flying seismic survey flights in Yemen, living in ever-moving campsites as Bedouins with an opportunity from time to time to return to Doha for a dust-down and shower. Or live on Kish Island, Iran, flying to the South Pars Oil & Gas fields. Both were appealing for three reasons: no more early starts, each attracted an allowance, where the average person residing outside the cities lived on US$100 a month and freedom from the Indian mafia running Qatar.

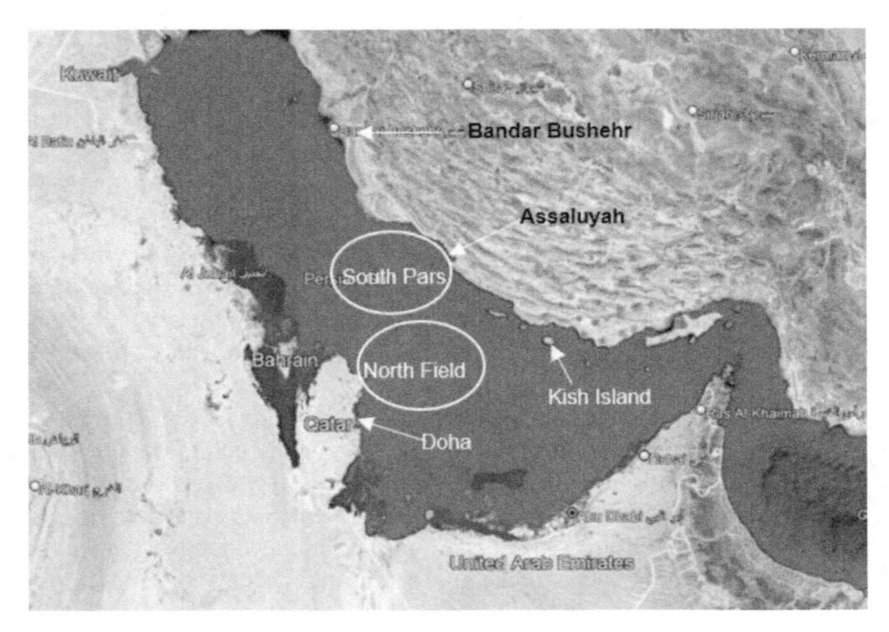

Fig 51. Approximate areas of oilfields North Field (Qatar) and South Pars (Iran). *Credit: Google Maps*

Iran presented a more attractive choice. Since the revolution in 1979, it has offered the opportunity to live in a country somewhat off-limits to Westerners. There is a ban on Americans working there. It was also the backdrop to a daring escape by Bristow Helicopters pilots in their Bell 212s. It was time to discover how much, or if anything, had changed.

.

*

In 1979, Bristow had three principal operations with seven Bell 212 helicopters on contract. An eighth EP-HBJ was dismantled and in the middle of a 'D' check. They were based on Lavan Island (a neighbour and northwest of Kish), Kharg Island (offshore Bandar Bushehr) and Gachsaran at the head of the Gulf. In January, Lavan's senior pilot informed Big Al the crews were flying at gunpoint. A Republican Guard is riding 'shotgun' in the back of each

flight; to ensure the pilot does not deviate from his planned routing around the oilfields, the weapon is loaded with the safety catch off.
Bristow's directors were against doing anything irregular. Instead, Big Al hatched a plan to fly his operation out. He recommended some of their sons fly the line for those aircraft left behind. After they had slept on it, they agreed to remove their aircraft. Two months later, they activated Operation 'Sandstorm'. Non-essential personnel and spare parts tagged as personal effects (Mr Bell C. Box, Redhill and so forth.) had been flown out of the country by the 20th of February in the company HS-125 jet. Being a day of prayer for Moslems, they chose a Friday in March; locals sleep in. The arrangement was to rendezvous at Sharjah, UAE, where air cargo transport was waiting. At 07:00 on the 9th, the three from Lavan left for Dubai, the two from Kharg to Bahrain; then nothing. An unexpected commercial flight comes up, delaying the two from Gachsaran. If they did escape to Kuwait, their problems would not be over. Kuwait had good relations with Iran and has notification from Abadan to look out for 'EP' registered Bell 212s. A bogus flight plan has been filed for two British-registered Bell 212s departing Kirkuk, Iraq, routing through Kuwait to allow for this possibility. It had to be updated. Later in the day, the remaining two managed to leave Gachsaran and refuel from a fuel dump en route. Engineers met them in Kuwait, where they calmly unfurled British 'G' registrations according to the bogus flight plan. These were genuine, except they were already allocated to 212s undergoing maintenance back in the hangars at Redhill. They replaced the Iranian 'EP' registrations with them. Suitably registered, they are finally on the way to their rendezvous. On arrival at Sharjah, engineers remove the main rotors and the tail section aft of their cabins. Then, fly them to Luxembourg on three Luxair freighters, a Boeing 747F and two 707s. From there, they were transported by road, arriving in Redhill 48 hours after leaving the Gulf. It seemed too good to be true. Big Al lamented they had to leave some smaller helicopters and the Bell 212 EP-HBJ behind. Altogether, they were worth US$4m. He brightened up when his financial director explained the value of the aircraft recovered was worth US$15m, and he owned only 49% of them. The remaining 51% he had stolen from their Iranian partners.
A former commander of the Iranian Grumman F-14 Tomcat fighter base on Kish Island now drove the passengers out to the helicopters. Out on the flight line, I joined the colonel on his bus. This audacious, dangerous, and successful mission had impressed him. Somehow, he might have liked to have joined them, too.

*

The law exam was oral and conducted by a flight operations inspector and a senior air traffic controller from Tehran. The controller asked most of the questions. His scant knowledge of the lower airspace was telling, yet he excelled with the upper airspace; mine was the reverse. With a twinkle in his eye, the arbitrating inspector agreed we compromise on our different areas of interest and to know what was relevant to our area of operations. With an Iranian air law exam completed and another licence issued, flying in Iran began on the 15th of May. Then, five weeks later, on the 21st of June, there was a stark reminder stuff happened here.

*

Farther up the coast, the Iranian Navy had captured three Royal Navy vessels crewed by six Royal Marines and two sailors. Their mission was to rendezvous with another unit from Basra on the Shatt Al Arab, then change out an unserviceable Combat Support Boat (CSB) with one of their own at Al Faw. They departed Umm Qasr North Port, and en route in their two support boats and a Boston Whaler, they noticed suspicious activity: a civilian speed boat was making close passes and stopping vessels in the main channel. They dispatched the Whaler to intercept it as part of a routine procedure to counter smuggling operations. When they drew level, they observed only one person onboard wearing loose pyjama-type clothing. He appeared to be unarmed. After exchanging greetings, they noticed two civilian Scarab fast boats with three crew members operating just inside Iranian waters. They, too, appeared unarmed and were moving between dhows and speaking to their crews. Taking no further action, the Waler re-joined the two support boats. They continued on their way when they detected what they believed to be their rendezvous party in four boats. They were travelling at high speed towards them.

It soon became apparent two of the boats were Iranian gunboats. Up to seven armed men crewed each. The other two were the Scarabs they had seen earlier. They, too, were now armed. The gunboats shot ahead and halted their progress as the Scarabs closed in behind. They surround them. With a 0.5” heavy machine gun trained on them, they were forced over the border into Iranian waters and then charged with straying into Iranian territorial water. Later, they were marched into the desert and halted in front of a ditch. Blindfolded, they heard their captors cock their guns – a mock execution. After three days of UK Foreign Office intervention, the Iranians released them; without their equipment, including international trade in arms regulations (ITAR)-sensitive night vision goggles (NVG), they returned to Iraq a day later.

*

It's a small world. In 1274, Marco Polo arrived in Peking (Beijing). From the gates of Vienna and east as far as the Pacific Ocean, Eurasia was still under the rule of Kublai Khan, grandson of Genghis. At the imperial court, Marco observed the Empress of Mongolia wearing a stunning pearl set. If you walk along the shores of the Pearl River, as experienced when operating out of Zhuhai, you will pass middens of oyster shells above the muddy high-water mark. Being a trader, he assumed they came from that region. Instead, much as we would refer to the Mayfair branch of Asprey, she replied: "Oh, I buy mine from Kish." It will not be until two years later she could access them from the Pearl River and cultured pearls called Nan Zhu from Beihai on the northern coast of the Gulf of Tonkin. The Song dynasty had controlled this area of Southern China and only fell to the Mongolian Empire in 1276.

*

At the other end of the spectrum was our local bakery making three kinds of flat bread distinguished by the different sorts of seeds scattered on them, or not as the case may be. These loaves were nân-e barbari, named after the Hazaras people from central Afghanistan, referred to as imposters, much as we were when operating in China, as barbarians, hence its name. They resembled small skateboards. Around 30 centimetres wide and 80 long, they were impaled on spikes high up on the wall, ready for sale. All you needed was a hod to carry them home, being invariably too hot to handle. And rollerblades. Instead of taking the company car, the last half-mile walk to the airfield was alongside a deserted dual-carriageway bordered by oleander and date palms. A rhythmic trundling invades this peaceful furnace - approaching rollerblades. Paul Micheletti – a CHC International S-76A+ driver. Australians! Surging by on the far side of the road, he'd holla across with "See you in the hangar!" then disappear around the next bend of this rural boulevard.

*

Kish Island is a small, nine-by-four mile, raised marine terrace. It formed after the last ice age and is set a few miles off the southern coast of Iran. Most of

the island slopes down to the shore except in the south. Some 60-foot-high cliffs border the shoreline, providing a glimpse of a former life under the seabed. Shells packed in the sediment, as rings in a tree, poke out of the crust with the most recent on top, much as they were deposited those thousands of years ago.
We had taken a crew change out to the Russian jack-up rig *Sakalinskya*. They were drilling in waters some 60 miles south of the island. As we approached, we disturbed Soviet roustabouts basking in the sun on the helideck between shifts. Coasting in later on the way back, I spotted a small, isolated beach carved out of the cliffs. It was a short half-hour cycle ride across empty country roads. Primarily flat, they are flanked in places with date palms, though mostly acacia shading small, nimble gazelles. Rockpools fringed the cove. Here, cowries hauled their brown-speckled, plumb-sized shells in slow motion; in contrast, the sandy shallows erupted with spooked shoals of small fry in a frenzy of silver. Deeper offshore lay a green turtle grazing ground where I'd swim with the sea grass below and among turtle turds floating above. Rarely would I be joined on these excursions more than once; was it the ridiculous heat of the journey or the predators and dung in the water? On the island's highest point at just 130 feet above sea level, the airfield is laid out with two parallel runways long enough to accept Concorde, an infrequent visitor during the time of the late Shah.

*

Above 1,000 feet, Tehran Radar controlled the airspace, and we flew with Iranian pilots as guards. No longer armed, they were insurance we did not disappear out of the country, Bristow fashion. An exception to flying with guards was when importing stores and spare parts. We flew these into the country as a single pilot to free up the payload. The other operator on the base was CHC International, with whom we shared a new hangar supporting enormous downpipes. Dew collected on the roof overnight flooded the apron when the sun rose. An open drive-through divided the company offices inside and at the end of this building. We sat in this area, where air funnelled through, sharing stories (Including one by Gilles Prégent. Bad weather terminated a shortcut through Columbia during a ferry flight in a Bell 212 from Canada to Chile. Landing on a riverbank with a cocaine factory in the bushes on the other side resulted in time as an uninvited guest of the Revolutionary Armed Forces of Columbia (FARC). They order him to fly the helicopter into the bushland where they can hide it. Rescue came six months later with the help of the Canadian Red Cross. Another by Ruud Heinen, my housemate.

He had acquired a time-expired Bell 205 – the civil variant of the UH-1 Huey. He swapped it for a brand-new model a museum had in storage. It was still in its packing cases. After all, they only wanted a static display. Ruud was not only a pilot but also a licenced engineer. After a few months, he was flying his deal too good to be true.) and kept cool by the breeze passing through and waited. Unlike Bergen, there was no imperative to go on time. The flight only went when everyone was ready. And in that heat, no one was ready to do anything. It meant there was much waiting. And Jab, a Persian engineer formerly with Pan Am, was no exception. When the flight eventually closed, it was time to grab three two-and-a-half-litre bottles of ice from the freezer and head out to the flight line. With two bottles wedged behind the cockpit seat, you had finished the third by the time the passengers had strapped in.

Fig 52. 'Jab' ex Pan Am engineer.

Line maintenance, Kish Island.

Author's collection

The co-pilot/guards came from two diverse sources. One was younger crews of Arab descent. Iranians. The other pilots trained pre-revolution during the time of the Shah at Fort Rucker, AL, USA. Persians. Today, the latter hope for better days and a restored relationship with the West. After all, as the Shah pointed out to Frank Prior, the chairman of Standard Oil of Indiana, in 1958: "You know – we are not Arabs, we are Aryans, and we are the same race as you are. We have a great history." As senior Iranian Navy and Air Force members, they included an admiral. They fought in the Iran/Iraq war (September 1980 – August 1988) and survived despite the enormous odds.

*

They don't shoot angels, do they? They referred to these pilots as angels because of their invincibility during this war. Immortal. One of them had considerable self-belief. For example, when the radar service vectors your flight after taking off on a collision course with an aircraft landing in the opposite direction on the parallel runway, it is usual to query the instruction. Unless you are this angel. And, when approaching the southern shore of Lavan on the way up the Gulf to South Pars, you'd see traffic rising and heading southbound on the way to their rigs. They are due to cross your track, climbing out through your level. The bearing is constant. It is on a collision course but on a different radio frequency. You plan to take avoiding action. Unless you're this angel. When you devise a resolution to the conflict, they sigh: ''Don't worry, captain. Inshallah," The engineers were mainly Irish (ex-Irish Helicopters), Australian and Persian, headed by Pete De Marzi and his back-to-back Pat McCarthy. Fortunately, they were not 'angels', well, not in this sense.

*

The company based four Bell 412s in Kish at any one time. They allocated their most worn-out machines, keeping the finest for their operation out of Doha, where maintenance could have been better. On an occasion when I arrived with Harry, a Brit engineer, in an aircraft from Kish, they removed the main rotor blades soon after we had landed. In exchange, they gave us blades in the 'too difficult to balance (track)' category. Harry spent the next three days observing the adjustments he had made from the left-hand seat until, after many air tests, he had trimmed them to perfection. We racked up so many landing charges they were glad when we returned to Iran with more stores and spare parts.
Each aircraft had two technical logbooks. One for Gulf Helicopters, recording the aircraft flying time from lift off to landing per European regulations; the other for the Iran Helicopter Company, logged when the engines started to when they stopped. The latter practice aligned with the tractors I drove on the farms in the South Hams of S. Devon. Having spent over five years operating under the sun and stars, cushioned by the hay stuffed in a West of England hessian sack on the seat and the air in the tyres, some of them were mine. For pressurised cabs to keep out the rain, snow and dust and a suspension to soften the ruts were a luxury, few farmers could afford: a proper day's work, every season, a memory. That was before taking up flying. And bar an hour or two, never having to do a *proper* day's work again!

The routes flown were mainly to South Pars, the northern part of the vast gas field spanning the Iran/Qatar (North Field) border. South Pars alone contains an estimated 436 trillion cubic feet of gas. The flights were routed direct or via where the gas was piped ashore on the mainland, Assaluyah. Here, you could refuel by pumping Jet A1 out of a barrel.
At the time, there were four gas processing plants at Assaluyah, with others under construction. Another, the Parsian Gas Refinery, was in a valley over the mountains at Khosh Abad. The latter was a struggle to reach. Following the gas pipelines ever upwards, when close to 4,000 feet, they snaked back down into the valley below. In the summer heat, it required a beady eye on the temperature gauges and torque metres to ensure they stayed within limits. At the top of the descent, the temperature was still over +40°C. On reaching the valley floor just to the southeast of Khosh, it was a question of finding a small concrete helipad set out in the open country of loose gravel, sand, and dust some two miles away from the refinery. Disappearing into a 'brownout' was guaranteed on arrival and departure. We rarely had to fly there; it was low on their visitor bucket list.
Total, the French oil company operated from Assaluyah. They provided a welcome Western touch on arrival at the heli-strip: a bag of freshly baked mini croissants and pain au chocolate driven in from their base. Yum! With the gas processing flares at the foot of this 4,000-foot escarpment, this place could reach +56°C on the aircraft temperature gauge in the summer – the max operating performance OAT (outside air temperature in the shade) for the Bell 412 is +52°C. Despite removing the aircraft air conditioning system to save weight, these days, it does not pay to be too heavy on the left pedal when departing. To clear the refinery fences and obstructions, easing the foot off provided a notional 10° to 15° extra lift to the main rotor at the expense of drifting off course. Still, the South Pars installations were good for tuna caught in nets by the crane drivers; they gave them away with their tails poking out of bin liners to take home, though, for the superior kingfish, they charged a few greens Iranian. (A green note: 10,000 rials = around 20 pence).

*

Illegal in Iran, it was possible to acquire good quality confiscated bootleg spirits from the Civil Police. It mainly originated from a duty-free area of London packaged in cans with a sell-by date just a few months earlier. One evening in the autumn, we were enjoying a sundowner on our balcony. Andreas Mouritsen, from the Faroe Islands, was my flatmate then. We could

hear a distant chant from the direction of the police stations at the end of the road.
There were two stations, side by side: one for the civil police (blue uniforms) and the other (green uniforms) for the military of the Republican Guard. After some time, a pick-up truck loaded with a rack of amplifiers mounted behind the cab came down the empty street into view. Twenty or so bare-chested men walking barefoot followed behind. This procession commemorated the death in 680CE of Imam Hussein, grandson of the Prophet Mohammed, killed in battle near Karbala, Iraq. The Yazidi victors later mutilated some of the dead. The urban area of Kish had been divided into sectors, and this evening, it was our turn on the edge of town to witness this Shia commemoration of Ashura.
As the truck moved along, on the bed in the back, an individual exhorted them to keep going. Attached to a chain, they were swinging small knives over alternating shoulders. First to the left, then to the right; the blades impart cuts evenly across their backs. Flagellated and with a rhythmic beat, they moved out of view. An hour later, they reappeared, having completed a lap around our part of town. It was pretty dark now. Yet we could see in the streetlights they were holding up no worse for wear. Not having witnessed self-mutilation before, it was a bit of a revelation - no wonder the Parsees left the country. Then, with tattered backs and blood-soaked trousers, the chanting procession continued its circuit into the wee hours. Somehow, tinned vodka with a sell-by date never tasted quite the same.

*

Dangerous goods could be concerning. The flight from Kish to Assaluyah usually coasted in over the small fishing village of Chiruyeh with a sweeping-crescent-shaped beach just off the coastal highway; small wonder, the Farsi word for landscape is paradise. Soon after landfall, we entered a lightning storm. Shards of light filled the sky, giving the sensation of golden ticker tape raining down on and around us. This time, there was no radio static or instrument deviation. These sferics are generally associated with an electrically charged atmosphere when their noise in the headset could grow from a low warble to a sustained piercing screech. Your only recourse is to remove your headset until they have dissipated. Still, there was no noise or turbulence this time - just the weather's silent flickering light show. And the engines didn't miss a beat as they continued to churn out their power to the C-Box, feeding the driveshaft between them back to the main gearbox and rotor head. After 15 minutes of this surreal phenomenon, we began our

thudding descent out of the hills. The route takes us past the Persian Gulf International Airport under construction and then over a vast roundabout (Iranians like them big and best viewed from the moon) leading to it. Next up on the left-hand side was the old airport still in use, with a naval detachment of Taregh patrol boats next door riding at anchor. We take care not to stir up their hornets' nest in the southern neck of the bay before entering the town coated with deep layers of dust. Upon reaching the harbour, sharp right to locate the fenced-off heli strip squeezed between gas processing plants.
Touchdown and shut down. Arriving back in the SUV after lunch cooked by French chefs at the Total camp restaurant on the edge of town, a huddle of men was hovering around a crushed cardboard box. It was leaking fluid into the concrete next to the helicopter. Two of them were Republican Guards and armed with semi-automatic weapons. My co-pilot, engaging in the (Farsi) discussion, became quite agitated when I told them there was no way we would accept this cargo.
The consequence of this input promised to exceed the afternoon temperature, already on the wrong side of +50°C. At this point, I drew him aside and headed out of earshot towards the fuel drums from where we had recently refuelled. He explained in this country, disobedience was not an asset. As a former policeman and part of the narcotics interdiction service on the Afghan border with his country, he understood hundreds of thousands of people had disappeared since 1979. A single round behind the freight office will ensure the flight went as planned – single-piloted. Together, we walked back to the helicopter. In case of trouble, I suggested he sit in the cockpit. I recommended the materials go by sea; when they admitted, the port security would not let them through with their sorry package, hence their efforts to ship by air. Disappointing as the real culprit were the owners – another Western service company. Worse, one that preaches and teaches safety to others, putting the locals and the popular heliport supervisor under unnecessary pressure. Afterwards, they respected the IATA dangerous goods regulations.

*

Some years earlier, working out of Aberdeen, we flew the fabled Sunday 'bomb run'. Not having flown this sortie before, we quickly learned it involved collecting hydrocarbon samples from offshore production platforms. These samples could have contained all sorts of corrosive and deadly gas. The containers looked like stainless steel bombs. There was no paperwork, a

terminal problem on this installation, or labels to identify and disclose their contents.
Moreover, no Dangerous Goods Shippers Declarations forms were onboard the dispatching platforms. They added to the equation by routing the flight through other third-party platforms where passengers were due to board. We declined the samples. An accident waiting to happen? After conducting a pipeline inspection to the oil terminal at Flotta in Orkney, we arrived back at Aberdeen, and ops asked me to speak with the oil company representative. He understood why we had refused the samples. And then the truth. A former BAH manager had advised them: on the provision, they did not inform his pilots of the actual contents of the cargo; they could load anything they liked. OXY did not renew the crew-change contract and gave it to British Caledonian Helicopters. Soon after this incident, on the 6th of July 1988, the principal source of samples, Piper 'A', exploded.
One hundred and sixty-seven lives were lost, and many were injured that night when the 20,000-ton platform succumbed to the inferno that lasted for three weeks.

Fig 53. *Piper 'A'* with *MFSV Tharos* in the foreground.
Photo credit Captain Lori Burn

This disaster eventually brought a new era for the UK offshore industry to better align with the one successfully pioneered by the nuclear and chemical industries – Safety Management Systems (SMS).

*

A licence to fly the Bell 412 includes the Bell 212, but there are differences. One side of A4 paper is sufficient to record them, and because we were not operating 212s at Kish, it was 'filed'. So, the day came to route up to Bandar Bushehr to collect an aircraft with a defective stability augmentation system (SAS – stabilises the aircraft in one or more axis). It would launch the helicopter into a sudden descending port bank, representing an un-commanded 'hard-over'. It was unnerving for the passengers. It was also the cause of fatal accidents when the aircraft had not responded to recovery inputs.

Taking the coastal route up was flying over a geologist's dream landscape with the most outrageous rock formations imaginable. It included the original seabed eroded into mushroom-shaped pillars or mushroom rocks. The wind and rain had eroded the soft sediment, leaving a hard dome on top; usually dispersed, these clustered together - a reminder of a drawing on the back of a plywood nav' board in BAH. It was a beautiful representation of a field of fungi with the caption 'Kept in the dark and fed on shit'. And past the Jashak Salt Dome (1,350m) on the way back. Letting down on the Bushehr VOR DME approach from the south is within 'touching' distance of the nuclear dome on the port side. The airfield, as most, has paved runways, except the ground intersecting them had mature bushes obscuring one manoeuvring area from another, an indication grass cutting was a rare event. And vegetation had done what it does best – take over. It gave the impression of a disused airfield, though maybe this was the best way to camouflage it in future hostilities.

Héli-Union (the French operator) was the other O&G helicopter operator on base with an SA 365N Dauphin. We approached them first to find our bearings in the absence of life anywhere else. Their hangar/office was in a long brick building near where we had shut down. Shellfire had blown out one of the long walls, forming a rubble access ramp of crushed bricks (Iraq had extensively bombed the area during the Iran/Iraq war). Inside, at one end of this bomb site, their engineer sat at a desk pebbled with paperweights anchoring his work. He indicated he knew of a helicopter behind some bushes, waving "Là-bas" in the general direction across the airfield towards the sea.

*

Soon after, the Gulf Heli engineer Colin arrived, and we exchanged tech logs. Bearings restored! (We were to meet again while working for Bristow International, out of Turku in Finland, in August 2010). It was then determined

the aircraft we'd come to collect was the Bell 212 EP-HUE. Casting the mind back to those brave ladies supplying our pilots with so many different aircraft types they flew from the factories during World War II, it seemed churlish not to have got airborne. The differences presented themselves on the walk-around, and pre-flight was obvious, so lighting it up, we flew back to Kish.
It reminded me of a Bell 212 Okanagan pilot coming off the flight line at Juhu. As I was walking out to the S-61N, he remarked under his breath to me, "You lucky bastard!" At the time, it seemed he was being a little unkind. But then, their S-61N was in the hangar, off-contract. Despite its age, the aircraft was a delight to fly; few instruments and space in the cockpit to stretch the legs out Harley Davidson style. Instead of returning it after sorting out the earthing/corrosion problem, we retained it, telling Bushehr there was still outstanding work.
An interception by NAVAIR McDonnell Douglas F/A-18 Hornets could be interesting. They operated off the US Navy Persian Gulf carrier fleet. Particularly when flying Iranian EP-registered aircraft. And more so when flying in stores and spare parts, single-pilot, from outside Iran. A stock answer given by former Bristow pilot Peter Morgan based in Bandar Bushehr when asked, "What are your intentions" as they moved in alongside was to reply: "To retire and open a corner shop!"

Fig 54. EP-HUE Bell 212 Kish Island, Iran 2005 – *Author's collection*

Note: the skid furrows after they have settled into warm asphalt.

This region was a volatile part of the world where anyone could make a mistake in this trigger-happy airspace. Most of us were aware the USS *Vincennes* had shot down EP-IBU, an Airbus A300, with the loss of 274 passengers and 16 crew - Iran Air Flight 655 en route from Bandar Abbas to

Dubai in 1988. The incident occurred when the US protected Kuwait oil tankers destined for the USA. These vessels were recently registered under the US flag to enable US Navy intervention and safe passage through the Straits of Hormuz. It was called Operation Prime Chance, and the derrick barge DB *Hercules*, a prime lifter during the Forties construction, was involved. Brown and Root had chartered her to the US Navy and Army unit deployed to the Gulf, where gunboats were launched from her deck using the heavy lift crane 'Clyde'. As one of its helicopters was under fire from Iranian gunboats, the USS *Vincennes* entered Iranian territorial waters. The guided-missile cruiser had assumed the A300 was an Iranian Grumman F-14 Tomcat supporting these Iranian gunboats. (The US sold these aircraft to the Iranian Air Force before the revolution in 1979). This error did not seem to register. It could have repeated itself when, more recently, during the second Gulf War in 2003, cruise missiles aimed at targets in Iraq ruffled the heli-lanes offshore Qatar. Fortuitously, with no strikes en route. And then I had an invitation to a tribunal.

Chapter 24. 2005 - 2010

Tribunal – Iranian Permit – Flying the F-35B.

Flying in from Iran via Dubai and London, the pre-tribunal proceedings convened in Aberdeen. The action began at 09:00. Together with Mick Brade, the BALPA Helicopter convenor, the four pilots (litigators) are represented by a Queen's Council (QC) from London supplied by BALPA. It became clear the other three pilots had, in effect, taken early retirement, and they were grateful to settle early out of court for what they considered a reasonable arrangement. Based on my homework, I instructed our QC to accept only 100%. Moreover, please reach a swift decision as I was making a presentation at the same time the following morning to the National Aeronautics and Space Administration (NASA) at Cape Canaveral. At this point, she cautioned CHC might insist on a full tribunal and then void the action through a technicality.

The other three pilots were not amused when she advised them their settlements would be off the table if that prevailed. Ten minutes later, after we had agreed 90% would be the minimum settlement, a smiling QC returned to announce the tribunal would not proceed - CHC had agreed to the amount requested. She was worth every penny.

Thank you, BALPA – for the third, and I hope, last time I would resort to a return on my union dues: 1977, 1990 and now 2005. At 09:00 Eastern time the following day, our Isocyanate Free Aerospace Coatings, a NASA exploratory programme to remove carcinogenic substances, was presented on schedule.

*

As autumn approached, the Islamic Republic of Iran Police requested I report to their head office on Kish Island. They did not want to discuss the traffic accident when I was 'T' boned by another driver, significantly damaging the company car. No, they were to issue me a Residents Permit for good behaviour. And that's fine, except it comes with a catch. It made entry into the country much more accessible. Travelling abroad was the reverse. Moving through provincial airports in the Mid-West USA with my Turkish business partner illustrates the point. Usually, security staff stopped him. Not now. With an SSSS (Secondary Security Screening Selection) code on my boarding pass, I have the full strip search, pad over and swab to screen for explosives. At the same time, he breezes through security and patiently waits, grinning back at me on the other side. Is that why people have more than one passport?

*

We established our presence in aerospace coatings nationally and internationally along with previous work at the UDRI (the University of Dayton Research Institute) Ohio, affiliated with the USAF and the NASAs program. We began in the UK the previous year in August 2003, coating a replica Gloster-Whittle E 28/29 jet aircraft mounted on the Sir Frank Whittle Memorial on the roundabout outside the main gate of Royal Aircraft Establishment Farnborough, GU14 0RP. This aircraft first flew on the 15th of May 1941. It propelled Britain into the jet age following a successful test flight from RAF Cranwell. Lutterworth, where they tested the original engine in April 1941, has the second example, also mounted on a roundabout leading into the town from the south.
And internationally, when I was passing through Ankara to meet my business partner, where he based his offices, research, development, and manufacturing premises. After Gerry Jones, the Vice President for Lockheed Martin's Corporate International Business, had invited us to his office, we moved forward another notch.

Fig 55. Sir Frank Whittle Memorial
Author's collection

Lockheed Martin F-35B
Photo credit LM Aero.

He asked if we were part of a Turkish Aerospace Industry visit to Fort Worth, TX. We were not. Events quickly changed. Being a foreigner, I needed

approval to join the mission from the Turkish Undersecretariat for Defence Industries. Later, at the Ministry of National Defence, we entered the office of the Turkish program manager for the F-35 Joint Strike Fighter. After a brief explanation, he signed off the necessary approvals.
Together, we met up in Fort Worth a week later. We spent time learning about the F-35 – and, in my case, how to fly it. The invitation came during an evening meal with Lockheed Martin engineers. They were aware I knew how to fly from my business partner and arranged for an instructor to meet me at their F-35B simulator. The morning arrived, and I climbed into the cockpit. Those who drive fast jets may be familiar with the layout.
Instead, I let the instructor lead the way. Once up and running, he asked me to power up the engines. Under my left elbow was a module mounted on a solid-looking rail inclined about 15° upwards towards the console. The module resembled the engine's starter switch box on the end of a Bell 212/412 collective lever. "Move it forwards to spool up the engines," he said or words to that effect. It had a heavy sensation of enormous power as I moved it against the friction up the slope of this ramp. The engine needles responded as they moved into the green. We were ready to taxi and take off. He then guided me through various flight regimes on and off an aircraft carrier and to launch missiles using the magenta head-up display. Some systems, such as the landing gear and an auto land from an 80-foot hover, were controlled by tapping an icon on the primary flight display. They later changed this to voice control as g-forces precluded reaching the screens to activate them. Well, perhaps not these two. There were plenty of others.
Before leaving the USA, a Lockheed Martin employee drove us to Dallas/Fort Worth airport. His task was to determine who I was and how I had infiltrated a successful all-Turkish mission, for they supplied around 40% of the components and systems. My English was suspect as it was better than their interpreter and one other thing. At this point, I left my business partner alone with him. On returning, he related they had been shocked. How had an industrial delegate's flight in their simulator exceeded the performance of their top guns? We never mentioned helicopter flying could be useful when handling vertical take-off and landing aircraft. The visit to Fort Worth generated invitations to engage in the Lockheed Martin F-35 Science and Technology workshops for a chosen few dozen delegates. We were on the F-35 development program. One of the venues was at the Joint Strike Fighter Program office in Arlington, VA. It overlooked the military helicopter traffic in the busy Potomac River heli-lanes. The workshops were a good venue to meet people from participating nations in the program.

Yet the work for us was worthwhile. To better understand the counter microwave radar technology, we developed non-toxic waterborne materials and acquired 20 UK NATO Stock Numbers, leading to program approvals. Thus, it may surprise many governments, customers, and taxpayers the difference in cost to them of an aircraft after radar absorbent material is applied can double the introductory price. They could easily halve this additional charge by applying a radar-absorbing coating, NATO stock number 8010-99-987-6166 (the '99' indicates this as a UK stock number). With a broad absorbing spectrum, it comes into its own as easy to repair; you can quickly return assets to the front line - no wonder Lockheed Martin wanted to take over this part of the business.

*

Despite having a resident's permit to live and work in Iran since October 2004, time was running out. The US Government was putting pressure on Western and Middle Eastern companies to wind down operations and pull out. I finished my flying days in the region with a one-tour notice to Chief Pilot John Toon in Doha.

Fig 56. Gulf Heli Bell 412s at sunset on the flight line. Kish Island, Iran.
Photo: Author's collection

Iran is a country of two parts: those who support the regime and those who don't. After all, records show the Persians gave Europe civilisation. Working with the ancestors of those that did, it was evident why. Maybe the taxi drivers on the island, former surgeons, scientists, professors, senior members of the armed services and others stripped of their professions by the regime should come to the UK. They could refresh our memories on how to behave, starting with courtesy and respect. It came as no surprise they wanted their country back. They implored me to take their case up with the UK Government. Insert a puppet instead of self-determination. These requests contrasted with TV newsreels portraying teenage girls in hijab with schoolbooks in their arms. They were queueing up to sign on as suicide bombers. As-salāmu 'alaykum Iran!

*

At this point, a call to CHC in the UK provided the position of contract pilot based in Aberdeen on the 'L2' working the North Sea again. Flying resumed in August 2005 and lasted a few years until the work ran out. By this time, I had more than 20,000 hours on helicopters. This milestone passed during a flight to the Brae Field with Andy Langman on the 19th of May. It did not include all those grilling hours in simulators. Things had moved on, though some of the managers did not forget. They sheepishly admitted they had kept their heads down; their behaviour in the spring of 2003 was wrong. They had a job to hold down, a young family to look after, or did not want involvement for undisclosed reasons. To them, I say. "Thank you for the experience!"

*

During this time, one incident stood out from others that would contribute to removing the 'L2' fleets from the North Sea. It was another tragedy waiting to happen.

On the 25th of March 2009, Bond Offshore Helicopter's engineers discovered a metallic particle on the epicyclic chip detector of G-REDL, an AS332 L2. The epicyclic module is part of the speed reduction gearing between the power turbine input speed of 23,000 rpm from the engines and the main rotor blade rotating at 265 rpm. The power turbine input shaft connects to the main module, which initially reduces the speed to 2,400 rpm. Mounted above it is the second stage epicyclic module containing eight planet gears. The engineers could not discount the possibility of a material defect in the planet gear or damage due to the presence of foreign object debris because, at the time, the existing detection methods did not provide any further indication of the degradation of the planet gear. A ring of magnets installed inside the sealed epicyclic gearbox further reduced the probability of detecting released debris.

After discovering this particle, the manufacturer was informed. "Due to a misunderstanding or miscommunication, the main gearbox was not opened", and the aircraft was released for service. A week and 36 flying hours later, G-REDL was operating BP flight '85N' inbound from the *Miller* platform with

14 passengers. This was one of many flights scheduled out of Aberdeen for 'DL' that day, including an earlier and uneventful flight to the *Bruce* platform. The aircraft was handed over rotors running to the '85N' crew with no additional defects to report, except one carried forward ice detection system malfunction.

Cruising towards the Aberdeen VOR on the 055° radial at 142 knots indicated airspeed, 1,983 feet above the sea with approximately 20 minutes to run, the co-pilot called Bond operations on the radio, "We've got er fourteen in the back. We are serviceable. Expected to be with you at one....one three one four" (13:14). The crew were unaware only a minute earlier at 12:53 the HUMS card had detected the last of four epicyclic chip warnings recorded over the previous minute and 43 seconds.
Within seconds of their call on the radio to Bond ops, the main gearbox low-pressure oil warning light came on. In one second, the pressure had reduced from 3.8 to 0.8 bar, with the helicopter deviating from the cruise accompanied by a grinding noise recorded by the cockpit area microphone (CAM). After four seconds, the recording stopped.

*

Two seconds after the oil pressure warning, the lift struts connecting the upper section of the main rotor gearbox to its base began twisting, preventing the helicopter from responding to normal crew inputs. The cockpit voice and flight data recorder (CVFDR) recorded the commander expressing alarm as multiple system warnings appeared on the primary flight display and navigation and mission display as he transmitted, "Mayday. MAYDAY. MAYDAY," followed one second later by the co-pilot transmitting "MAYDAY. MAYDAY. MAYDAY, this is Bond eight five November, 'mergency, currently on the zero five-five" followed by an expletive from one of the crew; this was the final radio transmission.
Twenty seconds after the loss of the transmission oil pressure, torque loading to the lift strut attachment points failed, releasing the main rotor head and blades from the helicopter. During the separation, the main rotor blades struck the helicopter's tail in several locations, severing it from the fuselage.

*

The Aberdeen radar controller acknowledged the MAYDAY and, after trying unsuccessfully to contact the crew of 'DL', asked another helicopter, callsign

'45B', outbound on a similar route, to examine the sea in the area where 'DL' was last seen on radar.

An eyewitness two miles away working on the offshore supply vessel *Normand Aurora* recalled hearing and seeing a helicopter descending rapidly into the sea. Shortly after, the main rotor blades followed and fell into the water. They were still connected to the rotor hub that had separated from the aircraft. Around this time, he heard two "bangs" close together. After the helicopter struck the water, a cloud of grey smoke appeared, soon turning black. A few seconds later, as he raised the alarm, he heard what he thought was an "explosion". They launched their fast rescue boat. In no time, it was making way to the scene. The flight crew of '45B' and the crew of the fast rescue craft described arriving at an area of disturbed water roughly 150 m in diameter. They found debris from the helicopter, two life rafts and eight people wearing survival equipment at the scene. There were no signs of life. Within 40 minutes, numerous other SAR assets joined it, where they recovered the eight bodies and other floating wreckage.

*

During the evening of the 2nd of April, the AAIB tasked the survey vessel *Vigilant*, on contract with the Maritime Coastguard Agency and already working in the area, to survey the seabed using its high-definition sonar system. By the following morning, her equipment had identified in good visibility the location of three of the main items of wreckage on the sandy sea floor in a water depth of about 95 m, 11 miles to the northeast of Peterhead. Late afternoon on the 4th of April, the diving support vessel DSV *Bibby Topaz* left Peterhead Harbour on charter to the AAIB to recover the wreckage and look for the remaining eight bodies. Saturation divers recovered them and, along with other wreckage, the helicopter's tail boom. It had multiple main rotor-blade strikes, with some at the base of the fin. Strikes on the tail rotor drive shaft were consistent with the shaft rotating when they struck. The damage to the tail boom also indicated that it had separated from the fuselage before it impacted the sea. When they recovered the main rotor blades, damage and paint marks were further evidence of striking the tail boom before they and their hub detached.

*

When the divers recovered the epicyclic gearbox, investigators found seven of the eight gears were intact and still attached to the planet carrier. The inner race of the eighth planet gear remained attached, but the gear/outer raceway and its associated bearings and bearing cages had separated from the inner race. Of the 51 teeth of this planet gear, they found 35 in three (9, 10 and 16 teeth) sections, leaving the investigators unable to determine the precise origin of the failure. Nevertheless, evidence pointed to a fatigue crack fracturing this gear.

Fig 57. Second epicyclic gear stage - as found.
Photo credit: AAIB

The 'L2' and the newer EC225 LR used the same type of gearbox. The more powerful engines on the EC 225 LR subjected the planet gears to 12 to 14% more loading, reducing the operational time limit (OTL) of 6,600 flying hours permitted for the 'L2' gears down to 4,400. It was common for gears to be removed before their OTL, though what was causing their defects was never established. Over the following days, they examined them and, to improve the probability of chip detection, ring magnets within the epicyclic were removed; the epicyclic chip detector was connected to the crew chip warning circuit and gearbox inspections are now every ten rather than 25 flying hours. A spokesperson from BP confirmed that "Until they had conducted a thorough review of Bond's operations and procedures, they would continue to use rival operators CHC and Bristow. However, it would take several weeks."

*

Following the investigation into the accident, the AAIB made 17 safety recommendations, including 2009-75. "It is recommended that the European Aviation Safety Agency, in conjunction with Eurocopter, urgently review the design, operational life and inspection processes of the planet gears used in the epicyclic module of the main rotor gearbox of the AS332 L2 and EC225

LR helicopters, to minimise the potential of any cracks progressing to failure during the service life of the gears."

Eurocopter responded and set up a test program to explore a second-stage planet gear failure scenario, validate propagation durations, increase understanding, and improve detection and means of monitoring. The 18-month completion timeframe agreed upon with EASA was (catastrophically) delayed due to resolving two EC 225 LP ditching events in 2012, described at the end of the next chapter.

Chapter 25. 2010 – 2012

Nord Stream 1 – Finland - The Tiger Den – Gotland

In 2010, the contract to fly the 'L2' with CHC ended, and I began contracting for Bristow International Business Unit (IBU) on the Tiger. The work involved supporting Saipem's Italian pipe-laying barge *Castoro Sei.* This pipeline was the first Nord Steam project laying twin gas pipelines from Vyborg, now a Russian town (stolen during the 'Winter War' of 1939) on the Finnish border, through the Baltic to Lubmin, near Greifswald on the German coast.

Fig 58. Bristow IBU AS332L1 (Tiger) Turku, Finland. 2010. *Author's collection.*

The project began in April to lay the first pipeline, and they completed it in June of the following year. A second was laid parallel to it. We operated initially from Turku, Finland, where I arrived in September, just in time for the crayfish season. Rosh Jaypalan, the chief pilot, hosted the base and the entertainment, including go-cart racing, in which he excelled. We last flew together in a CHC AS332L1 on the North Sea in September 2001. From Turku, we made flights working Tampere Radar to the barge as it slowly moved south, laying the 1,220 mm (4 foot) diameter pipe that eventually stretched 1,224 kilometres (760 miles) and became the longest sub-sea pipeline in the world.

Along with its twin pipeline, Nord Stream 1 will supply 55 billion cubic metres of gas per annum to Europe from the Bovanenkovo basin in Siberia, the primary source of natural gas for this project. The gas lies under the Yamal Peninsula, 40 kilometres from the coast of the Kara Sea. At over 1,000sq kilometres, this basin contains estimated reserves of 4.9 trillion cubic metres of natural gas. It is expected to last over 50 years, though pumping operations through a 917-kilometre-long overland pipeline to the Baltic to enter the Nord Stream pipelines have now terminated indefinitely. Turku town district is an area of two halves. On the outskirts, it supports vast shipyards where they construct some of the largest cruise ships in the world. The other half is a part rural community connected by miles of cycle paths meandering through the woods bordering the roads and offshore a vast array of outlying islets stretching way out into the Baltic. And over these, we flew out to and back from the *Castoro Sei.*

*

During the winter, the International Business Unit of Bristow seconded me to their European Business Unit (EBU) to fly out of Aberdeen, a surreal experience as the last flight I had planned in their ops was in April 1977. Some of the crews were not on strike. There was no animosity, just polite smiles and the subject was never brought up. Yet, the flying was different. Though older than many of the crew, seeing how these young captains dealt with the weather was always amusing. And so, on a few occasions, we met company traffic, having turned back in the face of storms. Then, that phrase 'it'll probably be all right' continued to hold good as we threaded a way through the weather. No dramatics. Just another day out on the North Sea. Later, it gave the pilot flying with me a glow of achievement back in the crew room. He had made it through and completed the crew change when others had not. It was also amusing to hear colleagues in CHC on the radio question my pledge never again to operate a Tiger over the North Sea.

*

As IBU did not immediately ensure this move back to Scotland, Steve Hogarth asked for assistance putting some operating manuals together for a potential Ghanaian Air Operator Certificate. Eight other staff members had turned the work down. Not knowing what the project entailed, in innocence, I agreed to help. After all, the postman doesn't knock twice. Experience has shown flight operations manuals were rarely well constructed, making information difficult to access. Here was an opportunity to change these aspects and create something useful without referring to the usual annexe and appendices wasting so much time. In parallel with this work, the Nord Steam 1 operation moved south to Visby on Gotland, Sweden, where I arrived in April 2011 in time for the asparagus festival. To save time, Rosh ran the flying program from a veritable North Yorkshire institution, the Black Sheep Arms. (The sea ice precludes pipe laying operations in the Northern Baltic during the winter). Visby is a medieval 12th-century Hanseatic town preserved within a stockade yet within an easy walk to the airport. Unfortunately, my stay only extended until the Libyan war started. The Bristow crews had evacuated their operations at Misrata to Malta to take stock. As permanent employees, they could displace contractors. And being a contractor in the Baltic, it is necessary to leave the Skandia operation for a final secondment out of Aberdeen for Bristow's European division. Most of the time was spent flying the line and constructing operations manuals. One of the latter was a template for future international projects.

*

The first of two events that delayed the Eurocopter test program to explore the second-stage planet gear failure on G-REDL (back in March 2009) occurred on the 1st of April 2012 when the Bond Offshore EC 225 LR registration G-REDW, callsign 'Bond 88 Romeo' "was on a scheduled flight from Aberdeen to the *Maersk Resilient* platform, 150 nautical miles east of Aberdeen. On board were two flight crew and 12 passengers. The helicopter was in the cruise at 3,000 feet with the autopilot engaged and at an approximate speed of 143 knots, indicated airspeed when, at 34 nautical miles outbound, the crew observed low oil pressure indications in both the main and standby lubrication systems for the main gearbox (MGB). This was followed by a chip indication on the vehicle monitoring system (VMS) and the main gearbox oil temperature starting to increase. They were flying in instrument meteorological conditions with a cloud base of 600 to 700 feet. The commander assumed control of the helicopter, reduced speed towards 80 knots indicated airspeed, turned back towards the coast, and initiated a descent. The crew activated the emergency lubrication system, and during the descent, the MGB EMGLUB caption illuminated on the central warning panel (CWP), for which the associated procedure is to land immediately. The commander briefed the passengers and carried out a controlled ditching 20 nautical miles from Aberdeen. The total flight time was 27 minutes. The helicopter remained upright, supported by the emergency flotation gear. After the engines were shut down and the rotors were stopped, the crew and passengers evacuated the helicopter into one of the life rafts via the starboard cabin door. A search and rescue helicopter rescued six occupants from the life raft; eight were transferred to an RNLI lifeboat from Aberdeen."

*

Then, on the 22nd of October, CHC's EC 225 LR, G-CHCN "was on a planned flight from Aberdeen to the *West Phoenix* drilling rig, approximately 226 nautical miles to the north of Aberdeen and West of Shetland. Whilst in the cruise at about 140 knots and 3,000 feet with approximately 81% total torque applied, the CHC crew of 'Helibus 24 Tango' reported the XMSN (transmission) caption illuminated on the central warning panel. They added that the CHIP warning and the main gearbox main and standby oil pump pressure captions on the VMS were also illuminated, and the main gearbox oil pressure indicated zero. The MGB.P (main gearbox oil pressure) caption is then illuminated on the central warning panel. The crew actioned the 'Total Loss of MGB Oil Pressure' checklist, which required activating the main gearbox emergency lubrication system (EMLUB). However, within a minute, the MGB EMLUB caption illuminated on the CWP, indicating that the emergency lubrication system had also failed. The crew carried out the 'Emergency Landing – Power ON' checklist and successfully ditched the helicopter close to a ship, approximately 32 nautical miles southwest of Sumburgh, midway between North Ronaldsay and Fair Isle. A fast rescue craft was launched from the vessel and recovered both crew and 17 passengers. There were no reported injuries."

*

Both helicopters experienced a loss of main rotor gearbox oil pressure due to a failure of the bevel gear vertical shaft in the main rotor gearbox, which drives the main and standby oil pumps. The shaft failed due to a circumferential high-cycle fatigue crack below the bevel gear where the lower part of the shaft driving the pumps is welded to the upper part driving the rotors. The stress in this area where the cracks had initiated was found to be higher than that predicted during the certification of the shaft. Because of these incidents, the manufacturer carried out several safety actions and redesigned the bevel gear vertical shaft. But the failure of this shaft in this area would not have been a reason to land immediately.

*

At this point, it is helpful to understand how the emergency lubrication system works. After the main and standby pumps have failed, the main gearbox is certified to run for 30 minutes on Hydrosafe 620 (a mixture of glycol and water). If the emergency lubrication fails and the system warning light comes on, the crew has no choice but to land immediately. The emergency lubrication depends on a bleed air supply from the left engine, a Hydrosafe 620 supply from an 11-litre reservoir, and a series of small pipes around and inside the main gearbox to deliver the Hydrosafe 620 in a spray. When the emergency lubrication system is activated, an electro-valve opens and bleed air from the left engine enters the system. At the same time, an electric pump supplies Hydrosafe 620 from the reservoir. Two similar sensors monitor the pressure in the Hydrosafe 620 pipes and bleed air lines; these sensors are mounted on the main gearbox. An MGB EMLUB caption will illuminate if low pressure is detected in the Hydrosafe 620 pipes or the bleed air lines. This warning is inhibited for approximately 30 seconds after the system is activated to allow the system to reach a steady state. The low-pressure signal is generated by either the bleed air or Hydrosafe 620 pressure switches if the pressure does not exceed a specified pressure value, P_{ON}, when the system is activated or falls below a set pressure, P_{OFF}.

*

An investigation later established that the emergency lubrication system had successfully operated in both cases. The problem arose when the system warning light came on in the cockpit.
It was traced back to when a company supplied the original pressure switches. The pressure switches have three output pins. The helicopter manufacturer's original specification was for Pin 3 to be common. Instead, the supplier delivered the switches with Pin 1 as common; the manufacturer accepted this change, and the wiring on the helicopter was changed accordingly. The original specification was not changed to reflect the different pin positions.

*

In 2010, the manufacturer updated the pressure switches and provided a new supplier with, wait for it, the original specification. They were delivered as interchangeable, part of a modification (MOD 0752520), with Pin 3 as common.

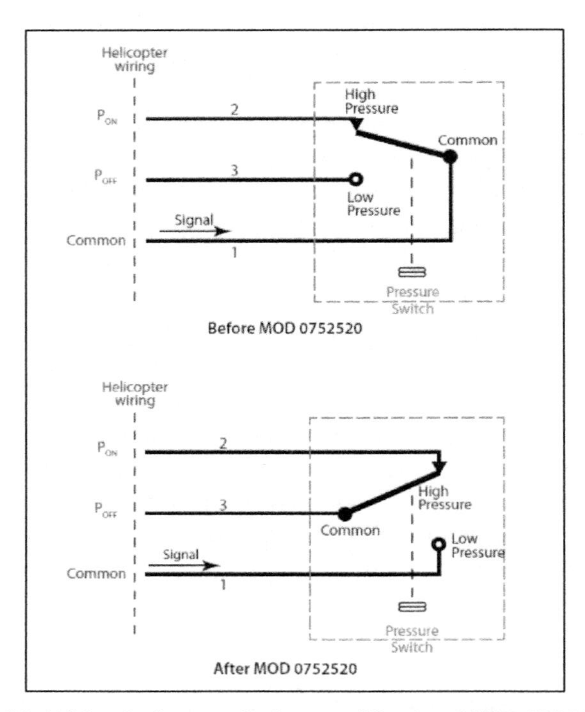

Fig 59. Wiring before and after modification MOD 0752520.
Photo Credit: AAIB

This explains why the MGB EMLUB caption would always illuminate after a 30-second delay after the crew activated the emergency lubrication system. On both occasions, the crew, now suitably misinformed, followed the emergency checklist instructions and ditched, despite 'DW' being within easy reach, eight minutes from Aberdeen, and 'CN' seven from the small airfields on North Ronaldsay or Fair Isle.

Chapter 26. 2012 - 2021

Reflections – Turkmenistan – Dar – UK SAR – Helibus 240 - Modern Times

But, by then, at the end of March 2012, I had hung up my headset. People ask if any unusual experiences offshore stand out. There are two that can prevail from the usual rig flight.

The description of the first, experienced twice over the years, is of a line of embedded funnel clouds with interest. And an interlude before the waterspouts develop. (Yet, if you see their beginning, their source is clearly defined. They appear as churned-up water moving across the surface, much as created by the wake of a large powerboat. When the force inside the cloud increases, twisting wisps of water develop. They usually appear under a cloud defined by an inky black horizontal base). I encountered the first when flying IFR in cloud during the summer of 1975 and again in 2009. The first time was a harrowing experience, having been on the North Sea for only a few weeks. On entering a series of these vertical airflows, the action begins, with violent deviations in altitude up to 3,000' a minute.

In effect, you are riding inside a form of line squall with a succession of air currents lining the walls of potential waterspouts. The outer walls take you down; the inner back up, then into the next to repeat the process. On the first occasion, we had not long been airborne from Aberdeen. To continue appeared fruitless as the gravity forces were significant both on the aircraft and the passengers. Not to mention the loading on the fasteners securing their seats to the airframe. We initiated a return to the airport, except it took over 20 minutes to turn and another 10 to exit the weather. We had returned through the same area, exacerbating the effort to free ourselves. After landing, it was apparent some passengers were in a bad way. The oil company rep organised taxis to take them downtown for a hospital check-up. On the second occasion, it was suggested the captain make a 90° turn and hold that course until clear; that worked.

Nowadays, North Sea helicopters have an Integrated Health and Usage Monitoring System - IHUMS equipment conceived by Alistair Gordon of Bristow Helicopters. The system was installed in North Sea helicopters following the accident to the Chinook G-BWFC on approach to Sumburgh to monitor the gearboxes, their connecting shafts, and rotors for vibration patterns. Minute changes are detected, as can defects such as a crack in a gear wheel (as happened on the forward gearbox crown wheel of G-BWFC), loss of a gear tooth or excessive wear in a bearing. A PCMCIA card collects all this and other engineering information. Even engine and rotor over speeds can be detected when downloading after every flight for analysis. They usually attribute these items exceeding their normal operating range to poor aircraft handling. A particular bonus provided by IHUMS has led to a much better standard of main rotor balancing and tracking. It is considered by some in the industry as the most significant advance in helicopter safety since mounting twin engines. In our incident, the Helicopter Operational Monitoring Programme recorded extreme deviation from altitude, among many other events. That did it! And this did not go down well in the subsequent enquiry when they delivered the IHUMS and HOMP records of the flight to the junior management. They were unaware of this kind of weather. As luck would have it, the chief pilot of Bond Helicopters in Aberdeen had heard of our incident. He had experienced it on another occasion. He volunteered to support our case. It was only then they conceded to believe the unbelievable.

*

The second experience occurs on the approach to land on an offshore helideck. It would be in snowstorms on winter nights with a high sea running. Essential to the scenario was a workboat. It would be waiting to unload and return with empty containers. The vessel would be positioned below and stern to the helideck you were due to land upon. An array of powerful lights just aft the bridge illuminates the deck cargo. These deck lights also pick out the snowflakes moving in unison with the vessel, like a murmuration of starlings, as it slips into deep troughs before heaving back up again. To simulate this movement, try this: with your eyes open, rock your head about as if on a gimbal to exercise the neck muscles. Focus, OK? Then imagine your head is the relatively static element (remember you're in a helicopter now), and what you see is moving simultaneously up and down, left and right. Back offshore in the dark, your principal reference is the lights defining the helideck perimeter. And they may be moving too if approaching a semi-sub alongside a workboat. As I say, it's all relative to the ambient environment where the world is out of sync, but not much. Focusing the mind on separating the third medium, the helicopter, as it is being pushed around in the storm's turbulence, leaves only a small matter of stabilising the arrival and deftly touching down. It is even more surreal when the wind is not blowing, with only snowflakes quietly slewing around as they heave up and down in the night.

Mid-February, Redhill Aerodrome. Working on a project with Steve Hogarth, we were sitting in his car waiting to go to lunch when there was a newsflash on the car radio. It was about a new Nationwide SAR contract. The preferred bidder, CHC, had been disqualified. Irregularities within their application had come to light. The police are launching an investigation to uncover how commercially sensitive information had come into the hands of CHC. CHC was part of a consortium known as Soteria (Thales UK, Royal Bank of Scotland, and Sikorsky). The Secretary of State had revealed he had received information volunteered two months previously. Someone or a group of the joint Ministry of Defence/Department for Trade project team evaluating the bids had passed information to CHC to secure employment with them. To Steve, I observed this was a great opportunity to be back in the game. And as my manager looked across, he gravely nodded, then smiled. Little did I know, it was also an opportunity for me. It was a long time since I had any involvement in SAR. The British Airways Helicopters contract in Sumburgh ended in December 1982 when Bristow Helicopters won the contract.

*

Over the years, Bristow provided SAR out of Sumburgh, Stornoway and Lee on Solent, with the remainder of the British Isles covered by military assets. When the Department of Transport (DOT) signed the contract for renewal in 2007, they awarded CHC with an Interim SAR five-year contract. Towards the end of the contract, on the 28th of November 2011, the DOT put tenders out for a nationwide all-civilian SAR service to replace the SAR provided by the RAF and Royal Navy. CHC, British International and Bristow hotly contest it. After a few months, it became apparent CHC was the preferred bidder when we heard this news flash in the Redhill Aerodrome car park. The current procurement process was now on hold. With the CHC bid now in tatters, Bristow slid into the preferred bidder position. They won the ten-year £1.6 billion contract the following year on the 26th of March 2013 to service all ten UK SAR bases. Initially, the SAR out of Sumburgh and Stornoway would be known as GAP SAR as they took over the operations formerly provided by CHC. New operations were constructed with hangar facilities and fed into the system. These now included Inverness, Prestwick, Humberside, Caernarfon, St Athan, Newquay, Lee-on-Solent, and Lydd. The new service, UK SAR, had its HQ in Aberdeen. Here, engineering carried out heavy maintenance for the 11 Sikorsky S-92A and 11 Leonardo AW189 aircraft. The contract replaced all of the military SAR Helicopters.

The Ghana contract did not materialise, though the work to create manuals for the EZ registered S-76A++ and C+ operating the Bristow contract in Turkmenistan did. Their operation into the Caspian was based at Türkmenbaşy, a port and gateway to the West. It involved writing the operating rules/air law for the Operations Manual Part A. My experience flying UK 'G' registered aircraft in Kazakhstan, where the former Soviet Union laws still prevailed, helped a little. It required more, especially when the result had to be a legal document both parties could cite in court. Then, digging deeper, it was a revelation to discover the Soviet Rules of the Air carried forward by these former republics of the USSR were so eminently practicable. For example: 'when encountering unacceptable weather phenomena or conditions below VFR, in addition to implementing conventional (fixed-wing, i.e., reverting to IFR) procedures, the helicopter pilot may land on an area chosen from the air'—a simple solution with a rule to support it. The State Civil Aviation Department (SCAD) - Turkmenhowayollary in Ashgabat approved the work.
Best of all was the Bristow/Everett joint venture in Tanzania. Part of this work in August 2014 was by the pool of the Southern Sands Hotel in Dar es Salaam, one of the better venues, more so in the evening with the fireflies out and from the neighbouring botanical gardens - flying foxes. These bats used the touch-and-go technique to drink water from the pool on the wing. This tropical interlude ended when IBU disbanded a few months later. Meanwhile, Bristow European Business Unit requested a rewrite of the Dangerous Goods section of their operating manual. It evolved from an ineffective few pages to 90 approved by the CAA. When the chief dangerous goods controller at the CAA asked why aircraft battery handling regulations had been highlighted, it was pointed out this was one of the more common dangerous goods to carry in the hold, for it was not unusual to recover an aircraft with a flat battery. On one occasion, we had taken the Wick Fire Brigade for an exercise at Flotta, the oil terminal in Orkney receiving oil from the Piper and Claymore fields. When the time came to return in the evening, the aircraft would not start; a flat battery. Fortuitously, it had not been an actual call-out. He overlooked this discretion. At the same time, Chief Pilot Matt Rhodes referred a film company to have their Unmanned Aerial Vehicle (UAV) Operations manual written for them; it turned into an interesting exercise working with the CAA. At the time, they were also feeling their way toward regulating what is now a burgeoning industry.

The UK CAA has now addressed many offshore incidents and outstanding operating procedures. They appeared in their Civil Aviation Publication

(CAP) 1145 'Offshore Helicopter Review' in 2014. It included 32 Actions and 29 Recommendations. During the subsequent rollout, my Flight Operations Manager, Steve Hogarth, asked me to represent them and provide a progress report. This review included safety on helidecks and dismay. The current Health and Safety Executive approved training for helideck personnel by enacting helicopter handling procedures offshore in a field with a Ford Transit van. Had they forgotten how the helideck personnel died in 1992?
Curiously, though reasonably, Action A9 took up the most time. A9 was to reconcile passenger body size, including safety and survival equipment, with the number and current size of the push-out windows and emergency exits on offshore helicopters. They were generally incompatible.
Moreover, those who did not fit through the latter will be prohibited from flying unless in an emergency. An emotive subject bound to conflict with political correctness, human rights – you name it! A casualty of these initiatives was the Sikorsky S-76. The standard seating configuration for this aircraft was three rows of four passenger seats. Reducing the number of rows to just two is implemented to comply with an exit window at either end of each row. It spelt the end of this superb offshore aircraft on the North Sea. It was no longer commercially viable to carry only eight passengers.
The Bristow Group HQ in Houston, TX, did not see a future for their IBU either, though fortunately, another door had already opened.

*

On the strength of my efforts with IBU, Mark Prior, head of Bristow Global Operating Standards, recommended UK SAR approach me to assist with their contract to provide Helicopter SAR to the Maritime Coastguard Agency. The 16-member SAR Standards Transition Team, headed by Tricky Dane OBE, had invited me to join them in October 2013. The basic mantra for all staff was, 'Do what you want as long as you can account for it afterwards.' Full circle, this practical modus operandi also rang true when I started on the North Sea 'back along'. Tricky asked me to develop a set of operations manuals along with training and checking forms. The principal manuals were for Flight and Technical crew training and a SAR manual based on three words: 'Techniques', 'Practices' and 'Procedures'. We called it Operations Manual Part F. The Flight Crew and Technical Crew (European Aviation Safety Agency terminology for Winch Operators and Winchmen, formerly, 'Rear crew') fed information to be collated into these three documents. Over time, Part F had morphed into over 900 pages. The contents of this tome and

the two training manuals illustrated a world apart from the life of an oil & gas line pilot.
The sheer volume of knowledge, skill sets, and equipment familiarity required to deliver a QC3 (Quality, Current, Competent Capability) is recorded in their manuals. And the currency checks. They are never-ending.

*

Meanwhile, on the 1st of January 2014, Eurocopter was rebranded Airbus Helicopters. A further delay was incurred in gathering information about epicyclic gear spalling (breaking down metal into small flakes or 'spalls') degradation and growth speed. This time, it was for test rig availability, which meant that results were not analysed until 2016. They were still discussing them in April, seven years after the loss of G-REDL, when events overtook them.

*

The previous year, on the 13th of March 2015, a helicopter's main gearbox, Serial Number M5156, fell off a small truck. The gearbox was in transit along a gravel road in Australia in an original Airbus Helicopter main gearbox container. When the driver swerved to avoid kangaroos crossing, the truck rolled over, and the container fell off. The upper half of the container was damaged, and the gearbox fell out, causing visible damage to the external parts of the gearbox. M5156 was returned to Airbus Helicopters in Marignane, France, for inspection and repair, where no anomalies on internal components were detected, and all bearings and gears were re-installed. It was released on the 5th of January 2016, sent to Bergen, Norway, and installed in a CHC Helikopter Service EC 225 LR, registration LN-OJF, on the 24th of January. M5156 had accumulated 1,080 flight hours.

There were many witnesses to this accident. Because it occurred on a main helicopter route into Bergen-Flesland for arrivals to R/W 17 from the western oilfields, usually, people took little notice of them as they flew overhead. Today was different. They looked up when they heard a loud noise from an aircraft coasting in over the islands. One was a man crossing the Turøy Bridge on foot with his wife and child. They were halfway across when he saw a helicopter emerge from the clouds to the west. As it approached, they heard a loud bang and saw the main rotor detach over the western end of the bridge. His wife and child kept going. Instead, he stopped and watched it emitting dark smoke and yawing, shedding parts that fell around them as it continued over the bridge. The five-bladed rotor continued to fly on its own as it veered off in a wide, erratic descending left-hand turn in a northerly direction and fell on the island of Storskora. With the noise of components striking rocks and splashing into the sea, his wife and child hurried away towards the end of the bridge as the helicopter continued falling until he saw it hit the rocks of the small island of Storeskitholmen to the southeast.

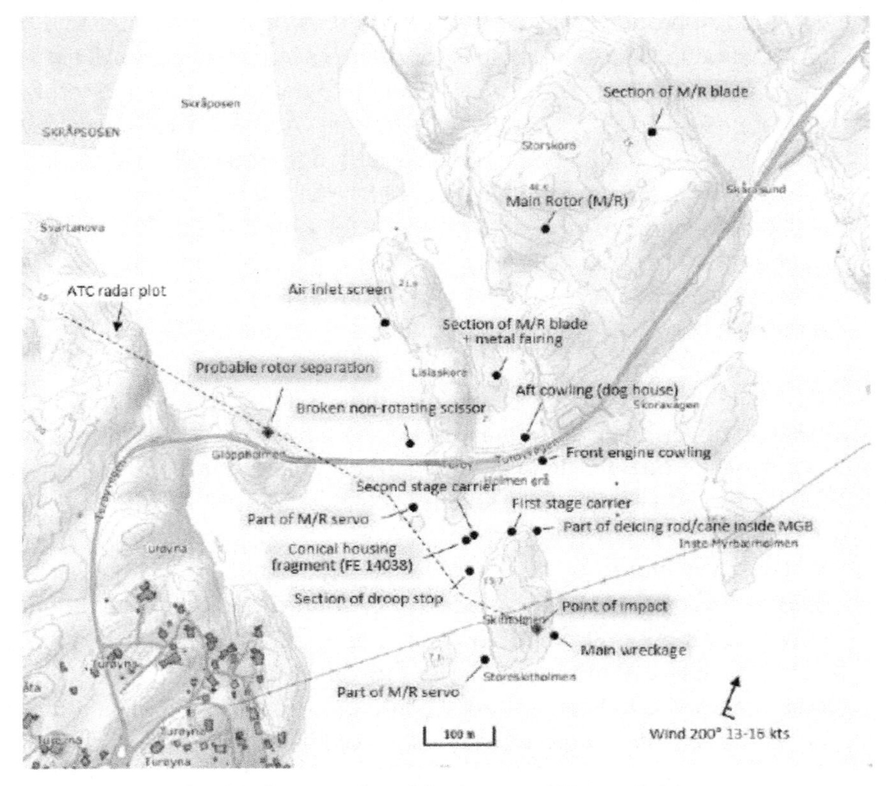

Fig 60. Scene of accident around Turøy Bridge.
Illustration Credit: AIBN

About 550 metres west of the accident site, a group of divers were onboard a boat at Turøy Quay. Two of them had helmet cameras. They realised something was wrong when they heard the noise and looked up. After the main rotor detached, their cameras recorded the helicopter falling in an almost horizontal attitude. It then made a half rotation to the right on its longitudinal axis before the aircraft struck the small island across the water from them at a 45-degree nose-down attitude. Impact forces destroyed the helicopter before most of the wreckage continued into the sea. A cloud of white mist appeared, ignited, and exploded on fire, burning the surrounding heather. Helicopter parts thrown from the wreckage churned the sea as a large black cloud of smoke billowed from the site.

The Canadian Helikopter Service AS Flight HKS241, callsign 'Helibus 241', was inbound to Bergen-Flesland from the *Gullfaks 'B'* platform. On board the EC 225 LR were oil workers for Statoil ASA. The radar air traffic controller at Flesland Approach had just cleared the crew from 3,000 feet to 2,000 feet with instructions to route directly to VENIN, a waypoint east of Turøy and ten miles from Flesland. The co-pilot confirmed the clearance and requested an ILS approach to R/W17. One minute later, Approach issued a new QNH, 1005 hPa. The captain confirmed receipt of the new QNH at 11:52:31. This was the last radio communication with 'Helibus 241'. After levelling out at 2,000 feet and cruising at 140 knots for one minute, the engine torque suddenly dropped significantly, and the main rotor started to tilt erratically. The aircraft climbed about 120 feet before the rotor detached, then followed a ballistic curve until it hit the ground at approximately 11:55.

As flight 'HKS241' disappeared from their radar, Flesland Approach tried to raise them on the radio multiple times without response before asking a Norwegian Coastal Administration surveillance aircraft in the area, callsign 'Midnight 1', to search for 'Helibus 241' near VENIN. At 11:57:50, 'Midnight 1' confirmed smoke in the area.

Within six minutes of the accident, a rigid inflatable boat (RIB), closely followed by two other small boats, converged on Storeskitholmen. Rising 15.7 metres out of the sea, the island consists of rock 97 metres wide and not more than 210 meters long. Heather on fire partially covers it. They found that most of the helicopter had slid into the sea, where the water depth was about five metres. There were no signs of life.

The effort to locate and salvage parts from the helicopter began shortly after the accident. Navy divers from the Norwegian Armed Forces laid out a matrix of lines on the seabed divided into 27, 100 x 100m squares, with divers from the Bergen Fire Department assisting them with the search over this area. A remotely operated vehicle searched areas not covered by kelp, and a purpose-built magnet sledge looked for steel parts. A vessel pulled this one-metre-wide sledge with 14 powerful magnets attached to flexible arms along the seabed. Two video cameras recorded the effort; one pointed down towards the magnets and one filmed in front. The search was called off on the 11th of September after the divers had made 354 dives, but with agreement from the AIBN, the Norwegian Naval Diving School used the area for training. They found a second-stage planet carrier during one such diving exercise in February 2017.

The main parts of the helicopter cabin, including the cockpit, were recovered as one piece, held together by bars, wires, tubes and pipes, but otherwise structurally destroyed. It was damaged to such an extent that it was almost impossible to conduct meaningful investigations of the wreckage. All damage was consistent with the helicopter's impact with the island.

*

This accident had similarities with the AS332 L2 accident off Peterhead in April 2009. Both accidents resulted from a fatigue fracture in a second-stage planet gear. The post-investigation actions over the interim seven years were insufficient to prevent the loss of another main rotor. The only difference this time was that there was no warning. No chips had been detected during ground maintenance or chip warnings in the cockpit of LN-OJF. "There was no evidence to indicate that maintenance actions by the operator had contributed to this accident, despite during transport in Australia in 2015, the main gearbox had fallen off a truck and suffered from unknown external forces. It was inspected, repaired, and released for flight by Airbus Helicopters without a detailed analysis of the potential effects of these forces on the critical characteristics of the component. Despite a possible link between shock loads and spalling events."

Within two weeks of the accident, CAA Norway and UK CAA grounded all EC225 LP and AS332 L2 helicopters, except for SAR flights. These decisions were based on national aviation safety considerations in line with the EASA Basic Regulation as a first reaction to a safety problem. One month after the accident, EASA grounded both types based on the Accident Investigation Board Norway (AIBN) preliminary report on the 1st of June 2016, and the CAA Norway and the UK CAA suspended all operations.

On the 7th of October 2016, EASA lifted the flight prohibition based on the return to service statements from Airbus Helicopter that included: "most particles collected in magnetic plug and filters assuring detection" and "safety is ensured by the current maintenance procedures (magnetic plug)". The AIBN investigation categorised the response as 'Not Adequate'. They had shown that the combination of material properties, surface treatment, design, operational loading environment, and debris gave rise to a failure mode which was not previously anticipated or assessed. They had expected a more precautionary approach given the detection system's inspection methodology and functional characteristics involving a critical part in which failure had led to two catastrophic events remained unchanged. On the 20th of July 2017, the UK CAA and the Norwegian CAA lifted the ban on operating the AS332 L2 and EC225 LR. But by then, no one was interested in using these types until a gradual acceptance crept in to use them for utility, including fire-fighting, heavy lift, and military purposes; if you have a spare (2023) US$20 million.

Fig 61. Newquay SAR S-92A G-MCGY.
Photo © Greg Caygill with permission from the MCA.

Back in Scotland, the UK Search and Rescue management determined a break from the Bristow Oil & Gas Air Operator Certificate in 2018 and have their own. This required a fresh set of manuals to be approved by the CAA.

With the new AOC up and running, the standards transition team was disbanded three years later, in 2021.
Over those seven years, Tricky often referred to 'the glue holding UK SAR together'. In truth, it was because no one else had the time; they had more important duties to carry out - Search and Rescue.

*

Much has changed with Oil & Gas Ops too. Remember that rope and the orange dayglow paint?
Health and safety had been in the way of a fast buck for years. Now, it is a growth industry. No longer can decisions be made using the captain's discretion unless you are a SAR pilot. Nowadays, rules and regulations replace this philosophy. These guide today's crews to make informed, uniform, and safe decisions in an evolving and different culture; the ability to take the initiative has been discouraged, a shame as the old can complement the new. The opportunity to explore the boundaries of resilience and capability is now a catalogue of risk assessments and a host of new, tighter, and restricting limitations, safety legislation and mandatory safety equipment. There are no more routine flights offshore when the breeze exceeds 60 knots (Force 9) to safeguard working on helidecks. Or depart if a reasonable prospect of recovery is not available (SAR) or the significant wave height (SWH) at the oilfield destination is greater than seven metres (maximum wave height ten in any one 20-minute period). The significant wave height is calculated by recording the mean wave height (trough to crest) of the highest third of the waves measured over a 20-minute period within 500 m of an offshore installation. The higher frequency of the significant wave height indicated the steepness of the waves. These limits dictated the ability to ditch safely and be recovered by an FRC launched from the standby vessel, also known as the emergency rescue and recovery vessel (ERRV). The oft-used phrase 'it'll probably be all right' is now just a fable and no longer in the aircrew lexicon.
The landscape has changed, and the culture has moved on. Operators no longer tolerate unnecessary exposure to danger. No incentives. No initiatives. No Challenges. No fun! As turtle fishermen from the Caymans used to say: "Modern time, Mon." So next time you travel offshore in a helicopter - you will probably be all right! And for the metropolitan intelligentsia, just maybe, this story has stirred your imagination to reflect on the work of offshore helicopter pilots.

Abbreviations and Acronyms

AAIB	(UK) Air Accident Investigation Branch
ADF	Automatic Direction Finder (NDB and radio receiver)
AFCS	Automatic Flight Control System
ALPA	(US) Air Line Pilots Association
AOC	Aircraft Operating Certificate
BA	British Airways
BAC	British Aircraft Corporation
BAH	British Airways Helicopters
BALPA	British Airline Pilots' Association
BBC	British Broadcasting Association
BEA(H)	British European Airways (Helicopters)
BHL	Bristow Helicopters Limited
BIH	British International Helicopters
BNOC	British National Oil Corporation
BOAC	British Overseas Airways Corporation
BP	British Petroleum
BV	Boeing Vertol
CAA	(UK) Civil Aviation Authority
CAAC	Civil Aviation Administration of China
C-Box	Combining Gearbox
CHC	Canadian Holding Company
DB	Derrick Barge
DME	Distance Measuring Equipment
DSV	Diving Support Vessel
EPIRB	Emergency Position Indicating Radio Beacon
ESB	East Shetland Basin
ETPM	Entrepose GTM Pour le Travaux Pétroliers et Maritime
FOD	Foreign Object Debris
FRC	Fast Rescue Craft
Green	Normal operating segment of the instrument.
HLO	Helideck Landing Officer
HMR	Helicopter Main Route
HOMP	Helicopter Operational Monitoring Programme
HS	Helikopter Service
IFR	Instrument Flight Rules
IBU	International Business Unit (Bristow Group)

ILS	Instrument Landing System
LSI	(IATA) Lerwick Shetland Islands (Sumburgh)
MOD	Ministry of Defence
MSV	Multi-function Service Vessel
NATS	(UK) National Air Traffic Services
NDB	Non-Directional Radio Beacon
O&G	Oil & Gas
OAT	Outside Air Temperature in the shade
OIM	Offshore Installation Manager
ONGC	Oil and Natural Gas Corporation (India)
OPEC	Organisation of Petroleum Exporting Countries
P1	Pilot in Command (Captain/Commander)
PROOC	Pearl River Oil Operating Company
QFE	Height above airport elevation – Altimeter pressure setting.
QNH	Flight altitude above mean sea level - Altimeter pressure setting.
RADALT	Radio Altimeter
SAR	Search and Rescue
VFR	Visual Flight Rules
VHF	Very High Frequency
VOR	VHF Omnidirectional Range

Bibliography

Air Accident Investigation Branch (AAIB) Bulletins and Reports:

Report 11/71 Sikorsky S-61N Helicopter, G-ASNM, in the North Sea, 50 miles east of Aberdeen 15th November 1970.

Report 6/77 Sikorsky S-58T Helicopter, G-BCRU, in the North Sea, Forties 'C' platform on 21st April 1976.

Report 8/78 Sikorsky S-61N Helicopter, G-BBHN, in the North Sea, northeast of Aberdeen, 1st October 1977.

Report 14/80 Sikorsky S-61N Helicopter, G-BEID, in the North Sea, southeast of Aberdeen, 31st July 1980.

Report 1/81 BAe HS 748, G-BEKF, at Sumburgh Airport, Shetland Islands on 31st July 1979.

Report 9/83 Sikorsky S-76A, G-BGXY, at South Kirkton, Aberdeenshire on 12th March 1981.

Report 2/84 Bell 212 G-BARJ, Brent Oil Field, East Shetland Basin on 24th of December 1983.

Report 8/84 Sikorsky S-61N, G-BEON in the sea near St Mary's aerodrome, Isles of Scilly on 16th July 1983.

Report 4/85 Sikorsky S-61N, G-ASNL in the North Sea, 75 nm northeast of Aberdeen on 11th March 1983.

Report 5/87 Boeing Vertol (BV) 234LR G-BISO in the East Shetland Basin of the North Sea on 2 May 1984.

Report 2/88 Boeing Vertol (BV) 234LR G-BWFC 2.5 miles east of Sumburgh, Shetland Isles, 6 November 1986.

Report 1/90 Sikorsky S-61N, G-BDES in the North Sea 90 nm east of Aberdeen on 10th November 1988.

Report 3/90 Sikorsky S-61N G-BEID 29 nm northeast of Sumburgh Shetland Isles on 13th July 1988.

Report 2/91 Sikorsky S-61N, G-BEWL at Brent Spar, East Shetland Basin on 25th July 1990.

Report 2/93 AS332L1 Super Puma, G-TIGH near Cormorant 'A', East Shetland Basin on 14th March 1992.

Bulletin No. 3/96 Ref: EW/C95/8/4 Sikorsky S-61N, G-AYOM Claymore Accommodation Platform, Central North Sea. 18th August 1995.

Report 2/97 AS332L1 Super Puma, G-TIGK in North Sea southwest of Brae Alpha Platform on 19th January 1995.

Report 3/2004 Eurocopter AS332 L1 Super Puma, G-BKZE on board the West Navion Drilling Ship 80 nm west of Shetland Islands on 10th November 2001.

Report 1/2005 Sikorsky S-76A+, G-BJVX near the Leman 49/26 Foxtrot platform in the North Sea, 16th July 2002.

Report 2/2011 Eurocopter AS332 L2 Super Puma, G-REDL 11 nm NE of Peterhead, Scotland on 1 April 2009.

Report AAR 2/2014 on the accidents to Eurocopter EC225 LP Super Puma G-REDW, 34 nm east of Aberdeen, Scotland, on 10th May 2012 and G-CHCN, 32 nm southwest of Sumburgh, Shetland Islands, on 22nd October 2012.

Other Reports:

Aviation Accident Report. United Air Lines Inc. Boeing 247, NC-13328, Western Springs, Illinois. 20th December 1934.

Aircraft Accident Report. Los Angeles Airways, INC. S-61L Helicopter, N300Y, Compton, California, 14th August 1968. National Transportation Safety Board Department of Transportation, Washington D.C. 20591.

Command History of HELATKLTRON THREE for Calendar Year 1970 (U). HA(L).3. 13th April 1971. Declassified Confidential 25th October 1972.

Transocean III (Sinking) (Hansard, 19th June 1975) – the API – UK Parliament.

Accident Investigation Board Norway. Rapport om luftfartsulykke I Nordsjoen den 26. Uni 1978 ca. kl. 115 med helikopter S-61N LN-OQS: 43.

RNLI Lifeboat Return of Service R.S. 809 Arun Class Lifeboat No. O.N.1050 on 31st July 1980; Lifeboat Magazine Archive Date: Autumn 1980 Volume: 47 Issue: 474. Scotland North Division. Ditched helicopter.

U.S. Department of Transportation United States Coast Guard. Report 16732/Glomar Java Sea. 28th May 1985.

Fax to Secretary, Chinook Disaster Legal Group from Speiser, Krause, Madole & Nolan., Counsellors at Law. Two, Grand Central Tower, 1140 East 145th Street, New York, N.Y. 10017. What the Group has Accomplished. 23rd July 1990.

Report of the Chief Inspector of Marine Accidents into the engine failure and subsequent grounding of the Motor Tanker Braer at Garths Ness, Shetland on the 5th January 1993 Marine Investigation Branch 5/7 Brunswick Place, Southampton, Hants SO1 2AN.

CAA Paper 99004 Research on Offshore Helideck Environmental Issues. August 2000.

CAA Paper 2002/02 Final Report on the Helicopter Operations Monitoring Programme (HOMP) Trial.

CAP 641 Review of Helicopter Offshore Safety and Survival. May 2002.

CAA Paper 2005/06 Summary Report on Helicopter Ditching and Crashworthiness Research. SRG.

CAA Paper 2007/02 Visualisation of Offshore Gas Turbine Exhaust Plumes.

CAA Paper 2008/03 Helideck Design Considerations – Environmental Effects.

Investigation and prediction of helicopter-triggered lightning over the North Sea. Johnathan M Wilkinson, Helen Wells, Paul R. Field, and Paul Agnew. Met Office, Exeter, UK.

UK Offshore Public Transport Helicopter Safety Record (1976 – 2002) John Burt Associates Limited / BOMEL Limited for the Health and Safety Executive.

Learning Account into the RNTT Incident – Shatt Al Arab Waterway. 21st June 2004.

Oil & Gas[UK]. Summary of 73 UK Continental Shelf offshore commercial air transport (CAT) reportable Accidents from 1976 to 2013.

AAIB Norway SL 2018/04 Report on the accident near Turøy, Øygarden Municipality, Hordaland County, Norway, 29 April 2016 with Airbus Helicopters EC 225 LP, LN-OJF, operated by CHC Helikopter Service AS.

Oil & Gas[UK] Emergency Response & Rescue Vessel Management Guidelines. Issue 6th May 2018.

CAP 1145 Safety Review of Offshore Public Transport Helicopter Operations in Support of the Exploration of Oil & Gas. 2014.

CAP 437 Standards for Offshore Helicopter Landing Areas. 10th February 2023.

Books and Charts; TV, Newspaper, and Magazine Articles:

HMRI. National Air Traffic Services.

Decca Charts Decca Navigation Company Ltd.

The Bridge: Natural Gas in a Redivided Europe. Thane Gustafson.

The Prize. Daniel Yergin.

Far Tortuga. Peter Matthiessen.

Catch 22. Joseph Heller.

Flying the Line. The First Half Century of ALPA. George E. Hopkins.

The Flying Sailor. Rear Admiral André Jubelin. 1953

Alan Bristow, Helicopter Pioneer. The Autobiography. Alan Bristow With Patrick Malone. 2009.

Fw 200 Condor vs Atlantic Convoy 1941-43. Rebert Forczyk.

Sea Float & Solid Anchor. GMCM (SW) (Ret.) Robert H. Stoner.

Arabs Halt Oil to Portugal, Rhodesia, and South Africa. The New York Times. Eric Pace. 29th November 1973.

400 Airlifted as Rig Moorings Snap. The Herald. George MacDonald. 10th January 1990.

Government Halts SAR Bidding Process. Channel 4 News. 8 Feb 2011.

U.K. Puts $11 Billion SAR-H Competition on Hold, Cites Irregularities. Defense Daily. 14th February 2011.

Setting the Standard. Kenneth I. Swartz. Vertical Magazine.

BP statement to P & J, 14th April 2009, following the accident to flight 85N.

Death in the City: How a lack of vultures threatens Mumbai's Towers of Silence. The Guardian. Bachi Karkaria. 26th January 2015.

Former policeman recalls horror of Chinook crash. Shetland Times. Peter Johnson. 12th November 2016.

Forty Years and Counting for Oil at Sullom Voe. Shetland News. Chris Cope. 23rd November 2018.

Early days of Sullom Voe: in their own words. Shetland News.co.uk.

Twenty-five years on - what really happened on the Braer. Shetland News. Jonathan Wills. 5th January 2018

The huge oil spill that Shetland survived. BBC News. 5th January 2018.

Charting the Oil Boom Years. Charles Woodley. 22nd October 2020.

1971 Indo-Pak War: Story of Pakistan's Surrender and Liberation of Bangladesh. News18. 15th December 2020.

Online Database:

https://. www.googlemaps.com

https://www.helis.com/database/cn/1420

https://www.helis.com/database/cn/1421

https://www.scottishshipwrecks.com/braer/

https://www.WorldHistory.Biz British International Helicopters Ltd.: United Kingdom (1986-2000). 18-03-2015.

https://www.ashpole.org.uk A collection of articles from a 36-year career in aviation. Captain Bill Ashpole.

https://www.brownwater-navy.com Historical accounts describing Sea Float 1967-1970

https://www.seawolf.org. US Navy Seawolves Detachments Det. 1.

https://www.brownwater-navy.com/vietnam/Seafloat.htm

https://www.heerema.com

https://www.rmg.co.uk/collections

https://www.thefreelibrary/KAZAKHSTAN

https://www.parkerwellbore.com/milestones-awards/

https://www.nytimes.com/1992/06/24/business/maxwell-s-mirror-group-has-loss-727.5-million-loss.html

https://www.belair.dk/about-bel-air/bel-air-history/

https://www.scottishaviation.org.uk/locations/114/raf-sullom-Voe

https://.www.moviequotedb.com/character_508/

https://www.nord-stream.com

Index

Intentionally Blank

Fig 62. Author. UK SAR Standards Transition Team Visit.
Portsmouth December 2019.
HMS *Queen Elizabeth* and HMS *Prince of Wales*

Printed in Great Britain
by Amazon

35266530R00185